The Management of Ignorance

*A Political Theory of
the Curriculum*

FRED INGLIS

Basil Blackwell

© Fred Inglis 1985

First published 1985

Basil Blackwell Ltd
108 Cowley Road, Oxford OX4 1JF, UK

Basil Blackwell Inc.
432 Park Avenue South, Suite 1505,
New York, NY 10016, USA

British Library Cataloguing in Publication Data

Inglis, Fred
  The management of ignorance: a political theory
  of the curriculum
  1. Education —— Great Britain —— Curricula
  I. Title
  375'.00941   LA632
  ISBN 0-631-14348-3

Library of Congress Cataloging in Publication Data

Inglis, Fred.
  The management of ignorance.
  Bibliography: p.
  Includes index.
  1. Curriculum planning.   2. Education--Great Britain--
Curricula.   3. Education--Philosophy.   I. Title.
LB1570.I554   1985   375'.001   85-9012
ISBN 0-631-14348-3

Typeset by Dentset, St. Clements, Oxford.

Printed in Great Britain by Page Bros (Norwich) Ltd

The Management of Ignorance

*To Lesley Aers
and Phillip Whitehead*

Contents

How did it come?
From outside, so it seemed, an endless source,
Disorder inexhaustible, strange to us,
Incomprehensible. Yet sometimes now
We ask ourselves, we the old citizens:
'Could it have come from us? Was our peace peace?
Our goodness goodness? That old life was easy
And kind and comfortable; but evil is restless
And gives no rest to the cruel or the kind.
How could our town grow wicked in a moment?
What is the answer? Perhaps no more than this,
That once the good men swayed our lives, and those
Who copied them took a while the hue of goodness,
A passing loan; while now the bad are up,
And we, poor ordinary neutral stuff,
Not good nor bad, must ape them as we can,
In sullen rage or vile obsequiousness. . . .'

Edwin Muir, 'The Good Town', *Collected Poems* (Faber & Faber, 1960)

Acknowledgements

In this book, as in the earlier ones I have written, an implicit but, as I intend, compelling theme is the idea and reality of friendship. Beyond that great name, I have sought to describe those values and beliefs, the disagreements as well as the mysteries of connection which hold men and women in friendship all their lives and at a greater depth than they understand. Further still, I have wanted to sound chords which resound not only in the membership of friends, but also join us to strangers who feel sufficiently the same about things to be counted, in a much-abused but still noble term, comrades. In the litany of socialism, the bonds of kinship are used to welcome those strangers who have come to ask for membership. I would like to think there are still thousands of teachers, whatever their institution or the ages of their students, who would be more moved than amused at the dignified and antique address of 'sister' or 'brother'. It is to them that I have tried to speak.

Directly also. For the book is dedicated to my sister Lesley, simply the best English teacher I have ever known in schools, and to Phillip Whitehead, loyalest of friends, sharpest of critics, and most faithful of comrades. In so far as this book professes a political agenda, then perhaps the best membership of teachers may still hope to see him pick it up on behalf of a future government.

There are many other friends who will, I hope, respond gladly enough to what I have written, but to whom in any case I owe much – in the way of ideas, hospitality, argument, kindness. Almost all this book was written while I held a Visiting Fellowship at the Humanities Research Centre at the Australian National University, Canberra. The extraordinary combination of generosity and comfort, geniality and intellectual energy which the Centre offers, cannot be exaggerated or too highly praised, and my gratitude to all its members, especially Ian Donaldson, who so unerringly combines kindness with acuity, and to his colleague,

Graeme Clark, is here set down. In Canberra also I learned to be glad of the rough and raucous way Peter Widdowson and James Grieve had with my ideas, and to take readily from Peter Herbst's prodigal store of learning.

I have often thanked Basil Bernstein and Quentin Skinner. I do so again. William Empson once said of T.S. Eliot, 'I do not know how much of my own mind he has made', and so it is for me with them. As much in their manners as in their thoughts, their patience and magnanimity are lessons in the good life of scholars, and there are few like them. Lastly I am grateful to my daughters for their fluent and fighting way with the educational obduracy reported and theorized in these pages; if the book *does* work for good, it works for them. Jessica also gave precious help with proofs and index, as did David Collins.

Acknowledgements are due to Faber & Faber Ltd for their permission to quote the lines from 'The Good Town' by Edwin Muir and 'East Coker' and 'Dry Salvages' by T.S. Eliot, and to Routledge & Kegan Paul Ltd and Harper & Row Ltd for the quotation from Martin Heidegger.

Fred Inglis

1

The State of the Nation

There is a battle being fought for the nation's soul. It is not a very military sort of battle. Its site is much more the familiar scenery of urban wreckage, of blasted and despoiled waste ground, smashed windows and kicked-in doors, ruined and rusting car chassis and derelict cookers, than a proud, archaic battlefield of Middle-earth, with banners and trumpets and lances. Half the time its soldiers don't know who's leading them on, or where the enemy is, and whether they'll be paid at the end of the month. Many of them, it is true, have no idea what the battle is about, or how on earth they would hear about it if they had won.

But there is a battle, all the same. And this book is meant to be read at the front and by the guerrilla. It is not for the General Staff, nor for the awful journalists from other countries who have come to watch the fight, to cheer on one side, and to vilify the other. It is meant to be a help, and help in a battle can only come in the shape of reinforcements – weapons, troops, food – or in the shape of intelligence (a good word) – reconnaissance data, secret information, maps.

I write as a teacher and parent of the taught. The battle now being fought, like all battles, is about power and territory; as a matter of necessity, it follows that it is also about freedom and justice, and the structures each denotes of property and habitation. As a result of victory or defeat, people may say, 'we've won or lost our home'. A just war is fought in defence of your home.

The battle of Britain now being won and lost has been going on for much more than a hundred years, and won't be finished for a long time yet. It turns on such essences of home as shelter, safety, protection from sudden injury, care in illness, a seemly veneration for the old, the promise of happiness held out to young children, the possibility of love, understanding, continuity, a live identity and an honest role for every man and woman.

The armies of the night arraigned against these fundamental qualities of a good home and a good society are multitudinous, headlong, and dreadfully destructive. To say that they are led by the grim horsemen of capital and old corruption is, however, like saying that Wallenstein or even Catholicism won the Thirty Years' War. For people give themselves crazily to bad causes, or are swept up into great currents of change, dissolution and ruin by mere accident, and just now these dark, poisonous forces incarnate themselves as indifference, hatred, vindictiveness, malevolence, greed, murder, all the unkillable deadly agents disguised in the bland reiterations of public communication as unemployment, robbery with bodily harm, racism, claiming sectarian responsibility, enterprise, rationalization.

To redescribe our nation in a harsher language is not to collapse politics into morality; it is, however, to seek to undo the lethal work of demoralization. Street murders in Belfast, the seedy running-down of decent nursing in London or Birmingham, the silent, workless wharves of Glasgow and Newcastle, the smashed and empty tenements of Liverpool, these are all the acted and individual consequences of political structures which have been put together and mechanized by the deliberate decisions of men and women. This is the damage inevitable in civil war, and the casualties – the old and ill and unemployed and beaten up (by the lawless or by the law) and very small – are as usual mostly civilian and all of them doggedly uncomprehending. The armies come in, and no one can stop them; you can't tell whose side they're on or what the sides are; but then more of the factories along the waterfront fall silent, or another wing of the hospital becomes half-empty and unkempt, or straight rows of once-decent terraces are boarded up and bricked in and become filthy with refuse, or a redbrick-and-railings school shuts.

Within this common, familiar present the lines of a very long, antique history can only be seen if the actor steps back for a moment and becomes a spectator. The great paradox of the thought that broke Europe open at the end of the eighteenth century in the name of enlightenment is that its spokesmen, whether in philosophy (Hegel), art (Turner), poetry (Wordsworth) or music (Beethoven), while committing themselves to the energies of progress, everywhere insisted on the certainty of tragedy. But only the spectator can see and feel tragedy; to do so requires exemption from everyday life, a compassionate leave of a kind that everyday life as lived by most people never grants, because the demands that business go on as usual are altogether too imperious and pressing. The spectator watches the action; the actor merely performs it. And so, within the deep disturbances, the abrupt and absolute fractures of present British experience, its fierce, sporadic conflicts and resistance, all of which are so chronically and complacently generalized as 'crisis', there is constantly the generation and actuality of tragedy.

Not many people speak of things like that, of course. For our public political language has long been devised in order to manage that same crisis in as harmoniously inequitable a way as its different classes of speech-makers would allow. In what may be designated the labour culture, in which work itself is the most powerful resource of meaning (and in which meaning itself is an increasingly scarce resource), the modalities of public language have for the duration of this century been those of negotiation. In the earlier days of its crisis, that language took as its master-symbols in all classes what were then renamed the traditional English virtues of fair play, ability to compromise, tolerance, a sense of justice.[1] These were the rights and attributes of the 'free-born Englishman', inscribed in the very principles and structures within which Englishmen argued after those decidedly unEnglish occasions in which members of the famously unified national family had crushed one or two brother-skulls or broken a few parental windows. Fair play, tolerance, and the rest – all of them morally excellent and necessary qualities in any class-divided society hoping not to tear itself open along the fissures of its stratification – are cashed at the conference tables of public negotiation as amounts of percentage pay rises, of welfare services cut and restored, of numbers of people sacked or taken on.

But those tables have, inevitably, a chairman to whose quiet authority the negotiators must turn when, in the nature of things, agreement cannot be found, and someone has to be autocratic. Then this public figure must call on this authority and the master-symbols to which he (*sic*) is responsible, in order to reprove other negotiators for failing to speak for the Britain it is everyone's common interest to defend.

'We may even say, well I'm here and you don't speak for me.'
'Exactly', the figure replies, with an unruffled confidence in
his role, for now a different consciousness, a more profound
dramatisation, begins to take effect; 'You speak for yourself,
but I speak for Britain'. 'Where is that?', you may think to
ask, looking wonderingly around. On a good day from a high
place, you can see about fifty miles. But you know some
places, you remember others; you have memories, definitions
and a history.'[2]

That unruffled figure, with his many different and identical
faces, is at his work of national importance now, drawing up
different memories, definitions, and history for us all to negotiate
over and agree to. The redefinition of what he calls Britain (and I
call, as it happens, the unbelievably beautiful reaches of Teesdale;
as for you, you'll have your own places) is going busily ahead. The
reassuringly named home counties continue to surround the
capital of capital; in a briskly modernizing metaphor, the
London-Bristol ellipse has become the service zone to the
quadrilateral of banks, property, insurance, and state which
provides the force-field for this late, cruel stage of (in a phrase)
monopoly capitalism, with its leading edge in communications
technology and its centre of gravity in the weapons industry.
Beyond the ellipse, in a wide arc, there are the new landowners
(though plenty of them with the old names) and ranch or factory
farmers whose patriotic success in over-production has won such
benefits from the Common Agricultural Policy. And beyond *them*,
there is the other England, Scotland, Ireland and Wales whose
dead estuaries I began by describing and whose people have
suffered or colluded with the invasions, forced evictions and
emigration, the loss of power and territory of all colonies.
    These are the movements of the history of the new Britain; it has
reminded several people of the old Spain.[3] In its absolutist days, as
its capital and administrative resources proved unable to organize
more imperial expansions, and as its markets in South and North
America became mere dominated territory with little yield and a
killing cost in jurisdiction and military control, Spain went
coasting down into its long decline. The new piratical imperialists,
in the Netherlands and England, proved much more buoyant,
ruthless and adaptable. Grim old Spain, held in the rigidities of

church and state absolutism, lost the competition worldwide. The Spanish left their names, their architecture, their language and their social forms at every point of the compass; their ruling class, regrouped in a small enclave at the south of the Iberian peninsula, hung onto their money, and simply petrified, while the rest of the country went to pot by way of going back to the direst poverty.

It is a history, with its powerful and inevitable tragedies, which it would be easy to adapt to Britain at the present time (the Netherlands' loss of empire is instructive in a very different way). And indeed trying to write the present as tragic history is part of my intention. But I seek to do so with a decided eye on praxis, on what may be *done* about the response to this history on the part of that corner of the systems of production which produces knowledge and meaning. As I said, I write as a teacher and parent of the taught, and in the human and the natural sciences alike there is to my mind no formal distinction, but only a procedural one between teaching and inquiry (or, as they say, re-search), as well as there being no knowledge without meaning. (To allege there could be is surely nonsensical.)

Is such a claim merely (as they say again) a matter of semantics? Well, if semantics is the study of meaning, then that is all it is. But there is more to the study of meaning than there looks. Think of all that we mean when we say, 'that means a lot to me', as well as when we ask heatedly, 'what on earth do you mean?' At once it is clear that by the concept 'meaning', as by that of 'value', we designate a concentration of significance, a density of vital experience and of precious activity and materials which somehow focus and order parts of our life, and therefore of life itself.

Such a definition is not so much philosophy as tautology. I have said that we find meaning where something is significant; now something which signifies, means. So the weight of interrogation falls less on what meaning is, and more on that something. We all of us try to make sense of our lives – in the phrase we often use, when we say that we can see no meaning in something that has happened to us, then if the event was important, our failure to find some meaning for it will press upon the very centre of our lives.

In all this talk, versions of which can be found in the most unphilosophical and non-technical of conversations, the effort to define and create meaning may be said to be itself a main purpose of people's lives. Notoriously, that purpose has been harder and harder to understand, let alone fulfil, since Britain became more or less entirely secularized. But it is not perfectly essential to call in God if you are making a new religion. The defeated, no doubt, leave us their symbols, thoroughly perfected and disinfected by death, but there is no promise that the symbols themselves will answer to our beseeching. Making meanings, the province of the sorcerer, the magus, the monk and the shaman, is now the work not of necromancers, but of a quite unmysterious cultural bureaucracy. Nor do I intend any bright irony at their expense. The victories won over monks and magicians and their royal masters were clear victories for freedom and reason and truthfulness, and if it turns out that the dispersal and dissolution of old powers has left us with a lot of meaning to make for ourselves, then that blossoming labour is the simple price of freedom, itself a great meaning in Europe and the world, at least since the English civil war.

So the fact that the meaning-makers have a lot to do is an exhilarating fact, part of the excitement of which is that such a freedom has turned out to be quite unrationed, and therefore anybody has felt free (in a phrase) to make a meaning in terms which suit his or her historical convenience. Thus and thus, in quite recent British history, the new classes and new nations have set to invent themselves brand-new traditions and freshly made longevities from the bits and pieces history left about the place. It is a supportable generalization that present-day culture was more or less completely made up between about 1820 and 1860; certainly, the age-old and immutable traditions of, for instance, ancient British regiments, similarly ancient public schools newly emerged from the sadistic barbarism and rote-learning of a few years earlier, even the timeless tartan of the Scottish clans, were all the invention of new, self-made and self-making social formations looking for forms and expressions with which to stake their claim in Victorian Britain.[4]

By the same token and with much the same energy, the harder business of inventing a history and a symbolism for those determinedly excluded from such processes of self-determination was carried on by the English working class,[5] at first in underground rituals of membership, and then with a public splendour in the summer shows of power at the union galas, banner marches, and wakes weeks. Similarly, the longer struggle of British women, especially its bourgeois intellectual women, to make themselves a different history, politics, education and literature out of the same material as the men had organized for themselves, started towards the end of the century and was brought to its peak with the success of the suffrage movement.

Such work is the most familiar version of human creativity, and its business is unstoppable. Perhaps by now the justification for the military imagery with which I began will become clearer. For although the waste and expropriation of industrial change are every bit as severe and, if need be, as deadly as I described them, the larger battle, as is always said by the bluff spokesmen for the military these days, is for the hearts and minds of the people. And the present civil war over the meanings and values of our polity is as fierce and contested as any in the past. Its honours are less geographically precise than those of Edgehill, Naseby, Marstor Moor, or the scaffold, but they will be as significant, even if those names themselves should remind both the over-sanguine and the downright bloodthirsty that clear cut victories are much less decisive when you come to the post-war settlements.

The civil and civilian battle for domination over the territory of meaning is all the keener for meaning itself having become, as I remarked, in a world of depleted and overspent resources, exceedingly scarce.[6] Not only the death of Gods (who none the less turn out, as the examples of Warsaw and Tehran remarkably bear witness, to have the amazing powers of immortality their prophets always claimed for them), but the failure of many modern myths, myths of life and death, and love and truth themselves, which have drastically faltered and buckled at a time when their ideological load was too heavy, have left whole peoples with no satisfactory stories to give shape and purpose to the way of things.

For I shall take these large, overstuffed, necessary words like meaning and value to be usable and intelligible only in the arc of a narrative, and each narrative as part of 'the ensemble of stories we tell ourselves about ourselves'.[7] And indeed the story of the stories[8] is both the subject and object of my book. For it is not only the oldest religious tales which have had to undergo some crisis of implosion and renewal, but some very much more modern ones, including the story of modernity itself and how to attain it (modernization). In Britain, this is still a story revised and retold at every general election, and since it is so familiar to us, it will serve as a short text for practical criticism.

The modernization story may be said to date from the advent of capitalism in political economy, and from the advent of a theory of natural rights in political ideologies, both as coinciding in the rough, wide world with the half-century of revolution and insurrection in Europe from 1789 to 1848. In the story, the heroes are the new class which tears down the narrow prohibitions, the superstitious traditions which not only uphold, but *are* the old order, and free their own energies and gifts, especially those of enterprise, daring, freebooting, individual *élan*, in a world of free thought and trade, where natural justice ensures the nice adjustment of reward to merit, once the controls of an out-dated tyranny have been broken.

By the middle of the century, this story was institutionalized in a dozen forms of the culture's expression, from tales of the origins of the new department stores and imperial traders as they appeared on tea-caddies and jampots, to the many romances of a true love which threw off tyrannical fathers (and their out-of-date way of doing business) in the name of newly successful marriages crowning newly cascading fortunes. The modern success story took its personal, or private morality from the romantics, and its public, or economic morality from utilitarianism and the free marketeers. Karl Marx, in a genial aside, noted this ingenuous complementarity in the drafts for *Capital* that he wrote in 1856:

> The bourgeois viewpoint has never advanced beyond the antithesis between itself and the romantic viewpoint and the latter will accompany it as its legitimate antithesis up to its blessed end.[9]

Marx no doubt saw it all ironically, but the success story of the bourgeoisie, still recounted on regular television since the record–breaking *Forsyte Saga*, has moved great segments of the world irrevocably forward, and fixed some versions of individualism ineradicably in our national and moral vocabulary. The mighty doctrines of progress, of social advance brought about by the unfettered zeal and sheer hard work of many energetic men, of unprecedented prosperity and comfort following inevitably the headlong train of industrialization, of personal fulfilment and civil weal guaranteed by the natural workings of honest, upright yeomen and their faithful wives, these all have found their way into the frames of mind and structures of feeling not only of our present Britain, but, in weird translations, of our whole world.

It has a very strong appeal. The principles of individual rights allied to the Romantic celebration of feelings has something in it for boys and girls; the spiral of effort crowned by success driving on to new effort inscribes forceful motivation in the essence of individual identity, and in constantly postponing ultimate success, ensures (when it works) that aspiration continues to impel labour throughout a man's life; to follow up the sacramental nature of privacy encloses a special frame of life within which wives may be loved, mothers protected, and the life of the feelings cherished by its custodians.

Put in such general terms, it is a very familiar story, still going strong in the admonitions of not a few editorialists, headmasters *(sic)*, Mills and Boon novels, and even, when suitably got up in blow-dried hair, chocolate blusher and homely swimming pools, re-issued in sexy television bestsellers. But the story carries less and less plausibility, which is perhaps why it is so easy to summarize. Once upon a time, that was how people lived and what they believed; *they* couldn't see it as a story. Now there are too many contrary tales, about what happens to those who didn't get on, about the different values and virtues of a different class, which looked so much more human and decent when you'd left them for the room at the top, about the absence of fulfilment and the sheer misery which attended some of the successes, about the hideous emptiness of working to make useless objects or weapons of death. Ours being a liberal culture, and it being a premiss of such freedoms that every story has its opposite version, or negation, the success story, successful as it still is, has had to contend with more and more compelling narratives in which it is shown up as a lie. And so, as I said, interested parties have seized in their partial way upon the stories which suited them, and discomfited their enemies.

This is the struggle for meaning, and the meaning-minders are in particular difficulties now, pulled between the obvious falsehoods of the success story, and the powerful situation of those who want it told again in an up-to-date version. For whatever truth the success story held on behalf of a smallish number of the bourgeoisie between, let us say, 1848 and 1968 – dates offering themselves for their historical flourish – not only was it never true for most people, but it has come to look as though to tell it now as if it were true is to ensure bitter disappointment for many, certain conflict for all, and even, in some portion of the world, absolute destruction. Indeed, one reason why the story is so visible now *as* a story is because it has begun to die (in writing, nothing is easier than to raise the dead).

What is more, those I have called the meaning-minders are themselves hardly disinterested. The cultural bureaucracy, like all bureaucracies (as Weber pointed out once and for all[10]) is there as an impartial arm of the state to serve its clients anonymously and efficiently, whether or not it approves of their purposes and persons; but at the same time the bureaucacy creates its own fierce purposes and compelling irrationalities within its own milieu. A bureaucracy, like any organism, struggles for survival. The meaning-minders, within the divisions of labour of the advanced economies, are to be found in all the welfare bureaucracies as well as the cultural ones – which obviously enough include the official and most explicit story-tellers of the culture, such as television producers and their vast teams for story-making, novelists and journalists and teachers. Their stories are told to themselves, as well as the rest of us.

Teachers, as I intimated, are my hoped-for audience. But the vicious class divisions of Britain bite connections off everywhere, and the word 'teachers' generally connotes only those teaching in schools, and occasionally those teaching in that carefully design-ated sector, Further Education. Those in what we revere as Higher Education are invariably known as lecturers, and even the thin air breathed at these Himalayan levels is divided between colleges and polytechnics, whose heights are still a little lower than the summits touched by the pinnacles of the ivory towers of the universities. In spite of these unignorable and assiduously maintained distinc-tions, I shall speak of teaching as the common activity of all teachers, just as I shall invoke the domain of official knowledge as a single geography and history, rather than as a form of cultural capital[11], whose senior bankers are the university staffs.

The metaphor 'knowledge as capital' is the real subject of the book. Nationalizing knowledge, drastically altering the way in which it is portioned out and withheld, ensuring that its production was co-operative and its benefits equally shared, such a revolution in social relations would be as great as the equivalent revolution needed to change the control of capital itself. And the idea for such a change comes from the other, opposing story about the course of modernization, the story of socialism. That story also has become incredible in its simplest and original forms, not only because the classical version of speedy revolution brought about by an immiserated industrial proletariat has *nowhere* taken place, but also because where a revolutionary mixture, always peculiar to its society, of intelligentsia, patriots, peasants and workers *has* wrested power to itself, the great names of freedom and justice have so often been fouled and degraded by the purported necessities of the politics. Yet, like all great doctrines capable of sustaining men and women in oppression and hugely moving whole societies towards unenvisageable ends, socialism in its many versions (its stories) continues to survive dishonour and its self-generated and horrible vengefulness,[12] in order to offer one of the very few plausible narratives of the future which has a happy and not an apocalyptic end.

In Britain, just now, and indeed in most of Europe and all of North America, to speak commendingly of socialism empties most lecture rooms pretty quickly and demolishes most electoral support. In academic and intellectual circles, there is, as national economies prove intractable and indifferent to the theories which have worked fairly reliably since 1945 or so, an unsurprising and repellently self-congratulatory recrudescence of the kind of conservatism which sets out to justify the way things are, in order to hang onto the comforts of academic gentility without any accompanying duties. And in the larger polity of Britain, the word socialism only connotes the intermittent decency, incompetence, deep philistinism, honest effort and regardless time-serving which was the Labour Party in power between 1964 and 1970, 1974 and 1979.

So to address an educational and academic argument to the possibility and admirableness of an imaginable British socialism needs both nerve and, it seems, fatheadedness at the present juncture. Plenty of venerable spokesmen have intoned a grave valediction over the god that failed,[13] and it is certainly a telling objection simply to point at some of the more extrme zealots in socialist sects, and wait for laughs. None the less, I hold in a modest way two largish ambitions. In the first, I would like to address those in the teaching community who still want to recognize the feasibility and admirableness of the socialist story as well as wanting more or less urgently to retell it in a different form for a new generation. In such a venture, there is no need for the spreading abroad of the greasier kinds of supreme unction to which such story-telling may incline. Quite without attributing all the evils of the world to the old bitch gone in the teeth, capitalism herself, it is clearer than ever before what a beastly unjust as well as abominably dangerous place the world is, and further, that – also as never before – all history is world history, that every fraction of each economy and society interlocks with every other, and that the complex and absolute mutuality and interdependence of the world is complete and precarious.

In these circumstances, and sensibly stepping off the world stage onto the smaller, friendlier platforms of everyday necessity, it is perfectly possible to speak on these of goodwill and some appropriate knowledge of human mutuality, of the justice, loving-kindness, equal freedoms and duties, prevention of avoidable want and resistance to cruelty, which are its material definitions. If an audience of those with such goodwill and knowledge is not to be found among teachers, where else is it? And having gathered itself together, for it to discuss the social structures and institutions which are the conditions of justice, freedom, equality, altruism, peacefulness and so forth, is in our time and country, with its deeply liberal and illiberal traditions, to discuss once more the practicality of a new socialism.

Any such debate, however, is grounded in a longer and larger one. For it is my second ambition to persuade those listening not only that the names of the virtues which in a quiet way they would stand by are the conditions and consequences of a decently socialist society, but also that their own best modes of thought are part of a long revision and recasting of the way in which Europeans (to go no further) do any thinking at all. That is to say, for over a century and a half many powerful minds have addressed themselves to correcting the distortions and to healing the wounds caused by the amazing triumphs of scientific thought-forms, and the depth and finality with which they have established themselves in Western culture. The dreadful monsters of modern weaponry are highly visible and crazy signs that the understanding of physical nature has vastly outstripped our capacity to understand human nature, and in the absence of a rational and morally adequate 'science of human affairs',[14] we are likely to destroy ourselves.

Such fearful adjurations before that hideous strength are very much of 1984. But the critique of a narrow scientism, of the view that man is a mind whose business is to know with certainty his surrounding natural environment as a set of objects open to his inspecting senses, a definition which includes other men also inspected as objects, has been going strong at least since the heroes of Romanticism launched it. Two heroes not always invoked as products of Romanticism may serve to fix my second ambition. The ambition is to reassure the teachers of goodwill, trying as gallantly as possible to criticize the depredations of their tiny corner of a bad dark world by the faint light of more human standards, that what they are doing, in the most actual, practical way, is to push forward a social and political theory of nearly two centuries in the making. Trying to match scientific knowledge of an *object* with self-awareness as a *subject* is roughly the same thing as trying to adjust scientific knowledge to fit a reasonable scheme of human interests. The two heroes are Hegel and Marx (our rural English versions could be William Blake and William Morris).

Hegel set off to criticize the monumental achievement of his predecessor Kant, and of the method of thought set out and advocated by Descartes, which identified epistemology, or the study which determines the grounds for saying that we *know* something (pretty well) for certain, as *the* subject of philosophy, and crowned philosophy queen of the sciences. In his great and baffling work, *The Phenomenology of Spirit*, which Hegel finished in 1808, he attacked the whole notion that knowledge and our claims about it stand in some immediate, direct relation to both our system of concepts and our unproblematic sense-experience. Hegel irrevocably relativized the whole inquiry, first by showing that all ideas, including ideas about reality and its unchangingness, are radically subject to historical change, and that, secondly as well as consequently, the subject who claims to know anything is himself historically and partially situated, and where he happens to be standing affects and inflects anything he thinks he knows. Accordingly, if we are to assess the validity of what people say they know, we have to evaluate *their* whole relation to their knowledge, and not just what looks like the simple knowledge itself.

Hegel's is the name we can pick out at the beginning of a movement now designated Romanticism which hugely disturbed the confident advance of thinkers and creators towards what they saw as progress and enlightenment, even while it exhilarated them with its powerful additions to the theories of human nature and society. In innumerable ways, Hegel's contemporaries individualized (and therefore made relative) the structures of experience, turned attention to the dark, passionate, irrational and unpredictable thoroughfares of the human heart, celebrated change and growth as new values in themselves, and drenched the European imagination in the sense of its own historicality, so that today even those millions of adults and children who share a general social amnesia troop helplessly past historical monuments and buildings in some token response to the changes of 1800.

These changes released the energy of those who wanted to criticize and resist the self-confident advance of scientific rationalism across the whole front of society. But as the nineteenth century proceeded, it became clear to many thinkers, and Marx was the greatest among them, that to take Hegel's critique of knowledge seriously meant also that the critic criticize the whole of the social conditions which produced knowledge. 'Turning Hegel on his head', as Marx himself put it, meant engaging with the totality of knower-plus-knowledge in his historical location, certainly, but rejecting Hegel's essentially conservative idea that full self-understanding, the unities of subject and object, knowledge and self-knowledge, can only come about retrospectively, and after the appropriate social conditions have been accomplished. Marx put away scornfully the idea, itself known as idealism, that ordinary finite men and women arrive at the good society by their successful identification with the absolute and infinite spirit of reason.

Marx made, for our genteelly thoughtful and educative purposes, two drastic innovations. First, he situated those finite men and women not in the uncircumscribed galaxies of inner reason, but in the finitude of their material, largely economically material lives. He at once theorized and demonstrated that only by patient, scrupulous attention to the material facts of life can we understand how the social institutions arise which make people as they are, and which shape the relations which define how they think and feel. Second, he sought to give this kind of knowledge prior purchase on these structures of society so that those in possession of it could *use* it, not as in Hegel's method for the recapitulative understanding of how they got to be where they were (though such historical understanding remains for Marx the logical first step towards praxis), but rather as an instrument for the transformation of society and social relations which are not adequate to the knowledge we have of them. Knowledge of material circumstances leads, in Marx's argument, to a self-knowledge that insists that our criticism of our present always asymmetrical ignorance (some of which is highly convenient to a few powerful figures) must lead to actions which, repairing that deliberate ignorance, make it possible to repair the want and cruelty it causes. For Marx, the dialectical play of thought over the methods of inquiry produces a knowledge capable, if properly understood and used, of unmasking the hateful irrationalities of actual, bourgeois society, and of guiding its transformation into the good life.[15]

Marx supremely gives those whose business knowledge is, the teachers, a powerfully liberating and inevitably subversive picture of that knowledge. This is not to profess any sanctimony on behalf of Marxism; as observed, too much foulness, lying and murder has gone on in Marxism's name for a comfortably middle-aged English academic, or some slightly younger denim Danny of the ILEA, still to be plumping for the slogans of 1917. It is to say, however, that no teacher should by now be unaware that knowledge is highly relative, that it may be highly critical and even, with the most liberal permissiveness, sharply subversive for both better and worse, and that the nursery scientist's view that facts are facts, and that theories are determined by observation and falsification, at least misses out on the whole realm of a different order of knowledge. Marx's name can be used to identify this different order of knowledge – order in the sense that ways of seeing and experiencing, objects of thought and the very things of the world themselves may be brought within its frames and made intelligible.

Later theories have given this version of the interpenetration of knowledge, inquiry, experience and values the title 'critical theory', and I mention this only to give my summary a ready handle, and to repeat that any teacher conscious of his or her responsibility to the changeability and uncertainty of knowledge (and the curriculum), and hoping, however mildly, for a better world in the future for the children to live in, should be able to take heart by standing on a few of these premises, many of them first assembled by Marx. (Beginners, as I noted, will find them paraphrased in honest and elementary English in William Morris's talks and lectures to working-class people.[16]

1 Knowledge is a product (and if so, it is more like a work of art than a manufactured object).
2 It can only be produced by the application to experience of theories.
3 Experience and theories about experience are dialectically related (that is to say, there is constant and reciprocal traffic between them).
4 This movement between theory and experience produces *reflexive* (or reflective) knowledge, i.e. it is endlessly subject to correction, as the theory is subject to history.
5 Such theory is aimed at producing enlightenment in the agents who hold them, i.e. at enabling those agents to determine what their true interests are.[17]
6 Such theory is liberating; it frees human beings from self-imposed self-frustration, and makes change for the better possible.
7 Such theory – critical theory – is reflexive, possesses its own valid epistemology and cognitive processes, and above all, is the essential, inevitable motion of *all* rational, self-conscious beings who are bound to strive (perhaps incoherently) for ever greater freedom, fulfilment, and self-critical awareness.
8 These three goals (or *telos*), freedom, fulfilment, and self-critical awareness, are the epistemes (or given grounds) of the epistemology which vindicates the knowledge produced by critical theory.

This necessarily technical summary leads to a conclusion any more or less awake teacher will want to endorse, that 'reflection' is an entirely valid kind of knowledge (and who on earth is the philosopher to tell us that it isn't), and that knowledge for educational purposes should always be, in a key word, 'relevant' to the best human project, as it conduces to the good society and worthy lives.

This potted history of ideas and small excursion into philosophizing is intended to restore to teachers at any level some sense of the necessarily intellectual form and content of what they do, and also of that engagement with knowledge, whether in helping 10-year-olds in their first decoding of fossils on the way to an idea of evolution or in aiding an HND student in his grasp on telephone electronics, as being powerfully and inescapably historical, and, in the most direct and most individual way, political and economic. While that 'economic' is no encouragement to the view that education is an adjunct to the gross national product, it is true for socialist and non-socialist teachers alike that they cannot get away without a commitment to standards and costs of living.

This is a reminder the point of which is worth sticking quite deep into teachers' sensibilites. We live, as remarked,[18] in a negotiation culture. Within such a culture, there is a public forum in which interest groups protest their desserts in an endless debate over the allocation of resources. Naturally, each group is obliged to break into wails of self-pity (sometimes justified, no doubt, but that hardly matters in the convention) when governments announce the year's rations. Only if they can represent themselves as badly done to, and always as meriting more generous treatment, will they be given a respectful hearing at the *next* debate. And so on. Such procedures institutionalize the structures of self-pity as framing dominant public feeling and serve to legitimate such mild political action as strikes, or measures against strikes.

It is therefore as difficult a task to persuade teachers as it would be any comparable and substantial interest group that theirs really is a voice to figure largely in that debate on national resources which issues in the many measures of our standards of living. 'Not us', they cry, 'no one listens to us. Now once upon a time . . . ' And in those good old days, teachers really were teachers, well-loved, well-hated, stern, gentle, telling you what, not asking what you want, sticking to the 3 Rs, and not getting mixed up in all this difficult stuff where there's no right answer. It's surprising how often these myth-heroes rise as giants from the folklore of teachers as well as parents; their great purpose is always to take the measure of a foreshortened present against an epic past. Beside these towering heroes, we can do nothing.

And yet teachers as never before are powerful, audible, visible, respected, *educated*. Such a claim cannot be put down either by the ghosts of popular novels or by the chorus of self-pity. Compared with the dismal barbarisms of the old elementary schools[19] and the arrogant instruction of the so much lamented

grammar schools,[20] contemporary teachers are models of cultivation, conscientiousness, judiciousness and a worthy attention to
the natures and rights of others. Set against the standing of the
dark-suited professions – doctors, lawyers, architects and the like
– then school teachers stand closer to academics than ever before
(however much the academics shrink shamefully away), and for
the same thing. By the exceedingly mixed tokens of, say, degree
status, autonomy over training schemes, professional associations
and research, their funding and public standing, proportion of
public expenditure spent on education, access to public communications (television and newspaper), by all these indices, school
teachers and tertiary teachers are indeed a vigorous, self-confident
and well-heeded estate of the nation.

This being so, then above all at a time of such lowering loss of
nerve on the part of all those whose public role it is to cherish the
best values of the political culture and to be guardians of as good a
life as may be lived in Britain at the end of the twentieth century,
teachers may be expected to fight for the light in the civil war over
meanings and values as reported here. The vocation of teachers is
to knowledge and its cognates, the good, the true, and the
beautiful. Their fight ranges over the terrain of what that offical
knowledge is – over what is known, who shall know it, and what
may be done with it for a living. They stand, therefore, at the
intersection of values and production. Consequently, their practice
is dramatically silhouetted quite near the heart of the action in
which different people claim to 'speak for Britain'. 'Where is that?'
we wonder once again . . . Well, let us agree that one place Britain
may be found is in the stories we tell ourselves about ourselves, but
particularly in those which are believed and believable. That rich
tapestry, in the immortal phrase, is the nation's curriculum; within
its variously coloured weave, every picture tells a story, and the
meanings of the stories, as Hegel and Marx advised us, are always
changing, according to who is in charge.

The stories have to change, as the nation's world-position, its
rulers, and therefore its identity change. To speak at least for a
corner of the British heart, through the vicious clamour of other
hateful British stories about such delicious topics as getting on,
doing well, making fortunes, killing other nationalities, booting
out blacks, trampling on the weak, and standing on that populist
form of transport, your own two feet, is to speak up for the

humanly admirable purposes to which what we as a people know may be put in a future which certainly looks sombre, but it is not at all certain to be deadly. There is much laid down in the veins of British culture which may ignite the lights of the future; to mine that energy is the work of teachers. It is an innocent datum of this book that in this single, modest moral barony much may be done to advance a decent version of a transfigured and domesticated socialism. The nation's curriculum, the forms and contents of its official systems of knowledge, is the fount and realm of the stories which make any such future imaginable.

2

Grammar and Narrative

The forces ranged against such a project loom darkly and portentously; indeed it is their military commitment to kill it off. But in the present confusion of things, there is, and will be, no simple alignment of those defending or advancing a warm-heartedly benign and socialist view of culture and the curriculum, and those resisting them according to the principles of whatever the opposite may be called. In which case, history having so many labyrinthine corridors, is it not ignorance rather than innocence to protest for some reborn version of socialism? Wouldn't it be more prudent to redraw the map of knowledge according to some very much more provisional and non-doctrinal world picture?

Non-doctrinal prudence still carries solid political weight, even in a polity which, as Britain's has, has lived for three decades on an overdraft of such prudentiality that it has left itself bankrupt and dishonoured, combining utter timidity and insane militarism, professing civic virtues, while practising urban ruin. But the vast changes in the world order, and the craven myopia of the country in refusing to see them, now force on the attention of us all the immediacy of choices about how we live which cannot be covered by prudentiality and caution, doctrinal or not. The kind of life the children of the present day – those, let us say, now in school and therefore in classrooms from infant reception through to the A-level examination hall – will be able to lead as members of happy families of owner-occupying, tax-paying, vote-casting, TV-watching, cold-war-waging citizens in the year 2010 is being settled by what we do now. Central clauses in that settlement are written in the contents and forms of the school, college and university curriculum.

This is a truth, after all, pretty well acknowledged, at least as a conventional piety or source of hope, by anyone who speaks earnestly in public to graduation ceremonies or bunches of school-leavers; it is spoken for by any parent cornering his or her child's teachers in order to get a forecast for O-level grades. It is certainly acknowledged by those who pay the heavy cheques to the mighty piles of venerable stone disposed about the south of England for the guardianship of standards of excellence at the Headmasters' Conference. Such cheques are paid for the deliverance of knowledge certificates, which in turn admit bearers to precisely differentiated levels of income. This handful of A-level grades may be expected to be cashable for membership of that profession.

Independent-school fees prefigure a very stark equation between knowledge and the future. In a larger and less simple set of relations, quantities are set upon gross domestic product as ensured by numbers of children who can spell and compute to the base ten, upon the realities of democracy as upheld by citizens whose autonomy and rationality is kept in trim by doses of liberal principle, upon the planned-for quotas of creativity, technical innovation, enterprise and initiative, or honest obedience and docility. Notwithstanding all the arguments about education as organization or as manpower planning, as milieu or as relations-of-production, the domestically intelligible and directly popular view of education as what you are taught and therefore learn, what (more subtly) you are allowed to be taught and what you are up to learning, remains the heart of the matter, as it is in all senses the heart of culture.

This is now well recognized. The recognition follows upon the shock of political change: accelerating economic decline, the dislocation of values grounded in images of perpetual prosperity, the dispersal of a nation's identity as it lost power, the centrifugal tendency towards a disunited kingdom,[1] all these readily purchased, off-the-peg explanations of social uncertainty carry through deep into the forms and content of what on earth that nation knows, and thinks it needs to know. So, in the past ten to fifteen years it has become a truism to say that the curriculum as formally approved by the public educational system of any society is a product of the history of that society, and that as a history changes, so does a curriculum. Consequently there has been, in and out of school, a new level of consciousness about the meaning and function of a curriculum, and the dispute about the often conflicting interests a curriculum may be written to serve becomes, as I say, fiercer. In Britain, even in Westminster, prime ministers and their secretaries of state have at last spoken with party unison and inter-party enmity about curricular content and educational standards, the decline of both, and the import of both for a national economy.

In all educational institutions, teachers have engaged extensively not only in the practical discussion of new contents and their relevance to children's and student's needs and wants, but also, and necessarily, with the tension implicit in such matters which is entailed by claims about the maintenance of high standards and the inherent difficulty of certain kinds of study. Indeed, the often deep-seated changes in certain curricular areas (and the no less significant resistance to change) over the past quarter-century may be understood as a conscious and determined process of cultural reinterpretation, the agents of which – the producers and reproduc-ers of social value, meaning and symbol – have directly addressed themselves to questions of national and personal identity as these dissolved under the impact of the new world economic order.

This is a large and round way of naming the lines of everyday teaching experience. For the present fractures in the political economy (to say nothing of the theories which seek to direct it), the facts of unemployment, of youthful dissidence (riots), of old racial and class hatreds and new poverty, all more crudely visible than for many years, require unprecedentedly thoroughgoing and imaginative responses from deeply tired schoolteachers and distinctly timorous university lecturers, who are trying to build a believable world-picture into a curriculum. Furthermore, the present attenuations wrought upon the popular political vocabu-lary force those responses towards the disingenously stark categories of the caricature left or right, and make entirely intransigent the definition of the moral and political meanings which may, in a difficult country, support a reasonable theory of the human interests, and an educative curriculum capable of expressing it. And yet it is not unduly pessimistic to claim that without our science of human affairs – or as one might say, a speakable, sane and affirmative political vocabulary, speakable moreover by a whole national community – then the headlong destructiveness of the world can only accelerate.

To raise such questions with the official forms of the curriculum in mind looks at first sight like megalomaniac bathos. And yet a curriculum is no less than the knowledge system of a society, and therefore not only an ontology, but also the metaphysics and ideology which that society has agreed to recognize as legitimate and truthful; it sets the canons of truthfulness. In the industrialized nations on either side of the Iron Curtain, the curriculum, widely forgotten and even more widely misunderstood as it is bound to be, is the reference point and acknowledged definition of what knowledge, culture, belief, morality, really *are*. Parents refer naturally to it all the time, even (perhaps most of all) when they never learned any of it themselves; their children at their most obdurate faithfully accept the school curriculum as official, at worst so that they can celebrate the unofficial as a ritual of defiance.[2] And clearly, the society itself maintains, reinterprets and revises the varieties of its curricular experience as a way of reproducing itself in the next generation. The curriculum is a message to and about the future.

It is in these many grand meanings that the curriculum, from the reception class in the infants' school to the newest doctoral thesis, is both public and political. To understand its message to the future is to see something of central importance about our whole view of how we wish the next generation – our own children – to live well in an exceedingly threatening world.

But to use the pronoun 'we' is to simplify matters impossibly, even though it gets that genial, unruffled spokesperson of the real Britain away from the cameras. The pronoun smoothes over the deep corrugations and ruptures caused precisely by struggle over how that authoritative and editorial 'we' is going to be used. The curriculum, it is not melodramatic to declare, really is the battleground for an intellectual civil war, and the battle for cultural authority is a wayward, intermittently fierce, always protracted and fervent one. Its different guerrillas include parents, pupils, teachers, bureaucrats, left, right, centre, nationalities, and the compelling mercenaries of the market forces. To join that struggle over the meaning and essence of the conversation of culture and the structures of educated discourses is to enlist under certain colours, largely reddish ones, and to claim that the dispute must be settled in the names of a decent theory of real interests, a valid sense of individual identity located in a believable moral polity, and a sufficient account of how to live well in (and not to blow to bits) the frightening new world now trundling towards us over the hill.

I have twice spoken of a theory of real interests; it is a phrase which portends much, and what it has much portended and then brought to frightful realization in assorted politics since Hitler came to power in 1933 and Stalin began the treason trials three years later has been mostly lethal. Other people's theories of your real interests were then and are still very likely to be hardly recognizable as such, and to promise such very long-distance satisfactions in return for such abrupt and present discomforts that many people lose interest at once, and go back to dreaming the dreams of the television advertisement, which even if it never comes true, is at least nicer than the alternatives. Yet it is surely uncontentious to say that the world can hardly go on as it is, what with famine and plague and war, and that even if it could it wouldn't, because men and womem, in the name of a preferred scheme of real interests, would intervene to stop it, and turn it in other directions.

Whatever the dangers of a theory of interests, everybody has one, and in devising new curricula, purporting to answer the needs and wants, the interests and purposes, of individuals, classes and a nation, such a theory is always and easily in sight. For the moment, however, I shall stay away from the severer implications of the word 'theory', and propose that, along with a number of family terms which for this context includes model, metaphor (and metonymy), picture, hermeneutic (which means a theory of interpretation), fiction, even hypothesis, we go back to speaking of all categorial frameworks and structures of ideas as constituting a story, a consequential narrative. I have already claimed that all political beliefs connote or make explicit a story about the world, and the two most popular in the West[3] remain the liberal and socialist stories of modernization. Having asserted the essential connections between political world-views and the forms and contents of knowledge, perhaps it makes sense to claim now that every subject tells a story.

This intellectual handhold – 'every subject tells a story about the world' – is first of all useful in a tautological kind of way if we agree to associate the loose group of cognates which have been listed. Model, metaphor, categorial framework, hypothesis, as well as story itself, may all be said to classify the linguistic figure (the hope) by which human minds seek to characterize the many dimensions of experience in as compressed and economic way as possible. This is to speak with a marked partiality. The classical view of science itself, together with one history of the advance of mind, is of a process whereby nature is rendered, in a pure naturalism, by a system of perfectly transparent symbols whose referential value translates without remainder. Mathematics is the ultimate scheme of such aspiration, and the subject has been famously successful in bringing within its transparencies and exactitude much that was once intransigent or unintelligible. But over the same time, such a story has been criticized for a reductionism not merely unfaithful to the facts of natural life, but also regardless of the necessarily manifold and validly ambiguous nature of language itself. By this token, metaphor is *the* type of thought,[4] and imagination the faculty which, in devising new metaphors, enables new versions of nature to be seen in such terms, and therefore new theories to become thinkable. This view takes to heart the reality of magic words and spell-binding. It insists that when we devise and apply metaphors to the world, then we see the world as those metaphors organize our seeing for us. A standing joke from the school dining-room makes this clear. Small boys routinely try to put other small boys off their meal by re-describing the school lunch as something else, disgustingly inedible – 'dead man's leg' (meat loaf), 'elephant's foot' (spam fritter), 'bogey pie' (cornish pasty). If they are successful in putting someone off their lunch, then what they have done is to persuade the victim to *see* their lunch *as* the disgusting object; they have indeed spellbound them. Such a view makes metaphor into the defining mode of apprehension of the world. That is, we may (as babies, for example) conceptualize some at least of what we see without language intervening; when, however, we name what we see, language becomes the lens through which we can see at all. Once we go beyond the very simple naming of objects in the material world, by which we teach children their earliest vocabulary, the manifold and multivalent nature both of objects and the cultural seeing of those objects can only be rendered by the transposition of qualities which we generalize as metaphor, but the many details and gradations of which are listed in the classic rhetoric books discovered and vastly extended after the Renaissance.[5]

Perhaps this elementary account of the relations between percept, concept and metaphor has much too nominalist a look about it for the professional, whether philosopher or cognitive psychologist. But what I am trying to represent is a rough-and-ready scheme of mind in which metaphor, as an essential feature of language (a feature without which there could hardly *be* language), meets the imagination, the human faculty by which the vision and re-vision of mere events is turned into experience of an intelligible, meaning-bearing sort. The case is that the structures of our metaphors not only frame our seeing and understanding of the world, but constitute that world; they are its ground and being.

The case, however, does not stop there. When we speak of the structure of a metaphor, we imply the power it possesses to inform and reform our articulation of the world. But the word metaphor typically suggests the formation: noun (and adjective); more rarely does it suggest: subject plus predicate. If we take a tip from literary criticism, however, we may treat whole poems as metaphors, and, by extension, a single poetic drama (initially, at Wilson Knight's suggestion, Shakespearian drama) and eventually a novel as 'extended metaphors'.[6] Such usage may seem too technical and local an occasion to justify the production of a straight line from metaphor to narratives of all kinds. But without going further into a tricky argument, perhaps it will do here to say that, as metaphors, especially those with an indicative predicate, attribute an association of qualities to a world-out-there, which, inasmuch as they are felicitous and economic, enable us to comprehend (which means, etymologically, to en-fold) that world more practically, scientifically, aesthetically, according to what our present purposes are, then a metaphor is an incipient narrative.

At any rate, then, I am risking the loose association of metaphor with narrative, as well as with theory, model, paradigm,[7] hermeneutic and so forth, in order to emphasize the theory-laden character of knowledge, even in its most primitive forms. So in order to be able to make such innocent remarks as 'I know that for a fact' or, as a teacher might say of a history essay, 'don't go in for theory; just give me as many of the facts of the matter as you can', we have to have a doubtless underived epistemology (that is, a theory of what the grounds are for claiming to know anything at all), a theory of interests (or, as one might say, a system which identifies *those* facts as those we need, out of the chaos of undifferentiated and inane materials and events which might be on show) and, lastly, a sort of *plot*, as a narrative has a plot, in the actions, characters, structure and sequence of which the facts may take on outline, significance and meaning.

It is at this intersection of many different -ologies (levels of knowledge as well as of signification) – ontology, epistemology, ideology – that theory generates facts and situates them in a story – a story which, as I say, implies a scheme of human interests, a history, and a *telos* or purposive onward movement. The different levels may be systematically distinguished[8] by the philosopher's stone; they need to be if, in the most commonplace inquiries of the primary-school classroom, we are not to make misleading errors in assuming commensurability, and radically confuse, say, classes of subjects, forms of data, or relevant criteria of evidence. Learning to think rationally, the ideal language of which process is universally appealed to,[9] if not observed in practice, requires all of us to make these distinctions and this totality. They harmlessly and fatally resound behind all the claims so unthinkingly made, 'that's a fact'.

But in claiming that every fact implies a story, I want to go beyond arguments about epistemology, and well beyond mere definitions of what knowledge is, or indeed what rationality is. These are substantial questions, and we shall have to return to them, but their substance is contained within the far larger, rounder ambit of the human story, and the innumerable versions of this story which knowledge authorizes (*sic*), confirms as true, organizes and vindicates. By this token, the facts are part of a story whose meaning is to give meaning, all knowledge is then acquired and pursued not for its own sake, as they used to say to freshmen convocations, but in order to 'edify'[10] the human life to hand, to give it meanings new and old, to educate in its passage from birth to copulation and death. These brass facts are gathered up into the larger story of how to live, and made as interesting as possible. The proposed demotion of knowledge 'for its own sake' from its central place in the curriculum of cant is only disconcerting to jobbing philosophers of a realist persuasion. Nobody, after all, seriously concerned either with edification or with old life itself intends to demote truth, let alone beauty and goodness, from being the heart of all matter. The enemies of truth are at and within the gates, and it is the homely and traditional claim of this modest proposal that the point of education (the meaning of edification) is that the educated girl or boy, man or woman, tells the truth and tries to be good. Shifting knowledge for its own sake from the centre of the intellectual and educational prizes is no more than recognizing the obvious feature of everyday assumption, that knowledge is intimately related to power, is a form of what has been called 'cultural capital',[11] which is to say the more you have of it and the more shrewdly you invest it, the more it will pay off, and that the disembodiment of its claims to truth until they reach a state of sakelessness is an old lie told by those innocently or disingenuously suited by the present distribution of rewards to those in possession of knowledge for its own sake.[12]

It is important not to be misunderstood at this stage. For I am about to go on and summarize the essence of the stories of the subjects: a synopsis of the intellectual gospels. Every subject tells a story about its own worth, its extrinsic and intrinsic justification,[13] its deservedly or unmeritedly low place in the hierarchy of the national curriculum, fights a gallant or a cowardly fight in the competition of subjects[14] and, above all, struggles to vindicate a view of human interests in which its own practitioners have a heroic place in the history of human emancipation, self-awareness and fulfilment. But to imply an amused, all-knowing and ironic distance from these stories is to fall into the self-congratulation of at least one school of history men, whose radical or deutero-marxist exemption from the little local difficulties of historicity enables them to spot the non-historical cooking of the books by everyone else. These demons of the times arraign everybody else for implying legitimations of their subjects that merely apologize for the subject's partiality, while at the same time defending an intellectual protectorate that safely marks in and out a terrain nobody else could possibly want or feel menaced by. On this account, such subjects and their defining structures interlock with all others to insulate their priorities from interference, to ensure the reproduction of subject-membership in assimilable and non-disruptive numbers, and to interrogate their preferred material in ways which never put in question their own dominant paradigms of thoughts and criteria of authority.

This critique derives ultimately from Marx's *The German Ideology*,[15] but more latterly it has been devastatingly reformulated in a home-grown version applied to all academic disciplines in the human sciences as practised by the British universities. In so far as they define the conduct of all subjects in secondary schools, both by their control of A-level syllabuses and university admissions, as well as by their formation of the students who become the teachers, the intellectual practices of British universities are indeed the ground and being of British education. Perry Anderson's celebrated onslaught[16] convincingly indemnifies the arc of the university curriculum marked by the useful heading (it comes from the French) 'the human sciences', which includes literary criticism, history, philosophy and aesthetics, as well as what are commonly called the social sciences in Britain. Of course this list, omitting both the creative arts and the physical sciences, is highly selective, but his charges of philistine mindlessness and self-seeking silence on major issues of social status, relevance and the generation of theories capable of putting in question the culture and society which support them are exhilaratingly plausible.

He was followed, in less heady prose as well as a far less brilliant and accomplished summary, by critics of the school curriculum,[17] reproaching it justly enough for favouring the language, characterizing thought-forms, and preferred subject-groupings of the professional middle classes and their children, and for devising time-filling and humanely time-killing activities for working-class children, which had neither content, status, nor purchasing power. The process, these critics argued, was as self-delusive among teachers as it was illusory for children, for whereas the teachers protested that they sought to bring children up to their individual and creative potential, what they really did was impose deeply conventional and anaesthetic frames of thought and being. These stifled creativity, foreclosed collaboration, and encouraged only a banal and docile readiness from junior school upwards to accept official categories of time, work and discipline, and then to retain the energy to subvert these when all forms of official patience and reward expire, as they do with the unemployables: the West Indians and the children of very poor, white and utterly unskilled, often single-parent families.[18]

Now there is no doubt that these analyses stick: that, in Marx's and Engels' tautology, 'in every epoch the ruling ideas are the ideas of the ruling class',[19] and that those ruling ideas are most audible and visible in the official version of knowledge organized as the curriculum at all age-levels. To say so is to follow the theory of ideology that systems of ideas provide a systematic masking of the

real relations of power and subordination, which are the spontaneous and inevitable consequence of capitalist production.
These ideas bring about a condition of false consciousness in those
who believe them, such that their more or less willing victims
accept the ideas, even though they work against their own best
interests – hence 'false'.

This potted version of a never very subtle thesis, which was
originally dreamed up to explain why on earth the working class
failed to deliver the proletarian revolution, will perhaps serve to
identify the 'masking' or 'fix' theory of ideology, according to
which knowledge systems are vigorously legitimated by those they
suit best in terms that pretend to show how they are also good for
everyone else. Thus the British bourgeoisie builds an educational
ideology, decent enough in its own terms, according to which each
child is a uniquely precious individual (the pleonasm is typical)
whose essential creativity and rich potential for selfhood may be
best brought out by the careful devising of educational conditions
which combine proper libertarianism with the inculcation of a
severe respect for hard work, personal effort, self-discipline
(especially as public examinations draw near) and the intrinsic
integrity of the forms of knowledge.[20]

That such a view may be viciously self-seeking is cruelly
apparent not only in the results of national selection for higher
education (and therefore higher salaries), but also in the most
mundane details of teaching the rich and poor subjects, or
teaching in the rich and poor schools. All the same, the bourgeois
ideology is not merely self-seeking. Its provenance lies somewhere
within the best doctrines of Romanticism, whose unprecedented
emphasis on the responsibility of the self towards its own deepest
feelings and its capacity for pure, spontaneous and passionate life
is its most serious and lasting bequest to the chance modern
society may have both for understanding itself, and turning that
understanding towards new versions of the good life.

There is therefore another version of ideology which sees it at
first as straightforwardly a structure of values. Values may be
thought of as never having meaning by themselves, but like
language itself only having meaning within a system of differences,
each inflection of which is articulated with another.[21] These values
are, straightly, values, not the property or product of any given
social class. However, as classes come to dominance in changing

historical conditions, so they bring to partial, peculiar embodiment those values which, fully embodied and lived, would
conduce to the realization of the project for human freedom. It is
this historically distorted version of real human values which
constitutes ideology, whether that word designates the fix or
hypocritical animation of ideology, or whether it more sympathetically indicates the always unsuccessful and local attempt to live
up to noble ideals.[22]

Ideology, therefore, is a concept which, as I use it here, strains
apart in the directions of two opposed meanings. In the first, it is
an advertising instrument on the part of the powerful, intended to
persuade the less powerful to accept a misleading story to their
own detriment and the continuance in power of the story-teller. In
the second, it is the interpretative structure of values which (to put
things very roughly indeed) the agent brings up to the meaningless
flow of events past and through him, and attempts to fit over the
events by way, as we say and I have already said, of making sense
of life and lives, and turning them into intelligible experience.

Either way, ideologies tell a story: are at the centre, as Clifford
Geertz puts it, of the ensemble of texts which compose a culture,
'stories we tell ouselves about ourselves'.[23]

On this arguable definition, educated language forms a totality
of discourses within which each subject draws upon the ideological field of the culture in order, on the one hand, to legitimate and
advance its own standing and membership, and, on the other, to
realize some recognizable version of its own ideal speech-forms
and exchanges. The stories that subjects may tell are therefore
complicated, and different groups of subject-members may certainly tell sharply conflicting versions of the subject story.

So, 'once upon a time . . .' there was the subject biology,
physical education, home economics, English, physics, French,
history. In each case, the story has its heroes, who determined the
subject in the face of uncomprehending and obscurantist opposition; its villains, who tried to keep an alien version going in the
name of a different elite; its arbitrary snobberies or anti-
Enlightenment cast of mind or mere self-protection. The story
includes a view of its past as surpassed, but mythologized, its
oppressions contrasted with present liberties won by its heroes,
and a strong account of its contribution to the post-enlightenment
trigonometry of human self-awareness, self-fulfilment and free-

dom. That is to say, the story nominates those human faculties which the subject uniquely prompts and cherishes (the intrinsic justification) as well as those social roles and necessities which it no less singularly fills and meets (the extrinsic justification). Like all good liberal novels, its heroes are individuals battling to free themselves from the dead weight of their parents' generation, and to find space for their own daring initiative within which entirely new freedoms, expressions and ideas will find embodiment.[24] Its history has beginning, middle and an end which begins in the present, and which, while not at all complete, provides ample scope for present self-congratulation. The largely unwritten novel of each subject includes, as one would expect, a canon of sacred texts which precede it, periods of exile and sudden revelation (peripetaeia), just as Aristotle said it should; less obviously, it implies a method of personal development and redemption, which is coterminous with the method of the subject itself.

Consider, of our short list, biology, new crowned queen of the life sciences, served always by her lesser sisters in the muses of science, zoology and chemistry, but assured of her own pride of place by her undoubted and undaunted contribution to the human project in terms of improved life-expectations, freedom from arbitrary epidemic, and therefore its triumphant warding-off of the last enemy. Unforgettably, Clive James has noticed that the history of the life sciences as represented in television is caught in a repetitive tableau on which are inscribed the everyday stories of solitary men with big black beards being thoroughly misunderstood by largish groups of other men with long white ones. Well, that is one popular version of the hero and his success story in the West.[25]

If we turn to the narrative of biology as told in a standard sixth-form and undergraduate textbook,[26] we find a happily pure version of the story of a subject. In the pages dealing with the great release of ideas in the early 1950s, which so dazzlingly applied the latest X-ray crystallography together with the earliest conceptual innovations of particle physics to molecular biology, the author recounts the interplay of collaboration and rivalry between the great prizewinners – Hans Krebs at Oxford and his work on citric acid structures, Linus Pauling at the California Institute of Technology, Fred Sanger at Cambridge – at the same time as he specifies both method and discovery. The geography is an essential part of the tale – Oxford, Cambridge, Harvard, Princeton, Los Altos, Santa Barbara, more occasionally Zurich and Moscow (it is a strikingly anglophone, not to say patriotic story). In each case, but often not until later in the texts, credit is given for the human and medical benefits of the discovery – for instance, Sanger's devising of a taxonomy for the amino-acids in insulin, the hormone notoriously secreted by the pancreas having the most obvious benefits for the control of blood-sugar irregularities in sufferers from diabetes.

The most glamorous heroes of the book are the Cambridge scientists, Francis Crick and James Watson, no doubt partly because of the drama of their discovery and their successful theorizing of the famous double-helical structure of the deoxyribo-nucleic acid (DNA), the vital molecular chain which carries the genetic messages of an organism, but also because the stops and starts, passions and divisions of their successful inquiry have all the ingredients of a popular movie about scientists. Watson himself biographized their research as a sort of novel[27] with an entertaining lack of disinterestedness, and surely part of their fame must be due to the smoothness with which their plot and its characters fitted the cultural-ideological space left open for the public acknowledgement of science.

In the sober, clear, confident march of the textbook's prose, however, what is as important as the drama, competition, and collaborative advance across the frontiers of knowledge is the homogeneity of metaphor, which rolled up these problems in the cellular structures of protein in a single, beautifully economic image. Krebs, Sanger, Pauling, Crick and Watson were all trying to adjust their X-ray photographs to the model of the helix, single, double or triple. They are caught in the magic icon of the scientist, gazing at the baffling and impenetrable phenomena until, in an intuitive flash, their meaning is released in a single, elegant and economic model.

The elegance and the economy are essential qualities in the story science tells itself and us about itself. Naturally, there are those who blow the gaff on this smoothly regulated and calmly successful practice. Thomas Kuhn[28] sociologized the placidly powerful conventionalities of paradigmatic science and how they work to exclude eccentricity or subversive inquiry until such time as the new science forces itself upon the scene and changes the paradigm. Then in no time at all, the new science establishes its conventions, and the old plot with its heroes, discoveries, human benefits, order, economy, elegance, calm and rational and intelligible *progress*, is rewritten to suit the new language, its tropes and forms. After the revolution, the new order. Roberts is the entirely believable and excellent ideologue of post-1950s biology. His is a good read.

Biology may stand here as a type of the natural sciences, and the tale they each tell of themselves. As I have suggested, the ideological strain of any such tale is between the fix which subject-members hope to put upon the world, especially their subordinates, in order to confirm and if possible strengthen their position in it, and their genuine aspiration to devise ideal speech-situations for their subject which will ensure the perfect harmony of truth and freedom, of the conflict of ideas and the eradication of personal interests.[29] The ideological strain creaks audibly in the story philosophy itself tells, a subject which has (extraordinarily) in Britain kept entirely aloof from all but higher education – it simply isn't taught in schools – and which has a highly self-congratulatory account of the ideal speech-situation.

Its history is of course a long one. In Britain, the official curriculum has worked steadily to present the subject as the public relations agent of epistemology, and the securing of science's unselfconscious and non-theoretic achievements as its most important work. It is hard, of course, to avoid falling into parody[30] in trying to sketch the outlines of philosophy's hero. Such a hero, mocked on stage by Tom Stoppard and in the pages of her novels by Iris Murdoch, goes to David Hume for a theory of human nature, to Kant for a rather gaunt, chilly morality, to Russell for scepticism and scientific realism, and to John Austin and A.J. Ayer for the repudiation of metaphysics, especially from France and Germany, as well as for the social, non-spiritual locating of self and mind in the many contexts of everyday language. The biography of this hero as he matures in the story of his subject is subject to a complete rainbow of political and economic metamorphoses, of course, but even allowing for his faint contamination these days in the murky languages of both Heidegger and Marx, he remains a liberal empirical figure, preferring the philosophy of science and modal logic to ethics or politics, and in his style and cast of mind, rationalist, empirical, sceptical, urbane, authoritative, social democratic, atheistical, tolerantly opposed to grand theory. It is also plausible to claim that his intellectual standards and the professional criteria of his peer-group are the highest in the academies and are apt to paralyse members of other subjects into a helpless deference. At all events, philosophy's self-justifications in its story are the most nakedly intrinsic of all: philosophy bestows upon its children the clarity of mind, the lucidity of argument, the sceptical provisionality of posture, the resourcefulnes of rationality, the certainty of the complexity and infinitude of things without which not just liberal, but *any* culture will lapse into barbarism. These are marvellously abstract values, and indeed to achieve junior appointment in philosophy is to be apprenticed to a senior, dead philosopher, and serve your indentures filing his universalizations and keeping his archive up to date. The story of philosophy as presently told, if we exclude assorted mad prophets reeling in from the transatlantic wilderness (Richard Rorty) or the dug-outs nearer home of the Marxist guerrilla (the editors of *Radical Philosophy*),[31] is a strictly academic one and being so, has to advertise less stridently in the educational market place. In the house of fiction, its room is a clean well-lighted place, small, neat, white, and well-appointed.

The stories of poorer, newcomer subjects, with no rooms at Oxford or Cambridge, and too much to do on too little money in comprehensive schools, are more badly written, much more prone to self-pity and the intellectually snobbish dismissal of others, nervous, awkward, and with a very doubtful family history. Indeed, they spend much of their time trying to find or invent that history, in order to license themselves as respectable in the present, and beneficent in the future.

Take a self-designatedly homely instance, that of home economics. The genesis of the subject lies, no doubt, in the decade before the First World War and after the 1902 Education Act, which established the new, national Board of Education and its Permanent Secretary, Robert Morant; indeed, in the *Regulations for Secondary Schools*, issued under his signature in 1904, we find a now-famous regulation setting out for the first time in Britain a simple codification of time to be spent on instruction in different subjects – 'not less than 4½ hours per week must be allotted to English, Geography, and History ... not less than 7½ hours to Science and Mathematics ...' and 'with due provision for

Manual Work and Physical Exercises, and, in a girl's school, for Housewifery'.[32] With that to hand, school teachers can remind themselves that they have come a very long way since then, but contributors to *Naked Ape*, as well as those less self-righteous and more doggedly social-conscience-stricken about not making girls do only girlish things, can acknowledge the significance of the 'manual work and physical exercises' for boys, as well as the housewifery for girls.

By a prime historical token, both items are an early sign of a time in which a nation realized that it was broken in half. The violent unsettlements and huge reconstruction involved in the unplanned or, in the phrase, free-market industrialization of Britain had famously torn an unmendable rupture in the taken-for-granted pieties and graces of the agrarian order.[33] Within eighty years, the urban poorest no longer knew how to bake bread or make butter or brew beer, even if they could have found the ingredients. Cheap fish, especially shellfish, had vanished, and reappeared on inaccessible porcelain slabs as expensive fish – oysters, shrimps, clams. Steak and sirloin had gone with it, to be replaced by what Richard Hoggart, writing of the dispossessed but still gamely gourmandizing Leeds poor in the 1930s, noted[34] as the cheap and 'tasty' cuts – offal, chitterlings, faggots, black (blood) puddings, trotters – 'those portions of the pig' as Dickens immortally put it in *Great Expectations*, 'of which the pig, when living, had least reason to be proud'. Whatever brave efforts Hoggart's Hunslet family made with its kidneys and Bath chaps, no one can doubt that by then the class stratifications of the English cuisine had gone deep. The very poor, who are reported by Mayhew and Rowntree[35] as living on bread and scrape and the meat extracts which came on the market to give that debilitating diet some flavour, had lost not only the knowledge needed to prepare and the money to buy the porter, claret, port and punch, the saddle of mutton, sage dumpling, chops and water-pastry pies eaten at such comparatively humble tables as Nicholas Nickleby's and (in *Bleak House*) Mr Guppy's, they no longer lived in a culture in which, in the strictest as well as the philosophical sense, the materials were there for such a repast.

It is always easy to utter maledictions over the decline of the times. Things have never been what they so surely were when he or she, or you or I were girls or boys; the country's short trip down to the dogs began for each generation as its youth began to fade. So to write a careful history of the British kitchen and its decline[36] would have to take account of complicated continuities which run strongly against the dread culture-killers of industrial capitalism – the processes of mass-production which ensure the standardization of parts, the concentration of capital, the Taylorizing of labour, the ruthless organizing and occupying of markets. But such a history, it is my insistent, repeated and *structural* claim, would come up against the incomparable changes wrought upon nineteenth-century experience by the amazing creativity and destructiveness of the world's first urban society. Somehow, between the vast upheavals of the Reform Acts, the Charter and the Chartist marches, the end of Ned Ludd and Captain Swing, the emergence of free trade unions, the bookish signposts of the political landscapes like William Lovett's *Life and Struggles in Pursuit of Bread, Knowledge, and Freedom*, or the many years of Cobbett's *Political Register*,[37] and the staid and stately prose of Robert Morant's *Regulation* in 1902, there came into being the apparatus of the modern state bureaucracy, at once protector and oppressor of the people.

This is the institution, vast, sprawling and incoherent as it often was, which was devised and committed by the governing classes to be sure, but encouraged and worked out by working people of all kinds, in order to repair the hideous depredations of the new political economy. And like its monstrous siblings, the institutions of capital and production themselves, the state sought to build a new order capable of holding down the new disorder. Inevitably it did so in terms borrowed from the culture which lay smashed and in ruins around the hitherto unseen machinery.

All over Britain, the business was in play to make such a new world out of these old fragments. Brand-new private-public schools were built with an architecture, an escutcheon, and sparkling-fresh traditions which declared their allegiance to the victors of the tribal Wars of the Roses. Equally neonate regiments were set up to police the working class, the Irish, the Africans and the Indians, which dreamed up battle honours and badges linking them to the vanished mercenaries and militias of a century before. Even nations rediscovered a sartorial atavism, and Scottish businessmen and agricultural industrialists put on the kilt and the dancing brogue craftily designed for them in Leeds,[38] and claimed they smelled of purple heather and less picturesque thistles.

Four countries and their different classes made up a new set of stories with which to connect themselves to the past, and to explain their present states of beatitude or misery, failure or success.[39] For such fictions to be plausible, it naturally had to be the case that some of them could be given a sufficient modicum of historical truth. But a very little went and goes a long way, and although the effort to practise historical truthfulness is no doubt essential for the perpetuation of virtue, such truth-telling must take its place in the given structures of narrative, and these are not so much legendary as natural, which is to say that without them there could hardly be either stories or histories at all.

These assertions are less of a detour from our smaller history of knowledge and its praxiology than they look. For it is a simple, platitudinous premiss of this book that all our key British narratives were hugely rewritten, reinterpreted and revised during the second half of the nineteenth century.[40] These narratives had to reach back to the imagined order before what is accurately called the industrial revolution changed the world (and like all revolutions, it was very long) and retrieve enough from that past to make the present seem intelligibly continuous with it. Morant's *Regulation* was inevitably part of that enormous and unco-ordinated marking out. Housewifery, our example, sought to put right the colossal rupture in continuity which left young girls unable to do what, according to the old narratives, they should be able to do: thrifty darning, simple seamstress and cutting-out work, laundering, bottling, preserving, baking. The old contexts for such work had gone, of course, those of dairy or kitchen in a large agricultural household of the kind we see Tess of the D'Urbervilles working on at Crick's farm, Marlott; the new kind is all too palpable in the awful inept poverty of her own family's life, especially after her father's death. The school curriculum was devised by the servants of the state out of the inevitable ingredients of their class formation to teach girls how to manage the tiny economics of a poor urban household and, no less pressingly, to obtain the skills necessary to domestic servants. The relations of agricultural production, which had been the proper context of (as we say) home economics and domestic science, had gone; the new terms of the small, sufficient consumer household had not yet been settled. The fragments of old custom were real, but insufficient;

the materials of the new curriculum were earnestly and decently reformatory, but lived only in schools. Out of the two, a school subject was made.

There was much, of course, to be done. The nastiness as well as the thrills of industrial and proletarian life since 1840 had released horrors unthought of on the grimmest farm – cholera, diptheria, typhus and meningitis joined the macabre and epidemic dance of unavoidable and deathly illness and deformation led by smallpox, rickets and tuberculosis. Custom and culture could do little about these demons; the new science, especially of hygiene and dietetics, could do and did much, and the liberal reformers rightly added that to the subject.

And so housewifery (cooking and needlework) changed into domestic science, and that in turn became home economics. On the way, the assorted inadequacies of the girls and the experience they brought with them had led other teachers to want to add elementary training in parlour and teatime manners, in the correct setting of places at table and entertaining of guests, and by the present day, when one has worked off all the irony and wryness one may upon the scoured formica and antiseptic tidiness of the home economics flat, its picture and its implied narrative of the good life, its genteel and decent regard for hearth and guests and hospitality is not so little but that, in social conditions which do so much to restore barbarism and brutality, we could readily do without it.

It is in some such form that I shall write of all subjects – whether disciplines, sciences, themes or topics – and their histories. Indeed subjects *are* their histories, on this purview, however much we acknowledge as we must that all knowledge has its realist form and content, and is truly a mirror of nature,[41] however distorting.

To understand each part of a curriculum, and to do so in order to change it on behalf of the future, we can only turn to its history, and that history recounted as a story it tells us of itself and about ourselves. Such a story, as I suggested, is a theory with which to find out what experience means, and how to wring knowledge out of it. Securing such knowledge is the work of a lifetime, and state education, together with its Victorian antecedents, is only one, though now a vast and powerful one, of its productive institutions.

3

Theory and Experience

Theory is vastly bigger than the province of intellectuals or even of universities, just as curriculum is a term which may take in all the price of experience, and certainly goes far beyond its present confinement to what is more or less officially taught to primary and secondary schoolchildren. Everybody has a set of theories, compounded maybe of fact and value, history and myth, observation and folklore, superstition and convention, but these theories are none the less intended to explain the world and, as I said, discover and confirm its meanings. Most of all, those who refuse all theory, who speak of themselves as plain, practical people, and virtuous in virtue of having no theory, are in the grip of theories which manacle them and keep them immobile, because they have no way of thinking about them and therefore of taking them off. They aren't theory-free; they are stupid theorists.

This stricture is no less fair if we define theory tightly, as a testable hypothesis for the explanation of phenomena. If theory is more widely taken, as a symbolic representation of the real world for the purpose of understanding it, and further taken that models, metaphors, fictions, systems of principles, and narratives are all versions of theory, then, quite without being committed either to relativism or naturalism, it is clear that using language is an action which cannot take place without theorizing, and that by definition we are all theorists.

None of this does anything to clarify the different contributions of imagination and reason in the making of theory. And certainly such a view of theory says nothing about the status of the theories made. If we define relativism[1] in a very reach-me-down way as the view that the truth is something which we make up (collectively or individually) more or less as we please, and realism as the view that whatever we make up less or more as we please, it certainly is *not* the truth, then to insist that cognition-plus-language formulates theory gives no particular opportunity to either persuasion, but only claims that thought entails theorizing.

It is surely the case, however, that the cultural rhetoric out of which theory is spoken in anglophone societies veers almost insanely between the view that knowledge is a realist product (as in the natural sciences) and that knowledge is wholly subjective, the only truth capable of making you free being the truth about things which is true and serviceable for you alone (because you, in the jargon, 'constructed' it for yourself). This baleful paying-on-both-sides of relativism and realism corresponds to deep divisions in the cognitive and emotional formation of all classes in the society, and understanding our knowledge means understanding them.

The first move in this enterprise has already been to revalue the idea of theory itself; but the second, which is more drastic and more ambitious, is to give far denser, more material (and materialist), as well as historical substance to the contrary term, experience itself. Anything – but largely the mere passing of old time – may be credited to the column marked 'experience' in the historical ledger. In our society as perhaps in any other, rewards, seniority, wisdom, power are accorded to those in whom the category 'experience' is thought to be stored and recognized. But:

> *Had they deceived us*
> *Or deceived themselves, the quiet-voiced elders,*
> *Bequeathing us merely a receipt for deceit?*
> *The serenity only a deliberate hebetude,*
> *The wisdom only the knowledge of dead secrets*
> *Useless in the darkness into which they peered*
> *Or from which they turned their eyes. There is it seems to us*
> *At best, only a limited value*
> *In the knowledge derived from experience.*
> *The knowledge imposes a pattern, and falsifies,*
> *For the pattern is new in every moment*
> *And every moment is a new and shocking*
> *Valuation of all we have been.*[2]

The interrogation was hardly heeded. Experience remains the champion educational category, along, perhaps, with intuition. Both are valued precisely because they sanctify the radically individualized and relativized view of life and its meanings – 'true for me' 'true for you'. The force of the primacy given to 'experience' comes out routinely when schoolteachers ask their children to write from 'their own' experience, or curriculum builders demand that children be given curricular material which begins from that same indubitable realm which is also their own property.

In the cases both of experience and intuition what is staked has a very high value: it is the personally possessed and unchallenge-able standing and meaning of these concepts as vindicators of free identity, of domains of personality, which escape all coercion and are the object of no social structures. You can't, conventional wisdom teaches, be deprived of your experience, and it is the fact of its inevitable accumulation, together with its uninterruptedly direct acquisition as *your own*, unmediated by anything between you and it, which is held to give it its resonant validity among our values. By the same token, even if somebody might be shown to be mistaken in their intuitions, agreement on such a score would be a consequence of changing your own mind for yourself: 'no one can make it up for you'. Once more, the significance of an intuition, like that of experience, is its standing as a personal possession which confirms the possessor in his or her deepest sense of self.

There is plenty of truth in these beliefs, as well as a clear justification in the value which accrues to the concept when it is understood in this way. Criticism and revision, however unpopu-lar, are timely on three grounds, none the less. The first and most obviously important is that, along with the truth of the beliefs, there is also serious falsehood; the second is that the emphasis on the possession and incontestability of experience has the conse-quence of further individualizing people's view of themselves and of life, of accelerating down the long slide from the genuine strengths of Romanticism to the consumer narcissism within which the employed and well-off three-quarters of the population devise an adequate picture of who they are. To cherish the personality of experience prevents your seeing your connections with others. 'Only connect', E.M. Forster's famous dictum, has a wise old owlishness about it which obscures the truth that connection in the many senses of common humanity and deep mutual interdependence is the ground of life. That being so, experience isn't just ours, but social and historical; it comes at us organized and shaped by all the experience others have had before us, as do our intuitions. An intuition cannot simply be felt along the heart, picked up and earthed there as though it were a stray electrical impulse. It means something, and it can only do so as it assumes shape within a conceptual framework capable of so shaping it. As I suggested, theory and experience are as mutually necessary as (and are in part synonymous with) concept and percept.

This antinomian insistence on the necessity of theories, paradigms and narratives in order to make sense of experience does not mean, of course, that each category is unanalysable. It is more a matter of starting from the premiss that such terms create the room for individual men and women to act as free agents by means of their choices and decisions, and bring these into some rough accord with their intentions and purposes, all of which deliberate movement is summarized under the heading 'voluntarism'. The strong counterweight to this easy-going assumption is that all such voluntary activity can *only* take place within and would be inconceivable without a complex network of antecedent structures. 'Experience' indeed is the name we give to the lessons learned in the often harsh encounter between agency and structure. It is not the transcendental talisman that life is worth something, as liberals and Romantics suppose; nor is it a term consigned by the determinate laws of a history without subjects[3] to the rubbish bin of politics.

Rather, as Edward Thompson tells us, while telling off the Marxists for jettisoning the notion,

> What we have found out (in my view) lies within a missing term: 'human experience.' This is, exactly, the term which Althusser and his followers wish to blackguard out of the club of thought under the name of 'empiricism.' Men and women also return as subjects, within this term – not as autonomous subjects, 'free individuals', but as persons experiencing their determinate productive situations and relationships, as needs and interests and as antagonisms, and then 'handling' this experience with their *consciousness* and their *culture* (two other terms excluded by theoretical practice) in the most complex (yes, 'relatively autonomous') ways, and then (often but not always through the ensuing

structures of class) acting upon their determinate situation in their turn.[4]

Thompson's rich rendering of what experience may mean need not delay us at the philosophical level. My purpose in this chapter so far has been to rescue the idea of experience as conventionally deployed by most teachers (and I cannot insist too often that by 'teachers' I designate all those who teach, including the men and women listed as lecturers or even professors) from the sacred, inaccessible groves of personal life and individual perception, and to restore it to the profane avenues, mean streets and main roads of history.

To say so, however, does not take us very far in charting the relations of experience to theory, and of both to the larger, no less comprehensive, but slippery concept, knowledge. Experience has its structures; these precede the individual's ordinance of his life; similarly, knowledge and *my* knowledge have their non-individual structures, and here too we come up against a system of categories whose familiarity and ease of handling seem to assure their accuracy of fit with a reality it is the business of language and other symbols to mirror faithfully. Thus, just as experience is happily supposed to be directly acquired and possessed by me, so knowledge is comfortably divided into the complementary domains of subjective and objective. The latter domain is ruled over by the natural sciences, whose precise methods of observation, framed by hypothesis and leading not to verification, but to the single absolute of falsification (that is, if my hypothesis is falsifiable, it cannot prefigure a general law; a working experiment is *always* liable to falsification), give them a jurisdiction, completeness and instrumentality whose prime materials are quantities and classes – which is to say, numbers and facts.[5]

This has been the victorious story of how to acquire knowledge and discover the truth since scientific method really began in the seventeenth century.[6] The colossal triumphs of science over nature and by means of technology have settled it in its place as the overpoweringly dominant model of inquiry in the curriculum of the industrial nations – which is to say, *all* nations of the world as they aspire to become or remain sufficiently self-determining and well-off.

Within the compulsion of this system of concepts, the standing of facts, of empirical obervation, of computation, of routine and method uninflected by changes of individuals practising that method ('value-freedom') for the reproducibility of phenomena, of reason itself as given structure and direction by its methodical framework, all these securities settle the natural sciences in their present position in the curriculum, and deliver their parallel dividends in terms of prestige, resources, cash and privilege in the society. The victory has been so complete that it is hard now to stand back a little way, to return science itself to the everyday battle of men and women to make sense of their experience, and to devise theories to select portions of life-in-earnest which will yield that kind of sense. In the past twenty years, the effort to show how even clinical and objective science has had its merely social distortions was initiated by Thomas Kuhn's famously subversive essay, and John Ziman's books[7] have continued that good work. At the same time, some of the most daring and original of mathematical theorems, notably Gödel's, have proved the limits of proof itself, and shaken the once secure and incontestably impersonal nature of numbers.[8]

In spite of this sapping of the underground of sciences, however, science defined as the successful wringing of objective knowledge from natural reality, and scientific method as the only true and reliable guide in inquiry still rule the national and international curriculum. For a long time, the human sciences struggled to gain the authority of the natural sciences by borrowing their methods, and history, psychology, sociology each conscripted their members into the ranks of the hunters and gatherers of numbers. There were, as will emerge from the next chapter, both good and bad reasons for this, but either way the tribute money and rates of interest were paid to the natural sciences.

There was always, from the inception of scientific method, another theory of knowledge and knowing,[9] one which, in specific opposition to the natural scientists, stressed the personal, intuitive, non-mensurable and non-provable actualities of knowledge. This other form of knowledge is the product of our human inter-subjectivity, with its forms of discourse and discursiveness, its unreasoned wrangles and chanciness, its gradual and experiential testing of circumstances until the results can be thought of as knowable; above all, such seeking to know goes on its humanly critical, self-reflexive, purposeful and intentional way about the world not in the name of knowledge for its own sake, but on urgent, voluntary errands, during which the knowledge is required to answer moral questions. Obviously, on one side, such knowledge is not rigidly distinct from the knowledge gained by the natural sciences ('hard v. soft sciences'); obviously, on the other, such knowledge carried a sometimes sinking fund of folklore, superstition, commonsense but nonsense, invalid saws and proverbs, mystification and jargon. Indeed it is exactly the business of the second science, in its various disciplinary, symbolic and productive forms, to chasten the folklore as well as to remind natural science that it, too, has its ordinary human ballast, to say nothing of its human crew, as liable as non-scientists to envy, greed, sloth, hatred and mendacity.

By this stage, without collapsing the knowledge yielded by physicalist method into the knowledge created by the reflexive (or human) sciences, it seems reasonable to point to strong affinities between both, and both as emerging from (being, in a rough sense, made out of) the stuff of a common history and customary ways of life. And indeed, while this book advances a tolerantly naturalist doctrine of knowledge (which is to say, it argues for a close enough correspondence between our symbol systems, including ordinary language, and a natural reality at once 'out there' and inside each of us, here), the use of such phrases as those which refer to knowledge being 'made out of something' and as being 'created' bring out, as a philosophic beginning, the significance of naming knowledge as some kind of social product. If it is such a product – and as chapter 8 insists, the production of knowledge, and then of 'work' as distinct from knowledge, is a main point of what is well called the education *system* – then knowledge, whether gained by the individual or by the society, is more a product like a work of art than a product Taylorized for the assembly line.[10]

The analogy is with the process of inquiry in, say, a painting, whereby the unenvisageable end – the finished picture whose finish can only be known when arrived at (and plenty of painters could never bring themselves to a finish, or put the picture away unfinished, because they couldn't find the end they were looking for) – constitutes a *discovery* when it is done. The artist knows something he didn't know before (and the discovery – the answer to his unspoken question – would probably have to remain tacit).

The knowledge, which is there somewhere in the symbol *and* the materials, the marks of paint and the grain of the canvas, may be of how to achieve a certain effect with the paint, or it may be that the world from which he took his picture really is as the picture is. In Cezanne's case, for example, Provence is in fact composed of those harsh, divided planes of umber stone. Either way, his way of working is a way of knowing, and what he has made, he knows.

A curriculum, however, is more than a map of knowledge; the two nouns are not interchangeable. I have spoken with deliberate looseness here of 'forms of knowledge' as if there were only the two, those as conventionally assigned to the natural and to the human sciences, 'Sciences' and 'Arts'. But in the larger divisions of the curriculum, the purported attributes of either scheme of knowledge, either in its methods of production or in the products themselves, are gathered into realms of meaning[11] which, according to the divisions of intellectual labour in the society, define key forms of consciousness, of social relationship, and ultimately of power itself.

A curriculum is no doubt, although only to begin with, the official register of a society's knowledge. But it is also dynamic. The word 'culture' is asked to bear very many meanings these days, and it will hardly emerge from this book any less heavy-laden, but if we take some such non-contentious definition (always hard to come by) of culture as the making (or production) and remaking of a society's values, meanings and symbols, together with the transformation of these as they circulate through different groups and different times, then the force of the adjective 'dynamic' may come through a little. For in the context in which I have presented the civil and incivil struggle for meanings and values, culture cannot merely repeat itself, any more than history can. A curriculum is embedded in a culture, and that culture reproduces and transforms itself such that to speak of its knowledge without asking what purposes and intentions that knowledge serves, or what questions the knowledge constituted answers to, is to speak meaninglessly. A curriculum is not just a matter of what someone is supposed to know, but also what they are supposed to do with it; it is, therefore, an *intentional* structure, at least in its origins, while at the same time its rates of change, its discarding processes, have their own erratic rhythms, and many even of its most prominent knowledge blocks may no longer be adequate to present purposes, and have strictly residual and traditional meaning and significance.

But there again, 'residual' and 'traditional' are not swear-words for the devoutly iconoclastic liberal to pounce upon and hold up to the bright enlightenment of derision. In the name of both an imaginable and a liveable continuity, any curriculum will house traditional materials and make space for residual activities whose most important meaning is just that: that they recognize the necessity of connection with a visible and audible past for its own sake, and the sake of a present which is perpetually becoming a past.

Such an argument[12] is, in all senses of the adjective, conservative. But the carefully polemical socialism of this book requires that conservatism to be taken seriously, in part as the voice of the enemy, an enemy who has been winning the day and doing the ruling for so long he *has* to be taken seriously. In part, however much socialism commits itself to a new start, you can't start from nowhere, least of all in a country whose condition of old age, decline, decay, traditionalism, immobility, and all the rest, are what you have to work with. Innovation theory as presently spoken is, then, a peculiarly inapplicable game, fun in its own way, but perfectly inconsequential.

So tradition and its cognates, custom, ceremony, habituality, accord, authority, ritual, worth, even value itself, are formal elements of being without which any social order would hardly be thinkable, and from which the new version of the good life, which socialism so variously claims to make possible, must make its selection. The battle restarts when the content of these forms becomes contended. For the argument of this chapter has been that the theories and principles of the hard and soft sciences, though importantly different in actual practice, alike emerge from the vivid actuality of human interests,[13] as these shape and are shaped by the immediacy of both nature in the raw and culture as cooked up by men. The argument has further been that our knowledge, although organized and allocated according to these interests and their categories, can only be understood and *used* in relation to exceedingly contingent and historically relative purposes, intentions, misconceptions and versions of the self. And we may furthermore claim that a curriculum just *is* this network of purposes, and far more than a map of knowledge, however much the cartographer of the curriculum must start from that.[14]

In other words, by implying a view of what to do with knowledge, the curriculum, like the culture, implies a picture of how to live and who to be; even in liberal society, it adumbrates the passages of the good life, in private and in public (and how the two are divided), and it proposes a structure of the self in relation to this praxis. Quite without any too large a dose of irony at its expense, since its strictly political and civic gains, however unevenly allocated, have been incontestably magnificent, liberalism may be indemnified as not knowing what to do about the good life. For if we pause for a definition of liberalism, it is its main, negative premiss that you must not tell other people how to live or what to believe, except in so far as they must learn not to infringe the liberty of others in such a way that the free development of each is at the individual's unfettered choice, and within a clear space he or she can call their own. Hence the primacy given by liberalism to the act of choice, the action which most defines the doctrine, and hence also the central place assigned to the individual as at once the realm (or domain) and the fount (or endlessly self-renewing origin) of value and meaning.[15] Liberalism, accordingly, has difficulties with the good life, since every individual chooses and creates the terms of that life personally. What tends to happen is that the immortal and invisible social structures, to which liberalism is bound by its premisses to deny determinate force, take over and shape visions of the good life willy-nilly. The honest liberal must, then, believe (the dishonest one need only pretend) that he freely chose the Habitat kitchens and Maples sitting rooms, the Volvo estate car and the Provençal holiday villa, together with the conscience-stricken opinions and *Guardian* morality, and not that they were given by the systems and relations of production, privilege and wealth in (as the phrase goes) late consumer capitalism.

This way of life, or, as we with suicidal accuracy say, this life-style, derives directly enough from the curriculum, as from the culture. The values it carries lead to the department store. But perhaps that line will be more fully drawn in at a later stage. For now, it will be clearer to list in two columns the terms which, betokening as they do the values, meanings, practices and principles which are conventionally, even popularly, held to organize and typify the soft and hard sciences, help to explain in this simplified form how social identity (of individuals and classes), subject or discipline membership, and the divisions of labour themselves, take the essence and substance they do.

SOFT KNOWLEDGE	HARD KNOWLEDGE
subjective	objective
evaluative	factual
intuitive	calculable
personal	public
imaginative	rational
emotional	cognitive
warm	cool
of the heart	of the head
artistic	scientific
indisputable	provable
feminine	masculine
moral	political

It is important not to be misunderstood. The prior argument has at least suggested the mistakes inherent in such a dichotomy; more to the immediate point, these are very broad designations of meaning, value and so forth which can only operate in the form of disembodied lists. As soon as one gets down to detail, plenty of people might be ready to acknowledge the imaginative quotient in physics, the cognitive core of philosophy, the moral necessity of politics. All the same, the roughness and readiness of everyday thought and action is what people live with; what they mean by science and the scientist is expected to look sufficiently like the right-hand column in its white-coated or laboratory actuality, just as the mere fact that the ratio of women to men in British university humanities departments[16] is 4.5:1 may serve to vindicate the claim that the left-hand column is widely believed to describe womanly knowing.

Either way, perhaps such a pair of lists will do to foreshadow the power of structures in everyday life to shape all our thoughts, and therefore to shape our very selves. Such structures may be ontic, which is to say they may be made out of all we think is the stuff of ultimate reality; they may be social, which is to say they are alterable as long as you don't forget how very permanent social institutions have a habit of being; they may be epistemological, in which case they are the deep orderers of all we think knowledge truly is. In all cases, however, they will be historical, and because this chapter is so much one of Hegel's numberless progeny, it is relevant to invoke his name again as the recalcitrant theorist of the curriculum and its culture as only discussable from the restless and precarious planes of history, old and new.

History is a cue for a new song, or at least for a descant on the tune of a personal knowledge. This is because the lessons one learns, in the doughty old phrase, from experience, become one's personal knowledge, but that knowledge looks out for confirmation from the same process in others, and in finding it, becomes less personal. Somewhere in these progresses, people have habitually distinguished between the learned, ineffectual clown, a joke figure all the way from *Love's Labours Lost* to Mr Casaubon in *Middlemarch*, and the man whose educatedness has been won from his successful insistence on finding the books that could, in turn, be made to order and make sense of his life.

That encounter – between known experience and an unknown book – is the heart of education, the moment at which you become the book. Such absorption is more than just being, as we say, lost in the story. It comes, presumably, from some deep recognition that what is said in the book comprehends (in the sense of en-folds) a movement of our own, but out of our own life towards some enclosure of the mind and heart which will satisfy them. In childhood, a single story can do this for us: we occupy the world of Swallows and Amazons or of the Chalet School[17] with a completeness and complicity which fulfil the promise of happiness such stories hold out. In adult life, the same absorption and the recognition it is token of may bring with it an excitement that is like terror, the consequence of seeing both the order and disorder made possible by a new understanding of a continuing life, one's own, one's wife's, one's children's, one's people's. Chaos threatens, because to relinquish old explanations and intellectual frameworks is to endanger identity; if you make a new past to replace present history, you might find no room for the person you think you were. Another order beckons at the same time with its invitation to a world made different, more beautiful perhaps, more intelligible perhaps, and one in which you and she and they will have greater power and freedom and wisdom, because you all know more.

A curriculum is not a moment, nor even a sequence of moments such as the one I have described. But unless a curriculum ensures such moments, then the individual, the class or the nation will alike remain ill-educated. Such a failure, whose results in terms of ruined lives and ways of life lie all about us, is not narrowly a matter of knowing too little. Neither is it a matter of self-congratulation on the part of those who are generally regarded as being well-educated at the expense of those who are not. The ignorance and stupidity which are the inevitable markers of an uneducated people are flagrantly visible amongst our oligarchies, as they are amongst the official custodians of education, in and out of universitites. One way of identifying what is wrong is to say that there is a rupture torn between knowledge and thought, so that we do not know how to use the knowledge we have in order to make the world a better place. Or as we might say instead, we cannot think with what we know in order to identify the ignorance which cripples us.

It is a premiss of this book that the social order of the developed capitalist nations is on the hinge of an epoch, that its forms and relations of production (in a phrase) are impelled towards great and submarine changes, one awful sign of which is the present busy preparation for nuclear war.[18] What this epochal movement may mean for the everyday business of learning and earning a living (or being paid to do nothing) is, certainly, my theme, but it would be an act of vertiginous megalomania to dive into an argument to find the right relation of thought to knowledge, and of both to action (let alone belief). Such have been the subject-matters of the greatest philosophers of this century: Dewey, Heidegger, Wittgenstein;[19] Merleau-Ponty, Lukacs, Adorno, Collingwood. It makes more modest sense to sit in the company of one or two men who had to make a curriculum to fit their lives (and vice versa); who battled to think in ways which the received books could not match; and whose determination to find ways of thought which would truly and truthfully order what they knew and what they wanted to know drove them to make an education for themselves well away from the main roads of the subjects whose bland powers of assimilation posthumously reclaimed them.

It is important that such reports come in the form of autobiography. Autobiography comes, as we might say, naturally, as the form in which to think out singular problems – it is sharply to the point to add that it is supremely the natural form for men and women whose education drastically failed to fit their needs and wants and interests, because their class or their race had no allotted identity in the present schemes of official education. Martin Heidegger set himself the task as a philosopher, one of the greatest as well as one of the wildest of the century, of posing the deepest metaphysical questions – about being and time, identity and presence – and proposing the modes of their answers, in a much homelier, speakable, but also corrugated and more physical idiom than that of usual philosophy. We might say, he tried to think and feel right through his body.

Such an enterprise was bound at times to lead to crankiness. But it is exactly this attempt to cancel conformities of mind, being and physique which I am hunting for as one of several versions of the story-guide, How to Get Educated. Heidegger wrote:

From the perspective of Hegel and Husserl – and not only from their perspective – the matter of philosophy is subjectivity. It is not the matter as such that is controversial for the call, but rather its presentation by which the matter itself becomes present. Hegel's speculative dialectic is the movement in which the matter as such comes to itself, comes to its own presence (*Präsenz*). Husserl's method is supposed to bring the matter of philosophy to its ultimately originary givenness, that means to its own presence (*Präsenz*).[20]

Unfamiliar readers of Heidegger have to allow some room for the queerness[21] of a vocabulary trying to break up the relations imposed by everyday terms upon everyday things. He is trying to change the rules and conventions of the discourse, to give us not only something different to think about, but also a different way of doing the thinking (Kant and Hegel did no less, of course). Reading such philosophy is a business not only of attending to the argument, but also of living its special strenuousness, physically as it were, and hence the importance of intellectual autobiographies, as I hope to show. Heidegger, therefore, is not easy to quote from briefly, because he is trying to render what it is like to think and feel these thoughts. He goes on:

But what remains unthought in the matter of philosophy as well as in its method? Speculative dialectic is a mode in which the matter of philosophy comes to appear of itself and for itself, and thus becomes present (*Gegenwart*). Such appearance necessarily occurs in some light. Only by virtue of light, i.e., through brightness, can what shines show itself, that is, radiate. But brightness in its turn rests upon something open, something free, which might illuminate it here and there, now and then. Brightness plays in the open and wars there with darkness. Wherever a present being encounters another present being or even only lingers near it – but also where, as with Hegel, one being mirrors itself in another speculatively – there openness already rules, the free region is in play. Only this openness grants to the movement of speculative thinking the passage through what it thinks.

We call this openness that grants a possible letting-appear and show 'opening'. In the history of language the German word *Lichtung* is a translation derived from the French *clairière*. It is formed in accordance with the older words *Waldung* (foresting) and *Feldung* (fielding).

The forest clearing (or opening) is experienced in contrast to dense forest, called *Dickung* in our older language. The substantive *Lichtung* goes back to the verb *Lichten*. The adjective *licht* is the same word as 'open'. To open something means to make it light, free and open, e.g., to make the forest free of trees at one place. The free space thus originating is the clearing. What is light in the sense of being free and open has nothing in common with the adjective 'light' which means 'bright', neither linguistically nor factually. This is to be observed for the difference between openness and light. Still, it is possible that a factual relation between the two exists. Light can stream into the clearing, into its openness, and let brightness play with darkness in it. But light never first creates openness. Rather, light presupposes openness. However, the clearing, the open region, is not only free for brightness and darkness but also for resonance and echo, for sound and the diminishing of sound. The clearing is the open region for everything that becomes present and absent.[22]

Heidegger was the child of a carpenter, and was brought up in the Black Forest. Thinking through such images as this of the clearing characterizes a thinker not simply in search of good analogies to illustrate an argument, but in search and research for identities in experience which embody less an argument than a way of living in the world. His philosophy, now called existentialism, belongs here not because I want Heidegger to win the day against an imaginary philosophic opponent, but because he so strenuously introduces the way each of us really thinks, feels, moves and *is*, when we address ourselves with the proper seriousness and commitment to questions which demand ultimate answers – questions, in Tolstoy's phrase, of 'the mightily important . . . men's relation to God, to the universe, to all that is infinite and unending'. It is these questions, and whatever answers we make shift with, which come up bluntly and obstructively when the forms of our official education and its curriculum do not fit the way an individual wants to think about his or her experience. Since it is another presupposition of this book that our present forms of thought drastically do not match our present experience, the important points for immediate study are those at which we find somebody sorting the disjuncture between what he wanted to think and how he was taught. Such a man, then, if he was determined and intelligent enough, built himself a structure of ideas and a method capable of handling the experience and joining the split between material and idea, or between what was past, or passing, and to come.

Such people, if we start in the academies, typically do not fit the received frames of subjects and disciplines. The great Oxford philosopher of between the wars, R.G. Collingwood, spent his life – and as he says, his thought *was* his life – wrestling his way out of what he found to be a deep unsatisfactoriness of prevalent evasiveness about ultimate questions, towards an adequate method for grounding what he called 'a science of human affairs'. The need for such a science was obvious to anybody who had seen as he had, from the laughably-named Intelligence section of the Admiralty, the pointless destruction of eight million young men and women in a few hundred square miles of France, Italy and Turkey, caused exactly by the presence of nescience, and who had gone on as a junior official at the Foreign Office to watch the triumphs of idiocy at the Versailles peace settlements of 1919.

Collingwood wanted to found an inclusive discipline which would make possible a structural investigation into the relationship between theory and practice. It may sound an impossibly large-minded and abstract way to put it, but I insist that some such purpose is at the heart of all education. That it is indeed general as a human enterprise is the message of this short excursus on autobiography.

For Collingwood summarized his life's thought in *An Autobiography*,[23] when, in a four-month convalescence after a sadly early stroke at the age of 49, he wrote a compressed, genial and brilliant revision of his ideas, in case he had no time left to write more. The form of an autobiography was pressingly apposite at such a moment: his own mortality must have been his uppermost thought in writing, and at the same time his isolation among his peers, his refusal of their way of talking, made some such polemical statement of his method and its necessary shaping of his morality and metaphysics, spontaneous, vivid, indeed 'auto-matic'.

Collingwood made his curriculum from the moral luck[24] and momentum of a life happy and successful, at least until its abrupt foreshortening and his last three years of fatal illness. His father was Ruskin's secretary and an accomplished painter; the early education provided for this dazzlingly precocious child was made up out of his own curiosity and his father's considerable efforts to teach him. When he later came to discard the routine tours of the text which passed for the history of ideas, and the pious refusal to answer urgent questions about how to live on the part of realist philosophy, he found in the paintings stacked against his father's walls a model of a method. The paintings were answers to questions which the painter put to himself, or which his experience (life, if you like) put to the painter. Some of the answers were unsatisfactory, or seemed to be becoming so, and therefore the painter left them unfinished. Some 'worked', and therefore were finished.

Collingwood thought again. He was an immensely gifted man – philospher, historian, painter, pianist, archaeologist, administrator, ocean-going yachtsman.[25] While on archaeological digs for Roman remains in his native Cumbria and Northumberland, he reasoned that on a dig nobody was 'just digging'. He himself had questions to put, first, to the patch of turf; next, to the bits and pieces he dug up; finally, to the ground plan he discovered. At each stage, Collingwood concluded, he was following a 'logic of question-and-answer', and each question sought to recover the intentions and purposes to which the artefact in front of him constituted the answer of those long-dead historical figures whose life, in terms of these objects to hand, the archaeologist sought to recover. But the method (the re-search) didn't stop there. The archaeologist, and the historian or philosopher – the reader of Plato or Shakespeare (or the Dead Sea Scrolls or the ciphers of an enemy military or the scrawled anonymities of a banned trade union in the 1830s) – was working to recover past thoughts and actions from their 'traces' in order to achieve a historical knowledge which would be 'the re-enactment of a past thought encapsulated in a context of present thoughts which, by con-tradicting it, confine it to a plane different from theirs'.[26]

The point is not merely to make the past live again in your present life, and the present lives of others, for it will do that anyway. It is to find a way of turning that past into practical knowledge, which you can use to lay hold of the present. That present, as his stirring last chapter tells us, will, as it passes, be represented by the gangsters, liars and hypocrites who are running it as if they were acting in the clear light of truth and reason, unless better men and women capture for themselves the historical knowledge that will give the lie to the falsehoods which disguise the cruelty and callousness of the time.

Collingwood ends his great, brief book with these words: 'I know that all my life I have been engaged unawares in a political struggle, fighting against these things in the dark. Henceforth I shall fight in the daylight.' An autobiography is the obvious place for a thinker to fight for his life, and Collingwood's is the best first advertisement for such a fight. Let his be the first account of what it is to make our own life and experience, and that includes as full a knowledge as may be won of all the other lives and experiences which are contained by our own, into our curriculum.

Collingwood is no doubt a bookish example with which to begin. Well, education comes from books all right. But he is exemplary in entirely accessible ways, which do not turn on his reading Kant at the age of 8 or becoming a great philosopher. He does all that, in the name of our education, we all should strive to do, what a teacher or a parent intends to show his or her children they should do. He makes his life as told in the autobiography into a work of art. The work of art then provides at once a way of thinking about his life and of fully representing it. Our education, as told in our autobiography, becomes a narrative – inevitably a work in a sort of fiction ('true' enough, but given an always retrospective structure), with characters taken from many parts of one's life, some of them fictional anyway. Think how a child makes its changing, constantly edited autobiography out of Mum, Dad, Dr Who, the Famous Five, the dog, an invisible friend, Dennis the Menace, the gang, the school caretaker, the Trumpton fire-brigade. In the best autobiographies, as in the best works of art, the central consciousness and the central attention are on how to make a life you can be proud of out of the fragments of history which you can win some command over. This is the lived question and its answer, the dramatization and an inward finding and realization of values through this extrinsic and historical medium.

Everyone has a history. That is why History with a capital H is made so much of in these pages. For the subject History purports to tell people's own stories, and the story of the people. But then each of us has to decide whether that story as told about us is true; whether our story can ever be told at all.

In another great *Autobiography*, the Scottish poet Edwin Muir writes:

> It is clear that no autobiography can begin with a man's birth, that we extend far beyond any boundary line which we can set for ourselves in the past or the future, and that the life of every man is an endlessly repeated performance of the life of man. It is clear for the same reason that no autobiography can confine itself to conscious life, and that sleep, in which we pass a third of our existence, is a mode of experience, and our dreams a part of reality. In themselves our conscious lives may not be particularly interesting. But what we are not and can never be, our fable, seems to me inconceivably interesting. I should like to write that fable, but I cannot even live it; and all I could do if I related the outward course of my life would be to show how I have deviated from it; though even that is impossible, since I do not know the fable or anybody who knows it. One or two stages in it I can recognize: the age of innocence and the Fall and all the dramatic consequences

which issue from the Fall. But these lie behind experience, not on its surface; they are not historical events; they are stages in the fable.[27]

Muir arranges the story of his life in three blocks. In the first, utterly formative stage, he is a child on his parents' rented smallholding in the Orkneys, and what this gave to him, as the quotation implies, was direct experience of the pure, innocent life in the Garden of Eden. 'That world', Muir recalls, 'was a perfectly solid world, for the days did not undermine it but merely rounded it, or rather repeated it as if there were only one day endlessly rising and setting.' In this Eden, held within the boundless freedom of his parents' free kingdom, Muir comes closest to living the fable of his and all men's and women's lives. The space of that great happiness almost fills and is congruent with the huge blue heaven of the fable assigned not merely to childhood, but to the human potentiality for freedom and fulfilment. From that early life, Muir takes the pure and mighty emblems of a traditional rural order, ideally unimpaired by brutality, poverty, degradation – stone and water, tree and leaf, roof and hearth – and uses these throughout the splendid picturesqueness of his poetry to prefigure the unnameable fable which every person seeks to embody, but can only find in a contingent history of wizened and misshapen outlines.

In the second stage of his life, after the age of 13 or so, when the family were driven out of their living in the Orkneys, Muir experiences not only the Fall, but the descent into Hell. Like thousands of families before them in the history of industrial capitalism, poverty drove them from the land to the more horrible privations of the city: dirt, disease, friendlessness, homelessness. His parents die. Two brothers die. Muir himself is ill and undernourished, making an education out of his tiny clerkly wage, the socialism then spreading with such justified-looking heat and fleetness through Glasgow and all the other cities of the industrial north, and the books read in a grim office or grimmer, bleaker bedroom, which registered this widespread, dreadful plight. Yet he confesses in the *Autobiography*, he could find no form nor metaphor for these lonely and pitiless years. They are a time he wishes simply he could cancel from his life, and there is nothing he can do to find in them a necessary meaning or to situate them in the narrative of his life such that he can perhaps make a virtue of their necessity.[28]

He cannot take subsequent condolence from T.S. Eliot:

We had the experience but missed the meaning.
And approach to the meaning restores the experience
In a different form . . .

Those years had no meaning, and he can give them no form. So the venture of the *Autobiography* fails in its purpose across the 'Glasgow' section. The best he can do is to recognize the stony barrenness in as truthful and bare a way as possible.

Restoration is achieved in the 'Prague' section, for here Muir brings together his successful emergence from his long, twilit depression by means of psychoanalysis, the happiness of his marriage to Willa Muir, his growing mastery as a poet, his love of a noble city, and his pioneering work with Willa in translating Kafka into English for the first time: Kafka whose deadpan and stoical rendering of insane state bureaucracies gave Muir a way of placing the hideous no-meaning of modern politics against the fable of an ideal city and its morally excellent polity, and therefore of understanding how Prague and the Czechs were again betrayed in the vicious history of 1948.

It is the claim of this chapter that everybody compiles an autobiography as they go, whether they write it down or not, and that it is the readiest, most common and most intelligible way in which to tie a knot between those large, counterposed abstractions, history and biography, thought and learning, knowledge and experience. This is most obviously true if we end by turning to the autobiographies of those who, recognizing that their experience was indeed, in Eliot's phrase, 'not the experience of one life only But of many generations', none the less could only tell their own story as they saw it (in the common phrase) and hope that others could recognize their lives there too.

These are the kind of men and women whose history had never been written down, either because they couldn't write, or because they'd been told the story was worthless. We hear them now, in the writings of those women who speak up for a view of the world, and of intellectual life within the world, which has been more or less ruthlessly excluded by the men who make and wield the power of that world. It is striking that, according to the divisions of labour and of value that I listed earlier, so many of these women have found their own voice by way of doing the different voices of university courses in English literature. Autobiography and novels were the natural forms for this class to take up, and a shelf of books under the admirable Virago imprint – including, say, Storm Jameson's *Journey from the North*, Vera Brittain's *The Testament of Youth*, and Naomi Mitchison's *You May Well Ask*[29] would, in the sound image, bear witness to the way in which these strong-willed brave women bent themselves and their books until they grew more or less together. And by the same token, the same is true of such an autobiography as Ezekiel Mphahlele's *Down Second Avenue*,[30] where the deprived, intelligent, solitary black South African reads and writes his way to the freedom of exile in an American univeristy.

These are, so to speak, the autochthonous, or born from the earth beginnings of writers on behalf of a speechless class. The voice is piercingly audible in the moving series of English working-class autobiographies which came out of the Reform, Chartist and trade union movements of the years 1830–70. Samuel Bamford, perhaps the most famous of these, friend of the agitator Hunt, reporter of Peterloo from under the scabbards of the cavalry, author of *Passages in the Life of a Radical* (1844) says of his own efforts:

> We had not any of our own rank with whom to advise for the better – nor many of other days who had gone through the ordeal of experience; and whose judgement might have directed our self-devotion.

That is to say, as (in E.P. Thompson's title) the making of the English working class was accomplished between 1790 and 1830, its leaders had to write a new history, create the forms of unprecedented political organization, and invent class traditions from a bookless and largely speechless past and present. This is how and why experience becomes theorized into knowledge, how in this case history becomes institutionalized, how it creates and holds a membership and thereby establishes a community of learning.

All Bamford himself could do was write an autobiography, and hope that it made sense. His narrative brings out clearly how hard membership was to come by for men used to the close, known community of friends who had grown up together in one place, who had then to organize associations of complete strangers in the fearful, bustling anonymity of the new industrial cities.[31] Similarly, Alexander Somerville, in his *The Autobiography of a Working Man*[32] had no theory of class or expectation to draw upon when he describes the poverty that drove him to become a soldier, nor could he name the nature of the system which set out to destroy him, when he and a group of other young soldiers published an anonymous letter advising both the Chartists and their foes in the established order that they as soldiers would not interfere with the demonstrations as long as they were peaceable. The army framed Somerville on a trumpery charge to do with a riding offence in his cavalry regiment, and he was sentenced to two hundred lashes.

It was, literally, a killing sentence, although he was cut down after half had been carried out, in case he died. The point here is that the whole frightful incident is very minutely described, the details of his being tied up, the wiping of blood and flesh from the thongs of the lash, all without any reflection on what it meant or who was responsible for such hideous cruelty and injustice. There being no theory, nor even a known community of listeners, Somerville wisely leaves the facts of the matter for the composition of later historians.

Autobiography therefore is the first foundation of identity. As personal identity[33] grows, and, let us say, becomes educated, it discovers extrinsic or even objective instruments and media of thought which permit it to reflect upon itself. The stories of art and of history are the first and last of these, as I have said. At the same time, these reflecting agents gather their own identity, so that reflection is (obviously) reciprocal. It is in these ways that objects of study become subjects, and we in our divisions of educational labour and value become subject to those identities even when, perhaps most of all when, we are students like so many who dislike, reject and do not comprehend the subject themselves.

4

Identity in Selves and Subjects

It is plain that in writing of education and the curriculum, which is its subject and object, we have to have some pictures of those who undergo that education. If it is true, as I claim, that the curriculum not merely implies, but actually teaches some versions of how to live a good life, then it follows that it, in turn, has subjects who are logically capable of living those variously good lives. There is, in other words, a necessary connection predicated and sought between what a society teaches its children and how it wishes those children to be: truth becomes truistic.

All the same, the formal connections between knowledge and learning, culture and action, are worth insisting upon at a time when many teachers will make a butcher's severance in the curriculum between who people are and what they can do. The blunt axeman of the staffroom can be counted on to dismiss considerations of the self in the philistine name of making sure that students get the skills which they may be able to turn to a living. His more sensitive colleague in pastoral care may shrink a little at his outspoken instrumentality, but she will largely connive at the distinction by treating the troublesome child from the fourth year as an individual whose selfhood and identity are not to be violated by any gross irruption from a more powerful being (the correct principle of liberalism), but more importantly an individual whose self is not a function of what he or she knows and can do, whose identity is uninflected by knowledge or learning. Either teacher might agree that a pupil may gain satisfaction from their instrumental skills – being able to reassemble an internal combustion engine, say – or may gain what is called self-confidence from some official act of teacherly recognition – the publication in a magazine of a piece of writing, perhaps. But the notion of identity, largely an unproblematic one in ordinary reference, is kept distinct from a repertory of skills and competences, and in the curriculum itself, the domain of instrumental skills – the practical, needful world – is kept distinct from the expressive life of a person, whose self and its values finds its voice and images in the strictly impractical world of symbolism.

There are deep confusions and incoherences here, and while it may be not only human but necessary to abide with muddle, or to keep apart both in the soul and in the society mutually incoherent frames of mind, the uses to which such master symbols of the society as 'identity', 'self', 'individuality', 'person', 'role' and 'character' are put in relation to the curriculum are often so radically self-deceiving that the results wound just those people such symbols are called upon to help, to liberate indeed, and enter into their own country. Our picture of who these human beings really are (let alone who we as teachers really are) is compounded of versions of all these concepts of individuality (including individuality itself), and it is only by sorting out a little of their entanglement in the first place that we can go on to say something about what knowledge and its modalitites can do to you, what difference it makes to you if you are learned or ignorant, as well as what it can do *for* you.

Identity is often seen to be in a critical state: 'crisis of identity' is the off-the-peg diagnosis of many a breakdown in the novel and in the psychiatric ward. But behind the diagnosis, whether sympathetic or offhand, is the large cultural assumption that the discovery, choice and affirmation of one's identity is a – if not *the* – key to a successful life. To generalize rather flatly in everyday language, that identity is thought of as something in me which, existing now, is identical with that something in a future me.[1] It is that something which is the test of survival after some drastic event has supervened – a severe accident, say, or going to prison for years – and which, being identical with a present something in me, *is* who and what I am, even if I were to have had a very different life.

Without launching into any very technical analysis, perhaps it will do to run quickly through the terms we habitually use to designate the agents of our individuality, in order to suggest the complexity and historical changefulness of this figure, together with the extreme difficulty of attaching much substance to this identity which is so truly you or me. As far as this chapter goes, it will be better to plump for a less solid picture of identity made up of our 'mental continuity and connectedness' (Parfit's motto[2]), in which what really matters in these terms is the holding of relations between an experience and our memory of that experience, between an action now and the intention to perform some later dependent action, between embodiments of present characteristic and later embodiment of developments of that characteristic, all this as well as these relations themselves being held in a continuous overlapping chain of many such relations.

Such a view doesn't make identity as a concept quite as loose and arbitrary as at first sight appears. Each of the many relations which compose the chain of continuity has its strong historical presence in our view of what we can be, and each, it had better be said, is assigned a particular path among the many routes of the curriculum, to be trained and cultivated accordingly. Thus, the concept of character[3] rests upon the givenness of the characters concerned. They simply are their powers and dispositions, largely in attachment to the adjective 'strong'. A strong character is someone who exhibits those characteristics in all circumstances; he is predictable and reliable, rather than subject to change or self-effacing. The term shades into indulgent derogation when we speak of someone 'being a character'; this someone exhibits, it is implied, an almost wilful insistence upon living out his characteristics. None the less, this usage also brings out the fixity and certainty of character; the nature of a character, even one with deplorable characteristics like Prince Hal or Falstaff or Grandfather Smallweed or Harold Skimpole, forms the structure of his experiences, rather than is formed by them.

Such characteristics are not of course individual; identity is hardly a word to use here. The distinct character which Arthur Lowe made of Captain Mainwaring in the television series, *Dad's Army*, turned upon the precise rendering of very general traits – a calm, complacent stupidity; a clipped, unselfconscious rudeness; a splendid and pompous incompetence – all externally exhibited, and wonderfully funny in virtue of their predictability as well as their awfulness. A character gives you little sense of what it is like to be himself; he can shed little light on himself, as witness that strong character Soldier George in *Bleak House*, who confesses to being as puzzled by and resigned to himself as his iron-willed mother is. What the character is, is powerfully present: as miser, as crook, as good tough guy, as leader, as lover.

We can gingerly venture the view that character at the present time is less preferred than 'person' or individual. The strong character looked for by the grammar-school headmaster as his head of prefects has faded a little in historical importance (though the pastoral counsellor will still speak as to the delinquent's character in the juvenile court). The head boy and head girl of character have been superannuated in a polity whose class definitions, though still so pervasive, are become abruptly soluble, and whose dominant meanings have been attached to freedom of choice and 'radical personalization',[4] which reject the fixity of the character. Indeed, one way to study the meaning and effects of a theory of (strong) character is to study what happens when one kind of character is overtaken by a social order that has no use for such characteristics: the daring and cunning adventurer when the war is over, the rugged frontiersman in the new business world, the *grande dame* after the revolution. If these people cannot change their characters, they will be destroyed.

In the present forms of our social change, as the modes of production shift acceleratingly away from manufacturing and extraction from nature towards service and consumption, the person takes precedence over the character, although the character retains strong residual life. The person, however, is defined by his or her personal responsibility for action. What she does is less important than that she is recognized as author of the action. To withdraw recognition of that responsibility, or to attempt to delimit it, is to fail to treat her as a person. This comes out clearly in the treatment of individuals or institutions as persons at law. The refusal of full rights or the plea of diminished responsibility (in the differing cases of children, or defectives, or aliens, or anyone else not counted under different judicatures as fully present) reflects and identifies the standing of a person as an issue of human or other *rights*, the exercise of which is both accorded to and assumed by that person as a function of his or her autonomy. Hamlet, for example, is caught on the historical twistpoint at which tribal obligations of revenge for his father's murder, utterly attested by his father's ghost, are contested by quite new demands of answerability to evidence and judgement in the court of law and not of ancient pieties. In this new legal and religious light (the advent of the legal doctrine in its Renaissance forms coincided with Luther's account of the individual's attainment to personal salvation), all men and, very gradually, all women came to stand equal at the bar of judgement. That is what it is to be a person, whether the person be a king's son or a court jester, and in judging persons in the light of their legal and moral responsibility, judgement increasingly turns not upon action (which, as Hamlet's case once more testifies, can go horribly wrong), but upon intention. What did you really mean to do? is the crucial question, and in attending to intentions and motives (a central aspect of legal proof, as the detective story underlines), the focus of moral attention wobbles and dissolves again, because the legally liable person is no longer directly answerable in terms of his role and its duties, but in terms of his personal duty and his moral adequacy. Morality is separated both from jurisprudence and prudence itself. So the person is interrogated for his motives and, beyond this, for who he or she really is, such that this was the choice made, and these the principles or lack of them that explain and justify that choice.

A legal person, then, is defined by his or her rights, and these are made visible by their property (the 'displaced person', as refugees were known after 1945, were stateless and without rights). But as individual human beings in the long transition of Europe and the New World from absolutism to a market and property capitalism came to acquire their rights in virtue of their personal powers, so they became selves. The quality of an individual self is determined by his qualities, as Amelie Rorty puts it: 'they are his capital, to invest well or foolishly'.[5] Their stories are then told in dozens of novels as their achievement in accumulating property and wealth, generally in a contest where victory has been won over those who tried to insist on power as appropriate not to powers, but to lineage and dynasty. The snob is the most easily derided figure in the nineteenth-century novel. Those vibrant selves, Jane Eyre and Heathcliff, make mincemeat of him.

The self, however, is rapacious. As Romanticism let loose a doctrine of self as defined by the irresistible beauties of spontaneity, the old civic virtues could no longer hold it. The self sought passionately for itself in the fulfilment of its own true interests, interests defined as knowable by their 'truth to oneself'. For a self to fail in truth to itself or to be negated is to lose an essential integrity (or, precisely, the integratedness of that same self). Of course, if fulfilment of the self is defined as the possession of inaccessibly distributed goods, there is an unfair fight on for the good life. This is very obvious in education: no use a university degree fulfilling you, if you can't get in or don't do as you're told – the point broken off by the film *Educating Rita*.

The self is in as deep trouble with its metaphysics as with its politics. In so far as the self is fulfilled by the unfettered exploration of its interests and passions, and in so far as it confirms itself by the acquisition of a rich store of possessed experiences with which it is at one, who is it who is organizing these intentions and this mobility of action? Where is its centre, if it is not to be a bundle of caprices? The difficulty is illustrated by Erving Goffmann's famous and subtle book, *The Presentation of Self in Everyday Life*,[6] which dissects the mechanism by which we variously show up and show off in the different roles society provides for us to occupy: customer, client, parent, daughter, plaintiff, lover, citizen, voter, mortgage-owner, and so on. The trouble is that nobody knows who is doing the presenting. The self seems to have no centre.

At this point, we call up the last and still the most rhetorically potent of our moral-educational symbolic figures, the individuals. He and she have appeared before in these pages, of course, and their present significance is largely taken from their alleged conceptual capacity to contain characters, persons and selves in a single nominative. That they cannot do what they claim to do is a discovery only gradually being made, and its consequence for the meanings of the curriculum and of education, indeed for the continuity of the social order, is of as large a significance for us all as anything we have to worry about. However, the largeness of that shadow looms over chapter 10 rather than this one, where what we are looking for is what is real about this individual who is so much appealed to, as both value and fount of values.

For a start, individuals[7] are their own entities, rational, self-sufficient, counterposed to the determinate force of Society with a capital S. The individual, like the person, has rights and duties, not given by law, but by the individual conscience; Kant is its honorary arbitrator, but even he, if the liberal individual were to meet and understand him, would be viewed with one auspicious and one dropping eye, because the imperative of duty which Kant universalizes may be overridden by the free demands which the individual makes of life (a way of putting it which gets round the charge of selfishness).

In trying to free itself from universal imperatives (in the other cant, 'laws are made to be broken'), the individual starts on the search to find absolute uniqueness or originality. His individuality is then a function of his difference from others, his serenely sufficient capacity to live free of others. D.H. Lawrence's hero and heroine in *Women in Love* aspire to this condition, helped on, as Lawrence readily admits, by a small private income, and Lawrence is perhaps the most fervent and profound explorer of the country to which a commitment to one's own flaring and vivid singularity will take you. Dedication to that singular vitality is the criterion for seeing others; and by this intolerable light all the rest of social life – as in Lawrence and as so often in Henry James – is shown up in its socially conformist, hypocritical, lying and self-betraying impurity.

The only answer, then is, to go into exile, and Lawrence, never afraid of following the logic of his beliefs, did just that. But exile is a lonely place, and the individual who, like Ibsen's doll-wife Nora in *The Doll's House*, strikes out for the fiords as the locus of individuality will find it a cold going. The individual is then at the mercy of her own choice, in a world of mad individuals living the consequences of *their* choices, with no means of acknowledging their complicated mutual interdependence nor the necessity of altruism.[8] The individual, seen as *the* realm of meaning, can have no scale for situtating itself in a history, nor a means of restitution for the gross structural inequalities which prevent the realization of individuality for all those individuals on the wrong side of opportunity.

The queasy condition of all these key points of appeal is of direct significance to the subject-matter of the curriculum, whether we take it large or small. The curriculum at large is another name for the officially sanctioned and world-political picture which we produce, circulate and reproduce in our society; it *is* our politics. And when the question of the curriculum is, as they say, an academic one, then its theories or its unexaminedly ready reckoning-up of what a person, a self, or an individual are, are at the heart of its praxis, in the natural as in the human sciences. For natural science is investigated and developed *for* someone; it cannot be purposeless, any more than any human activity can be purposeless. Its proponents cannot work without a theory of interests, and those interests can only be human. The point is even sharper and more penetrative in the human sciences; the very subject of the subjects is the human being,[9] and so are the student and the teacher. Their view of what that subject-matter really is – whether individual, character, or mere porter of the forces of historical evolution – is product and producer of the conduct of inquiry, and no one can escape this as a condition of teaching and studying, whether their fellow-students are in the reception class of the infant school or the reading room of the British Museum.

Furthermore, either form of the sciences has gone forward since the Enlightenment[10] on the view that science is both the doctrine and vehicle of progress, and that the vast project of human emancipation will be brought about under the clear light of its new system of human reason. Even now, when faith in progress has been so badly damaged at Auschwitz, Gulag, Hiroshima, and in uncountable smaller torture-chambers, that project of emancipation is still appealed to in the schools and universities of the rich countries of the world as guaranteeing personal development in the terms of scientific rationalism and educated subjectivity.

There is therefore a direct reflection from our preferred name and notion of a human subject onto the methods of inquiry by which we turn experience into knowledge, and both into values. It is worth extending the implied criticism of the dead-end reached by too enthusiastic a pursuit of selfhood and individuality, by saying that now that progress is faltering as a master-symbol in a world poisoned by its own effluent, bleeding from its own weapons, and deformed by its simultaneous gluttony and starvation, we would do well to return the individual to his and her lived and social history. In classrooms and seminar rooms, of course, there is still much necessary play to make with persons, selves and individuals, if we are to understand anybody else at all, but a useful corrective to the studiously anti-social connotations of 'radical personalization' is to stress again the proper significance of character as a locus of intellectual being, to turn sharply away from a narcissistic preoccupation with the state of self, and strongly towards the development of character traits which might make for a better world. It is so obvious that a more provident and humane economics[11] would make more for a benign world would encourage structures of behaviour in which the character traits of naked piracy became at least mildly recessive.

The connections between character and learning are never

direct, and paradise cannot be introduced by the curriculum. None the less, if the official institutions of education do not think about virtue and reason, and how one may engender the other, no one else will. The sociology of knowledge may be paraphrased as the study of the structural conditions within which knowledge works for or against the good life, just as sociology at large is the study of the social structures of being. Now the structures of knowledge may doubtless be antecedently the product of the way our concepts work upon our percepts in the name of understanding. But necessarily conservative arguments[12] about the logical form and grounds of knowledge still leave an awful lot of room for sociological impositions, and it is these that are too often represented as natural ontology, when what they really are is an unnatural ideology, locally self-serving and self-righteous.

Social structuration produces agency, which in turn produces structures.[13] To put it less propositionally, we make and are made by formal arrangements and dispositions which occupy the frames of our social identity, issue in actions which are our own, though involuntarily mediated by those structures, which same actions constitute subsequent structures for the future actions of ourselves and others.

The most immediate way to study social structure is to find the boundaries of classes of people and things: to understand the principles of classification. In a celebrated book,[14] Mary Douglas, starting from the implicit premiss that all human beings fear the unclassifiable as a danger to identity, studies a series of examples of strongly classified taxonomies, violations of which may in some societies lead to very severe punishment, as in the list of Jewish food prohibitions and permissions given in *Leviticus*. In an endearing example, she cites the case of family friends who, while converting an old and backward house, had made a bathroom out of a ground-floor corridor, to which there were two doors. One door was kept locked, and the other became the official bathroom door, but the bathroom itself was still 'polluted' by impure elements which belonged to the back-of-the-house corridor it had recently been: a gardening mac on the unused door, a pair of heavy wellingtons, assorted garden implements, old shoes and gloves, and so forth. The room was perfectly big enough to take all the clutter, but Douglas recalls that, though herself 'naturally tolerant of disorder', she felt uncomfortable with the bits and pieces which didn't belong there, and the locked door, which might suddenly open upon the privacy – the sanctity, even – of a bathroom. These are tokens familiar to us all. A dirty plate, knife and fork are in place beside the sink, out of place on the bedroom dresser; the unmade bed prevents the bed-sitter becoming a sociable sitting room. Whether simple rules of this kind derive from innate instincts to order (which obviously some people lack) or are culturally learned doesn't matter here. The point is that principles of classification are the same thing as principles of order (dirt is only matter in the wrong place) and may be detected at work wherever society opens or closes its forms and structures.

This can be quite a literal as well as an experiential matter. When shops, factories or schools close for the day, you find the line drawn between work and leisure for the classes of people involved. Where doors are only opened on request or at a summons (private houses, office doors, prisons), you find the regulation of access according to the criteria of privacy or power. So with telephones: the more calls you have to make on the way to speak to somebody, the more powerful they are. The fewer people allowed into a particular place (the bedroom, the shrine, the morgue, the study), the clearer the message about the sanctity of its space. Where combinations of substances or identities are forbidden (girls and boys, white and black, ceremonial and casual), there too are the personality-creating classifications of a society. And where these classifications are flouted, as when men grow long hair or women wear men's clothes, there you find a struggle for different forms of classification, and a reconstruction, sometimes trivial, sometimes important, of the sources, forms, and control of power itself.

Once upon a time, a London East-End working-class Jew brought up a Catholic, having edged his way into the mixed classifications of the still superciliously regarded and 'so-called' (in the Olde English put-down) social sciences of about 1950, found Durkheim as his way of sorting these impossible contradictions, and of recognizing the fact (in his own words) that 'out there it's all ambiguous'. Basil Bernstein, in two volumes of his collected works,[15] has devoted himself to an anthropology of British education along the planes, as he puts it, of its 'classification and framing'. Classification refers simply to the principles by which knowledge is organized into subjects, areas, disciplines, and so forth, just as elsewhere in sociology and anthropology it refers to ways in which openness and closure are socially effected. Framing is Bernstein's instrument with which to analyse the ordering and organizing process of teaching itself, as opposed to what is taught. A teacher frames his classified knowledge by his timing and sequencing of his material, above all by the degrees of freedom allowed to students to interrupt these sequences, displace and reorder them, or the extent to which students may glimpse and move towards quite new and untimetabled fields of study. In either case, classification and framing are strongly coded where the insulation of social relations is heavy and impermeable, where process and order are thought of as difficult to alter, inevitable in their momentum, and immune to idiosyncratic preference. The textbooks, notably in maths and science, of the 1950s, were strongly framed and classified in this way: arithmetic, geometry, algebra; Euclid, Pythagoras, trigonometry; multiplication to the base 10, long multiplication, logarithms. O-level children went solidly through these sequences in the order required by Messrs Hall and Knight and their rivals without any comprehension of how it all worked, but some sufficient address at cranking the mathematical handles and turning out answers which nearly corresponded with the answers at the back of the book.

Bernstein introduces a third articulation of what he calls educational knowledge codes, and this is the ordering system which controls evaluation – or more crudely, examining. The strong evaluation system is inscribed in the three-hour examination paper, with its terse commands and its imperious variations in typeface ('Candidates must . . . four questions only . . . go on to part III . . . write clearly on ONE side of the paper'; 'Failure to comply will result in execution'), which, however unfailingly comic, indicate great confidence in what the examiner–evaluator thinks of the realizable knowledge of the course. Now to 'realize knowledge' means just that: to make the knowledge 'real' in a public form – to answer questions publicly, accessibly and approvably. An essay question or linguistic exercise or scientific experiment is intended straightforwardly to give practice in the subject and to reveal whether the student can do what the teacher wants her to do. Strength of coding is always easiest to see in the evaluation system: just read the examination papers.

Bernstein wrote the first of his papers on curriculum analysis in

1970. Its occasion was the sudden quickening of interest in integrated studies, that is, studies in which classification and framing were radically weakened in the name of the universal dovetailedness of knowledge, and of important advances in learning psychology which, with Piaget's name to hand, asked for pupils to organize the pace and scope of their learning for themselves. Bernstein is often misunderstood as positively recommending the desirability of integrated studies, but his concern is much more to show what is involved, and to connect the upheavals in curriculum development with seismic displacements in all the classification systems of society. In an exceptionally subtle and symmetrical analysis, he identifies the surface forms of integrated study as congruent with those of Durkheim's mechanistic society, in which the principles of solidarity are mutual and equal; but he then points out that this is only made possible by the making of explicit, statable premises and arrangements of the kind necessary in Durkheim's other, organicist society, in which solidarity rests on an interdependence born of the many divisions of labour. The mechanistic society does not need to make things explicit; simple and limited divisions of labour make for implicit systems of order and verbal redundance. Complex divisions of labour, in which the relations of production cause marked differences between producers (not just between, say, engineers and designers, but as between electronic and mechanical engineers), require highly elaborated and verbally explicit systems of order. Paradoxically, integrated studies are of this order.

So far, indeed, from advocating integrated studies, Bernstein points out that a frequent failure in making principles of order explicit and intelligible, or the no less frequent tendency of teachers to devise order merely from a trivial or arbitrary topic ('the breakfast table' on the primary-school display table, or, vaguer yet, but respectable-sounding 'prehistoric man', the 30-million-year jump from dinosaurs, stalwarts of the junior school, to flint axes, all made in a couple of models) leads to bewilderment and disorder in the individual. The child can't make sense of a mess. The deciphering of knowledge from inquiry has no clear procedure. Value is dissolved.

It is at such moments that Bernstein fixes for us the social structures which make or unmake individuals, as persons or as characters. For there is nothing much to comfort those who want to start 7-year-olds off with a rock-tight timetable divided into history, geography, maths, English. Such teachers are endorsing the high insulations of the 'collection code', the consequences of which are hardly less arbitrary than its opposite. By its directives, pupils in England collect their bagful of O levels, a collection whose contents are dictated by no more educational purposes than that those are the subjects which are available in their school, those the ones they seem on a pretty random estimate from trial examination to be sufficiently good at, and those which university boards of examination define as available at O level in these versions.

Beyond O level, the same topography deepens like a coastal shelf. The separation occurs between the academic A level and the technical Higher National Diploma, a division which advertises the worldwide privileging of mental over manual accomplishment. A levels are managed by universities, who are embarrassingly unselfconscious about the mixture of historical chance, redolent snobbery and ideological self-seekingness which is the real structure of their subjects. There are supposed to be 'natural' groupings of A levels – maths, physics, chemistry, for instance, or history, English, French – admission to which is largely won by doing well enough in O level, but membership of and identity in which becomes more and more compelling. It is now that the value-systems I listed in the last chapter lour strong and permanent in their pressure – fact against value, objective against subjective, science against arts – while those who have been successful in getting as far as A level learn to be proper members of their segment of the divisions of labour.

At university, the marks of Cain are those of success. Membership is confirmed by confinement to the language of the discipline, and anomalies are watchfully controlled. In an ingenously flagrant exemplification of Mary Douglas's thesis, certain subjects are even designated 'pure' – pure maths, pure science – as opposed to the social inferiority of 'applied', with its overtones of labour and of manual effort, as in 'applied engineering'. And all through English-speaking universities, in Australasia as well as those of Western Europe, mixed categories, either of a collection kind (Russian and mathematics) or of an integrated and inter-disciplinary sort (cultural history and mass communications) are either hunted down, or exiled to junior institutions like polytechnics and colleges of advanced or higher education. Within these strongly classified institutions, individuals who have been gradually marked out for success by way of A levels and university entrance learn the structures that confirm their membership of a subject and their place within the divisions of labour and of value.

They learn by heart what characterizes a subject as *there* in its own right. It is first a way of marking off educational (or school) knowledge from non-educational, non-school knowledge. This is the most battled-for boundary of all – between what they tell you at school and the customs of the country. In one narrative, the strong classifications of educational knowledge deny to a man or a woman what each thought they knew, hard and real, out of their customary life. As we shall see, such a battle was once fought most callously over language itself – 'You're not going to talk like that here'. But in the other, educational story, knowledge must be somehow objectified, made to stand still in the library or the laboratory, and thereby rendered immune to the variations of transient passions and separate wilfulness. For any science to be a science, it must simplify and rigidify experience to make it studiable.[16]

There are, however, accidents and unevenness in the development of any subject, and the accumulation of its properties and empire are fortuitous and piratical. If a subject may be said to become such by its attachment to certain regular experiences, by its view of what constitutes its special system of concepts, by its chosen techniques, its tradition of authority and its past masters, by its list of great achievements in its field, it is not hard to see how the characterizing features of such a landscape, its main roads and landmarks, may quickly seem at least disputable and at worse capricious. And the same goes for the so-called realms of meaning and forms of knowledge. The conceptual division between practical and aesthetic thinking took place sometime in the eighteenth century; there was nothing necessary about it. Although it is obviously true that physics typically deals with a different set of materials to psychology, and even though some schools of psychologists have tried to treat their material human beings as though only physical things could be said about them, neither subject-matter excludes the other in an ultimate way. Neither set of methods expels the other's. Indeed, one of Hegel's greatest contributions was to notice how sets of ideas, once liberating, supple and open, become hardened and constricting after a certain length of time, and explanatory models of action obstruct and disable thought until it can find innovative models and metaphors.[17] that carry it past the dead end into new intellectual possibilities. This was obviously the point reached when physics began in the 1920s to collect the data inexplicable on the old terms, and the break was only made when Heisenberg used Janneau's maths to bring into order the eccentricities now known as quanta.

Subjects, it seems, have an aetiology. They are liable to arthritis and hardening of the arteries. The brilliance, insouciance and daring of John Austin's analystic philosophy and Ayer's scepticism in Oxford of 1945, which did so much for the very closely finessed understanding of everyday language, trickled away into social triviality.[18] Mathematics, always an exacting and exiguous subject, was suddenly released into disorientingly new dissolutions of its own premises by the last work of Turing, and then by Barnach and Ziman, as well as Gödel in the 1960s. For once, most unusually and beneficially, what intellectuals thought changed what happened in school classrooms. In a rare case, the line from the genius to the 10-year-old was quite direct.

These and many others are occasions for speaking of the decay and resurrection of fields of study. Some of these histories are intoxicating; but whatever the subject-matter, our immediate concern is to notice the way in which those who are successful in their education are more and more deeply socialized into their intellectual difference from others. Understandably, the longer you have been doing a study, and the more it has contributed to your advance (teaching is the best-known, most thronged avenue of social promotion), the more you believe the story it tells you about itself. Who in teaching has not been confided in as to the preposterousness of upstart new disciplines? – 'not really subjects at all' as the bluff and bluffing voice has it. To revert to Bernstein, the pervasive classification and the mechanistic framing of traditional subjects at degree levels of education deepens loyalty to a subject (and hostility to others) as well as membership of its intellectual community (compatible, naturally, with the English educational class system: higher, further, secondary, primary) in order to make the very self (*sic*), its criteria of authenticity and sincerity,[19] into a soldier of its subject-regiment or its constituent-audience – physics, biology, French, drama, junior children.

These fidelities are visible in the most commonplace social life of the staffroom; they are even enviable there. The divisions of labour ensure that the biology department takes its instant coffee in the lab, the PE hide their inferiority complex with the horsebox and the steel-yard next to the gym, the English department sneers politely at the alleged thickheadedness of the geographers, the mathematicians walk alone. And it won't do to say that these things only impinge on that small minority of children who do A levels and take a degree. The symbolic violence, which Pierre Bourdieu speaks of[20] as being done to the masses (as socialists used to say), who do not comprehend the ultimate porousness of the curriculum and the swampy, saline and enveloping grounds which undermine the foundations of all knowledge, is violence done in the name of the integrity of the discipline, which cannot be polluted by the stuff which would make it intelligible. The one thing children feelingly understand about what they do not understand is that they are not good enough.

5

Access and Prestige

It is this that the national curriculum of any country does with great efficacy: it makes clear to its students who is any good and who is not. And here it is important to put down the myth that four-fifths of the school population are unmarked by school anyway, so whatever we do makes no difference. The strong legend of teacher powerlessness is not only rebutted by everyday experience – look at how clearly people remember their school-days, even if they hated them, and reflect a little on how intensely and clearly all children take in the experiences of early years, and lastly notice how absorbed one's own children are by their school life (how popular *Grange Hill* is): it is, after all, where they live. And if we need the backing of formal research, there is Jerome Bruner's summary[1] of a mass of cross-cultural inquiry into the effects of schooling which shows, so far as such conclusions can be shown, that children who have been to school the world over are more like one another in their handling of abstract concepts and their consciousness of different points of view than children in their own countries who have never been to school at all. From the age of five on, children live and learn the essential divisions and structures of their society as these order the immediacies of time and space . They learn the difference between work and leisure till time and times are done: schoolday and weekend, termtime and holiday, lessons and play: they learn that lunchtime is, within polite limits, if not theirs, then not the teachers' either, but those weird social officers, the dinner-ladies'. They learn that Friday afternoon is a special time because it's nearly, but not quite, the weekend, and the teachers are allowed to feel exhausted and entitled to the easier time marked by 'story', 'activity' or games.

Thus and thus are children and students initiated into the individual-making structures of curriculum and life as we live it. It is often overlooked just how fundamental and unnatural such arrangements are: we turn to what they signify as the necessary meanings of the bureaucratized state in relation to production in chapter 8. For now, however, there is the more intractable question of what kind of individual the society does want its curriculum to help make children and students into, and then, more complex and elusive still, how it will organize the curriculum in order to produce these in more or less recognizable versions and in the required numbers.

In the first question, we are returned to the protracted struggle for personal and social meanings from whose historical battle-ground we started out in the first chapter. This time we shall need to be more precise. Capitalist economies (to go no futher) are undergoing a drastic redistribution of their productive centres of gravity. The four waves of communication revolution which have been at once the dynamo and the common condition of capitalism since it took off in the nineteenth century – railways, motor cars, aircraft, electric and electronic communication – are widening outwards in a series of irregular and colliding circles, leaving some economies at once stagnant and stormswept. Britain is the case in point. The modes and relations of production in the nineteenth century required (we may say, following Bernstein[2]) a durable and relatively inflexible proletarian workforce, commanded by an entrepreneurial class in which the successful traits of resolution, ruthlessness, personal authority and strength of will were likely to be the character formation the system looked for and sought to mould. By the present late stage of British monopoly capitalism, with its investment entirely overseas and its home markets dominated by imports, the booming of its finance sector and the collapse of its manufacturing one, a very different human creature is needed in order to maintain the social order on the road of tranquil and relative decline. In its workforce, what is looked for is docility, certainly, but also flexibility, readiness to move, change and retrain, as well as to adapt quickly to new keyboard technology. In its managerial and professional classes, what is needed is a science of management, which is to say, of persuading people nicely (as opposed to the nineteenth century method of telling them nastily) to do what you want, including take the sack, and a controlling style which as far as possible works through the personalized procedures of negotiation. These are the control systems of liberal political economy, the product less of successful resistance by trade unions and more of the needs of new conglomerates for whom finite capital, resources, and above all finite markets with dangerously unstable international currencies demand the delicate balancing act and mutual collaboration which world communications now make possible.

It seems a far cry from the Bank of England to A level, or from the world economy to a 16-year-old's ambition to be a hairdresser. But there is choice as well as the determination of circumstance in these processes; the school wants to see its pupils in employment, so it recommends jobs where there are jobs, in the service industry: there is less riveting for Rosie the riveter to do now than there would have been on the Tyne or Wear in 1948. It is a platitude to say that investment patterns determine available employment: which A levels would *you* pick in Port Talbot?

More invisibly, however, the new forms of the instrumental curriculum, shaping the ideal manager, sales representative, software operator, word processor attendant, fast-food servant, or amiable unemployable, run up against the powerful and entrenched forms of the academic curriculum. And this is no bad thing. As we have noted, the curriculum carries a picture both of what to do for a living and how to live a good life. Being instrumental about things should not mean that people will offer themselves as instruments for anything whatever, so long as they're paid. Inasmuch as curricular forms and the requirements of manpower are at odds, then at least education has its small autonomy and is not merely a processing house for the systems of production. What is the meaning, purchase and leverage of that resistant autonomy we shall hope to estimate. But the combination of the academic curriculum, with its many internal battles between revisionists and traditionalists, and the strong pressure from very recent subjects such as business studies or computer science, make curricular discussion sound at first like babel; it is only where we understand how efficient it is at doing what's wanted, and this in spite of universal complaint (and everyone has always complained about school), that argument over the curriculum sounds less like the tower of unnumberable tongues, and more like the Stock Exchange.

Within the strictly academic battle of the books, the immediate competition is between the old and the new. Now any such battle has its vigorously ideological squadrons in it, as well as more crudely repellent weapons like money, numbers and resources, and 'ideology' is a word much and rightly invoked in arguments about the curriculum. It has two versions, but in both versions I will claim[3] that there are three planes of ideological admonition. The first version of ideology derives not from the earliest usage in the *Encyclopédie*,[4] where the word meant straightly the history of ideas, but from the first influential use in Marx's and Engels' notebooks, written in 1847 and ultimately published as *The German Ideology*,[5] and their celebrated formula, 'The ruling ideas of any epoch are the ideas of the ruling class'. Marx and Engels propound the brutal, but convincing view that since the bourgeoisie was the historically necessary, but drastically unemancipated arm of victorious capitalism, the self-justifications of that bourgeoisie would have a comparably ambitious reach as well as an inevitably sanctimonious and inadequate grasp. That is, the bourgeoisie would devise legitimations claiming the conditions and the quality of their own fulfilment and emancipation as being the conditions of liberation for all men and women; their apparently startling success in persuading those in the proletariat whose interests were so patently *not* served by the happy triumph of the bourgeoisie was stigmatized by Marx as the victory of 'false consciousness'.

This is the Marxist doctrine of ideology; it may be labelled the fix theory of ideology.[6] In a safer, more everyday version, ideology is the loose designation for the structure of values and beliefs with which we take or dare the assorted strains of the universe. The strain theory and the fix theory are alike in that each sees ideology as the inevitably distorting lens through which individuals and classes must look at the world from their historically relative position, although Marxism has a notoriously optimistic programme about the regrinding of the Marxist lens until what it will finally permit is a vision of the world as it really is. Furthermore, the analysis of ideology preferred here nominates three levels of its operation: a first, metaphysical level, of what Collingwood calls 'absolute presuppositions', which is to say the given premises of a thought-system which you have to hold if you are to think within it at all – the God-created nature of the universe for Christians, for example, and the motions of economically driven change for Marxists. The second level connects these data and assumptions in an explanatory form with the actualities of history, such that

Marxism can represent striking workers or insurgent guerrillas as determinate actions in a class struggle born of the collision between contrary motions of the systems of production, and Christianity may present an actual, but miraculous cure or the saintly courage of a single figure as the revelation necessary in the circumstances of divine providence. The third and final level, which sustains the practical and everyday workability of an ideology is that of the precepts which join data to explanations by telling believers what they should do about it. Ideologies typically admonish their supporters about how to turn belief into action: Marxists must work for the revolution, Christians for redemption, both carry a clear picture of the need for self-sacrifice.[7] But the prominence of Marxizing inquiries into ideology is due to their need to explain the failure of Marxism itself to make more headway in the West, and the potent explanation is the power of ideology itself.

It is for this reason that education and the curriculum have drawn the close attention of theorists of ideology. These are indeed 'the ruling ideas' which have ruled successfully. If people believe them so comprehensively, they must have unusual penetration and staying power in order to overcome the weight of obviousness which surely shows that the real interests of the masses lie with taking things into their own hands. This is the basic position from which Western analysis has proceeded, and the analysts, looking for help in the Marxist tradition, found Antonio Gramsci, the Communist leader of the Fiat workers in Turin in the early 1920s, their best guide.

This book is not a Gramscian handbook.[8] Gramsci is merely the occasion for mentioning his rather catch-all, but much-quoted concept 'hegemony', by which he meant the all-pervading and saturating power of cultural control, a power whose omnipresence caused people to think of as natural and unalterable the circumstancs which made for their own subordination and oppression. Such hegemony, it is claimed, is won by the curriculum and reproduced by education generally.

The lesson for radical critics of education within education is then logically taken to be, change the curriculum, for by changing that you will be able to change what is done to popular thought, its frames of mind and its mentation. The straight way into such a change is to start by exposing the present self-interestedness, arbitrariness, hypocrisy and lies within a given discipline or subject area. There is no need to be radically unctuous in this adventure – always an infectious, but also noisome tendency in curricular criticism. *Any* field of study (or realm of meaning) will be distorted by mischance and misdeed, and will be tautologically ruled by its rulers. To criticize content is to try to alter the historical location of a subject, to free it from its boundedness in a position in which it holds students down, narrows and constricts them, makes them less able, rather than more to live up to their times and to imagine boldly and well in them. Education, like any art, is a way of learning to think well of the future: the artist, as John Berger puts it,[9] gives us reason for thinking the best possible thoughts.

This is why the battle of the books is always between the new and old, a battle of generations,[10] though there is never any saying who in either generation will pick which side. Nor (again) is there any hidden sanctimony in that remark. Bernstein observes placidly that 'in a period of heightened social change, it seems likely that continuity can only be maintained at the expense of a false yesterday or a mythical tomorrow'.[11] Discuss, as the exam papers say. It seems just as likely that both are always the expenses of continuty; the efforts of keeping faith with a sufficiently plausible yesterday or a not too dizzily apocalyptic future is what initially determines enlistment in the colours of old or new.

See how they run in a particular subject, English. It is a complicated subject, moreover, because in schools, obviously, it is the medium of instruction, hence the rallying cry, 'Every teacher is a teacher of English',[12] and it is also nominated by many employers as a qualification for large numbers of clerical occupations in terms of strictly instrumental competence – which is always held to be declining in standard ('the youngsters we get, can't write, can't spell, can't speak properly, – now in my day . . .'). At the same time, for historical reasons as well as because of the nature of the subject, which is after all the native language itself, a vanguard of teachers themselves turned English into the vehicle of progressivism, the legitimate occasion for the development of personal creativity. The latter energy derived from theories of teaching, which in England took great heart from the doctrines of Wordsworth and then of Romanticism and liberalism by way of John Stuart Mill, Matthew Arnold and T.H. Green,

about the educability of all children, about the power of what
came to be called high culture to transform and redeem those who
had known only poverty and humiliation, and about the universal
capacity to create.

At the same time, in the universities (which meant Oxford,
Cambridge and London) some of these same strong stirrings came
together to challenge the dominance of the ancient tongues Latin
and Greek in the name of a now distinctive and immensely
distinguished native literature. The classics, known at Oxford as
'*litterae humaniores*', had been long studied in two forms: the one,
by hard learning of declension, conjugation, voice and mood,
followed by grammar and etymology; the other a direct engagement with the texts, with Thucydides and Tacitus, Aristotle and
Plato, Catullus and Martial, not historically, but as though these
were living and contemporary masters with whom one debated
and from whom one learned the history, morality and aesthetics of
the day. If English was to match them, it had to have respectability
in its antiquity, formality in its study of language, and immediacy
in its moral substance.

The argument broke up in different directions. Oxford's English
course plumped for scholarship and antiquity – students had to
study the linguistic origins of English in Anglo-Saxon and
Norman-French, and the official literature stopped, until the
1960s, at 1832, a fine symbolic date for conservatives. The
Cambridge English course made Anglo-Saxon optional, and out of
the chance assortments of interests present at its early years,
prescribed as the content of its curriculum the historical, classical,
and genteel medley which made up culture in its roughly
anthropological sense (it called one group of exam papers 'life,
literature and thought'). Its architects attached to this framework a
highly selective version of the development of English literature to
which nevertheless the student was invited to make his or her
personal response. The formal results of the discipline were to be
the taste and judgement which the procedures of what was called
practical criticism, or the very close reading of the words on the
page for their tone, meaning and organization, would inculcate.
This latter was, as it turned out, the crucial innovation. For, in
Bernstein's terms, once you as a student are able to interrogate the
pacing, sequence and significance of what is taught, the authority
bases of the classroom are dissolved.

The date as well as the membership of the formation of Cambridge English was crucial. Discussions were active in 1917; Oxford's had been settled before the war. By the time the war was over, a new generation of teachers and students had arrived who were committed to discovering a method and object of study which would provide for the ideals and the determination of the best remnants of the ruling class in 1919 to make a land fit for heroes to live in. Well, most of the heroes were dead: the essentials of power and property in bloody old England were unchanged. Yet without sentimentality, perhaps it can be claimed that the forms of Cambridge English were in part provided by and for the idealistic men and women who came to university in order to discover a way of living well and on behalf of others unavailable in a moral philosophy empty of anything to believe in, and for whom no cultural authority existed in a society whose intelligent members could only despise a ruling class of such hideous incompetence and callousness as were to be seen at work in Flanders.

The immediate relevance of this compressed history is to show just how complicated the formation of an educational subject area is and with what variously ideological voices it may speak. As devised by the venerable universities betwen 1900 and 1920, English was compounded of grammar, etymology, what was then the canon of honoured literature (Shakespeare to Dickens), and a running fight between modernists and traditionalists about the worth of the new writing – T.S. Eliot, Yeats, D.H. Lawrence: an American, an Irishman and a sexually arousing coalminer's son. At this distance we can see the terms of the disputes pretty clearly, made raw and painful as they were by the terror and haemorrhage of the war. The struggle for continuity *and* for a new, decent start, the confusions of restoration and retribution, made teaching stand in much more direct relation to life than usual. It is not just dead old history that is being told, however, it is the origins of the same arguments in the present. Continuity and connectedness in the subject as in the self are the criteria of identity, and they exact a fierce loyalty.

Consider, therefore, the terms of membership in present-day English. The traditionalists take their stand in the admirable name of a necessary continuity, a 'storehouse of recorded value', on a canon of literature which, although only settled upon by the ideological upheavals of the 1920s, indeed *because* only so recently agreed, should be left to see us through the bewildering and patternless proliferations of the new technetronic culture. For them (putting it crassly), first films and now television are inadequate for academic study because they are mass produced and mass watched also; the cultivation of delicacy and wisdom, which is the life of culture, demands the deliberate pondering of what is written by the best who read it, and literary culture on this definition is the canon. The canon excludes enormous amounts of writing, certainly – of what is classified on the library shelves as philosophy, theology, most history, all working-class writing until it has been promoted into an individualist category, most American literature but not all (Henry James is admitted, but not Hemingway), crime writing, thrillers, translations, or anything which might be discomposingly political.

Put like that, the arbitrariness is plain to see; but it is my ecumenical point that any curriculum is similarly arbitrary. The traditionalists, battling in the name of continuity and a coherent social memory to value a past which tells a worthy story, pick on *The Prelude, Jane Eyre* and *Middlemarch*, because those stories provide such a past. Yet that past and its story only fit a particular historical biography, the tale of someone for whom the great surge of Romanticism gave a proper belief in the truthfulness and ardour of their deepest passions, but only as validated and judged by the strength of a mature, scrupulously self-conscious conscience, whose intelligence was bent on balancing the life-significant claims of sincerity against duty, choice against wholeness.

This is to moralize literature with an ideological vengeance, and a vengeance that falls on infidels alone. For the severities of membership allow the arbitrariness of the canon to go out of focus; in the battle of the books, the standard of the canon is defended against the tatterdemalion vandals who come on with a new, wild and hoarser cry about different, bloodier worlds and more sudden climaxes. And after my best efforts at fairminded-ness, in this short analysis of ideological preference, I shall come out cleanly on the side of the hooded hordes. For the great and unironic strength of the canon as set up in the forums of English in its first phase is exactly its historical responsiveness to the image of the brave, sensitive, freely choosing and responsible soul. But once this soul takes on the body and clothes of the respectable and petty-bourgeois English lecturer and teacher, its merely time- and self-serving imagination strikes you like a bad smell.

Even at its best, the traditionalist view has been broken open by the facts of cultural prodigality and the obliterating deluge of its electronics. The modernist English teacher, following the precepts of his great most recent forebears – of T.S. Eliot and Yeats and Lawrence among the writers of the canon, of F.R. Leavis, Denys Thompson and Donald Davie among its theorists – follows language and, in Leavis's fine phrase, 'the inevitable creativeness of ordinary everyday life' wherever they lead him. His own responses and his students then take him to some academically insalubrious places: to the innumerable fictions of that everyday life in exceedingly non-canonical literature, to more of the same in films (since, as is the way of things, a handful of different films are now edging into the very canon of the traditionalists built to keep them out), and to the whole unstoppable rout of television. This, the modernist says, is where the imaginative life of the present is really being lived, and if you try to interpret it with the forms and manners of the old canon, one of two things will happen. In one action, the old canon will break up, and you'll have to acknowledge that, wonderful novel as *Middlemarch* is, its incontestable, settled moralizing goes with a settled order and doesn't easily transplant to disorientingly different frames of feeling. In the other, those teachers whose final commitment is to the strictly pedagogic fiction of the moral Romantic and the passionate puritan withdraw from the undoubtedly awful mess which is modern culture into that smallish number of enclaves hidden in a few schools and universities where the tones, forms and manners of that fiction and its structure of feeling still hold. Those places being where they are – cells of rigorous and principled intellectuality in socially exclusive places – the University of Bristol, say, North London Collegiate School for girls, Rugby or Westminster schools for boys – then such teachers may still touch for moral good a small fragment of the power elite. But their ideological self-justificaiton no longer holds on a larger world. Their enemy the modernist, seeking to make sense of an English curriculum in inner London schools or to build a cultural studies course at a polytechnic, has to try out every new strange language to see if it will hold down the mad disorder of things: hence, structuralism, neo-Marxism, semiology, socio-linguistics, post-Freudianism, hermeneutics.

The political inflection of most of these, whether borrowed from Paris or Bologna, Yale or Chicago, is the key to this fragment of ideological analysis. For the latter pages have not been an idiotic tale told merely to English teachers; they have been an essay in the politics of knowledge. Now by politics is meant no more than is usually meant, the struggle for and control of distribution in power, privilege, rewards and resources. In England (the emphasis is deliberate: the other three countries stand at the wrong end of the axis of power), English, our example to hand, is defined by its history in universities as a way of thinking about literature with fairly clever members of a particular social class, a fairly senior fraction of the clerical and servicing bourgeoisie, many of the recruits from which become producers and distributors in the cultural industries. If your formation and your experience take you that way, you'll stress continuity and tradition and end up with vehement ideological justifications as a soldier of reaction. If you go the other way, you'll plump for identification with the common experience of unprecedented amounts of new fiction and its dramas and for membership of a wide linguistic community, and end up as spokesman for the children rather than their rector, and as their archivist rather than their guardian.

The English story and its ideological meanings are amply corroborated in the European languages most usually studied in schools, French and German. Both languages are longer lived in universities than the native tongue, and both for obvious reasons retain satisfyingly heavy emphasis on the difficulties of an inflexible correctness in grammar and vocabulary. One much-noted consequence of this was that until fairly recently – the 1960s, say – all their attention went on writing the language, and very little on speaking it, which is what people do rather more. In addition, both languages, and their poor sibling, Spanish, share with English a stern definition of the tongue as defined by its novels, plays and poems, plus a few of an elusive genre known as 'essays', largely known to be such by a lack of any substantive content (Montaigne, Chateaubriand), specially promoted biographies (a few non-theological ones), and a selection of collected letters, either those famously by poets (Keats, Rilke) or more of the substanceless, aesthetic and 'personal' kind (Gautier, Walpole). Philosophy, history, let alone art and music are excluded from as queer a looking canon as could be imagined, the more as German literature so classified is extremely thin, and German scholars have to make too much of Goethe, a very scattered genius, and preposterously more of the puny achievement in *Novelle* writing, while all the time the great giants of German philosophy from Kant and Hegel via Marx to Nietzsche and Schopenhauer go disregarded. If instead, as is surely reasonable, students of a whole culture and its language were, with German, to take in philosophy, music and a little science, and with French, to take in art with a little politics, then to read either subject at A level, let alone learning to speak rather than write it at O level, would already have made for rather more understanding of and admiration for our sisters in the Community than is to be found in the columns of rancid xenophobia which fill the press.

These are topics, I repeat, in the politics of knowledge, and in this as in any other kind of politics, they are focused by the concept of power. But power is not a merely coercive force, though the concept most certainly and centrally includes coercion.[13] Power is also whatever it is that gets things done, and metaphors for its effectuality may as well recall electricity as machine guns. Power, that is, is not merely brutish and not merely in the hands of other people. In spite of what is a neurotically self-exonerating propensity to self-pity among them as among any other of the official authority figures of the society, teachers have real power of their own, and that power is unevenly, but circumspectly distributed not only according to seniority and what is defined as responsibility, but also according to subject membership and loyalty.

This is true from the infant school chronologically upwards to higher and further education, and is intricately, but cartographically linked to the hierarchy of knowledge in the society at large. Such truths may be propositionally put, for the benefit of method in curriculum theory.

1   Power in the curriculum is hierarchically ordered in direct and systemic relation to the parallel power of comparable areas of knowledge and inquiry in the society.

1.1   This systemic ordering, however, is refracted by the interposition of universities between schools and the economy, and the university's curriculum hierarchies are reproduced by its own class fraction which mediates and resists the wider economy.

1.2 The relative power of subject-areas increases and consolidates with the age of the student.

1.3 Power in the curriculum is only over resources; no subject-area has power over the content (or existence) of another subject-area. Eliminative power is strictly political.

1.4 Political power of this sort is assigned to members of high-prestige areas.

2 Prestige in the curriculum is determined by resource allocation in the parent economy in torque with culturally situated definitions of conceptual difficulty as determined by the dominant class.

2.1 Prestige loss or gain fluctuates as the dominant class revalues or devalues the significance of longevity or innovation, but only as these are invisibly loaded by the mode of production (which is not fixed).

3 Crises of power and prestige, such as are now being undergone, are signs of important shifts in the mode of production.

Thus all disputes of power in schools or anywhere else are regulated at first and ruthlessly by the supremacy of mental ways of knowing and inquiring over manual ones. This distinction has its slipperiness, if the quickness of the hand, or anyway its importance to physical comfort, is allowed to deceive the category and is backed up by heavy theory. This is the case with medical and veterinary surgery and with dentistry, an interesting anomaly not noted for conceptual difficulty or even for demanding very marked locomotor co-ordination, but assertively on the right side of the divide.

The theoretic understanding of power in the curriculum, according to the short list of propositions, needs to work in a number of dimensions, which are best suggested by example rather than by the sort of generalizable propositions which lead quickly into jargon.[14] Broadly, therefore, we can say that those subject-areas are most powerful which command the largest amounts of timetable, staff numbers and salary allocation: in universities, science and medicine; in secondary schools, science and English; in primary schools, numeracy and literacy. In the competition for time, space and money, these areas win easily, with science, leaning heavily on its alleged material necessities – laboratories, safety conditions, ostensive methods of teaching with very low teacher-pupil ratios, expensive apparatus and so forth – assuming and getting the share due to a lion with a big mouth and a roar to go with it.

But power is built up across a wider geography than is measured by numbers, money, time and space within a school. The case of reading in primary schools illustrates this. The model for understanding its rise to power is much more like that expounded for classic imperialism[15] than by the everyday story of a country subject. First the explorers, then the missionaries, then the settlers, then the soldiers. Then, when everything on the ground is safe, along come the agents of not-very-great-risk capital. So the researchers, eager for colonizing all early educational life after the vast achievements of Piaget, opened up the ground of reading – how on earth children do wring meaning out of black runes on white paper? With a few areas staked out – look and say, colour coding, early teaching alphabet, phonic method – the zealot missionaries came into schools, hot-eyed and fervent, to convert the new world to the new method, and the settlers, hoping for a new life with new degrees making possible their bright new standing, and underwritten by a special trading station at the university, brought their agronomy with them and broke up the old customs for the promised increases in productivity. Lastly, the colonial police patrolled the classrooms making sure that no new laws were broken, no old primitive ways revived by recalcitrant natives (whether parents or teachers). And so the first of the three 'Rs' was replaced by a fully administered literacy, bureaucratized by the publishing industry in a dozen well-capitalized schemes.

Telling the history this way throws into relief once more the politics of knowledge. It also brings out its anthropology. Very little of what is asserted to justify power and prestige or even method in the curriculum is justifiable. Teaching reading has certainly altered the relations of production, but it can't be said convincingly to be a better way to teach. The great prestige of research and even of phoney expertise conceal the old human hugger-mugger of hand-to-mouth practice, folklore and super-stition, honest effort and individual intelligence.

Such obfuscation works everywhere. Sometimes it works shamelessly, as when the University Grants Commission in Britain, enjoined by the Minister in 1981 to cut the budget and itself dominated (of course) by Oxbridge scientists, indefensibly privileged pure science at the expense of everything else, especially applied or technological science (mental over manual again). Usually it works so much in the grain of everyday life at school that we hardly notice. Thus when the powerful subjects in secondary school move in on sixth-form resources, which, naturally, are higher per head than the resources made available to the children who don't understand and leave early and uncomprehending, they need to hold their numbers as high as they can compatible with good exam results, while for the sake of prestige they make themselve sound difficult.

An intricate and long-lived ceremony of difficulty-incantation has gathered over the year in reinforcement and signification of these last meanings of power and prestige. It is discoverable at work on any parents' evening: 'No, I don't think your child can quite manage O-level biology, how about CSE?' 'It's not been a good year, they all did badly in the mocks', 'He's not really a bookish boy, but very good with his hands', 'She's really artistic so you can't expect her to be good at maths as well', 'No, she's got a real feel for languages, so why not drop general science?' Without in the least wishing to deny the reality in childen of great gifts suddenly declaring themselves, of the varieties of intelligence, of the facts of difference between being a good painter and being good with animals, of, indeed, being a boy as opposed to a girl, it is by this folklore and these quite unexamined premises that power and prestige in the curriculum subtend the arc of privilege and reward in the society.

There is a well-known curricular verb which all teachers instinctively conjugate at parents' evenings. It goes like this:

I am clever and bourgeois: I shall do nuclear physics or Russian at Cambridge.
I am clever and working class: I shall do electronics and Telecom will pay for me at polytechnic.
You are middling middle class: you shall do geography and estate agency by correspondence.
You are middling and poor: you shall do home economics and a catering course at the tech.

*She is dim, and very well off: she shall go to finishing school
and train to be a receptionist at the Dorchester.*
He is dim, black and effortful: he shall do car maintenance.

These are the conjugations which get as far as the examination
hall. In a worthy effort to fill time without killing it, and to
acknowledge the entire lack of fit between the official forms of
educated life and the customary forms which are their out-of-
school experience, a wholly different mode of work and its
relations is being gradually devised for those who are designated
unexaminable. The power commanded by those busy with this
design is, as we shall see, considerable, but their prestige is low.
These are courses the occasion for which arises dramatically in
circumstances of economic crisis, but political fluidity. They don't
fit the dispositions of usual curricular allocation, and only swim
up from deep curricular waters when politics can no longer be
neglected, but must be transposed to the ideological realm.

They do pose, of course, critical questions about what education
is for; what the worth of a human life in our society is. Each
subject or area, as I have argued, has an answer to that question
couched in its own terms, and the answers change with history.
The history which is life in earnest corrodes the old hierarchies,
and the answers to the question 'what's it all for?' have to change,
or – as happened to Latin and Greek – the subject gets stranded
and left behind. Subject-areas rise and fall not so much according
to their merits, but according to their creative capacity in
accommodating the troublousness of the times within the frames
of their ideology. If they tell too sharp a truth, they are rebuked; if
they tell a good tale, complicated, but ending happily, about how
to recover the good old days for science, for man, or for God, then
that's just fine.

6

The Social Mobility of a Subject

The hierarchy of factors that exacts change from areas of the curriculum is not easily diagrammatized. Certain kinds of curriculum handbook are much given at this point to a set of interlocking circles like the Olympic flag, which are as conceptually vacuous as it is possible to be, particularly when they are marked solemnly 'knowledge' 'culture' and so forth, and are much set about with dotted margins outside which monstrous powers called 'change' or 'society' prowl in black letters with many arrows darting at the circles, but themselves hemmed in by nothing but the acute limitations of two dimensions.

This book is of a sufficiently Marxisant persuasion to admit that it loads one factor in the hierarchy much heavier than the others, and that factor is the uneasy conceptual duo, the systems-and-relations-of-production. These, whatever they are, hugely inflect the 'classification and framing', the power and prestige, the totality of relations in the curriculum. But the excursion in the last chapter into the theory of ideology should illuminate just how tricky a process it is to account for changes in the curriculum. The decline of Latin and Greek by 1919 was no doubt overdetermined by the expansion of state education, by the rise of a new segment of the bourgeoisie to academic power professing the ideological strengths of a different class culture, by the triumphant advent of a monopoly capitalism and its conglomerates – Wills tobacco, Brunner-Mond, Firth-Vickers, Handley Page – insisting on a new technical elite from their local universities, by the deadly slow passing of the Empire, by the proper demands of the working class for a decent and democratic education.

The whole tale can be put together from these prefabricated causes, arranged in a plausible order, and made to fit the unutterably banal generalities of curriculum innovation theory. But, however determined, they were unpredictable in that form. It is only as a history that we can watch the comprehensible decline of the classics. And there too we might pause and wonder about the presence in that immediate past still immediately with us of a powerful amnesia which is not so much a consequence as a parallel force with that well-known actor on the historical stage already introduced in Chapter 1, modernization. Latin and Greek have been more or less scrapped, because they stood on the further edge of the tradition crevasse which opened up in 1918. They went down slowly: Latin was still a compulsory O level for admission to Cambridge in 1955; but they went because they had no sufficient answer to any of the historical factors listed with sloganeering bravado in the last paragraph. Their humanizing claims had been wrested from them by English literature, their training of the mind according to the precepts of the first philosophers superseded by the new mathematical logics of Russell, Wittgenstein and Carnap. The trouble now is of course that their disappearance from state schools and their tiny numbers of students in higher education signify a major act of forgetting on the part of the society. Amnesia is a horrible and frightening condition. A European society which knew no Latin and Greek would be amnesiac, the more so at a time when the recovery of the past has so vastly opened up the world over, and understanding how we got to be the way we are (the only adequate position from which to see what to do next) has been so changed exactly by way of the astonishing discoveries of classical archaeologists, biblical and textual scholars, and ancient historians working on the Levant during the past generation.

The response to the threat of amnesia is to start the equivalent of the World Wildlife Fund, whereby a special subject threatened with extinction is caught and bred entirely in the library-equivalent of a zoo. A new academic profession comes into being: curator of the knowledge in danger of being wiped out of the memory. It recruits from very high-prestige training grounds in tiny numbers. But of course its practices, intensely specialized and hermetic like so much learning, are removed from the main lifestream of the society.

This is not a threnody on broken ways of life. It is a description of how the resources of meaning drain away. Now the still legally empowered meaning-maker of the official curriculum is religion, and it is instructive to plot its history, when faced by the great wilderness of incredulity and incredibility which defaces the century. Religious education itself possesses notable legal power, as every head teacher knows. The celebrated 1944 Education Act requires the school to conduct some form of religious worship and religious instructions, the only subject-area so singled out. In 1944, with victory in the war seeming to be so very much to God's and British credit, and just appeals to the rightfulness of the cause satisfactorily combining religious propriety and patriotism, such a clause looked vastly more justifiable than it does now, forty secularized and multiracial years on. In those days, the classification of what was revealingly called divinity or scripture was watertight and Christian: the Bible was the text at all ages, and the New Testament at least was taught as a true narrative, whose precepts were God-sent and to be followed. Pupils were tested for the straightforward recall of their knowledge of the Bible, and the advance of a final secularization, which Engels had so confidently predicted exactly a century before,[1] was still so diffuse and slow that whatever the degree of sullen or amiable incomprehension and unbelief on the part of the pupils and their parents, Bible knowledge was for the devout strain in the official culture a necessary part of becoming a Christian, which naturally children should be taught, because it was true and because they should learn the road to salvation. For the liberal–agnostic strain, the strength of whose determination to do nothing explains why Engels's expectations was disappointed, Bible knowledge was a necessary part of a worthwhile education, an aspect of the inheritance of English literature into which a student must enter to be counted as educated at all. Either way, the subject remained comfortably within the ample space of the Authorized Version, and was taught as something pretty well immutable (as well it might be).

But it is now forty years since these days were made secure, insular and insulated, exactly because the adversary, the devil, was walking abroad all over Europe. Secularization is still not at all finished, and certainly no Secretary of State would have the nerve to declare religious instruction redundant. Indeed, he would hardly be right: the terrific revival of radical Islam, the recent and colossal surge in recruits to British Catholicism and, on a smaller scale, to evangelism in the Church of England, to say nothing of sectarian successes of a dottier kind from Mormonism to the Moonies all give the lie to optimism on the part of the atheists, but leave the question of what to teach of religion piercing and unanswerable.

To answer at all, the subject had to break its institutional allegiance to the Church of England. The church itself, however, was trying to accommodate the same splitting social strains as the subject in schools, and living within the deep irreconcilables of commitment to the revealed truth of God inside a society possessing no language except Christianity to express its Christian unbelief, but retaining its continuing devotion to some kind of sanctity in the central questions and ceremonies of life, it had to provide a serious answer to the question, 'what is a human life worth?' at the occasions of birth and death. Both church and curriculum had to encompass this question in such a way as to defuse three very touchy and explosive charges. The first was the danger of the ultimate detonation of the force of atheism, which would displace both institutions to a marginal terrain visited only by tourists and educational custodians on Sundays. The second was the enormously disruptive force of other religions flowing into the country as immigrants: from Italian Catholics via the Greek Orthodox members of the Mediterranean countries and on to the many and factious adherents of Islam and their old enemies in Hinduism, concluding in the Far West with the boisterous ostentation of new Rastafarianism, all watched sadly and tranquilly by long-standing exiles in the churches of Judaism and Buddhism. The facts of conflicting belief and the keen danger of racial warfare demanded of the home church, and its teaching, major concessions about tolerance, the relative nature of the revelation and of truth itself, and a thoroughly tolerant liberalism which really made that much derided doctrine live up to its own profession. The third force, another bastard child on one side of the hungry generations just listed, was the new theology within the church itself. The names of Tillich, Bonhoeffer and their unchurched Christianity were given popular rating by Bishop John Robinson in 1964.[2] Their device for restoring Christianity to everyday life was to empty it of historical and intellectual content, and ask the Christian to bear witness to his or her Christianity by the fullness and holiness of being and bearing, since, as Robinson briskly vulgarized it, we may 'Let God be the name for whatever is of deepest significance in Life'. The trouble with this remedy for doctrinal conflict and social irrelevance is that it can only work in a practical way in circumstances of high historical drama. As MacIntyre ironically notes,[3] Bonhoeffer could bear, as he heroically did, Christian witness in a Nazi prison; it is less clear how to do the same thing as a rich stockbroker in Virginia Water.[4]

To define Christianity as a state of being removes the difficulties with truth and dogma, and also answers the question of how to be a Christian during the week. You behave much the same as everyone else, but more seriously and in a quieter voice, in order to indicate humility. But the repudiation of dogma leaves belief with no religious specificity; the gap is then filled by morality. This had to be the answer for religious education. Its study of and recommendations about action become ordinarily moral, and because conscious of the teachings of liberal morality, these were largely grounded in strictly interpersonal dealings and attempts to devise techniques for what are emetically known as life-skills, in order to ensure the sufficiently frictionless dealings of class with class, and both with other races. In a dozen worthy ways, religious education bereft of a curriculum turns to the encouragement of understanding and sympathy in face-to-face encounters. Heaven knows, of course, these are important qualities left shrivelled and deformed by the way the world goes, but the cognitive vacancy of the teaching materials, together with the hopelessness of designating religious study with no account given or looked for of truth, God, belief or mortality, means that whatever 'life-skills' and 'educating for personal relationships' may do, they accelerate the loss of belief and help to expunge religion, as well as all forms of spirtuality.

Writing this way does not constitute a cry for the restoration of Bible-bashing and the proclamation of the one way to salvation. I am tracing, as the chapter heading advertises, the social mobilities of the curriculum. Religious education, following its church, is not so much mobile as vaporized. What can or should be done about it[5] is in issue at the heart of the culture.

On a sanguine view, we shall eventually face the wounds and severances of our experience, and name for what it is our failure to resolve the deep and killing political and moral contradictions in what we teach and how we live – all of which is hardly imminent. Such an act of self-definition on the part of society might enable the slow construction of a secular and socialist ethic which left due space for the constituent religions of its polity, and offered a language for the recognition of these without deranging the civil and civic order. Poland is the obvious example of a social order in which religion is used politically by the people to deny official politics. Iran is the contrast, in which religion, being coterminous with politics, obliterates the necessary polity of tolerance. Both are repellent. It is only in a few corners of developing countries and their specially desperate straits that an admirable juxtaposition of religious and political education seems to have emerged. And they will hardly serve as examples to Britain, or Europe and the anglophone countries.

On the other hand we can anticipate what we are likely to get. And that is the continued evaporation of religious content into therapeutic forms. For the pretty certain evasiveness of the fair-to-middling rich industrial societies before their own lies, hypocrisies and cruelties will lead them to patch up social agreements in terms borrowed from an imaginary and pacific past, which has always had many historical stations, but is often about halfway to the horizon – nowadays about 1959. These agreements made very exclusively by our social managers will then be used as ideal references for everybody, and the great engines of manipulation will continue to organize the world not for an openly held moral and political debate, but for its manipulable assent.

It is in this large context that the social mobility of the curriculum needs to be understood. Religious education is only one, though obviously crucial, of the forms of knowledge (or, again, realms of meaning) that have abandoned content, because the old content would no longer do, and filled the hole up with mere skills and techniques. In this, they blend with the huge tendency of capitalist society to devise ways of organizing agreement to its prior and determinate ends, and to find space for all its members within which they may make themselves sufficiently happy not to challenge those ends, but to leave the system to go on producing whatever it pleases, including its own destruction.

This tendency, naturally and irresistibly, has deeply invaded education from two directions, and teachers have flocked to study the new subjects created by society for its self-manipulation. It is important here to bring out the full, conscious ingenuousness of my critical analysis. For I will be reminded that the business of counselling and the necessity of studying and improving administration have arisen because ours is a society which, having recently progressed from barbarism, has to find ways of bringing often obdurate and always bloodyminded delinquents within the adjustments of society.[6] Furthermore, it is merely sensible to acknowledge not only that our society is bureaucratized, but that this process has brought great benefits in efficiency, social justice, the elimination of want, illness and public danger, and that not to study it for its greater improvement is irresponsible.

Now both reminders are true. And it is further true that our encounters with the public bureaucracies of health, welfare, production, travel, communication and education constitute our public lives: our public self is defined in relation to these institutions, so to turn and accuse the practices of counselling and of administration as being the complementarily private and public mechanisms of the manipulation of consent to incontestable ends is to sound naively ill-at-ease (or Luddite) in what are infallibly classed as the realities of the modern world. Subsequently, you meet the charge of Utopian (another familiar dismissive), if you suggest the possibility of a profoundly different, free association of men and women in forms of production immune to the techniques of manipulation and the management of assent.

Management indeed turns out to mean persuading others to agree with a more or less good grace on ends which are systemic and unavailable to question. Technique and skills are key words in these trainings, never judgement or reason, nor admiration nor disgust. Indeed the strange ring of this latter coinage takes the measure of its exclusion from the vocabulary of social (and therefore moral and political) arrangements. Such concepts denote, at least in their earlier sense, a moral meaning whose reference could be settled by appeal to an impersonal rationality independent of personal preference.[7] Quite rapidly, the complex but consistent advance of the doctrines of the unfettered non-social self (radical personalization, the freeing of the self from all structures), the detachment of the true person from the occupation of social roles, and the making almost synonymous of the expression of personal feelings with the structure of morality – the moral theory known as emotivism – all served to bring about a social order whose principles of cohesion are no longer open to critical reflection and dissent, but are consequently irredeemable, though constantly changing.

For the free self, possessing as it does no theory of moral value beyond its fulfilment of its own feelings, has no teleology, or scheme of admirable human purposes. Radically individualized as it seeks to be, it possesses neither politics nor civics, nor of course the politeness and civility which derive from the same urban root, but are now reduced to the trivial details of a class-assessed niceness. Deprived of a social theory, the self takes its ends as given by the power of superordinate systems: in the case of Britain in 1985, a failing, but still fleet, portly, arrogant and unchallengeable capitalism. Management becomes the refinement of techniques for ensuring complicity in its systemic ends (think of the well-named arbitration and conciliation services devised for settling industrial disputes). Counselling, a process in education reserved for those who in one way or another have been chewed up and spat out by the system, becomes the administration of similar techniques which console or in other wise (at times pharmacological) sedate the victim over his or her anti-socially lived disappointment. Emotional satisfaction, however, is now too high on the shopping list of all good consumers to be laughed off it, and counselling for an adequate dose of such satisfaction is now the pastoral half of systems maintenance, and a new and stongly expanding section of the curriculum. After all, these are the only ways to sort out a world in which morality and politics are subjective and immune to reason. It is your business, as both manager and counsellor, to persuade those who disagree to see reason, but reason then turns out to mean the reasonableness of giving way to superior power.

At this point, the honest counsellor or the pastoral head of the third year bursts indignantly in to say that finding something for his emotional satisfaction is not why she spends hours fishing William Brown out of the juvenile court for assault. Absolutely not. My point is at first sight the simple and familiar reassurance that awful as William is, the system and the place are at fault in being at least powerfully responsible for making him as ghastly as he is. The point at second sight, however, is that it just *is* both its meaning and function that therapeutic counselling, once it leaves the psychotic ward for the counsellor's office, is the highly personalized arm of a total control system, even whose minor and modest officers like the head of the third year have no criteria of personal worth, meaning or virtue, other than their own effectiveness and efficiency, kindly as they always are (as according to programme they *must* be). They do their duty by the criteria of bureaucratic authority, which on this showing, as MacIntyre says, is 'nothing other than successful power.[8] That duty turns out to be part of a moral-political structure of manipulation and management in the name of the compliant hedonism which subtends the inhuman goals of endless production. This extraordinary rise to prominence of manipulative techniques and what once was carelessly called 'man-management' is one measure of the controlling the curriculum is asked to do.

The same is even more thoroughly true for the complementary arm of therapeutic and management curricula, which is the study of administration itself. Now especially at the present, one supreme criterion of bureaucratic efficiency is its alleged cost-effectiveness, and the study of management is now directed towards the competitive capture of resources and devising means of putting them to efficient ends.

> Every bureaucratic organisation embodies some explicit or implicit definition of costs and benefits from which the criteria of effectiveness are derived. Bureaucratic rationality is the rationality of matching means to ends economically and efficiently.[9]

MacIntyre points out that we owe this maybe overfamiliar thought to Weber (even though it is not the giant Weber, but wizened nonentities who are the men actually studied in so-called business studies, in and out of school), but he goes on to put an asseveration borne out by both research and everyone's everyday observations, that all senior managers justify their authority by influencing the motives of subordinates, and ensuring that subordinates argue from premises which will produce agreement with their own prior conclusions. Any school head of department will jump to recognition of that process. The manager's function is 'that of controlling behaviour and suppressing conflict in such a way as to reinforce . . . bureaucratic authority'.[10] Oddly enough, this is even true in those schools that have taken in and been taken in by theories of organizations and their collective sentiments advanced by such agencies as the Tavistock Institute.[11] For the slow public exposure of inner feelings advocated by these theories are made with a view to the ultimate control and containment of difficult conflicts. They are not to do with the rational discussion of what the good life of a school or a factory should look like. They have no political morality, but a preference for this dissolution of principle.

The manager wants a curriculum therefore that teaches him how to persuade people to accede to organizational ends not accessible to criticism or alternative. The counsellor devises one in which the discussion of personal satisfaction and values is completely central, but without conceivable resolution in an inherently social and strongly characterized life, since its ends are already decided upon by the regulative machinery of the bureaucracy. The counsellor is the bureaucrat's odd-job woman. Her contingent defence is that she, at least, is in direct touch with what each of us is taught to see as a fact, and that is our position as an autonomous moral entity. She is stuck with protecting that small redoubt by advocating the techniques of adjustment and of self-expression, which are the self-congratulatory description of the manipulation of others. But her experience requires her theory to stand that close to moral facts.

Not so the senior or middle manager. He disclaims fervently and explicitly any relation to morality, at least of an imperial kind. It is his business (*sic*) and his duty to ensure the maximally effective administration (the phrases offer themselves) of the means and resources available for the bringing about of ends always chosen somewhere else: by the local authority, by the society, by the Minister. He wants to construct a curriculum that will continue the effortless separation of means from ends, define all problems as soluble technically or by the sensitive application of skills, precisely because he has effected the precipitation of morality from his own domain, which is the rational, accountable (key word), professional (ditto) and effective control of the system which he serves. It is wearisome to have to keep saying it, but the practitioners themselves insist in such assured accents that *they* are self-aware, self-critical aspirants to competence in an unavoidable action, that I have to say again of many managers beyond, but particularly of vice-chancellors and University Grants Commissioners, of principals of colleges and headteachers and deputy heads, that what they have to do is contrive manners to manipulate large numbers of people to do as they are told according to means the managers cannot handle and in the name of ends which few people would support.

To bring off this monstrous and well-named confidence trick, the managers must devise consultative techniques and skills of referral and delegation which are validated by an unrecognizable spectre, the expert, and could only be generated by knowledge which is unobtainable. The making of the subject has to rely consequently on what are reassuringly called case-studies, which might be of use if what they were was careful history or intelligent fiction, but which are used predictively or exemplarily when all they, in turn, really are, are superstition and folklore. Nothing wrong with folklore, of course, as we must nowadays all say; but they don't justify a subject, let alone the subject's power.

For the manager's authority to be justifiable in the language of present bureaucracies, he must be intending to organize his institution according to ends which he sufficiently endorses. In order to do this, he must intend to manipulate others according to his own purpose (whatever his disclaimers). To open things to the possibly different and indeed destructive purposes of others is to relinquish claims to his effectiveness. Happily, such extremities rarely arise, if only because senior managers talk mostly to middle managers, and the common interest of this whole new class[12] is in maintaining the illusion that sanctions their power. Of course, when things come out their way, they will cheer themselves around and up by saying that the stamp of their own authoritative rationality is on this happy event.

These are the practices, complacencies and self-deceptions of what are so accurately called, especially in the case of head-teachers, civil servants. (For such figures to be neither civil nor servile requires the unusual latitude now only conceded to primary schools, conventionally marked by a worthy, affectionate, but absolute mindlessness.) They are circulated in the curricula of management courses and pollute the work of ancillary departments such as drama, a subject whose chronically low status caused its members to seize on the new usage of 'role-play' and 'life-skills' in the management sciences to promote their own indispensability. The deadly banalities of the management consultant and the technocratic expert are universally deployed to justify arbitrary closure, redundancy, the dereliction of building (plant, as they say), as well as the gross, philistine and self-seeking foreshortening of a humane education. We all of us have innumerable such stories to tell. But through it all, with unshakeable self-satisfaction, the managerialists pursue their unimpeded way, entitling new courses 'the management of contraction', 'the organization of decline', or most risible of all, 'falling rolls'. The inanity of the disciplinary diction should have been enough to kill it off. Stuck with a latter-day and pretentious account of the policy sciences as being capable of bringing about rational progress and the accurate predictions which would permit this consummation, no senior manager ever has recourse to such traditional concepts as wisdom, sagacity, utter accident, sainthood, passion, tragedy, historical understanding. No curriculum advises middle managers to pick at random from Hegel, Turgenev, Dickens, Kierkegaard, Einstein, the Buddha, Aristotle, Prince Kropotkin, Hannah Arendt, Rosa Luxemburg, Chinua Achebe.

I do not for a moment deny that we must administer our society. But whatever version of desirable human relations we advance, our administration can only be grounded in the wisdom, maturity, learning, recklessness and intelligence with which we use the specific kinds of human knowledge that we have. To use intelligence upon such subject-matter is to devise a fiction the *form* of which will be congruent with the forms and materials of human life. Such forms have included proverb and saw, as well as allegories of chance, fictions and narratives of endeavour, and even case-study; but there is no substitute for the sort of reflexive thought and inquiry now called critical theory, of which the most usual and useful version is, simply, history.

There can surely be no management theory that is not flagrantly manipulative and no less flatly obligated to self-contradiction. All managers' purposes will always be thwarted and resisted not only by their subordinates' insubordination, but also by their creativity, for which routines cannot be planned. If managers then say, as they fatally do, 'Ah, but we seek only to balance routine and creativity, to enable initiative *and* predictable efficiency', their own persuasive skills intoxicate them, just as they are supposed to. What they exercise is arbitrary power, and the distinguished advance of their subject is merely a measure of the credence given to that power by their society. In its old sense, their only skill is Rhetoric.

It is at this moment that history is brought forward to stand, if not for queen of the curriculum, then as its magus. Now for anything to count as a subject not of the curriculum so much as of inquiry itself, it must possess cognitive content and substantive evidence. In the case of psychiatric therapy, these are provided by the history of the patient; in the therapeutic and bureaucratic subjects, there are no provisions made for what the philosophers of science call counterfactuals (examples that rebut the theory), nor for conditionals (what if something different happened?). The same defect terrifyingly afflicts so-called war games, even in their maddest flights to worst-case instances. At the same time, management theory in the personal or the institutional domains has no critical history, no method for asking, as we all *do* ask in the course of ordinary lives, 'how on earth did I get to be in this mess?' Devoid therefore of principle to guide reflexively understanding backwards or thinking forwards,[13] it is condemned to be the prisoner of its own endless circulation of the present; the purported agent of change becomes in thrall to its own hidden purposes, the warder of changelessness.

The same could not be true of history either in logic or in experience. Of course it is clear that plenty of people lie about history for their own grisly ends, and it is also clear that, in Quine's phrase, '*all* theories are underdetermined by the facts'.[14] Telling a history therefore leaves ample room for partiality, log- or drum-rolling, sentimental twaddle, and downright propaganda. The stern self-image of the historian as the value-free judge of the value-free facts is as big a fiction as the disinterested manager of effectiveness, as all good historians know. The point about history is that we all have one, and therefore can if we are of a mind to and *have* a mind to, check and criticize the history we are told against the one we have lived. It is in this sense that history is logically reflexive. At the same time, the story of history depends on life-in-earnest, and although within and without this story there are no facts which are not inscribed with values, there are determinable events and actions whose truth may, ideally speaking, be established. The way it is usually put is to say that the historian verifies the facts and then interprets, the interpretative frame being subsequently brought up to the true facts and screwed round them for the sake of museum presentation.[15] It seems far better to say that the historian who is in everybody as each of us battles to make sense of our lives, tells and retells, criticizes, edits and confesses a dialectically renewed narrative, whose actions and reactions (as we may say, instead of riding high horses over the facts) are given sequence and meaning and revision according to the beliefs and purposes which the interested agents saw then and see now in them.

This is to put things in an introductorily abstract way. But the present history and historiography of Britain is the best short illustration, in schools, in universities, on television, in the culture at large. The history we told ourselves for half-a-century will no longer do and was always disgusting. It told, as everyone over the age of 40 knows, of a country unequalled in its benignity and resolution, which brought gradual emancipation to its own people and the benefits of both industry and democracy to the Empire it ruled with a firm, wise hand. The tale told of a loyal and utterly adequate military quick to resist the always malevolent piracies of other countries, to defend the weak, and to keep a just and due order in what were thought of as its rightful possessions.

The author of this tall tale was Whig imperialist, and in the present openly contentious climate, he is still doing a brisk trade. But there was always a different history in circulation, much of it necessarily oral, some of it as in the working-class autobiographies I have mentioned,[16] successfully ignored in the list of set books, but still there as a very different version of the narrative, in which the oppressed classes only won any kind of freedom by their own dauntlessness. And as the imperial history went sour, a much glassier eye was turned upon it by novelists like Nadine Gordimer and Paul Scott[17] and historians like James Morris,[18] who were trying to square their own credulous but vivid idealism for what was best in British imperialism with the reality of dire snobbery, venality, cruelty and corruption in its mighty decadence. Meanwhile, the post-colonial states themselves set their new clerisy the task of writing a history and a literature from the wrong side of the imperial police, and in promoting black consciousness, Pan-Africanism and Pan-Indianism, told their own gross falsehoods and in turn violated their own minorities, until once more, in Nigeria, Bangladesh, Zimbabwe and elsewhere, the clash of personal history with official History took place not on paper, but in the streets and in the bush.

The whole action has been muted in Britain, as one would expect, but no less important.[19] Put in a synopsis, we could reasonably say that with the reality of equal treatment and common purpose embodied in the Second World War and made

visible in the triumph of the Labour Party in 1945, a sufficient
number of young historians turned to the old interpretation of
British history in order to subvert it with a new account of what
came to be called 'history from below', a new narrative in which
the people of England who had been entirely excluded from the
drums, battles, kings and constitution history of the old days
would be given back a history that returned to them an
honourable past with which to live in the present. These men,
notably Christopher Hill, Lawrence Stone, Trevor Aston, began
from the sixteenth and seventeenth centuries and what Hill
renamed, Marx in hand, the English Revolution, bringing out of
the historical dark the masses of chiliasts and millenarians,
Levellers, Diggers, Muggletonians, who gave the Commonwealth
its radical and egalitarian energy and who went under in the
landed class settlement of 1688.

This new history placed the motor of change in the class
struggle. It went on to find the many different documents that
would reconstruct the life of the subordinate class. In this its
practitioners were aided by similar developments in France, where
the post war historians of the great journal *Annales* also brought
Marx and Bloch up to the details of domestic, local, class and
political life all over France. They worked in the relative miniature
of particular towns (Beauvais, Rennes, Plodemet) and in the huge
design of Fernard Braudel's 'total history', *The Mediterranean in
the Age of Philip II*,[21] which called on the fullest definition of
dialectical materialism in order to include a historical geography,
economics, theory of uneven development, and a history of
relations of production in hamlet, farm and family.

Braudel may be said to have recast his academic subject. But at
the same time, the labours of intensely local historians like W.G.
Hoskins[21] brought to light the forgotten lives of obliterated
villages and read back the making of a people from the living
details of its landscape. He was joined in an adjacent field by Peter
Laslett,[21] who worked to reconstruct the daily life of ordinary
seventeenth century families, rich, poor and middling, in terms of
what they ate, how they brought up their children, how they
married and with what settlements, how they died. There is no
need to go further into the making of an extraordinarily rich and
careful historiography to vindicate the claims that the work put
history back into ordinary life, but within a large narrative,

explaining so far as it could the disappearance of places, the deaths by starvation, the conversion of souls, in terms of a far larger political economy.

Perhaps the clinching works in this great rewriting took as subject the second epochal upheaval of actual British history since medievalism, the advent of industry, well called the industrial revolution. Working, like the historians of the seventeenth century, from local records, parish registers, magistrates' reports, broadsheets and newspapers, police reports and illegal minutes, E.P. Thompson and Eric Hobsbawm[23] brought back to life in the present the agitators, demonstrators, footpads, highwaymen, paupers and rick-burners who made a culture of class resistance out of those crucial years. It is not too invidious to speak of E.P. Thompson's masterpiece, *The Making of the English Working Class*, as being like a great romantic-Marxist novel of history, in which the years from the naval mutinies of 1794 to the Reform Act of 1832 are populated by a series of working-class heroes, many of them anonymous, who not only won bloody ground from the class enemy, Old Corruption, but brought their own people to a consciousness of their huge strength and resolution. Thompson and Hobsbarm, in turn, have been followed by historians whose records of resistance and creativity come up to the present by collecting orally the reminiscence of the originals, and restoring judicious memory to its rightful place in the conversation of culture.[24]

I write, it is plainly audible, an encomium. But this history gave a whole education system not only the tools of discovery (and the discovery of history is, to say it again, self-discovery), but the crossing of biography with the larger, more destructive and creative forces which can only be seen through the lens of theory. Primary schoolchildren working on the parish register and counting and dating the gravestones, secondary schoolchildren asking their grandparents about the Blitz, undergraduates busy with *Hansard*, *The Times* and *Reynolds News* are alike occupied in reclaiming a past which is capable of being made their own and yet with every re-presentation (the tense is important) is directly open to critical revision and the consequent learning of dialectical knowledge: that is, knowledge which only signifies as such in virtue of its difference from what it is contrasted with.

History is offered as the object-lesson of how knowledge and learning work upon each other to produce an education worth the name. My potted history of History is not sentimental, it is a song of praise. More than that, it indicates a praxis capable of realization at every level of education, and lifts the word education out of its deadlier resonances onto the plane of edification and of human flourising.

7

Class and Culture

Liberation and control, management and resistance, these are the inevitable plays of forces within the mobility of our industrial and class-defined societies. The story of the stories is bloody in all senses, as partisans of different versions try to gain sway for their side; revolution and counter-revolution are merely the names historians themselves have given to the men and the moments at which the machine gun became a more telling way of telling the tale of the society in question. Nor is this a melodramatic way of drawing attention to what has been persuasively seen as a class-struggle in the classrooms. Only one thing is more certain – to say it again – than that there will be no social revolution in Britain, or the United States, or any other country normally and complacently[1] listed as one of the Western democracies, and that is that if there were, the Right would win. In Britain, it would be highly unlikely to be typified by mass rallies or parades of tanks, but far more probably by what E.P. Thompson has called[2] 'steady, vegetable pressure' by a state power grown to an exceptional authoritarianism in a hothouse of economic forcing, and – as Fascism must be – amply supported by a popular mood.

This being so, the class-struggle of the classrooms is not at all a clash of historical titans, nor even recognized as such by many of its protagonists. Those who do, as I shall suggest, give its contradictory, tussling shapelessness a simplicity and starkness of silhouette which has its pictorial attractiveness, but which quite fails to fit the much messier facts of life themselves merely outlined in chapter 1. And yet class is the grammar whose rules enforce the conjugation of our curricular verb according to which children are sent to study pure maths, or business studies, or commerce (typing and shorthand).

So we can repeat the platitudinous premise of social theory since the great contrapuntal duo of Marx and Mill first set themselves to write their contrary economies in the middle of the nineteenth century, that class is 'the dominant cultural category'[3] of our societies, and our societies may be neither understood nor governed without it. But what does it mean to say so? If we go no further than a round up of staffroom folklore about class, we are likely to be able to group what people fairly crudely say into the following fairly crude sectors of that left-to-right continuum which is drawn with such facility to fix in a single axis all the political positions of an antique polity.

First, there are those (conservative, let us say, with a small c) for whom the model of their society is as a sufficiently steady, occasionally and frighteningly tottering building with spacious and ill-kept accommodation in the basement and on the ground floor, where poor and black and working class live, and a limited succession of floors above that, in each of which the available space is progressively more comfortable and rich in its appointments as it is less crowded in its population, until we reach the grand rooms at the top, furnished with great desks, opened into by immense, discreetly closing mahogany doors and occupied by a very few, dignified men in pin-stripe blue suits. Within this house is a single, hand-driven lift, to which access is only granted to those universally and unenviously acknowledged to be meritorious enough. Such people may subsequently and by their own energies alone cause the lift to rise to the spacious summit whose long, penthouse windows look out upon the kingdoms of the world and the glory of them. This is the house of meritocratic Jack, whose fiction,[4] not without its truth, is that worth in society is that of personal attributes, which should be rewarded according to their inherent value as well as their value to society, and that social structures should be allowed to evolve according to these immanent energies. Let us name this old headteachers' and principals' home from home, the meritocratic-conservative hotel.

Second, there are those whose metaphors for society are synonymous with their metaphors for class. These are the 'radical personalizers', whom we met in Chapter 4, and without too remorselessly insisting that they pay for irony at their own expense, we may call them liberal individualists, or Nietzsche's children.[5] They too tell a fiction which it must be the business of liberal democracies to keep credible and therefore in enough cases true, and according to which class is a dead weight of chains, fetters, balls and gyves, whose archaic historical symbolism makes a prisoner of the individual beneath them. It is, then, the self-creative purpose of that individual so to remake his or her consciousness that the dead past's dead weight is thrown off in an act of will determined by the energy of the subjectivity, so that what remains and is there to grow into fulfilment is unmarked by its class inheritance, freely and purely itself. Such adjurations may at times be incongruously heard from certain schools of feminism who declare allegiance to Marxism, but whose real emphasis is on an existential act of self-determination, brought on by seminars and rituals of transfiguration. Given Marxism's view of itself as the one true science of humanity in the modern world, there can be little room or relevance for such narrowly subjective moments. But the best programmes for re-education which, in this example, address themselves to women's consciousness[6] are far more conventionally of that wide constituency in the society which invokes as master-meaning in the value-system the journey to self-discovery and the achieving of self-fulfilment. Nobody is any the worse for using Marxism as a name to advance the claims of liberal and Romantic individualism, but it is as well to be clear that this is what is happening. A large number of meaning-minders in the cultural industries who offer a radical and often valid critique of class in society have no theory of class beyond its actuality as imprisoning, and personal redemption as always being within the capability of the individual, if only he makes sufficiently strenuous efforts at self-education to merit it.

The third common-sensible account of class has taken much more solid account of Marx-derived theories of class, and is much more inclined to offer an image of class not in terms of the shaky building which houses all of society, nor as a heavy encumbrance bolted onto individuals by their natural enemy, Society, but rather as the dynamic source of historical energy which powers *all* the actions of social agency and is therefore the source of the unintended and uncontrollable motions of structuration which are history in action and life in earnest. This distinctly abstract way of putting it implies no particular endorsement of this third assortment of images for an everyday theory of class. But as the terms 'dynamic', 'energy' and 'power' indicate, they do have some account of the force of destiny, some way of acknowledging that individuals live their society right through themselves, their lives and bodies; they do not merely experience it as oppression (although of course it may be that alone), nor as residence, but as conflict, friction, the ceaseless chafing of an engineering in which they are part, which will no doubt wear them out and break them up, but without which nothing at all would move and they would be inert fragments in a stopped story.

Perhaps the mechanical metaphor tells us something about its provenance. Marx himself wrote[7] of the relations between economic base and ideological superstructure as though the former (the systems of production and their intercalation of capital with labour) were the vast machines in some underground powerhouse which drove all the little mechanical figures on top through the motions of civil society: the law, the military, art and science, education, religion, domesticity. Marx himself, like all of us, took his most compelling metaphors from the dominant public practices of the time, in his case, capitalist technology; indeed, it is a datum of his own analysis that he was bound to do so. Inasmuch as more or less Marxisant criticisms of education have been the source of some of the most vigorous and progressive ideas in the field for the past twenty-five years, then it is worth illustrating this variety in two brief instances which bear particularly on the analysis of the curriculum: the Althusserians and, less precisely, though a bit offensively, the New Left Hegelians.

Louis Althusser, born in 1920 and now sadly confined to a mental home because of his apparently murderous bouts of depression, stands best to exemplify his own influence. That influence may be readily traced in a clutch of recent primers.[8] But Althusser addressed himself directly to theorizing the leadenly anaesthetic properties of a French education which he sees as the state's own processing apparatus functioning always on behalf of the elite bourgeoisie (the social-analytic vocabulary of English cannot do without the French conceptualizations) in order to ideologize and inculcate a mute, quiescent acceptance of the way of a world ruled by its present rulers. We have already glanced at the theory of ideology, and in a now widely invoked formula, Althusser wrote[9] of 'ideological state apparatuses', largely encompassing the whole educational system, which functioned as printing machines whose inscription of dominant ideologies upon helpless individuals left them incapable of voluntary agency. At the same time it reduced them to bearers of ideological standards, emptied historical momentum of their will and their very presence, and made of history 'a process without subjects', in which juggernaut structures clashed at night out of their own formative and dialectical drive.

The theory is subtler than this rather crass synopsis makes it sound. It enables a theory of social-personal formation which gives proper place to the notion cheerfully propounded by this book, that individual identity assembles itself out of the inevitably ideological narratives which cultural structures spontaneously produce as the expression always of human interests and their interested parties.[10] But putting things thus certainly domesticates the harsher edges of Althusser's distinctly ruthless view of human inaction. He was, we should recall, writing from a Paris in which a cadre of severe and ascetic *maîtres à penser* [11] (and he the least of them) set themselves in about 1960 or so to repudiate the doctrines of classical humanism, deny the central images of Man as the agent of progress which the human sciences of enlightenment would help to bring about, and dissolve what his colleague in the enterprise, Jacques Derrida, later called 'the metaphysics of presence',[12] which the grim old bourgeoisie keeps in trim to disguise its entirely partial privileges.

In spite, however, of these seemingly remote and academic lucubrations, the Althusserian model of class in our terse review of class and the curriculum has its short significance. For he insisted, in the company of others, that education was a process which only seemingly could be said to lead to individual enhancement and self-awareness, but which in the harder way of social things really taught pupils to stay quiet, do as they're told, and more largely, to accept with docility the world they step into as adults. Althusser was then faced with the entertaining indignation of very large numbers of his teacher-disciples, who furiously denied that they were no more than carriers of ideological radiation to dissolve any resistant marrow in the pupils' bones. Under this attack, he devised the useful, though very approximate notion of 'relative autonomy', subsequently and rather more tightly theorized, as we have seen, by Basil Bernstein.[13] This left teachers some space for political and intellectual manoeuvre, and uncoupled the flatly one-to-one connection between economic base and ideological (that is, educational) superstructure which Engels wrote into official doctrine after Marx's death. Such a connection is the surely far too simple-minded foundation of even such a powerful book as *Schooling in Capitalist America*,[14] the main assertion of which is that schooling is no less and no more than the manpower-training-and-providing machinery of capitalist society.

Relative autonomy is the slogan, rather than the concept, which releases teachers from the rigid determinism of this description, and allows them a degree or two of critical freedom.

It is never a view to be paltered with, even though, as Marx himself observed, to become aware of the limits on your imagination is to move them, and therefore to understand that too much of your teaching day is taken up with holding pupils to the bureaucratized lines of arbitrary work is to become capable of not doing so, and opposing the imperative that you should.

This is the shadowy realm in which, as I have quoted Anthony Giddens as saying, structure produces agency which reproduces, in a changed form, structure. In a more homely idiom, we can only do what we do according to the rules and conventions of the place; but when we do so, we may change them as we go. As the observations on selves and identity in chapter 4 insist, no one can make themselves an identity *outside* social structures, but equally it is extraordinarily difficult to distinguish spirit and culture, an essential life from what life makes of it. Wherever the knife falls between shadow and act, it never quite cuts at just the point where structure and agent, or society and the spirit, truly meet. Psychologist, linguist, sociologist, political scientist and novelist are all trying to throw their intellectual net over those moments and make them universals.

This chapter-long inquiry into the reality and elusiveness of class can hardly do more than point out the difficulty as a central conundrum in the human sciences, although it is of course no accident that this huge question arises so bluntly and disobligingly in connection with the official knowledge-system of society. The magnitude and density of the issues released by the question of how structure turns into action, or in a more staffroom diction, how class organizes both the knower and the known, are staunchly faced in a well-known book which may be listed as a product of Althusserian inquiry without its ever falling into the more plonking versions of mechanistic explanation. Paul Willis's *Learning to Labour*[15] takes the most recalcitrant boys of the school-leaving year ('the lads') and alternates vivid ethnography with structural explanation, whose import is that such boys, cheerful, truculent, anarchic and resigned as they are, learn thoroughly the superordinate lesson of the curriculum as being that it is work itself which defines their week, their year, their life, that further it is pointlessly allocated in fixed and necessarily boring quantities by superiors from whom the only self-authenticating escape is to dodge or skimp what is given to do, and replace it with directly remunerative and subversively illicit alternative production. Thus and thus the lads learn to labour and not to labour, to endure dead routine and to keep as much of the profits as may be feasible without trouble from authority.

These are the homely and economic class lessons of old England. But Willis's book intends no simple minded victory for Althusser's grim theorists.[16] For as every teacher knows, as that first-rate film *Gregory's Girl* so touchingly brought out, he and she piously work and think with him and her in the same work-endorsing, work-dodging rhythm. The teacher in charge of the metalwork rooms and the antique Morris Minor engine does repairs for his friends and neighbours with payments in kind or out of kindness, while he allows the lads themselves to mend unlicensed motorbikes on the quiet and off the syllabus. The third-year head cooks the books and the law in allowing her tiny bunch of incipiently delinquent girls to evade the dance and movement lesson which they hate and are very bad at, in order to practise the hairdresser's and beautician's art in the toilets as the only job they have a hope of getting, as the only pleasure they have in awful homes and dreary schools, and as a reasonable way of keeping them quiet anyway. It will not do at all to come down with a radically sanctimonious thump upon such versions of pastoral care as covert forms of 'social control'.[17] These practices are not forms of control, they are forms of *life*.

It is, of course, the rigidly fixed nature of the whole scheme which makes its critics so impatient, and this fixity characterizes even the subtler formulations of new Marxism. Such theory has become a badge of dissent worn by those who wish, admirably enough, to delay, qualify and deflect the undoubted inclination of schooling in capitalist modernity to plan production of smiling, polite, obliging, compliant little bearers of a changeless social order situated in the lotus-land of about 1960. But few of them take seriously the Arctic immobility of their pet spokesmen. Thus

Nicos Poulantzas, defining the location of class as found in the struggle itself, a definition given by Marxist epistemology, goes on with necessary generality to say:

> Social relations consist of class practices, in which social classes are placed *in oppositions*: social classes can be conceived only as class practices, these practices existing in oppositions *which, in their unity, constitute the field of the class struggle.*[18]

'Practices' become synonymous with relations of production and the situation of struggle in the realm of everyday life, because such life in class society simply *is* a matter of class-struggle. So whatever you think you are doing – resigning, giving up, getting tired, or merely dying with a little patience – the significance of structure is such that intentional action is impossible, and your own sign is that of struggle. It follows, for this dogmatism, that 'social classes coincide with class practices, i.e. the class-struggle, and are only defined in their mutual opposion'[19] . . . and 'in this sense, if class is indeed a concept, it does not designate a reality which can be placed in the structures; it designates an effect of an ensemble of given structures, an ensemble which determines social relations as class relations'.[20] If, indeed! Well if it is, by this token class is entirely caused by the interlocking dynamics of a historically singular, but ubiquitous mode of production, and then what is both vindicated and abused as functionalism comes into play.

Functionalists, whether under that or more everyday titles, claim that all social behaviours similarly function to maintain the system of that society, and that understanding social action is a matter of inserting that action into the structure of society in order to see what it does to maintain that structure. Conversely, it may be removed from the society and understood by asking what its absence would do to unsettle that society such that the behaviour's restoration (or its creation in the first place) enables the machine to function better or indeed at all. Thus, even ceremonies that turn the world upside down (as teachers coming to school on set days of the year – 'for charity' – dressed exaggeratedly as schoolchildren in gymslips and long black-stockinged legs or crammed into grey shorts), such ceremonies by definition function to maintain a systemic structure which without saturnalia would have no

disinhibiting release of tension or dispersals of unspoken resent-
ment at the necessities of authority. In the revealing cliché, this
'safety valve' view of the social machinery is a routinely familiar
reference to functionalism. It may come in many political
colours,[21] but for our immediate purposes it is its Marxist guise
which has both disguised and discovered the art and craft of the
state as it devises education and culture for the liberation and
control of the people, intended or unplanned.

But whatever the discrediting of Marxism and the alternatives,
it is probable that the mental modes of all teachers – and, most
likely, of all citizens – will continue to include the house of class,
the lone ranger *and* the Left functionalist. This being so, what
more accommodating, discontinuous, but also experienced
theorization of class will do to explain by redescribing the
pervasion of the curriculum by the fact and values of class
formation? Looking for a different model in the natural sciences to
the old brass and iron steam-engine, which for Marx and Engels
both symbolized and *was* the agent of alienation and accumulation, working always for and against men, we may come up with
the metaphors of a particle physics, in which class is a field of force
whose wave functions pulse down the channels of production,
investment, labour, and so on, and whose highly various, systemic,
but unpredictable atomic life is carried in the realms of family,
friendship, school, cultural form, and as many other charges of
electro-social life as you care to name. Some such formulation has
the merit of acknowledging both power and pervasiveness, as well
as inertia and chance,[22] and also acknowledges that fields of force
have their own rules, but are at the same time subject and object of
study. They may be harnessed by those who know their working,
and given specific, alterable purposes.

My illustration (the metaphor purports no more than that)
arises from two longish essays with which the piously political
student might begin practical reasoning about class.[23] Both heroes,
E.P. Thompson and Jean-Paul Sartre, are intensely practical in
their reasoning about political life,[24] to the extent of famous
interventions in the living praxis of their day – Thompson's
intervention being indeed still very much alive, in the movement
for European nuclear disarmament. In their writing, both emphasize the interconnectedness of individual life with a larger social
life, itself a commonplace enough thing to do, but both seek to

bring out the quickness and vivid spontaneity of that individuality, its distinctiveness of silhouette and of effectuality, as well as its atomic self-sufficiency, the degrees of freedom which allow a mass to become just that: a bloc of discrete, active, but causally inefficacious motions of indifference. When activity-in-indifference characterises large groups, as for example when internal events cause mass, but separate response – a torrent of refugees from a bombed city, or crowds of unemployed across Britain – then Sartre identifies this as 'seriality' (his coinage): a continuous, multitudinous situation of passive or oppressed help-lessness. Against *and* within these motions of creative individuality and the seriality of (causally speaking) passive co-existence, Thompson reaffirms the necessary *fight*, that compound of bloody-mindedness and the will to freedom, of independence and leader-ship, as well as (less attractively) of organization and ruthlessness, which compose class solidarity.

As the two activists (*sic*) think of it, a militant class is, in Sartre's words, never 'simply embattled, nor simply scattered in its mass passivity, nor a bureaucratic machine (as in political political parties). It is a multivalent, mobile *relation* between these different forms of practical life.'[25] And he precedes Thompson, though in a very different language, in reminding all social thinkers-and-actors that the many forms of practical life 'cannot be enclosed by any single category of interpretation'.

Seriality becomes solidarity, and dissolves back again; these are the rhythms of history, in its homely and its historic forms. So it was, say, in Prague in 1968, the process being helped along by Russian tanks; on my reading of British history, so it was in Britain between 1943 and 1947. Either way, both seriality and solidarity may find either their life or death in the spontaneous actions of 'bonded groups' (Sartre's phrase) or in formal institu-tions like political parties or schools.

Perhaps these metaphors may prompt a richer vocabulary of class analysis in the conversation of the curriculum, for the obviousness of class advantage, hypocrisy, mercilessness and apathy is all the more painful to point out as it is denied, ignored or neglected by teachers of every kind, from infant schools to universities. Yet it is class which organizes who does which subjects in what numbers at every level of education. That same process of organization and selection determines admission to the privileges of the professions (the mental forms of production) and to the less obvious rewards of semi-skilled labour (the manual). These things are everywhere known and bitterly commented upon,[26] but almost changeless in the proportions of reproduction. It is always worth insisting upon them, and ensuring that a still popular sort of falsehood, that everybody can 'get on' and 'do well' and reach the top of every tree if they have a mind to, is regularly put down by new figures confirming the old truth, that Britain is a monstrously and arbitrarily unequal country, and that such unforgivable injustices flout the first principles of a decent moral republic.

These circumstances are the results of policies and structures of access and admission in education – of, as they say, input and output. But class is no less present in all that happens to the curriculum in between. It is there, if you want to see things that way, in the very presence of the teacher teaching the class-inflected definitions of the curriculum to working-class pupils who, in the relevant phrase, just don't want to know. Truly enough, as I have noted, there is a dire tendency among teachers to combine in their picture of the good life as realized in the curriculum those qualities which put so many of them where they are: obedience, faithful repetition of all they have been told, docility, quiet, hard work, stifling small-mindedness and attention to unimportant detail, respectability. These are some of the moral and intellectual attributes of the European *petite bourgeoisie*, and malediction comes easily to all radical tongues when they are named.

No doubt there is truth in such charges. Teaching has long been the avenue of social promotion for working-class children with the wits and the opportunity. To obtain that promotion, they had to do as they were told, and if so-called reproduction theory has anything in it, it is (to compress drastically) that educators seek to make students in their own image. Now critics of teachers and teaching who hold this view – and all rational people must be alive to its frequent accuracy – have been at pains to point out that, for instance, even in the most liberally self-conscious classrooms, the teachers do most of the talking.[27] They have picked up Bernstein's famous distinction between restricted and elaborated codes, in which the former modes of speech are context-specific, personal, allusive, disjointed and concrete, and the latter generalized, abstract, sequential and complicated. In his wake, they have suggested that teachers speak the latter, 'educated' code, and working-class children fail so frequently because they can't make the conceptual, as well as the linguistic shifts (and the one failure because of the other) which are required of them.[28] And thereafter, these critics have gone on to suggest that a petty-bourgeois teacher population selects and advances those children with nice manners who smile politely and write clearly, and ignores, bullies or puts down all the others.

By this stage we have travelled out of the realms of inquiry into class towards the mean streets of everyday abuse. Well, abuse has its justified targets. There are indeed battalions of teachers, in the deep complacencies of universities as well as the dismal mediocrities of many primary-school classrooms, whose effective preferences for cowed submission and leaden, truculent concessiveness are actualized in curricular practices best vivified in Michel Foucault's analysis of the ideal modern prison,[29] in which the warders' surveillance of the prisoners would be made total, and therefore totalitarian.

No one can ignore the deep drives of industrial culture towards what Poulantzas calls 'the exceptional State' and its 'populist authoritarianism'.[30] Indeed, it is the whole purpose of this book to call such teachers as read it to the standards of resistance to these dreadful and dangerous forces. But the last enemy is not the first, and in criticizing the class formation of teachers and its effects in the ideological distortions of the curriculum, it is important to be sure of where real power and its menacing coercions lie, as opposed to the trivial irritations of manners and morals we happen to find unimportantly limiting. This distinction comes out with massive inescapability when we turn in the next chapter to consider the 'modes and relations of production' as these issue in the making of work by the systems of the curriculum. But for now it will do to say not only that it doesn't much matter if teachers still tend to send girls to home economics and boys to metalwork, or if they pretend that writing poems is creatively self-fulfilling when several children find it very boring, but that such actions are hardly expressions of a class hegemony whose universal saturation ensures that class values, class organization of knowledge and culture, and ultimately class retention of capital and production are kept where they are.

There are, after all, *values*, not merely class values. The value of severe and lonely dedication to the creation of a painting, a performance of a Mozart piano concerto, a piece of philosophic inquiry, unites Cezanne, Solomon and Wittgenstein in what it is dumbly incomprehending as well as wrong to call a class activity. Without such austerity, there would be no art nor thought, and without these no history, only the repetition of inanity. By the same token, the virtues are virtues, not modes of class oppression: the compassion and gentleness shown by Jesus to Mary Magdalene, Cordelia to Lear, Bonhoeffer to his Gestapo captors, are themselves virtuous. They are not class property, any more than they are only Christian; they recur in classical Greece, primitive East Africa, contemporary Buddhism. Courage is courage in the battle of Bataan, before Agincourt, at the Hot Gates.

Opposing the deformations of class in the curriculum is a deeper matter, therefore, than taking the side of the students against the teachers because they, like your parents, are the ones who are there and get upset, whereas the ideological state apparatuses and their policemen are hard to find and somewhere else.

Sometimes the depths are perfectly clear. When all is said and done about the class favouritisms implied in particular ways of teaching, it is surely the case that, as never before, the British primary and secondary-school systems are the sources of decisive social progress, even at a time when progress itself has such a threadbare referent. It is argued[31] that the pedagogy of discovery and of self-pacing, the curriculum of concept-building and thematic fields of study, are peculiarly congruent with ideological tendencies and social relations of the meaning-minding industry as presently disposed in the various cultural bureaucracies of church, education and media. Their preferences are for loose, informal modes of control, for 'persons' rather than 'characters', as I put it in chapter 4, for ways of knowing rather than states of knowledge, for delaying the divisions of intellectual labour in the interests of fluid agglomerations of cultural reference (politics, art, science, gastronomy, travel, humanitarianism, sexuality). All these, the case goes, are best suited to their own children and their social advance.

It may be so. But it is also true that the threats to educational freedom and the reality of repressive control are rather less marked[32] in the amiable excesses of infant-school finger-painting and secondary-school sessions on personal relationships than they are in the dead ends of the Manpower Services Commission and the various efforts now being made to run secondary and further education from the Department of Employment. There are no doubt severely *intellectual* strictures to be made of bits of awful curriculum; some have been made here already. But those have only at several removes a relevance to questions of class. Indeed, at a time of such lowering and ungenerous uncertainty, it is worth reaffirming the great contribution made to the sum of human happiness and freedom, especially if freedom is thought of less as a right to individual space and more as a virtue, by the development of the comprehensive school for children from the age of 5 to 18. That development is still in its babyhood, in places hardly begun, but starting from the straight abolition of the eleven-plus selection examinations, the legal insistence that all but the fee-paying handful of the nation's children go together to school through the same gates, followed by the enormous extension of both study and opportunity – of subjects, equipment, travel, and methods of teaching – the changes in schooling reflected in the rewriting of the whole curriculum have made unmistakably for a better world. In the teeth of continued and dreadful ignorance, bigotry, illiteracy, and the rest, the citizenry as never before can speak up for itself, knows more of the great world and respects what it does not know, refuses servility and loves freedom, honours culture and tolerates variety in ways which still give meaning and believability to the great project of human enlightenment and emancipation.

Of course, such boldness of affirmation risks shouts of derision at a bareness of face which to the old self-appointed guardians of culture is synonymous with cheek. And of course these embodiments of progress may have all kinds of things about them which we don't like. Children may so far have learned, as teachers claim they intend to teach, to think for themselves, that they get up and leave the classroom. They may have won for themselves the knowledge that some hands in the curriculum dealt to them are part of a pack of lies. Maybe this and maybe that. But in so far as the intentions behind the move to comprehensive education in schools was that all children should be given access to common culture and a curriculum as realizing a shared, mutually accessible picture of the good life, then – allowing for the slow historical construction of all new institutions – those good intentions have not been dishonoured, and the best teachers who may without priggishness be said to act as the conscience of the institution have surely kept their faith with and in those ideals.

Looking on the bright side has its presumptuousness, no doubt. But it doesn't win or lose the day for progressivism. The all-important significance of class is not only that it is so ubiquitous and material a fact of life in Britain and the world, that nobody can understand what is going on without some picture of class, but much more that the effects of class are to have wounded and poisoned so many lives in such irrevocable ways. The point of this short tour of class theory is, as ever,at once theoretical and practical. It is to indicate that the picture (or theory, if that seems preferable) you have of how class works, frames and directs what you will do about it. My brief apostrophe to the victories won by and on behalf of teachers and pupils in comprehensive schools (which, to say it again, denotes both primary and secondary) connects theory with practice in the easily forgotten platitude that political and moral gains, like military ones, have to be held onto and renewed. Given that class is the mobile, elusive, but invasive thing it is, then like power itself class may be transformed in one social action on behalf of the good life and its truth and beauty, while at the same time it reappears elsewhere with its new mutilations and imprisonments.

This is indeed the process of our history, and it is formally and repetitiously inscribed in the curriculum. Indeed, the making and remaking of any curriculum is a collective, but also contested act of cultural revision. In the view of the comprehensive curriculum as well as that of polytechnics and even the corners of some universities, which I have taken, for the present chapter, from the sunny side up, this revision as it has been conducted over the past thirty years or so has consistently, though fumblingly, sought to rejoin lived experience to offical knowledge. That is to say, as the temporary surges of feeling came through from a working class only just counted into the benefits of capitalism, teachers responded by altering the structures of recognition extended to their pupils. Where once the school had insisted on the absoluteness of the boundary between school and out-of-school, between street wisdom and book wisdom, between speaking properly and talking like a lout, an entirely new, irregular, but vigorous movement began to acknowledge the culture and experience which the children brought with them so inalienably in order to attach it to different forms of knowledge itself, and the purposes and actions which are the end, the telos of knowledge.

So, speech changed. Talking improperly became limitedly possible. Especially in primary schools, the child herself moved forward on the plane of reception; she was put in a slightly larger, more prominent space in which to make some shift at creative action and a personal discovery of the world in her own language. What she wrote, she wrote 'in her own words'. When she measured the playground and counted gravestones, devised histograms of passing traffic and built a collage with her friends from her table, whatever the sentimentalities and trivialities of some of the work done, such a curriculum enormously extended the purchase of her own experience upon the inscrutability of learning.

There is no need to rehearse the various, polemical, and often moving literature which has been a sign of these times. But a personally chosen, memorable handful will perhaps do something to bring out what I am trying to name: the strenuousness of physical, moral and intellectual effort which men and women put into the battle to make sense of their lives, and then, most moving of all, the way in which at the right time, in an indeterminate place, these efforts rise above the merely personal and surge into a common stream. When Brian Jackson and Dennis Marsden[33] wrote the small history of their associates' experience as working-class boys who passed the eleven plus and went to Huddersfield Grammar School, they showed in a vivid tableau the way the school first put down and then tried to wipe out the experience those boys and girls brought with them; and they restored to life the intransigence with which some at least resisted their orders. When Richard Hoggart[34] described the working-class life of the Hunslet he grew up in – when indeed in almost as good as a book[35] Brian Jackson copied him – he not only restored to value the class life he so richly described, he extended recognition to a whole treasurehouse of recorded value which all children of the 1940s brought to school – comics, thrillers, the Light Programme, the Home Service, the sentimental song and the stand-up comedian – and insisted on its shaping spirit and memorable force, as well as on the spirit and force of all such experience in the lives of all children. When David Holbrook wrote his significantly titled *English for the Rejected*,[36] even when the Royal Commission delivered up its muffled prose under the chairmanship of John Newsom,[37] a new educational constituency had been named and, if at times condescendingly (this is England (*sic*), after all), recognized as having, in the phrase, its own life to live.

This is what I mean by cultural revision. It transpired in the Newsom Report and in the Plowden Report three years later on primary schools. It issued in such successful curricular projects as the Schools Mathematics Project and Nuffield Science, in *Science 5–13*, and a dozen others whose advances and withdrawals may be read in the very formation as well as the publications of the Schools Council.

Any such tide comes in on a very uneven front. As tides will, it goes out again. But the tide metaphor will not do to describe the doubling back and forth of historical progress and regress. It will not do to say, with the new Marxists,[38] that the educational changes I have summarized and applauded are no more than the machinations of social democracy trying to make the world safe for post-1945 capitalism. Class, as I have remarked, is inseparable from power, and power is not just the ability to coerce in either two or three dimensions the wills of others:[39] it is what it says it is: power, the essence or force which is effectual, the nature of causality (or efficacy) itself.

There is no need for this to sound melodramatic. This side of warfare, history only moves very slowly and, as we might put it, in its own time. But if the changes in the curriculum on behalf of a slightly less lethal class system which emerge from recent British history may be seen as energetically willed, voluntary and worked for, they have to operate in the field of structures – structures of regulation, production and systematization – which have *their* deadly and inflexible presence.

8

Work and Meaning

I have spoken much in these pages of structures, and as many people have noted, the word and the concept are fatally liable to merely modish use, as well as implying a real existence out there, instead of its having a strictly metaphoric life identifying otherwise nameless and uncontrollable eventualities.[1] But it is in speaking of the structures of economic production that the idea has one of its strongest applications. As we have noticed, the value, meaning and functions of work itself are taught to and learned by children from the moment they enter the reception class, and days are divided into worktime and playtime. From the age of five, the deep distinctions between work and leisure, production and holiday, weekdays and weekends, clocking on and off, productiveness and unproductiveness, conscientiousness and sloth, all come to shape not only the innumerable individual identities, but our profoundest sense of space and time, continuity and culture themselves. Indeed to complete education is to enter the present as an adult, and such entrance is marked by stepping over the thresholds of production into the society of other free, productive men and women. Of course, as we see around us every day, many of those thresholds either give onto tightly locked doors or open into derelict premises, but the effort to keep that entrance to work universally open remains the central, collective enterprise of the society. To have work is to ensure your own freedom.[2]

For work to be work it must be contained within the recognized structures of the mode and relations of production. It must be made visible and given value as production by its actualization as a commodity. Only then is it official work, and gathered as such into the relations of production which define social life. Within capitalism, these mean that whatever commodity is produced, including the so-called invisible commodities of the service industries – driving a truck or a train, working in a bank, mending teeth or lecturing on ancient history – that commodity must be defined according to the criteria and categories of profitability, productivity and efficiency. Once a social practice is organized in such a way that the time it occupies may be divided into remuneration and surplus-value (Marx's phrase), then that time encloses the occupation as commodity, and separates labour from capital accumulation.

In his famous formulation of these processes, *Capital*, Marx himself simplified the argument by speaking always as though the commodity were a palpable, manufactured product which, as he saw it, the slightly crazed brain of both worker and employer thought of, fetishistically, as possessing value in itself and not just for its social uses. In a famous passage, he wrote:

> A commodity is therefore a mysterious thing, simply because in it the social character of men's labour appears to them as an objective character stamped upon the product of that labour; because the relation of the producers to the sum total of their own labour is presented to them as a social relation, existing not between themselves, but between the products of their labour. This is the reason why the products of labour become commodites, social things whose qualities are at the same time perceptible and imperceptible by the senses . . . To find an analogy, we must have recourse to the mist-enveloped regions of the religious world. In that world the productions of the human brain appear as independent beings endowed with life, and entering into relation both with one another and the human race. So it is in the world of commodities with the products of men's hands. This I call the Fetishism which attaches itself to the products of labour, so soon as they are produced as commodities, and which is therefore inseparable from the production of commodities.
>
> This Fetishism of commodities has its origin as the foregoing analysis has already shown, in the peculiar social character of the labour that produces them.[3]

It isn't a satisfactory account, unspecific as Marx is about what it is which does the 'presenting' of the sum total of their labour to all men, and so presents it moreover as at once a social relation and a *thing*, with its curiously autonomous life. And Marx has been subsequently and seriously criticized, even by economists much influenced by and sympathetic to his thought, for precisely this crucial notion of 'surplus-value' and its operational slipperiness.[4] But the importance of the passage as of the book is that it shows believably how a very particular, not at all inevitable system of providing for human needs becomes a structure of meaning which attaches men to things, in a telling phrase, in spite of themselves.

By 'mode of production', Marx and those who follow his analytic lead mean the economic system dominant in any one society which seeks to create and distribute abundance. It is a phrase by means of which to conceptualize not whether a particular economy is, say, dependent on extraction from nature (mineral or energy mining, for instance) or on manufacturing, but rather the ratio of subsistence to surplus, of use to exchange (and profit, if any), of money to its reproduction, and all of these ratios at *any* point of historical development, not merely at that point at which money is replaced by capital. Now the 'relations of production' are conceptually inextricable from the mode. For the mode sets limits to the ways in which men and women may associate with one another as they pursue their vital interest in food, shelter, property, freedom on behalf of themselves and their families and friends. Most simply, once the mode of production operates with the categories of capital and labour, and the drive to accumulate begins, then classes are alienated one from another, and workers alienated from work. Capitalist relations have begun.

The magisterial reach of this theory is clear. It accounts for some of the deepest conflicts, contradications and pains of contemporary experience. It places the acts of production at the centre of that experience and brings out that failure to fulfil which makes us strangers to ourselves, and fixes them as inevitably contested, in so far as the pointlessness of profit accumulation for others rides our acts of making and makes us their slaves.

Putting things like this is only possible, of course, in an analytic framework that sets itself in opposition to the totality of what it analyses. But opposition entails position. In other words, Marx, like any other critic of the industrialization he first identified as capitalism, at least in a full-blown theory, has to situate himself somewhere else in order to gain leverage on the object of his criticism. He stands on the foundation of two traditions: from the first, enlightenment position, work is criticized as having lost the creativity and potency of self-fulfilment, which Marx's very various Victorian contemporaries located either in the medieval guilds and their crafts or in the practice of the artist, the very type of free, useful and humanly enhancing production. From the second position, however, hugely more long-standing, work is Adam's curse, the condition of his discharge from the Garden of Eden and the enduring burden of a humanness severed from beatitude.

Either way – and few Victorians, certainly not Marx himself, distinguished between their dual inheritance – industrial work was what had come to deprive men and women of the living connection between them and their creativity, the connection broken in the theodicy of the Fall before which, either in Biblical truth or mythical longing, the provision of subsistence was entirely harmonious with the rhythms of nature. Alternatively, industrial work was what, in its killing repetitiousness and clear severance of the 'hands' from head and heart, had sundered – through the agency of the boss – the maker from the made, the whole person from the activity of creative work.

This is the long appeal to an ideal of work as self-sustaining, fulfilling, slow, rhythmic and true, to which Left and Right alike appeal[5] from the early nineteenth century until a present in which teachers of all kinds seek to keep apart in the minds and efforts of their students work which is satisfying, true and creative, and labour (best seen in exams) which is repetitious, uninvolving, false and deadly. The distinction between live work and dead labour is Hannah Arendt's,[6] but it is implicit in all criticisms of what happened to the daily work when industrialization took over.

Of course, it is an act of hysterical self-obsession to suppose that the possibility of eternal indolence has not been a transhistorical fantasy, as all myths of Paradise, in which work is so ambivalently present and absent (is harping work?), testify. Equally, however, it has been methodically underlined in the last chapter that transhistorical values take on their distinctive historical character and outline. Work is a human condition, but who on earth ever came to think that it could possibly be a good thing in its capitalist version?

Trying to explain work in its typically capitalist origins, Max Weber[7] propounded the famous thesis that Protestantism, in both its Calvinist and Lutheran versions, obviously shifted the locus of grace and redemption from the church to the individual. In spite of insisting on the arbitrary nature of that redemption, placing the individual soul in such a bright, universal light gave to all actions an equivalent potentiality, either as a source of damnation or grace. Any sin might be *the* sin which damned a soul. Any virtuous action might redeem it.[8] It is therefore hardly surprising if, in the attempt to take this chance of grace, the most vigorous adherents of a doctrine with no hierarchy of well or evil doing, but only a belief in the power of actions to change the world, one without (furthermore) any ritual of absolution, should have evolved a mode and structure of being in which conscience-stricken rectitude, brief, austere self-examination and ceaseless activity were predominant. Weber then suggests that as the contextual and dogmatic beliefs dissolved under the impact of science and its 'disenchantment of the universe', the formal structures remained as the necessary poles of being within which a man kept himself upright. The character of the capitalist was made within such frames of being.

Weber's has been an extraordinarily popular thesis, so much so that the phrase 'the work ethic', compressed from the title of his great book, is habitually referred to as the prevalent meaning of the labour culture, whenever anyone puzzles over what to do with the unemployed or seeks to explain how it is that some people simply renounce the contemplative virtues and work pointlessly on. Like Marx's theory, however, but on a larger scale, Weber's has great gaps, or rather, is one-legged. He is doubtless right to return the power of *ideas* back alongside economic production itself as the motors of history, but he gives no sufficient account of the genesis of classes nor of the actualities of cruelty, unhappiness and oppression, which are at the humanist heart of Marx's thought. Neither man in practice properly credits human beings under capitalism or any other industrial system with their undoubted powers of resistance, of making concessions and compromises which also leave them room of their own to move, of evading and dodging the points at which coercion hurts in order to do and to make do for themselves.

The drive for a totalitarian control and surveillance of the minds of men and women seems at times – and nowadays is one such time – to be coterminous with modernization.[9] And yet the supreme theorists of modernization, Marx and Weber, never see the facts of an alternative life, a counterculture, simple expressions of the episteme in all human lives which, as naturally as breathing, seeks and finds corners for its freedom. There is no complacency in this. The corners made available for such freedom by concentration camps, or even the officially benign institutions of modern bureaucracies like schools and hospitals, are not very great. The unforgettable point of, say, Solzhenitsyn's great novella about the Gulag, *A Day in the Life of Ivan Denisovitch*, is that we make the best of them.

The mention of schools brings us back to the curriculum. For this short history of work as meaning, in which Marx and Weber are the first, essential teachers, still has a little way to go. Both thinkers knew that the values and meanings to which people give their lives are, because of that significance, the site of bloody disagreement. Of the two, Marx both weighed the costs of that disagreement, in terms of terror and bloodshed, and was more hopeful about the outcome. Still speaking from a tradition that reached back, though the Enlightenment and its faith in progress, to the Christian and Greek formation of ideals that nominated, in Aristotle's word, *eudaimonia* or human flourishing as the goal or telos of a man's life, Marx wrote his critique of capitalism from an ideal of undivided human creativity, the happy operation imagined by both Aristotle and the Romantics. The defeat and supersession of capitalism was the biggest step towards achieving that ideal. Teachers may have learned some such lesson more from folk-memories of what Wordsworth and Ruskin or, further back, Thomas More and St Benedict may have said, than from fierce old Marx and the besotted optimisms of Rosa Luxemburg. But the notion of human flourishing lives on in the far from empty appeals made in the curriculum to happiness and satisfaction, and to the epistemic trigonometry of that flourishing: freedom, fulfilment, and self-critical awareness in *praxis* and *poesis*, action and making.

Weber, on the other hand, had a bleaker and more sombre view of the developments of industrial production. Glancing aside at the Marxists of his day in Germany, when the attempted social revolution of 1919[10] failed and Luxemburg was murdered with Liebknecht, he observed thinly, 'They summoned up the street. The street has dispatched them.' He not only had no great faith in any social movement; he saw the march of modernity as advancing more and more completely with the bureaucratic forms that had become the inevitable expression of the advent of the state, and further considered that the only opportunity for making things a bit better lay in ameliorating the working of those bureaucracies according to the criteria of efficiency, and a rationality which strove always to adjust ends to means in some more or less adequate fit. The characteristics of the good bureaucrat might then make the depredations of a blind state and ignorant masses slightly more orderly to live with.

In effect, Weber provided in fine detail a map of the very relations of production diagrammatized in Marx's mode of production. Taken together, they show us the way of the working Western world since 1900 or so. More bureaucracy, no revolution: the organization of consciousness[11] deceives all parties. (Until, of course, it reached Tehran, when the Ayatollah, as I remarked, rebutted Weber's predictions and dispatched him with Marx to the attic of history.) The trouble is that the slogans of a mindless individualism, as set in bold type for the banners of the tabloid right, have turned 'bureaucracy' into a swear word. Nobody on the sane side of idiocy, however, can suppose that Western societies could possibly function without bureaucracies, and those remaining few whose enthusiasm it is to imagine them no longer in function, have no picture of a redeemed society capable of taking decisions, defending itself, caring for its sick, raising its children, and burying its dead, which does not require a scientific administration and a handbook on how to run it.

Weber wrote the handbook.[12] He saw that bureaucracies must have a purposive rationality expressed first, in the equitable treatment of all clients, secondly, in an efficient knowledge of the files and perfect accuracy of record and retrieval, thirdly, in anonymity in the referral of cases and an infallible routinization of their handling, and lastly, a clear subjugation of means to ends, of process to aims and objectives. And as Peter Berger ironically sees, these ways of sorting experience are now part of all our everyday experience, not only in our necessary traffic with public life – banks, doctors, police, supermarkets, schools – but also in the way these impinge on the everyday living – keeping the deep-freeze full, getting the children to school or ourselves to work on time, keeping out of the red on the current account, paying bills and remembering favourite programmes on television. All experience is partially bureaucratized, for better as well as for worse.

Admittedly there is some difficulty in recognizing the moment at which the shaping of experience, identity, time and decision moves from mere regularity and routine to becoming bureaucratized. Perhaps we can say that the passage is made from routine to bureaucracy when the agent treats another subject (feasibly including himself) as a *client* or, in the revealing term, patient; when formal records and files objectify everyday arrangements in a transferable form; when time dictates the action and not the action the time.[13]

These termini may serve to mark the moves to bureaucracy in formal action. As the Bergers bring out so well, bureaucratic habits deeply penetrate and reshape the modern consciousness. What they do not bring out is the connection between these shapes and pervasions and the relations of production which are controlled and made systematic by the special forms of modern bureaucracy found in those great institutions of modern capital, the corporations.

It isn't quite enough, however, to say flatly that some bits of bureaucratization are good for us and some bad. The official symbols of liberal individualism are such that the notion of bureaucratic organization and its central structures of formality, anonymity, efficiency, justice and regularity are thought of as in themselves deadly and inhuman. Anyone who insists on their proper working can be dismissed as one of the faceless and repressive automata who people Kafka's *The Trial*: creatures whose only purpose is the purposeless maintenance of their system and the eradication of human inconsistency. Consequently, the new developments of bureaucratic systems into the forms of managerialism and counselling that appeared in chapter 6 have to present themselves as warmly and sympathetically concerned with individuals in order to achieve people's compliance.

Such self-presentation works all the better if its practitioners believe in it. So, teachers will organize the curricular culture of schools, self-deceivingly confident that creative activity (art and craft) is not less so for beginning prompt at 9.30 a.m. and going on until, although impossible to stop before, 11 a.m. when it's playtime. ('Play, boy', Estella and Miss Havisham commanded Pip.) The kindly headteacher of a devoutly progressive, childcentred primary school, conscious of his personal care and, indeed, generalized affection for his children, cannot without pain see the files and times of school life as the agency of state bureaucracy.

His difficulty is, however, only the start. Anybody might reasonably agree, after a brief dose of Weber, that the rational adjustment of means to end in the name of efficiency is imaginably a help towards the good life in industrial flourishing. They might reasonably go beyond Weber, with the help of Kafka's warning and recent political history,[14] to make a strong separation between the bureaucratic and the informal realms of life, more or less in parallel to the distinction between public and private life, and the latter as being the domain of all that is informal, flexible, warm, sympathetic, creative, and so on. Something can be made of the argument; it is the way in which most of us hang onto meaning in private life, both at home and at work. But it suppresses the fact of dominance by the public over the private (a dominance inscribed in their lexical meaning). We have rather to think of all lives, in and out of production, as conducted in a *milieu* in which means-end rational planning only applies to specific and short-term problems.

It is, however, the dominating premiss of bureaucratic planning that *all* thinking is defined as amenable to means-end rationality. That is to say, there is a law of its motion which drives together within its own effective field all the activities of its milieu. We may risk a proposition: that bureaucracies are intrinsically driven to attain hegemony over all human action.

If this is thought too near the view of the *Daily Mail* or the worthy headteacher, perhaps it may be more politically astute to say that in the tense, gigantic dialectic between individual liberation and industrial production released in Europe at the end of the eighteenth century, bureaucracy represents an always veering effort on the part of the state to mediate between the two poles, mutually repellant and attractive as they are. It cannot be doubted that veering at the present time is all the way of the systems of production.

It is a loss of balance widely felt, but little grasped. In school life generally, the change in pressure comes through as the weight of committees, of increases in record-keeping, in the minor, irritating, but ceaselessly fracturing interruptions of the day: the dreadful bell, the special appointments, the movement of equipment, the checking of stock, the allocation of resources, the public address system, the notes and chits, the sanctions and punishments, the assembly. But the pressures upon the curriculum of bureaucratization are felt, as it is the point of this chapter to show, with profound and enfolding power as – once more – mode and relations of production. What then comes though is a particular account of work, work for its own sake and organized in these ways because those are the ways which turn doing into production. In a celebrated paper, E.P. Thompson[15] provided an early history of the tropes which accomplish this conversion, when he identified the moments in the seventeenth century when capitalism combined with Protestantism to make time itself into a commodity which should be *spent* valuably, not wasted, and thereafter the way in which the image of the clock ('clocking on') came to dominate production. It did so symbolically as well, even to the extent of clocks and watches becoming the talismans given in honour of the service rendered by those retiring and as a token of their prior gifts of the time of their lives.

The turning of time into a commodity ('overtime', 'part-time', 'time-and-a-half') has been going on since then, and the fitting of time to space in order to provide a unilinear calculus of reward is now a commonplace of educational production. It is most ostentatious in examinations, where the production of set quantities in set periods is what is required, produced and examined. Even when schoolteachers themselves rebelled in the name of non-productive *poesis* and, after the Beloe Report of 1961 and the early Schools Council examination bulletins, moved some examining towards the submission and assessment of coursework folders, bureaucracy and production exerted their logic. In order to regularize production and make assessment just, anonymous and efficient, teachers had to organize techniques of statistical moderation,[16] worked out in endless hours of committee discussion, and issue definitions of quotas and types of production – essays, projects, experiment reports, 'oral talks' *sic* (not more than ten minutes), notes, poems. The same principles hold throughout the curriculum. At tertiary levels, the production of coursework and answers for three-hour examinations is organized by the same inevitably bureaucratic principles. The striking difference is that so very few university examiners (colleges and polytechnics are better educated) have any knowledge of parametric statistics. Singled out for stardom by its purity, they continue to believe that the first-class honours award is identifiable in terms of incontestable qualities rarely to be found in contemporary decadence, and perfectly immune to the demands of a curve of distribution.

These myths are noticeably strong in university humanities departments, but they are present everywhere: over here, amongst teachers who mark down the mock O levels in order to make the pupils work harder: over there, in polytechnic modular courses, where tutorial timorousness in anticipation of the external examiner, custodian of both comparative and absolute standards, causes all students to be awarded a lower second.[17] As most myths do, these seem to obscure the facts of life, in this case that examinations are best understood as boundaries marking access to the next stage of education, and therefore as stages of allocation at the appropriate age (16, 18, 21; O level, A level, BA) in the required numbers for further training or its withdrawal.

Given the mostly arbitrary, but drastic significance of examinations, it is not surprising that their ideological and legendary mass is as great as it is. In representing the culmination of years of work, they enforce the imperatives of work at all previous stages. Given also that teachers made their own mobility out of working hard for examinations, they vehemently endorse what in any case the whole culture teaches: that to become a citizen, a home-owner, a parent, a grown-up member of the world, you must join the society of freely productive men and women, and produce with them. So all children are made to produce, preferably in quiet, and largely by themselves, for it is taken for granted in individualism that that labour is best which you do for yourself, and which when completed is your own property, not to be shared, collectively produced, or stolen (copied from). Such work is also best if it is produced in measurable amounts ('You've done a lot this morning, Garry', and the old *canard*, 'No need to read PhDs, just weigh them'). The rates of production are then subjected to innocent forms of operational research, and the natural way for these to be controlled is in the bureaucratic mode. Hence, pieces of work must be finished by Friday, or by the end of term, must be handed in on time (unless you have a note of exculpation from parent, tutor, or policeman), must represent enough bulk for the time spent, must be all your own – with the possible exception of art which can be occasionally collective, the occasions being school plays or concerts, the odd mural, a magazine.

It is hard not to smell the presence in all this of the deadly machinations of F.W.Taylor and 'Taylorism', the time and motions techniques first devised to accelerate beyond belief the mass production of Ford cars in the USA of the 1920s. Versions of Taylorism, [18] and then later revisions which brought to bear the tenets of a liberally inclined industrial psychology, were the intelligible and widespread expressions of a monopoly capital competing fiercely with itself to ensure that no resource, especially wage-time, was wasted. It gave severity and discipline to the novel forms of an efficient bureaucracy. In state or private capital corporations, those techniques emerged (between 1920 or so and the present day) that fix the terms of planning for production, define the meaning of efficiency as cost-effectiveness, and ensure that the multiple division of labour, but the denial of interdependence, characterize all production, including intellectual production. The anthropological PhD, the primary-school zoology project and, supremely, the increasingly successful efforts of the Manpower Services Commission to control the curriculum, and therefore the lives of an insurgent age-group, are all alike subject to these vastly inclusive processes.

What is more, these processes of necessity frame the minds which do the planning. It is a valid criticism of industrial society that it turns all human activity into the solving of problems which, when once named and defined as problems, are then amenable to the development of techniques which gradually overcome them. A question is not on this account an attempt to direct inquiry and discover the telos;[19] the self-confident, science-minded theoreticism of the rational planner must pose questions capable of defining realizable goals, goals which in turn may be reached by technical, foolproof means.

Well, any fool may use a technique, helped out where necessary by operational managers. The curriculum, as another product from the systems of production, is naturally available for rational planning, since its aims and objectives are determinate and definable, and techniques may be found to attain them. Such has become the conventional wisdom of education's administrators, and as only to be (rationally) expected, curriculum and staff development are linked in the planning of all up-to-date institutions; a manager manages everything and everyone according to their 'needs' and the objectives of production.

The wide, enveloping tendency is totalitarian, even if in a very genteel, vegetable sense. It may be that economic production is humanly improved by these disciplines; it is certain that in all our public life bureaucracy will and must continue as the only mechanism we have for controlling the enormous potentiality for misery, epidemic, destruction and disorder our mass society might realize any day. But – to go no further – the complex milieux of domestic, educational and welfare life should be vividly alive to the mortal dangers of means-end planning, the irrelevant application of cost-effective criteria, the technicizing of both poesis and praxis in the human capacities for creation and action.

If, as I propose, the curriculum as a product is more like a work of art than a manufactured item, it is a work of art like a cathedral or a city, rather than a painting or a concerto. In other words, it is a collective, historical expression of men's and women's purposes and preoccupations, and inasmuch as the word expression connotes a single historical moment, it is also the tradition and ground which make purpose, making and thinking themselves possible.[20]

For no one can intelligibly say that they have aims and objectives in building a cathedral or a city. Or indeed a novel or painting. They are purposive actions with 'unevisageable ends'.[21] To perform them, we standardly look back to see how we got to this position in the first place, and for this short historical reckoning, move forward to make the step. Such thinking is directly contrary to the approved lessons of design theory and the managerial sciences. It has inherent inclinations towards the philistine, the complacencies of common sense, towards (alas) conservatism. These can be avoided with a proper intelligence, as we shall see in chapter 10. But the lived criteria of 'seeming right', of properness and propriety, human suitability, of delicately recognized desires, of practical usability and likely pleasure at beauty are the conditions of art. And if these sound too comfortable, then comfort in the biblical sense of solace is not much in evidence in our relations of production, and in any case I subjoin to the notion of good art the rather more terrifying requirement that it be virtuous and truthful about life as it is lived, and life as it might be lived better.

The curriculum as a work of art has a tale to tell of a better life as well as one to tell us of what and how we do now.

9

Values and the Future

It has been continuously argued in this book that the curriculum should be understood as an ensemble of stories told by one generation to the next about what the possibilities are for the future and what it may be going to be like to attempt to live well at the time. But although I have made blithe play on many occasions with the term 'the good life' and although − Richard Briers and Felicity Kendall notwithstanding − I use the term quite unironically, it would be irresponsible to pretend that the phrase connotes a shared picture of things. Indeed the whole point of my military metaphor at the beginning of Chapter 1 was to show that different world-pictures are fought over continuously, and that this struggle over meanings and values is inextricable from the struggle over territory and wealth. But because the whole curriculum, from that of an infant to that of a doctor, from cradle to grave, is securely settled as, above all, official and at the same time assented to, then we have in it a statement of the instrumental and the expressive realms of the society. That is to say, the curriculum is both the text and the context in which production and values intersect; it is the twistpoint of imagination and power.

Neither this way of putting things, nor the recommendations I shall want to make about the content of the curriculum should be taken to imply that I think that what is taught in schools, colleges, polytechnics and universities is the most important aspect of a nation's life, and that changing them means changing it. The most virtuous curriculum in this world would not prevent of itself our being blown into the next one, if those in power had a mind to it, or no mind with which to stop it. None the less, unless our assorted and disunited nations devise a rational and virtuous science of human affairs − R.G. Collingwood's noble phrase, which I have so much invoked and to devising which he gave his life[1] − then the human prospect is fairly bleak. Given also that it is the business of an intelligentsia to imagine the good life and to teach how to lead it, then the national curriculum certainly begins to loom as large in importance as, say, television newspapers or other instruments of public communication.

Indeed, it *is* one such instrument itself, and as the striking title of the well-known research reminds us,[2] it is one to which every citizen is required to be, with however impaired hearing, audience for 15,000 hours of non-returnable life. Moreover, it is an excellent premiss of liberal or social democratic societies that the content, form and organization of the curriculum is constantly open to public debate, and in point of fact, that debate is regularly and quite decently conducted. Primary schools run parents' classes to learn the new maths, older parents come loyally together with teachers to try to prevent sixth-form work and syllabuses disappearing from their schools, and polytechnics have been known to incorporate students in curricular review and (as they say) evaluation.

These are a few of the signs whose signified reality is the mildness and docility of the society, no doubt, as well as the successful ordering of a cultural consciousness by the dominant interests – that saturation of the *Zeitgeist* named in a rather blank and baffled way 'hegemony' by its enemies. But the reality includes the widespread sharing by the constituency of British society, its many overlapping minorities and its fluid coalitions, of the main principles and politics, the meanings and metaphysics of the national curriculum, however incoherent and inequitable these undoubtedly are.

Understanding the curriculum of British education is therefore to understand a text and texture of social meanings at their most open and readable. But it is also to construe a multivalent and ambiguous text, whose ideological structure is at the same time arrestingly firm and monolithic. In a valuable metaphor, this humdrum, municipal, but solid edifice occupies and holds the wide middle ground of society.[3]

The phrase was first applied to the analysis of television news magazines, where the standing of the presenter – the William Hardcastle, Robin Day, Alistair Burnet and Ludovic Kennedy figures – became such as to guarantee the impartiality of coverage in the programme, together with its judiciously representative mediation on behalf of each of us, the common citizens, as we face up to and interrogate the inadequacies, mistakes and vanities of our rulers. Kumar's convincing case is that such programmes search for the middle ground of social exchange, a geography by definition away from extremes and planted comfortably in a position across the middle of the road whence, the hope is, it will cause all the traffic on left and right to swerve into the ditch. The trouble with the metaphor, as with the politics, is that the middle ground won't hold, as the end of an epoch cracks the highway right across. Plenty of people, television presenters included, go on driving across the bumps and holes as though nothing has happened, and a lifeless assortment of clichés are to hand which partly acknowledge, partly deny by their casualness the real state of affairs; fingers in the dyke and paper over the cracks serve well enough, in a short interview, to keep the old bus on the road.

But Kumar notes that in order to hold this gregarious ground, the agencies of public communication have to widen their exclusion zone enormously. If the nation's broadcasters claim to speak peace unto the nation, as the old nine o'clock news slogan more or less put it, then peaceful speeches had to include as many people as could reasonably be thought of as, in turn, constituting the main membership of society. Those excluded had to be outlaws. But it follows that if views about our life and times are increasingly fractured and contested, then to hold the middle ground you must include a lot of people you would rather exclude. That is, your very principle of solidarity drives you seek controversy in a doomed attempt to resolve it by hearing both sides of the case (the constitutional, but spurious myth of 'balance'), and by asserting a reconciliation found by presenter-knights Robin Day or Alistair Burnet exactly on the fulcrum of the counterposed positions: left v. right, management v. labour, war v. peace, men v. women. Hence, Kumar concludes, public debate on key social issues, as conducted by the BBC and the ITA, is driven veeringly down a spiral of controversy and conciliation in the search for an irrecoverable community of political assent.

I think it is possible to prefigure the whole cultural framework of 'stories we tell ourselves about ourselves' as similarly a holding of an ideal middle ground where most of us are supposed to live, publicly and privately. Kumar, in other words, gives us another homely, intelligible and comprehensive way of understanding ideology and its workings in many different quarters of social life.

I shall apply the notion to the curriculum, but perhaps it brings out its domestic strength, as well as throwing into a kind of relief the way in which the unofficial curriculum of television shadows, extends and echoes the official curriculum of education, if we enlarge the focus of Kumar's concept to take in all television narrative.

We can then see its subtlety and flexibility in acknowledging potential exclusions and even outlaws breaking away from social solidarity (whole peoples at a time, as with the nationalist surges in Wales and Scotland, and the unfinished battle of Ulster). Television narrative constantly recognizes new groupings, and – by giving such groups space in the texture of national narratives – assimilates, perhaps sedates, and sometimes liberates such groups. Thus, soap operas about amiably dotty punks and student revolutionaries (*The Young Ones*, itself a friendly placing title), about single women making their own, post-divorce professional and sexual career (*Solo*) or the same women fluttering safely on the married side of the same sort of life (*Butterflies*), about Geordie workmen finding employment on the other side of the EEC (*Auf Wiedersehen, Pet*), about the wretchedness and splendour of black ghetto life round the dole queue (*Black Joy*), even about the bitter tensions and murderous vengeances of fidelity in the six counties of Northern Ireland (too many Wednesday *Plays for Today* to recollect), all these varied expressions of new, often unsettling group life in contemporary Britain appear in 625 lines and dazzling colour in order to renegotiate the terms of our membership of its society.

The edge is taken off the unsettlingness of these stories by the dazzle of colour television; as every good painter knows, it is very difficult to prevent dazzle becoming either glamorous or nostalgic. But to put things a distinctly functionalist way, it may plausibly be claimed that the range of narrative on television about the multitudinous forms of the good and the bad life in our Britain helps a country *recognize* (the key verb) its own tolerable variety, and therefore helps to keep it tolerant, as well as sympathetic, even compassionate, understanding, mutual, perhaps friendly.

The discordant ring of this insurance company list of the cardinal virtues – mutuality, friendliness, assurance, protection, relief, benefit – declares its lack of harmony with the real, grimmer virtues of our streets: endurance, bloody-minded independence,

146   *Values and the Future*

scepticism, loyalty, dogged pride, kindness. Television, as we might expect, uses soap opera to soap over the lacerations and wounds of a class-hostile life. One of its main qualities is, in liberal society, certain to be soapiness. But the curriculum – the story of the subjects – has another set of tropes which, while quite unable to assume salvation or to prevent the end of the world, may at least hold up if the world ends. And in any case, its more settled (conservative, if you like – how could it be otherwise?), less febrile, local and domestic temper and circumstance immunize it against the demand for news (which must be new) and entertainment (which mustn't hurt) that belabours television. With the best and most radical will in the world, education systems are, functionally *and* intentionally speaking, providing for the reproduction, in some recognizable and therefore conservative form, of contemporary society. It is therefore the duty of teachers in virtue of their role – a moral and a sociological point – to make their necessary changes within a pretty stable and solid framework. By its social definition, a state school cannot train the revolutionary cadre.

Not many teachers would put things in these terms, and are quite right not to do so. But the structure of their daily lives is such as to prevent most of them being *required*, precisely by the public definition of their role and its duties, to endorse a mindless conformism and an obtuse bureaucratic correctness. The tendencies are there, of course, and more marked always in some roles rather than others: it is no accident that headteachers and their deputies are so much miscalled by their staffs for pettifogging triviality of mind, structural timidity before their superiors, and the dismal extinction of their imagination. Similarly, it is not unjust to say that, as professions, the reproduction of themselves by university and polytechnic law departments and schools of medicine is typified by narrow self-protectiveness, by the dull turning into technique and technology of the baffling complexity of human actuality and encounters, by simple greed, pretentiousness and witch-doctoring. These hideous strengths are those of the politics of special knowledge as mediated by the power of the present forms of bureaucracy. But they are escapable: change social structures, and you change what they make people into.

People – in this case, teachers of all kinds – have their own intransigence, and (like children) do not need quite so much care and protection as the self-importance of the very earnest is apt to insist. Indeed one essential way to understand theory and practice in the curriculum is to study the many forms of subversion and resituation necessarily performed by all teachers on all aspects of what they teach. The uniform and unilinear diagrams of curricular instruction give no play to these wide margins of inevitable creativity in everyday teaching. The creativity may be all the wrong way according to the flow charts, it may indeed be less cheerfully interpreted not so much as creative play and more as downright error, or quite unintelligible. But this is the nature of human communcation, which is not to be mapped in the more simplistic forms of the communication handbooks onto a neat little tree-diagram. Supposing it can be leads to one of the more chronic expressions of banality in present-day management, that human problems are a result of 'lack of communication' or 'information leakage', which would go away if communication were improved or restored or otherwise mended by a plumber. Human attention is not like a wheel, turning over and over on the ground of its study, touching at every spot. It is more like a child on a walk, running, skipping, stopping to look closer, coming back over the same ground for something left behind, going on again with strides of varying pace and length. Indeed the old clichés of the school report reflect just this metaphor: 'she has made great strides', 'he has difficulty keeping up', 'his attention wanders'. It is worth adding that a child on a walk isn't only a metaphor, but is the realization of human attention itself.

The complex play of human attention and its infinite capacity for perhaps creative misprision[4] is one powerful guardian of freedom against brainwashing. It is also the provocation of good curriculum planners, who long for the unattainable perfection of fit between their aims and the students' learning. It is cheerfully declared hereby that such a fit is impossible, and would be lethal if it were possible. Let us return instead to the notion that the curriculum, in all its conceptual and unsystematically varied hierarchy of learning, teaching, knowledge, praxis, skills, has stories to tell the world of its constituency, and that these, takeable in many different frames of mind, are marked onto the vital map of human interests.

I shall further say that such a map has five realms of value,[5] each realm lived according to the particular, history-bound absolutes or master-symbols of an epoch. Now it is the claim of this book that we stand at the gate of an old epoch, and as new epochs will, the land outside the gate looks like a wilderness. The evidence is all about us, quite apart from the fact that we have to hand the instruments to make the new epoch into the most literal wilderness the world can imagine. That evidence reposes in the distinctly material ways people have of choosing and living their values in terms of what practices and possessions they really hold on to; what changes they make at those points in their life where they are touched most nearly; what they want for their children; what they will give up.

Whatever people do, for good or ill, they do it within these following essential orientations and vital interests: in time, to their past, present and future; in space, to property and sexual relations; everywhere, to the knowledge of death; and all of these as known and lived through the singular lenses of the master-symbols of the day. The curriculum as the most stable meanings-bearer of a secular society must carry a sufficiently coherent organization of each realm of value, both internally and in relation to all the others. It is plain that such coherence is now largely absent, and that the whole structure is fractured down every join.

Consider how the messages and enigmas of the curriculum place a pupil in time. There is a dead rationalism which supposes that all the information of the curriculum should be entirely lucid. It is wrong. Any knowledge system must have its ratio of mystery to message, or else the unsolvable conundrums of experience are subjected to the fatal techniques of algorithmic thought. When I speak of coherence, I do not mean that a curriculum should be without its mystery, only that the mystery should be settled in life itself and not in the mystifications of what we may well call the showmen. Now to be placed by your parents and teachers in time is not, as the time-line[6] of the primary-school history project confidently proclaims, to situate yourself neatly on the moment at which an orderly past produces you, on your way to occupying an orderly and continuous future. Finding yourself a place in time depends on a large number of factors of the kind that impinge on the exceedingly chancey nature of identity as we reviewed it in chapter 4,[7] and provide that elusive essence with bits and pieces of place, nation, myth, morality and behaviours to attach itself to.

In this always provisional process, the story of the past, as I have been at such pains to emphasize, is strictly crucial. For the epoch now ending so slowly, the past has been surpassed, but mythologized behind a faintly golden haze. That is to say, the past is what we have left behind in order to attain our present freedoms and comforts, and its trajectory is understood by having led in a more or less deliberate development to a present in which the old miseries and brutalities have been eliminated. Surpassing the past, in a necessary pun, leaves us also able to honour its great heroes who made the present what it is, but whose like we shall not look upon again. This is the ambivalence of the past's meaning for us: things were bad in those days, of course, but those were also the good old days whose central figures took part in decisive and heroic battles titanically above the puny deeds of us, their successors.

This avenue upon the meaning of the past is open in many textbooks, but is most widely and handsomely visible in assorted revaluations of the past performed in the more durable of television serials. In the globally popular *When the Boat Comes In*, the poverty and bitter inter-class rancour and inequity of 1920s Tyneside were vigorously portrayed. We are well past all *that*, was the clear political message. At the same time, the simplicity of the political silhouettes – the Rolls-Royce, the blunt, dauntless, trenchant working-class Labour Party man – make it easy to feel and say that at least you knew where your loyalties were in those days, and what the enemy looked like. There is nothing like a reliable enemy and a pungent theodicy for making sense of the past and yourself.

When the past arrives at the present, it is simply converted as meaning into the opportunity for production. Chapter 8 had much to say about work as the central meaning of the so-called 'labour culture', and the individual, indeed the nation, situate themselves in the present by working. It is through working in the present that time is given structure and then allocated to the past, a process controlled, as Keynes theorized, by the handling of money, and its containment of our great expectation of life through the keen excitements of saving, accumulating and spending. The present is the space in which we produce and are paid. The future is then the time in which we will spend and consume. It means what it does as the land of future plenty, a plenty purchased out of what we produce at work now (that the exigencies of credit constantly bring the aspired-to and enviable future nearer and nearer is only one of many disintegrations in the allocation of time).

It is obvious that the curriculum carries and expresses its specific versions of these very generalized meanings. The tight connections between schooling, employment, the forms of study and the methods of assessment are both taken for granted and pretty well understood; what needs a renewed emphasis is how completely (and how partially: plenty of children and students expect not to get work or, if they do, to dislike it) individuals and classes are constituted as people doing time by their access to work. The strong ceremony of the parents' evening in primary or secondary school, or of registration at the technical college, displays in its most ingenuous and touching encounters how it is that forms of work animate and embody the hopes of the future, and the hopes *for* the future. Parents ask about their children's prospects with a strained love and anxiety going far beyond the notion of financial reward, profound in its significance as that is as a meaning-giver to the uninflected passage of time. Getting the right qualifications for admission to a good job is, then, the point of education and its curriculum, and even when this harmless ambition is unloaded of its commonplace snobberies about 'getting on' and 'doing well', it is still an authentic and powerful source of energy and resource of value. As I insist, every subject tells a story, and the best-loved story is the one that connects conscientious study to social promotion and satisfying production and service.

It is perhaps to toll a surly, sullen bell to claim, as I want to do, that the curriculum formalizes and indeed teaches, at least implicitly, an attitude to death, given that it is so important to all of us that death be itself believably transcended beyond the individual end in the good of those we love and care for. One's own death, at least in the offical tales of school told to children, which decently canonize our very best impulses and qualities, is assured of its meaning as a memorial in the future lives of our prosperous, happy, protected and well-loved children. The length of a generation would seem to be, in the global danger and local uncertainty of modern life, the sanest measure of choice and consequence. To ignore the consequences of action which put the first generation of children at risk in the name of distant future benefits is to lose hold on the only safe moral scale we have. (Such ignorance was at the heart of the dreadful and murderous Khmer regime, starting a new world in Cambodia with Year Zero). Well, the curriculum tells quietly its worthy tales about the memorializing of our parents and of the teachers who, ideally, stand beside our parents, in the bright hopes of better futures.

If there is sentimentality here, then that is a quality which is deplorably lacking in all but discussion of primary education. Stories of progress and modernization, of individual creativity and fulfilment, of co-operation and mutuality, of productivity and obligingness, are all variously told by the teachers and what they teach. However distantly, the bell tolls for all of us in each of them, in their images of praxis and poesis, of gift relationships and, in the reiterated phrase, human flourishing.

And so it is as the curriculum places its students in space, especially according to the coordinates of property and sexuality. (The closeness of the two is brought out by the convincing feminist critique that what has been wrong between men and women since capitalism got going strongly has been men's treatment of women as possessions.) Within their many dimensions, boys and girls learn the articulation of a self and a society as they perform the actions of owning and relinquishing; or as self and society shape their freedoms and their dependences. Once again, this is straightforward enough not to need much elaboration. The now substantial literature of gender-definition[8] has much to say about sexuality as shaped by the curriculum, and the definition of knowledge largely as private property is, as we saw, inscribed in the principles of work, particularly at examination time.

The matter is more subtle, of course, than a glance in the exam hall or getting girls to do metalwork will reveal. Property and sexuality are the ground of our spatial being in *any* society, not merely capitalist ones, and what we do about them entails bloody quarrels about the commitment to what men and women really live for. The owner-occupier and the romantic lover are highly specific answers to the questions, where do I live? and whom do I care for? but the questions recur in all human societies.[9]

What is, then, important is to understand how historically specific values transform universal questions into the highly specific generation of answers. For the curriculum as it is represents those answers, always mobile and contested, as they are taught at the end of the eventualities of the present. My contention is that our ending present is also an ending era, and in common with thousands of teachers at all levels I believe that many of the commonly accepted answers to the old questions are incredible falsehoods. But to authenticate this, it is necessary to sketch out the rainbow of our era, and where it ends.

To attempt this in a few paragraphs is only to align some very crude, but not vacant headings. I shall say, flatly, that bourgeois society is ending. This is also to say that the vastly powerful political economy centred on Europe since the early nineteenth century is breaking up. The economic centres of power have been moving west for several decades, but are moving again to the South Pacific. Within this huge and uneven formation, Britain, as the first capitalist and first imperialist nation, had far more in terms of wealth, privilege and power to lose when the balance of things shifted. Since the end of the European Civil War of 1914–18, that loss has been going on steadily, apparent in the erratic alternation of boom and slump, managed or abandoned by its rulers. The terms of that decline and how it shall be endured are the terms of British politics, and its curriculum is an even readier text than its newspapers in which to read how the settlements and treaties have been negotiated.

The arc of the rainbow is not smooth, however. For when the Second World War was over, and the world became divided into its two mammoth ideological alliances, the new political economy led in Britain to a ratification of personal values for which much in the century had prepared the nation. The absence of strong Communist parties with an honourable war record such as marked France and Italy, the purportedly special relationship with the USA, where individualized values had a long record going back to 1776, the strength of domestic and low-key Romanticism, all combined to give a renewed push behind the expressive values still so celebrated by our education system.

We have to call the values individualized in order to differentiate them from their contraries in a more institutional order. Perhaps it makes for lucidity to set out the values in question as though they may be merely counterposed, in order to bring out the emphasis of liberal culture in its official, curricular forms, upon the conscientious, singular, subjectively approved values, rather than those which ask for allegiance to larger structures and institutions. Indeed, we can say that British society, like all others in the West, is remarkable for the present porousness of its institutions, their loss of holding power.

INDIVIDUALIZED	INSTITUTIONALIZED
sincerity	goodness
honesty (truth to self)	truth
freedom of choice	duty
integrity	loyalty
dignity	honour
rights	right
fulfilment	asceticism
experience	endurance
independence	humility
freedom of being	obedience
passion	wisdom
morality	politics

To talk of values is not to cut off discussion about the so-called instrumental side of life, in the curriculum or in production. That is to assume the truth of the fact–value severance that it is part of the business of this book to deny. A value is merely the organizing concept which identifies a field of activity or practices as making sense and being worth while. By this token, all human activities are values-impregnated, and cannot be interpreted without them. They would simply make no sense. My assertion is that in the forty years since European and Japanese Fascism was defeated at least in its military uniforms, British society has taught itself in its classrooms and on its television screen that the good life is lived by the left-hand list of qualities, and in any conflict between the two, preference should go to the first. In other words, this is the specific structure whose ideological premises give their present actuality to our human preoccupation with past, present and future; with the space of property and face-to-face relations; with the circumambient globe itself.

And it is the globe which has begun to resist them, to turn monstrously upon them and crush their ruthless hedonism with the elemental necessities of earth, air, fire and water. For the conjunction of the values I have named with the drives of capitalism has produced what is neutrally called consumerism. This drew on the centuries-old habit on the part of men to regard the earth as an inexhaustible bank of resources, his own space for the exercise of his demands. As long as technology remained slow in its advances, the globe contained the demands. Once technology joined with the triumph of capitalism, it became clear across a century or so that the globe's tolerance of its exploitation and pullution had rapidly approaching limits.

This is an argument which has made extraordinarily rapid headway in a very few years. Of course, the spoliation of the earth has been horribly visible for a century in the filth of industrial cities, the ruinous erosion of arable land and pasture in America and Africa, in mere starvation, and the poisoning of the habitat by the chemistry of both war and peace. But it is fair to claim that only recently have suitably authoritative sources[10] pronounced on the precipitous danger of these circumstances. What is then really remarkable is that, thinking only of our smallish subject and its province, the warning has been so quickly heeded and absorbed. The growth of the happily renamed life sciences and the advent at all levels of school of subjects such as environmental sciences provide the readiest, most widely discussable example of the way the old value-system and its vigorous hedonism is breaking up. Of course growth economics are not going to come to a stop. Of course economic development is so uneven, so subject to local caprice and incompetence, that much of the Third World is in no position, short of starvation, but to go blindly for growth, at whatever penalty in terms of rates of interest and the new imperialism of aid disguised in the godless alliance of ruling elite and international corporation. Of course.[11] But it is still amazing that, all over Britain, children, students and teachers are so rapidly well informed and anxious about the ruin of resources. That they are is evidence of how the school and higher educational curricula have done their considerable bit towards discrediting the beautiful people.

For the post-1945 scheme of the virtues is crumbling fast. Work, as I have said, is less and less likely to provide a dominant meaning in people's lives, or not as tied to profitability, to mass unemployement, to making destructively useless products. The future can no longer be promised to the present by prosperous parents, and the past has many mansions, some of them morally much more admirable than the present, or the sombre-looking future. Institutional virtues a long way from either Nuremberg or the Holy City look to have their attractions.

Neither revolution nor moral regeneration impends. Things look bad rather than better, and in any case only the most febrile commentator would speak of 'new moods of realism' and other clichés. What we can say, however, is that the breaking of the old world picture makes it increasingly clear that the curriculum must treat morality and politics directly. While it is certain that, for a season, the difficulties of recovering political consensus are insurmountable, and that therefore there will be no agreement on a curriculum embodying a single picture of the good life, there is no way out of this quandary through the amiable evasions of liberal pluralism or philosophical relativism. A decent curriculum and its honest toilers will have to engage with an adequate scheme of human desire, and a fairly stern sense of physical necessity.

10

The Language of Politics in the Conversation of Classrooms

As soon as anybody mixed up in education takes the risk of speaking of the good life, a chorus of obloquy is likely to go up. For all its present manifest failures, liberalism is still the official intonation, and one extensively declaimed, of classroom and lecture hall. Even the givers of the philosophy and politics seminar, who have begun to take such a risk again recently,[1] only do so gingerly, and their professional obligations to think about the conditions and nature of virtue in the republic have been little met for a very long time.

For the loose premiss of liberalism is, of course, that nobody has any right to tell anybody else what to think, but that, since the central good of human life is individual freedom, which is exercised in the making of choices, the good life is best organized by clearing as large a space as may be cleared for the choosing activity, compatible with not infringing the choosing space of others, and validated by more or less optimistic trust in the innate goodness of people. If, however, that trust turns out to be misplaced, liberalism still upholds as a paramount good the freedom of individuals to go to the bad, as long as that is their choice.

The consequence of this in the conversation of classrooms, as in that of the civil society, has been to attenuate to the point of vaporization the ideas of the good and the true. If the good life is what you lead as a result of your free choices, then what is good for you, while not being good for me, is indisputable, can only be known by you, and cannot be taught. The compliance of such a world-view to the irresistible but inexplicit invasions of consumerism was mentioned, though untheorized, in the last chapter. For now, there is little need to go beyond pointing out how completely people have acceded to the notion of the good life purveyed by television glamourizations, in and out of advertising, because the area of human choice has been successfully allocated to the purchase of consumer commodities, from houses to holidays; in the world of domestic subjectivity, liberal individualism and the life of the limitless desires of the consumer go comfortably together. For the 75 per cent of the British adult society in employment, there is much to be said for this private, mobile life and its satisfactions: the car; the camper; the decent garden; the package holiday to the kind old sun; the modish, informal clothes, themselves forever quoting the ideal informalities of a healthily sporting life, on the ski slopes, at Le Mans, at the country club. In an incomprehensible world, private politics on the scale of your own and your children's lives are defensible (you can vote for its providers) and morally palpable. I have no wish to deny the delight and attractiveness of such pleasures, nor to limit access to them in the name of asceticism.

But the life-weaknesses are obvious. Not only will the globe stop supporting such easy-going extravagance: the petrol will run out, and the limitations of poverty will spread; but also the pleasures themselves are socially limited. Lying on sunny solitary beaches is what Fred Hirsch[2] calls 'a positional good'; however, it stops being a good if the beaches are polluted by a filthy sea and covered with too many people. Not only do these objections thrust their way into the private, mobile lives, but the way of life itself is morally repulsive in its disregard for any scheme of the duties that have to be set against such privileges, a disregard on which it is only too likely that the less privileged will want to take their vengeance.

Such maledictions over the consumers' instantaneous gratifications are familiar enough and cheaply bought for a *frisson* by the social conscience-striken segment of the meaning industry. The real costs would only be paid if anybody tried to act upon such a different view of the way the world ought to go.[3] But the cerebral displacements attendant upon taking quite so heavenly a curricular view have been criticized already. The classroom point, like the political one, is blunter. It is this.

The mobile, private consumer's view of life simply *is* the unacknowledged good life of contemporary liberalism. The hold of the consumer's heaven upon our imagination is very powerful.

The classroom and the political criticisms that have got through the private enclave of consumer mobility are the ecological critique, and the less focused, but numerically vast resistances of the peace movements and of feminism; the three taken together presently constitute in Britain a momentous and diffuse surge in popular consciousness against the dominant forms of rationality, action and purpose. These arguments, however, have to get through assimilably; that is, the criticisms are largely to be understood only in so far as the liberal frame of mind absorbs and decodes them. Thus the ecological critique impresses people as a threat to their present homes and lives, not as a statement about the interdependence of a world which in any case is moving its attention to the South Pacific. If the notion of a positional good had any acceptance, naturally enough it would intensify the competition to gain one such good, rather than induce a universal acceptance that such goods must be equitably shared and conserved. If someone can afford the last country cottage, then he or she will buy it, not leave it to the so misleadingly named National Trust.

Similarly, the best way to understand the meaning of the one unmistakably non-routine public movement of the day, the peace movement, is as the private individual's display of his or her public powerlessness and the terrible menace each sees as looming over private freedoms; to signify this, all wife, husband, lover or child can do is bear visible witness. Their sign is to be seen in their quiet helplessness. The feminist mode of opposition is also an individualist one. Their case is correctly and with justice understood by most people as for greater space for the exercise of personal freedom, and more opportunity to gain the political power which decides on how such space is portioned out.

These three overlapping pressures of public consciousness upon the received definitions of the free, fulfilled and self-aware individual living the good life according to his or her good luck each constitute a radical criticism of the way of the world, especially in its capitalist formations. But each of them is still refracted through the data and precepts of liberal individualism which, lacking as it does any sufficient theory of human interests attached to a realistic classification of desires, can do nothing much about the state of the nation beyond loose moral exhortation of a deeply unattractive sort to raise niceness to others to the level of universal principle. Each contribution, from the ecologists, the feminists, the disarmers, involves drastic and accurate criticism of things horribly wrong in British society; for good measure, I should probably add to the list the vigorous critics of the evil and deep-seated racism now boiling up in Britain, but in spite of so much busyness about multiracial education in local authorities, liberalism is hard put to it to situate the very idea of racism in its scheme of things, and has consequently failed so far to acknowledge its poisonous presence.

Indeed, the present treatment of multiracialism would serve as an example of the difficulty of coming at agreement about common desires and interests, and framing these envisageably in a form of life. Since it is a worthy premiss of liberalism that you must not tell people what to believe and how to think, but that they must be left to make up their own minds, it can only be possible to consider multiracial education in schools as an individual issue in which different social lives may be studied (for example, as different religions) and from which, it is vaguely hoped, an undifferentiated relativism may be somehow inhaled by students. (The issue doesn't arise in universities, since they are habitually blind to their own structural racism, except in the few honourable cases of single scholars,[4] who opened up the study of the origins and reality of British racism.) By relativism, as I have said, I mean the view that all world-views as between societies or even as within individuals are adjusted to fit distinctive circumstances, for judging which there is no common court of appeal, and therefore nothing to be said about different ways of life, beyond that they work satisfactorily in the circumstances.

Hidden in this perspective so far as it applies to whole societies is often an unrecognized functionalism, or (to repeat) the view that everything in a society functions to maintain that society on its own terms. Hidden in this secondary view of separate people is the doubtlessly fairminded attitude that others have their own, unknowable motives and what impels and organizes them in their world need not at all be what impels and organizes oneself. Either way, actions, beliefs and behaviours are only intelligible as relative to their own context, within which they function to hold those different from ourselves in truths-for-themselves which we may not share, but which are strong in their own validity.

It is a powerful argument often dottily applied.[5] Its strength and truthfulness are that there are indeed many different forms of life and good lives across the world, and it sounds a convincing moral precept that you should not judge what you do not understand, even less that you should interfere with it from outside. There are powerful counter-arguments to the effect that transcultural claims on common humanity give each of us authority not to condone a practice which is plainly inhuman, and the obligation to try to prevent it if we can, especially if its victims within the culture just as plainly think the practice is as horrible as we do. The dottiness comes in at the point at which people not only claim that any practice or expression or belief may be valid for the practitioner, that there is no agreement possible on any moral or political values and ends, but indeed that goodness and truth reside in their being strictly good-for-you or true-for-me. Both claims are absolutely relativized and stand on the self-contradiction that they make absolute the principle of relativism, which is that nothing is absolute.

The deep obstacle which this inevitably confused and wide-spread habit of mind set up, even among well-meaning teachers intent upon educating children decently, is that they cannot get beyond this variegated relativism, compounded with the justified fear of the totalitarianism implied by too-ready use of the word 'indoctrination', to a discussion of what a feasible human flourishing could look like in the future, and what interests and desires really are basic and what are changeable. There is a fear of agreement on moral ends which derives from the unexamined notion that individuality, resting upon the free exercise of choice, must further rest upon moral pluralism. So in curricular planning, as in classroom discussion, the right to be wrong – or, as it is more genteelly put, the right to your own opinion – is volunteered as an ideal in such a way as to expel the truth as a controlling concept. Of course, in the real life of classrooms, children are told to shut up and listen to the facts in order to reproduce them in their examinations, but I am invoking the implicit ideal of communicative rationality as shaping the form of the curriculum, the context of its learning and teaching.

It is important to get clear that I am talking about the universal models of what it is to be rational which the whole curriculum endorses, and not just about what happens in the discussion lessons of the humanities. These models are endorsed as much by the primary-school project as by the university physics laboratory. Indeed, given the enormous public prestige and visibility of physics, its account of rationality and relativism, truth and *telos*, is omnipresent and all-powerful. Physics is of course a hugely self-confident field of study: together with certain kinds of biochemical inquiry, its dominance of university study is assured and absolute: it commands the research grants, the numbers of appointments, the social elites of the academies. It is largely ignorant or contemptuous of the recent relativizing and sociologizing of its knowledge base, because its triumphs have been so incontestable.[6]

Those triumphs have depended upon a methodical separation of the facts and values of the world, which was historically grounded in the founding of empirical inquiry and philosophical science in the eighteenth century. But as has been repeatedly declared in these pages, the division of thought and experience into reason and emotion, calculation and imagination, fact and value, becomes irreversibly established as what ontology is, during the settlement of bourgeois society in Victorian Britain. Pure science instructed technology, and technology suffused the culture with the belief that science dealt with the objective world of facts, but that its strictly disinterested purpose was the enlargement of the field of knowledge for its own sake, and not the organization of its inquiry for human benefit. The benefits might accrue, certainly, but they were subsequent to the business of enlightenment.[7]

Such a method of defined rationality itself according to its own, collegiate success. Hypothesis-making, evidence collection, verification by experiment; classification, counting, formulation of laws; these became the dual process whereby reason itself sought and found knowledge. Since values are by this canon separate from facts, and since facts are objective, it follows that values can only be subjective and impossible to agree upon. Rationality and values are themselves sundered, and there can therefore be no way of resolving disputes about values rationally. Opinion is the individual's sovereign. Only if the human sciences can obey the adjurations of Carl Hempel and Ernest Nagel,[8] and make themselves formally, conceptually and methodically, members of the physical sciences, can politics become a rational subject. But they cannot.

It is well-known how extensively this position has been

attacked, both in the name of a dissolution of the fact–value distinction, as well as in fully documented claims for the status of a reflexive and critical human science well able to stand up for itself in a third realm of knowledgeability that breaks open the antinomy of subjective and objective. But the grim old picture of the factual, infallible and omnipotent science prevails. The liberal belief in the autonomous individual and the scientific faith in empiricism combine in the doctrines of moderation and balance, evidence-counting and observation. There is in such a world no form of rational praxis (only the impulses of psyche and structure) and no inquiry into the good life, unless it has what cannot be granted to it, problems and techniques.

This can only mean that questions about how to live must be placed in the rough and reach-me-down calculus of utilitarianism, which science allows as the making of the best of a bad job. Utilitarianism as a social philosophy[9] holds that, in a mass society, questions of public policy can be resolved by reducing all questions to a calculation of the outcome of political actions in terms of the material benefits it will bring to given proportions of the population. These benefits are laid along a single scale of materiality, and the numbers they affect are measured. Policy is then decided upon according to Bentham's slogan 'the greatest good of the greatest number'.

In Bentham's time it was a radical doctrine. But it is quite unable to handle incalculable but vital concerns of human being. It has no picture of human flourishing beyond the material welfare which, however important, is *not* synonymous with happiness, let alone virtue or *eudaimonia*. It is the utilitarian calculus, ratified by a bourgeois society under the lights of liberalism and scientific empiricism, which is now breaking down so vastly. In the not unimportant corner of human desires and interests marked 'the curriculum', what can be done about it? How can the state of affairs even be talked about?

The first help I offer comes from the study and the content of British television. For a start, British television provides much of the subject-matter of everyday conversation as well as being a very substantial and audible part of the whole conversation of the culture. Let us get the disclaimers out of the way first.[10] Of course there is awful rubbish on all channels; of course the family quiz and the competitions can make any remotely sensitive person shrink with embarrassment; of course tired old scented soap operas on the sexy or on the sugary side are deeply lowering in their top-rating success and stomach-turning in their popularity; of course the suppression of certain intractable political subjects like Northern Ireland and the fixing of the fight in any trade union dispute violates natural justice and demeans intelligence; of course Mrs Whitehouse is sometimes right about disgusting movies and all of us are right to recoil from the silliness and nastiness of the latest dose of the horrors. No discussion of television can start without a due declaration of one's own taste, judgement, immunity to its insidiousness, diminishing use of its programmes, preference for older, established cultural genres – book, piano, art gallery.

Once that is done, however, perhaps we can see and hear in television what it tells us of ourselves. In my earlier extension of Krishan Kumar's argument that broadcast political discussion intends to 'hold the middle ground', but that such an intention of itself pushes such programmes onto controversial terrain, I suggested that the whole ideological field of broadcasting is mapped onto the programmer's sense of that field of the culture that is permitted public legitimation and expression. The narratives of television act as integuments, holding together the many pieces of the culture, and because the medium is so fluid, swift and responsive, it can do so in many different voices. Subjects can come up in the conversation of culture and be admitted to broadcasting very quickly; once admitted, the same topic can be very variously treated – as material for drama, as issue in the public forum of the studio audience, as comedian's joke, as the vehicle for a serial, as documentary.

Much has been made of the difficulty of breaking open the frames and conventions of television. The so-called 'tyranny of the slot', which dictates length of programmes as well as time and cost of preparation, date of screening and so forth, processes dense, subtle and delicate human experience into routine and rapidly assimilable forms. The conventions work to exclude the unsettlingness of the best art, the chiasmus of aesthetics and morality present in, say, a great novel, but smoothed and plasticized by the modes of camerawork and the manners of actors and actresses. None the less, its relative openness, the very operation of its modes of production, which make it an entirely unpredictable agent of both liberation and control,[11] its amazing quickness of ear and eye and responses, its obsessive self-discussion, the sheer bulk of its provision, all make television a powerful curriculum builder in the society, both senior and junior to education.

Both institutions organize a medium of public communication. Television obviously has a great deal more glamour (always a tricky concept) especially among schoolchildren, but education has more direct power. Both command between 5 and 6 per cent of the gross national product. Television's fleetness in devising new agenda is vitiated by its transience; it is driven always to seek the new. Education's comparative dullness and stolidity is compensated for by its stability, the settled nature of its knowledge and its discursive practices. But each sets the curriculum of the other, and neither may be understood without the other.

Such understanding needs to go deeper than a list of contents, though this would be a start. Trying, for instance, to match the forms of television science to the science of schools and universities would not win the battle for either, but would bring out their sturdy reciprocity. Science comes in many forms: lecture courses like Jonathan Miller's *The Body in Question* or Bronowski's famous *Ascent of Man*; magazine programmes like David Bellamy's or James Burke's; regular documentaries like the incomparable rivals, *World About Us* and *Disappearing World*; lastly, but perhaps best, dramatizations of famous careers in the history of science, like the magnificent *Voyage of Charles Darwin*, which brought to exact and vivid life the patience as well as the reach of Darwin's genius, and both the historical context and physical endurance of his adventures in Christian heresy, world geography and sea-going actuality. These are essays in a humanist science, and no one could doubt not only that they are deeply edifying but also that they arise from the official curriculum of our education system. They are mapped onto the culture in a way that endorses it, certainly, but also makes possible criticism of a science taught and philosophized as though it all took place in Karl Popper's laboratory,[12] and not in the battle to work out answers to questions which declared themselves in the case of Darwin and in that single mind as a deep life-question which could not be put in any propositional form.

A history of television history would similarly include admiring reference to the 26-parter on ITV *The World at War*, a vast revision of the Anglocentric view of the Second World War, which drew on remarkable finds amongst abandoned newsreel footage left in their cans by all the combatants. A parallel inquiry might turn to the hardly less drastic revision done on the British Raj by the dramatization of Paul Scott's quartet about the British withdrawal from India, *The Jewel in the Crown*. The two examples serve to do no more than indicate how important to the understanding of national identity such an enterprise would be.

But the tropes and tones of television are no more varied than those of classrooms, only more ephemeral in content and less stolid in manners. What is more important is the implied conversation of television culture, and what its ideal speech-situation, or in other words, its implied model of the best, most sympathetic, respectful, disinterested and egalitarian exchange of human knowledge, wisdom and counsel would look and sound like. The phrase 'ideal speech-situation' is generally credited to Jurgen Habermas, and he set out its conditions in my paraphrase as follows:[13] first, that truth or validity are the object of all discussion; secondly, that no force is exercised, other than the force of the better argument; thirdly, that we seek to exclude all motives except the motive to discover the best argument for what may be called valid (and true).

It is this picture of the conversation of culture which needs to be held over against the vapidly judgementless holding of the ring of argument, in which the professional broadcaster (or the teacher) merely acts as broker-umpire at the assertion of contrary points of view by opposing parties. This is the balancing act which expels truth and merely draws conclusions that sufficiently mediate different views in a passable compromise. All that is sought for in such negotiations is agreement, a sufficient correspondence of interests. This is the management of consensus.

There is quite enough of this kind of thing in schools, as on television. It represents the worst kind of threat to truth and therefore to virtue, but also to the rationality that must have truth as its first principle of mind (as justice, for Plato, is the first principle of the republic). And the broker's balancing in turn threatens the idea of democracy and our political obligation towards it,[14] because, in the event of irreconcilable disagreement, there is no court of appeal (all opinions being equally valid), and it follows that someone must be autocratic, probably with the help of policemen.

On the other hand, even if it looks an ingenuous thing to say, the ideal speech-situation is, ideally, invoked by all good lessons and seminars, and is broadcast widely by the whole montage of both television and the curriculum. Each, that is, lives in the reciprocities and exchange, the dialectical juxtapositions of form and content, their inevitable reflexivity in the play of subjects over subjects, which together make up the texture of their narratives. The whole curriculum, like the whole programme system of television, may be taken to contain as immanence the ideal speech-situation, which is to say, a conversation whose politeness embodies the best political language of the day. A conversation, however, is not just itself; it is *about* something. Ideally, again, it is about the good life. The best parts of television and the curriculum have this subject-matter in common, and, with Aristotle in mind, we could say that the good life is not something you plan (nor conceivably could plan), but what the good man lives, only known fully for itself when it is over.

If I am right, it is possible to learn a rational and admirable mode of thought from the intercalation of these official and unofficial curricula, and while learning it, so join a conversation about how to live which may be accurately called political. The obstacles are frightful, of course, both in terms of the ordinary noise coming from Vanity Fair, which drowns that conversation, and from the deadly but astute enemies of the people, who have accepted that the end of the twentieth century is a very dangerous place, but who are prepared at whatever risk to bend those dangers to their own advantage.[15] But so far, the small voices of the conversation of culture in the best classrooms, seminar rooms and television studios remain just about audible.

The unpredictable play of liberation and control in these places is in part structural, in part intentional. I have vigorously named the defects, hypocrisies and contradictions of liberal society, but its continuing strength is, as Bernard Williams puts it that:

> to someone who recognizes the ultimate plurality of values
> ... *there are such values* ... Put in that blank way, [such a
> truth] can be taken to speak for an objective order of values
> which some forms of consciousness (notably the liberal form)
> are better than others at recognizing. But that way of putting
> it is very blank indeed. It is more illuminating in itself, to say

that one who properly recognizes the plurality of values is one who understands the deep and creative role that these various values can play in human life. In that perspective, the correctness of the liberal consciousness is better expressed, not so much in terms of truth – that it recognizes the values which indeed there are – but in terms of truthfulness. It is prepared to try to build a life round the recognition that these different values do each have a real and intelligible human significance, and are not just errors, misdirections or poor expressions of human nature. To try to build life in any other way would now be an evasion, of something which by now we understand to be true. What we understand is a truth about human nature as it has been revealed – revealed in the only way in which it could be revealed, historically. The truthfulness that is required is a truthfulness to that historical experience of human nature.[16]

Now the curriculum is *intended* by its many authors to express these truths in its forms and narratives. But its structural strength upholds the same freedoms.[17] That structure of its nature generates reflexivity; the states of knowledge and ways of knowing are not yet separated from one another, although the accelerating drives of the divisions of labour in our society tend more and more to make them so. Each realm of meaning, in Phenix's useful phrase, can play upon the other in ways capable of altering them or of producing new theories.

I mean this on behalf of all those joining the political conversation. This is not abstract talk about high theory in the upper air. The essential form of all learning (all learning about life, that is) is a narrative. All narratives might have ended differently. The human mind in virtue of possessing an imagination can experiment with different endings. A schoolteacher working against the grain of a syllabus out of natural bloody-mindedness, a small child busying away with her own bit of botany, or one of the lads wrecking a lesson by his murmured insolence are all providing themselves with a different narrative, a momentary living of a theory about how the world might be made to go in a different direction.

Not much to build on there, except that absolute indoctrination is impossible without the aid of drugs and torture. But people are all too apt to heed the worst voices, and however much the different narratives of the curriculum ensure a continuing critic-ality, criticism in itself is only the exercise of freedom, it is not freedom directed to any purpose. Since I am much preoccupied both with understanding how the entire curriculum works *and* with directing it to better ends, it will be useful to identify some of the voices which speak among its many messages, and consider how they may be received in such a way as to become effective.

For any message to be understood, there must be some kind of fit or common focus between the two frames of mind in communication. A successful lesson is presumably one in which the fit is more or less complete; where the teacher's frame of feeling and structure of intention coincides with the feelings and motives of his or her audience as praxis. 'Encoding' and 'decoding' are mutually transparent. Each process may be thought of as built upon common structures and meeting in medium and message, as in figure 10.1, in a model of the mass communication transaction.

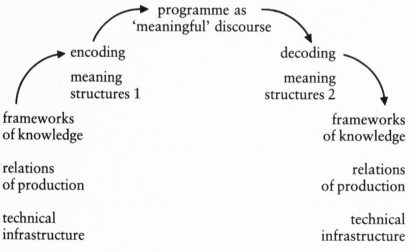

Figure 10.1   A model of the mass communication transaction

Perhaps this language is unnecessarily abstract.[18] The technical infrastructure of the classroom or seminar room is first given by its immediate technology – tables, display cases, blackboards, VTR, and so on – but beyond that, by the technical production of the institution's own life through books, the reproduction of paper, telephone calls, typing, all the apparatus through which work is done and by which it is actualized. (In the case of a television programme, this infrastructure is easier to see: it includes the cameras, the recorders, the radio and recording apparatus.) By relations of production is meant most of what I have already written about work and its meanings: the hierarchies of pacing, sequence, collaboration and study in the transmission of education. With embodied meanings, we come of course to the central preoccupation of this book, a term which I have used more or less synonymously with value, taking both words to be the concepts which identify a field of activities as visible and valuable, and not therefore intelligibly subsequent to technical modes and relations of production as Marxists would have it, since they must be logically prior for there to be some such activity in the first place.[19] And although we have learned that concepts are the interweaving of their usages, and that therefore the practice of an economic mode alters the meaning we attribute to it, all that follows from these minor reflections is that embodied meanings are inscribed in every stage of encoding and decoding (or meaning something and understanding it), and that whatever meanings and values there are, they can only be *for* somebody and *in* a context.[20]

I want to propose that there are three such fields of meaning which may be heard among the many voices on the different wavelengths of the curriculum and of television, and that all three are ideally understandable to any member of British society of whatever sex or racial origin or social class, even though it must naturally be true that each will be differently spoken or heard, according to the presence of whichever sex, race or class. The three are: usefulness, humanism, criticality.

Each of these insulates the field of meaning within education as opposed to production. Now it has been a main premiss of this book as it is a truism about society, that education is distinct from production. Indeed it is a main point of educational discourse that it keep its account of its subject-matter in an ideal state. It is a condition of science itself that, in the search for simplifying and ordering the impossibly recalcitrant facts of life, it must constantly remove itself from the immediacy of those facts in order to devise the most concise description capable of formulating (*sic*) the facts. By the word 'science' here, as elsewhere in these pages, I intend what the philosopher of the eighteenth century intended, the space and standing of all knowledge and the knowable.

In one of the most famous and purest examples of idealization in this sense – that is, making the material into idea – the equation $E=mc^2$ represents the equivalence of energy to mass, when mass is annihilated at the speed of light in empty space. From the equation, itself derived by Einstein from his own theory of relativity, glowed the hideous detonations brighter than a thousand suns, as well as the so far contained and smouldering peacefulness of the world's nuclear reactor stations. No one, however, could think of the equation as *close* to the seething invisibilites of the electronic interbombardment which is both mass and energy. Its success as theory is a necessary (though not sufficient) consequence of its economy and beauty, both of them in turn consequences of their intensely idealized formulation. Originally hypothetic, the metaphors of this symbol were none the less capable of application to reality. Like any true narrative, they passed from hypothesis to theory through the frame of experiment.

On the argument of this book, these are the motions and emotions of all cognitive effort and effect. It is also my argument that they characterize all stages of thought, and their assorted logical forms. Indeed, rather than arrange these spatially, as educationists in ivory towers as well as ministries have latterly told us to do,[21] let us go back to adapt and paraphrase R.G.Collingwood in one of his earlier books (1924) *Speculum Mentis, or The Map of Knowledge*. There he sets out what is at once a hierarchy and a chronology of the forms of knowledge. According to this chronology, all societies begin the metamorphosis of experience into knowledge through art. Art is the first means human beings devised for idealizing (in the strict or philosophic sense) the facts and events of life, in order to make them stand still long enough to be tested and used as instruments for the interpretation and control of that life.

In his argument, Collingwood writes of the whole scale of civilized development in terms of each stage of thought, and the conceptualization followed by the control of the world which each made possible. He further insists that each stage is superimposed upon its predecessor, so that the initial form of thought, art, is not only the necessary beginning, but remains as foundation and immanence in all subsequent thinking and in the knowledge which is secured.

The moral of this is both social and personal, and it is brought out in the most practical way by the everyday life of primary schools. Whatever else may be goofy or wrongheaded in the usual primary curriculum, its teachers have got hold of Collingwood's point, that thought starts with art, and that without the arts of story and symbol, rhythm and form, the children can hardly learn to think at all. The practical emphasis of most primary classrooms on painting and modelling, music-making and music-listening, story-telling by teacher and children, in books or drama or movement, carries the marks of grace, even when these activities are as dire as they can be to all but the parents. Hence the whole emphasis of this book on our telling stories of so many kinds (every picture tells a story), on, that is to say, framing things in a narrative.

It is, however, the awful mistake of liberalism, as I have argued, to suppose that any story is as likely to be true as any other, indeed to attenuate truth itself, as I have argued, either to what happens to be agreeable to think ('true for me') or to any comfortable-looking midpoint between the extremes of opinion. But art combines as naturally as may be the love of beauty with the search for truth, as Aristotle impressed on us against his master Plato's judicious banishment of the poets from the republic.[22] Even that same art of the primary school, in writing, music or modelled forms, seeks not only to tell a tale, but to tell the truth. By the same token, the humanities discussion class for the school-leavers and the philosophy seminar on abortion at the university have in common and immanent in their practice a model of the ideal speech-situation which I have already invoked and Habermas has codified.

In a high-handed passage of his splendid novel, *The French Lieutenant's Woman*,[23] John Fowles makes the doctor Grogan, who in his crusty, vigorous, slightly provincial and bibulous way stands for the brotherhood of scientific inquiry, tell these (as we say) home truths to the hero, Charles Smithson, himself a slightly dilettante, but honestly intellectual Darwinian:

'You believe yourself to belong to a rational and scientific elect. No, no, I know what you would say, you are not so

vain. So be it. None the less, you *wish* to belong to that elect.
I do not blame you for that. But I beg you to remember one
thing, Smithson. All through human history the elect have
made their cases for election. But Time allows only one plea.'
The doctor replaced his glasses and turned on Charles. 'It is
this. That the elect, whatever the particular grounds they
advance for their cause, have introduced a finer and fairer
morality into this dark world. If they fail that test, then they
become no more than despots, sultans, mere seekers after
their own pleasure and power. In short, mere victims of their
own baser desires. I think you understand what I am driving
at – and its especial relevance to yourself from this unhappy
day on. If you become a better and a more generous human
being, you may be forgiven. But if you become more selfish
... you are doubly damned.'

In the teeth of the facts about cynicism, callousness, incompetence
and indifference towards the best meanings of the country's
education, it is still both possible and necessary to affirm that the
structures of both making and thinking in our education, however
distorted and debased their practice may sometimes be, entail that
the space and conditions in which the truth may be found, beauty
made, and goodness defined, are always kept open. And in its
much more fluid, electronic and ephemeral way, the same is true
for television, becase British television takes both form and
content, structure and essence, not (as in the USA) from the
dominant power of capital, nor (as in the USSR) from the power of
the state, but from education, as both institution and discourse.
    Education maintains, by means of its curriculum and in spite of
education, the twin discourses of truth and freedom. Such are, in
liberal or any other kind of society, both its function and meaning.
I prefer to put things this way, rather than to praise mere
rationality, because the terms truth and freedom, understanding of
which is a precondition as well as the structuration of rationality,
alert us to those great names as the necessary virtues of education
as well as of educated men and women. Against old-fashioned
liberalism and (indeed) on intelligent behalf of the human future, I
would want to claim, as before, for freedom the standing not
merely of the condition of individual action[24] (freedom *from*
wanton constraint, freedom *to* act as one chooses in self-

definition). Rather, let us say that to live, in thought and action, as a free man or woman, is to live one of the virtues.[25] By the same token, for living freely to be virtuous, it follows that the agent, whether an individual or an institution, must stand uncompromisingly on the side of truth. Indeed, the free man is, by definition, truthful. It is hardly surprising that a book such as this on the curriculum moves towards the conclusion that all children and students should be taught to be good and to tell the truth.

The pious resonance of this excellently Victorian admonition rings no bells for any particular secretary of state, however. Teaching virtue and truthfulness is always likely to make things uncomfortable for the system of structural lying built into the political negotiation which defines the intersubjectivity of the culture. Indeed, a main characteristic of many official statements issued by Elizabeth House is that they seek the complicity of the education system, especially by means of the curriculum, in the official and constitutive discourse of state lies and propaganda.

Resistance, I have claimed, is inscribed in the structure of pedagogic discourse itself, and the justification for this mouth-filling phrase is that it signals the formal separation of *all* educational conversation from the business of production.[26] Production being what it is under the pressures of locally failing capitalism, that separation creates the margin of a few degrees of freedom, and the structural space whose presence ensures the impossibility of indoctrination (which is the pedagogy of the infallible deduction). Of course there are circumstances – writing this book is one example, putting on the school play or concert is another – in which pedagogy is forced into production, and schooling becomes creative work. When this happens, as anyone who has been a teacher knows, the dangers increase with the exhilaration. What is being made is new; it is not the recontextualizing of the already known. It is therefore an instrument of praxis.

The distinction needs developing. Pedagogic discourse (teachers talking teaching) in order to be capable of critical analysis has to become, as I have argued, 'idealized', which is to say turned into usable, testable, formulable metaphor. It has to be kept as clear from experience (the materials of real life) as possible, compatible with that experience remaining in its reach. It occupies the realm of the imagination. But in that realm, critical analysis is only enabled if critical thought comes up with what the philosophers call counterfactual conditionals, which is to say, that we play the game of 'just suppose . . . ' and imagine feasible alternatives that could as well be the case as what is. To move into the imaginary is to create new worlds: the acts of criticism and creation stand in an essential relation to one another, forever spiralling from one to the other in the essential motion of thought. To imagine freely is a partial definition of the practice of education (as opposed to schooling). At the same time, free imagining becomes merely fantastic and enervated, unless it maintains energizing contact with the real.

When this contact fails, we lose ourselves in daydreaming, the private novels of the powerless whose imaginative life is their consolation for their incapacity to direct anything in the real world to their purposes. Such fictions, widespread in the controlled helplessness of so much modern life, are theories of a kind with no empirical content. Their standing as truth (and not many people believe that they *are* true, of course, not even their eponym, Walter Mitty) is perfectly unaffected by facts and events. In so far as narratives or educational discourses are all imagination, they are ineffectual. They mirror the real, but they cannot affect it. This is what it is like to be stuck in an ivory tower.

A theory of practice [27] is what it purports to be: a discourse which re-situates the real in the contexts of the imagination, and in so returning the facts of life to the field of possibilities from which they came, makes those facts resume their shadowiness so that they may be seen again as given the force of actuality only by chance and contingency. The interplay of criticism and creation is, then, the theory of practice and the disturbance of what Bourdieu calls the habitus, which is to say, the system of durable, transposable dispositions which works as the generative basis of structured, objectively unified practices.

Such and such, as Kipling endearingly observed of the Python, is the way sociologists always talk, but the frightful and aridly necessary abstraction of their speech is also an example of what I am discussing. Only when we can imagine a habitus, will we understand how dispositions are made systematic by the order of schooling, and become the basis of how people really live. All too readily, that is to say, most children learn terribly well to do as they are told, and most students are dismally adept at keeping the imaginary well away from the real, at accepting that criticism has no purchase on creation, and that both discourse and habitus are changeless forms for the reproduction of that timeless entity, bourgeois society. Since a sizeable proportion of those students who spend longest learning the pedagogic discourse become pedagogues in their turn, it is hardly surprising that what teaching does to teachers, as David Hargreaves unforgettably wrote,[28] is to make them boring, exhausted and hate the job. More subtly, I may repeat an observation earlier implied, that because teaching has been a safe and steady avenue of social promotion throughout this century, and rewards in education largely go to those who politely repeat after the teacher what the teacher has said, the fractions of the working class and the *petit-bourgeoisie* (especially their daughters) who are the teaching force are heavily weighed down by the durable dispositions they have acquired towards docility and intelligent conformism. So many in the staffroom lack either solidarity or critical resistance (bloody-minded teachers rarely become headmistresses, do they?), and show a deeply ingrained preference for petty private rivalries allied to a killingly small-minded individualism.

Not much light or space in such a habitus. Against its narrow constriction may again be set the structural advances made possible in the discourse of education by extensions in knowledge and by the changed place of these in both the politics and hermeneutics of inquiry. As I have so much protested, the moves against the deadly dogmatism of the hunters and gatherers of numbers, against ludicrously oversimple models of human behaviour, and against the lethal reductions of utilitarianism have gone a long way. The criticism and creation of learning in its long historical progress themselves give the discourse of education its power of liberation. The shock waves of these against the solid walls of the late capitalist habitus is one engagement in the civil war whose battlefield I began by describing.

I listed rather cryptically three linguistic weapons with which teachers and pupils in different parts of their being might arm themselves on behalf of human freedom. There were: usefulness, humanism, criticality. I spoke then of these, in a clumsy metaphor, as being voices broadcasting on the wavelengths of culture, continuously available to any audience which could tune in. Each carries its own version of both truth and goodness; each, in other words, is necessarily teleological; it has human ends and improvements, the betterment of the world and the perfectibility of man in view.[29]

At this concluding stage of my argument I want to bring my three weapons – sword, chalice and golden orb – into specific relation with *telos*, a view on our human future. Schooling is a small and a large enough subject to spend a lifetime on, and the curriculum – what we learn and what there is to learn – is the official point of going to school, college or university. Now it is clear that the curriculum, which is the heart of education, increasingly fails as a means for binding our children to life. Its structure of values cannot do this, because the view of life those values frame is no longer believable. To put the same point another way, the theory of life implied by so much of our curriculum does not fit the form of how we actually live. Hence managerialism and therapeutic counselling are dreamed up in order to persuade us that lies are truth; the process of persuasion has naturally to begin with those who will teach us how to be managed.

The best of our teachers, and of our students too, know that our curriculum cannot 'bind them to life'. What they can then do is tune themselves to what is useful, what seems likely to serve a human future (humanism) and what enables critical resistance (which is at the same time the creative imagining of alternatives). This selection among the wavelengths goes on as teachers and students alike pick out the usefulness of, say, these novels as opposed to those, or given the chance, of learning Russian instead of Spanish. Usefulness in this sense is not the same as practicality; it is as useful to be able to mend an old car as it is to be taught *Timon of Athens* instead of *The Winter's Tale*. Both may be made different use of, in the present moment of history. Either takes the strain of that history better than some of the alternatives. So, too, with a humanism which no longer looks much like Matthew Arnold's, but is still not an empty concept, whatever the French *maîtres à penser* say. A workaday humanism leads an honest biology teacher to insist on life in the life sciences, and to spend much time on industrial pollution, nuclear waste and the exhaustion of resourses; a similar humanism encourages a home economics which can propose the usurpation of take-away pancake rolls, sodden beefburgers and the eternal sugary confectionery by decent bread, fresh fruit and the democratic cuisine of the good supermarket – let alone launch an inquiry which had much to say of factory farming, Franju's terrifying movie *Le Sang Des Bêtes*, and the effects of cereal-to-meat ratios on world starvation. A mildly theoretic criticality, of a sort sometimes more evident in the exigencies of a comprehensive-school fifth year than a university seminar in fine art or psychology, makes immediate play with the discrepancy between History and my life-in-earnest, which will eventually be part of a future historian's History of Britain. There is no necessary salvation in criticality; it may be blindly philistine or mostly self-referring. But there will be no future without criticality.

These are forms of the discourse through which the curriculum, and therefore a different future than that envisioned by our present masters, may be fought for. If I also say, as I do, that these small weapons may best be wielded for something that may be described as a socialist view of that future, I hammer no Stalinist anvil, nor fantasize none of the more barmy dreams of anarchism or syndicalism as sung by the initialled sectarians of motley revolutionary groups. It is clear, furthermore, that although Marx was the greatest analyst of capitalism there has been, Marxism as a theory of social advance no longer will grip upon the facts of our society. As that society in its classical bourgeois form breaks up – that is to say, as bourgeois class formations, the stark relations of *rentier* capital to propertyless labour, the long lines of Old Empire, as all these disintegrate and world economic power moves vastly both in form and geography – so Marxism, as a total account of old capitalism devised from within that capitalism in order first to oppose and then to destroy it, disintegrates into its earlier compositions, that mixture of socialist allsorts made up of Owenites, Saint-Simonians, Blanquistes, Left-Hegelians, Chartists and so forth. Lacking any coherent theory, each affiliation then gave its allegiance to some domain of human desires and needs crying for recognition as the social order of mass and free-market industrial capitalism became established. Thinking of those programmes, variously compounded of profit-sharing co-operatives, pantisocratic communes, welfare militants, anarchists, libertarians, and suffrage reformists, we may only see any socialist interest on the part of present-day teachers and curriculum developers as finding rational expression in a combination of altruism with mutuality, of peacefulness with a sufficient independence.

Put like that, a manifesto for the human future would ring with resonant platitudes. I am claiming that, in the present vertiginous uncertainty of the world, its runaway debtors and acceleratingly out-of-control imbalances of payments, its raging and horrible wars, its similarly headlong starvation, the small barony of Britain, certainly becoming modestly but unequally poorer, cannot afford the luxuries of predestinarian Marxism. Thinking about socialism,[30] with no more than a national curriculum in view, commits the teacher-sympathizer to repudiate, especially after the longed-for and terrible upheavals of impossible revolution, the simplified paradises of Marxism. But given the same teacher's clear duty to imagine the good life and to fight against the so simply horrible manifestations of late capitalism both home and abroad, what is to be done, which will be feasible, honourable and effective?

> In the last days, perilous times shall come, for men shall be lovers of their own selves, covetous, boasters, proud, blasphemous, disobedient to parents, unthankful, unholy, without natural affection, truce-breakers, false accusers, incontinent, fierce, despisers of those that are good.[31]

It is only sensible and not at all melodramatic to think that the last days of the world may be at hand, without some huge effort of both will and compassion, the two great elements of humanism, to stop making the weapons of ultimate destruction. But other, less globally final days impend, so long as one looks no further than Britain's minor, but not temporary impoverishment and steep decline in power, and the dissolution of bourgeois imperialist society which has caused it. In these circumstances, the steady-nerved teacher-socialist will take what he or she can from the motley of pre-1848 socialism, and use it to make human and liveable the small space of European Britain and its post-Keynesian systems of production and education. He, that is, will take the stories of the subjects and retell them, in order to give much more room to the meanings of altruism and peacefulness, of independence and mutuality than is usually allocated in present-day environmental science, peace education, physics or machine maintenance.[32] She will take the art of the curriculum and give its symbols and images much freer, bolder and more homely play than is dreamed of among the egg-boxes and tambourines of the present.

It is important to make clear that such a vein of thought and feeling runs deep in radical culture. I am not trying to make something out of nothing. Nor am I trying to do down the great pleasures of private life, the deep satisfactions of consumer living, nor the delights of a well-upholstered leisure life. I am insisting that these may only be enjoyed as part of a worthy, just and generous life, and that it is the function, meaning and duty of being a teacher to think about how this may be done, and how such lives may be made out of the materials of classroom and street. It is not easy to see how to be a teacher without engaging with the strenuously contested, but essential notion of a common good.[33] That good lives in the just, tender-hearted, merciful and generous dealings we may make with our resources – our wealth and our attributes certainly – but also in our membership one of another. In a secular time, it is likely that only some severe, forgiving, dedicated and highly sceptical version of a new socialism will have the language to imagine and the power to manage such a brave, small world. These are indeed the politics of knowledge, and it is still possible to hope that their products will be precious and repeatable versions of human flourishing.

Notes

CHAPTER 1   THE STATE OF THE NATION

1 The argument I borrow is Alasdair MacIntyre's, in *Secularization and Moral Change* (Oxford University Press, 1967).

2 Raymond Williams, *Drama in a Dramatised Society* (Cambridge University Press, 1975), p.15.

3 Most notably, J.H. Elliott, in *The Revolt of the Catalans: A Study in the Decline of Spain*, (Cambridge University Press, 1963.

4 The documentation of my examples is to be found in Eric Hobsbawm and Terence Ranger (eds), *The Invention of Tradition* (Cambridge University Press, 1983).

5 See, of course, E.P. Thompson, *The Making of the English Working Class* (Gollancz, 1963).

6 Much in this analysis follows Jurgen Habermas, in his *Legitimation Crisis* (Heinemann Educational Books, 1975).

7 Clifford Geertz, *The Interpretation of Cultures* (Hutchinson, 1975), p.448.

8 The title is Dan Jacobson's in his methodologically (as well as textually) absorbing study of the Old Testament, *The Story of the Stories* (Secker & Warburg, 1982).

9 Karl Marx, *Selected Writings*, edited by D. McLellan (Oxford University Press, 1977), the *'Grundrisse'*, p.357.

10 In, classically, *Economy and Society*. Weber, famously, is the first and bleakest prophet of the triumph of managerialism, to which we shall return. See especially his essay 'Politics as a Vocation', in *From Max Weber*, edited by H.H. Gerth and C.W. Mills (Routledge & Kegan Paul, 1948).

11 The metaphor was first used by Pierre Bourdieu, in, variously, *Outline of a Theory of Practice* (Cambridge University Press, 1978) and, with J.-G. Passeron, *Reproduction in Education, Society and Culture* (Sage Books, 1977).

12 The difficulties of handling poisoned ideas are stirringly listed by John Dunn, in *Western Political Theory in the Face of the Future* (Cambridge University Press, 1979).

13 The title of a now celebrated conference of apostates. See subse-

quently Stuart Hampshire and Leszek Kolakowski (eds), *The Socialist idea* (Weidenfeld & Nicolson, 1974).

14 The phrase is R. G. Collingwood's, in *An Autobiography* (Clarendon Press, 1939). Collingwood believed that history was that science; I have tried to build on his views in my *Radical Earnestness: English Social Theory 1880–1980* (Martin Robertson, 1982).

15 I owe much of this summary of Hegel to Charles Taylor's *Hegel and Modern Society* (Cambridge University Press, 1981), and, in the brief reference to critical theory which follows, to Raymond Geuss, *The Idea of a Critical Theory: Habermas and the Frankfurt School* (Cambridge University Press, 1981).

16 See William Morris, *Political Writings*, edited by A. L. Morton (Lawrence & Wishart, 1973); see also my treatment of Morris, in *Radical Earnestness*.

17 This premiss is quoted from Geuss, *Idea of a Critical Theory*, p.2.

18 Following Charles Taylor, once more, in his 'Interpretation and the sciences of man', now extensively reprinted, first appearing in the *Journal of Metaphysics* (January 1971).

19 For atrocious memories of which, see S. Humphries, *Hooligans or Rebels?* (Basil Blackwell, 1981).

20 As represented famously in Brian Jackson and Dennis Marsden, *Education and the Working Class* (Routledge & Kegan Paul, 1962).

CHAPTER 2   GRAMMAR AND NARRATIVE

1 See Tom Nairn, *The Break-up of Britain* (New Left Books, 1978).

2 Much documented in S. Hall and T. Jefferson (eds), *Resistance Through Ritual* (Hutchinson, 1976).

3 The view that modernization is the inevitable motion of all societies has been vigorously set back in Iran: Khomeini has more or less single-handedly rebutted Max Weber.

4 The classic analysis of these two traditions of inquiry into metaphor, while favouring the transparency side, is Max Black's in *Models and Metaphor*, (Cornell University Press, 1962). For the cloudy, or hermeneutic view, see Paul Ricoeur, *The Rule of Metaphor* (Routledge & Kegan Paul, 1979). A widespread examination of metaphor in all forms of science, human and natural, is provided in the anthology edited by Andrew Ortony, *Metaphor and Thought* (Cambridge University Press, 1979).

5 See R.R. Bolgar, *The Classical Heritage and its Beneficiaries*, (Cambrige University Press, 1954). The structuralists, especially in France, have returned the study of rhetoric to the centre of the human science by their emphasis on language rather than man as the subject of study.

6 Thus, F. R. Leavis of Dickens's *Hard Times* in *The Great Tradition* (Chatto & Windus, 1948).

7 A notion which T. S. Kuhn makes almost synonymous with narrative. See his *The Structure of Scientific Revolutions* (Chicago University Press, 1962).

8 It is done for us by Stefan Körner, in *Categorial Frameworks* (Basil Blackwell, 1970).

9 The conditions for realizing ideal language are sketched in Jurgen Habermas, *Legitimation Crisis* (Heinemann Educational Books, 1975).

10 I take the substitution of 'edification' for 'education' from Richard Rorty, *Philosophy and the Mirror of Nature* (Basil Blackwell, 1981), and am grateful to him for the chance to escape the more dire impress of education with a capital E, as well as the case for an iron epistemological philosophy.

11 By Pierre Bourdieu, as noted in *Outline of a Theory of Practice* (Cambridge University Press, 1978) and elsewhere.

12 Innocent proponents of this view, who have none the less influenced formal thinking (for want of a better word) about knowledge and education, are best represented by Paul Hirst, most accessibly in *Knowledge and the Curriculum* (Routledge and Kegan Paul, 1975).

13 Coming in that order, in the history of all subjects. The process is entertainingly described by Frank Musgrove in *Patterns of Power and Authority in English Education* (Routledge and Kegan Paul, 1969).

14 Karl Mannheim first drew attention to competition in ideology in his example, generationally, in *Essays in the Sociology of Knowledge* (Routledge & Kegan Paul, 1952).

15 Here and afterwards used in T. J. Arthur's edition (Lawrence and Wishart, 1970). It is relevant to remember that *The German Ideology* was written with Engels during 1846–7, and never published during the two men's lifetimes. It is not therefore a systematic work, and certainly not the procedural handbook some later Marxists have used it as.

16 Perry Anderson 'Components of the national culture', *New Left Review* vol. 50 (1968), reprinted in *Student Power*, edited by A. Cockburn and R. Blackburn (Penguin, 1969).

17 Most popularly in the anthology edited by M. F. D. Young, *Knowledge and Control* (Routledge & Kegan Paul, 1972). The criticism in the same terms of primary-school pedagogy was made by Rachel Sharp and Anthony Green, *Education and Social Control* (Routledge & Kegan Paul, 1975). The best of a now substantial reading list is Michael Apple, *Ideology and Curriculum* (Routledge & Kegan Paul, 1979). See also his *Education and Power* (Routledge & Kegan Paul, 1981).

18 Notoriously, the poorest white families have the highest proportion of single parents. See Peter Townsend, *Poverty in the United Kingdom* (Penguin, 1979), especially chapter 7.

19 *German Ideology*, p.64.

20 I have no wish to make Paul Hirst the villain of liberalism. But he conveniently expresses the classically liberal view of education as the successful deployment of a freely choosing rationality in the domains of knowledge, a view which prefigures the ideal speech-situation of most classrooms.

21 This is the classic theory of semantic difference proposed by Fernard Saussure, in his *Course in General Linguistics*, edited by Charles Bally and Albert Sechehaye (McGraw-Hill/Collins, 1974), part I, chapter 4.

22 The whole summary of historical partiality in these paragraphs is a sort of nursery Hegelianism. It derives from Charles Taylor's tips in his *Hegel and Modern Society* (Cambridge University Press, 1979) or, for those who want the original, J.W.F. Hegel, *The Philosophy of History*.

23 See Clifford Geertz, *The Interpretation of Cultures* (Hutchinson 1975), especially 'Ideology as cultural system'. See also my *Ideology and the Imagination* (Cambridge University Press, 1975).

24 John Fowles's wholly admirable and classic *The French Lieutenant's Woman* (Jonathan Cape, 1969) boldy makes the Darwinists, and by implication, the feminists, torch-bearers of the new science.

25 Just how differently science has been done in the East is brought out by Joseph Needham in the greatest work of scientific history ever written, *Science and Civilization in China*. My own glimpse of this giant work was gained from the anthologized version, edited by Needham with Colin Ronan (Cambridge University Press, 1978).

26 M.B.V. Roberts, *Biology: a Functional Approach* (Nelson, 1971).

27 James Watson, *The Double Helix* (Weidenfeld & Nicolson, 1967).

28 Thomas Kuhn, *The Structure of Scientific Revolutions*.

29 see Habermas, *Legitimation Crisis*, pp.102–10.

30 The best such parody is Ernest Gellner's of the linguistic philosopher, in *Words and Things* (Penguin, 1959).

31 See Rorty, *Philosophy and the Mirror of Nature*. *Radical Philosphy*, a journal of faintly *samizdat* air and presentation, has done much from junior establishments in the hierarchy, especially polytechnics, to alter the stereotype described here, and to push philosophy back towards the insistent unacademic questions about meaning in life, good and bad societies, acting and living well.

32 Quoted from Stuart Maclure, *Educational Documents: England and Wales 1816–1968* (Methuen, rev. edn, 1969), p.159.

33 For the history of late-eighteenth-century poverty, see E.J. Hobsbawm and G. Rudé, *Captain Swing* (Lawrence & Wishart, 1969). For

the significance of the late-eighteenth-century bread riots, see E.P. Thompson, 'The moral economy of the 18th century crowd', *Past and Present* 50, 1971.

34 Richard Hoggart *The Uses of Literacy* (Chatto & Windus/Penguin, 1957) pp.37–8.

35 For a useful selection from their relevant writings, see Peter Keating, *The Victorian Prophets* (Fontana, 1978).

36 A vivid synopsis of such an essay is to be found written by the man who, in his lifetime, was best equipped to try it: Raymond Postgate in his introduction to *The Good Food Guide for 1965–66* (Consumers' Association with Cassell, 1965).

37 All given classic but novel relocation in the narrative of E.P. Thompson's *The Making of the English Working Class* (Gollancz, 1963).

38 All documented in the self-explanatorily named *The Invention of Tradition*, edited by Eric Hobsawm and Terence Ranger (Cambridge University Press, 1983).

39 It is my point that this is a long-standing human faculty, a view powerfully supported by Dan Jacobson's *The Story of the Stories* (Secker & Warburg, 1982).

40 It is a claim upheld by much recent historiography, best exemplified by Stefan Collini, John Burrow and Donald Winch, in *That Noble Science of Politics: A Study in Nineteenth Century Intellectual History* (Cambridge University Press, 1983).

41 The reference is to Richard Rorty's now deservedly celebrated *Philosophy and the Mirror of Nature*, which tries to do away with philosophy as the agent of a realist epistemology. I shall come back to the question of what realism means in chapter 4.

CHAPTER 3   THEORY AND EXPERIENCE

1 As, with distinct partiality, John Dunn does in 'Practising history and social science on "realist" assumptions', in his *Political Obligation in its Historical Context* (Cambridge University Press, 1980).

2 T.S. Eliot, 'East Coker', part II, in *Collected Poems and Plays* (Faber & Faber, 1976), p.179.

3 The phrase is Louis Althusser's in *Lenin and Philosophy* (New Left Books, 1977).

4 E.P. Thompson, *The Poverty of Theory* (Merlin Press, 1978), p.356. This definition is fairly criticized by Perry Anderson for its lack of an operational taxonomy, in *Arguments within English Marxism* (New Left Books/Verso, 1980), especially chapter 3.

Compare also Pasternak's novel *Dr Zhivago*, where the grim, but sympathetically treated revolutionary, Strelnikov, tells Zhivago that in revolutionary Russia the personal life, the individual life of the feelings, is over and done with.

5 I hope this very crude and foreshortened summary of Karl Popper's description of scientific method in *The Logic of Scientific Discovery* (Hutchinson, 1959) will serve the purpose of this chapter sufficiently.

6 The historical record is valuably, if uncritically summarized by A.N. Whitehead, in *Science and the Modern World* (Cambridge University Press, 1938).

7 T.S. Kuhn, *The Structure of Scientific Revolutions* (Chicago University Press, 1962). John Ziman, *Public Knowledge* (Cambridge University Press, 1972), and *The Force of Knowledge* (Cambridge University Press, 1976).

8 Gödel's Incompleteness Theorem is illustrated in many hues by Douglas Hofstadter in *Gödel, Escher, Bach: an Eternal Golden Braid* (Harvester Press, 1979).

9 A very partial history of its career is given by Marjorie Grene, in *The Knower and the Known* (Faber & Faber 1965).

10 I owe the idea of knowledge as a product being like a work of art to my friend, Gordon Reddiford. Taylor was celebrated in song and story for first working out in intense detail the methods of mass assembly, in which each worker performs thousands of times per day one single brief action. See Harry Braverman, *Labour and Monopoly Capital* (Monthly Review Press, 1974).

11 A good phrase coined by F. Phenix in *Realms of Meaning: a Philosophy of Curriculum*, (McGraw-Hill, 1964).

12 It is put with a dogmatism at times proper, at times merely supercilious, by Roger Scruton, in *The Meaning of Conservatism* (Penguin, 1980).

13 A singularly critical history of these relations is offered by Jurgen Habermas in his *Knowledge and Human Interests* (Heinemann Educational Books, 1974).

14 I keep using the time-honoured phrase, map of knowledge, with a particular eye on R.G. Collingwood's use of the phrase in his book of that name, *Speculum Mentis* (Clarendon Press, 1924), to which we return in chapter 10.

15 I extend my own definition here, as taken from *Ideology and the Imagination* (Cambridge University Press, 1975).

16 DES *Statistics, Yearbook*, 1979, 1980. The comparable ratio in, for instance, civil engineering is $1:18$. The university *teachers* of the humanities are largely male, however.

17 I am relying on a phenomenology of the imagination which I try to portray in my book on children's fiction, *The Promise of Happiness* (Cambridge University Press, 1981).

18 They are called, of course, preparations *against* it. But see Geoffrey Barraclough's *From Agadir to Armageddon*, Weidenfeld & Nicolson, 1982) for chilling parallels with 1911–14.

19 Readers familiar with Richard Rorty, *Philosophy and the Mirror of Nature* (Basil Blackwell, 1981), will recognize my indebtedness with the first three names. The others are my idiosyncrasy.

20 Heidegger, *Basic Writings*, edited with an introduction by David Krell, Routledge & Kegan Paul 1978, p.383.

21 Unforgettably parodied by Paul Jennings (via Sartre) in his essay on 'Resistentialism', reprinted in *The Jenguin Pennings* (Penguin, 1962).

22 Heidegger, ibid. pp.383–4.

23 R.G. Collingwood, (Clarendon Press, 1939), *An Autobiography;* reissued, with an introduction by Stephen Toulmin (Oxford University Press, 1981).

24 Collingwood is a good example of what Bernard Williams means by the term, in the title essay to his *Moral Luck* (Cambridge University Press, 1981).

25 I have written at some length about his life and work in my *Radical Earnestness* (Martin Robertson, 1982).

26 Collingwood, *Autobiography*, p.114.

27 Edwin Muir, *Autobiography* (Hogarth Press, 1954; Metheun, 1968), p.48.

28 It is Alasdair MacIntyre who suggests that within the terms of present ethics, the only virtue (and the ethical life for MacIntyre simply is the pursuit of virtue) is to live as continuous a narrative, which one can then be proud of, as possible. See his *After Virtue: A Study in Moral Theory* (Duckworth, 1981), especially chapter 15.

29 Storm Jameson, *Journey from the North*, 2 vols (Collins/Harvill, 1969; Virago, 1984); Vera Brittain, *The Testament of Youth* (Gollancz, 1942; Pan 1980; Virago, 1984); Naomi Mitchison, *You May Well Ask: A Memoir 1920–1940* (Gollancz, 1979).

30 Ezekiel Mphahlele, *Down Second Avenue* (Faber & Faber, 1956).

31 I take this point from Bernard Sharratt, in *Reading Relations* (Harvester Press, 1982), p.313.

32 First published in 1848; valuably republished by MacGibbon & Kee in 1967.

33 I rely here on Amelie Rorty's anthology, *Identities of Persons* (University of California Press, 1976), especially the paper by Derek Parfit.

CHAPTER 4   IDENTITY IN SELVES AND SUBJECTS

1 I follow Derek Parfit in this argument as rejecting common-sense accounts of identity, and going for a more slippery and less reassuring

philosophical account. See his paper, 'Lewis, Perry and what matters', in Amelie Rorty, *Identities of Persons* (University of California Press, 1976).

2 See also Derek Parfit's singular and tremendous book, *Reasons and Persons* (Clarendon Press, 1984).

3 And here I rely on the editor, Amelie Rorty in her postscript to 'Characters, persons, selves, individuals', in *Identities of Persons*.

4 The phrase is Basil Bernstein's, in his *Class, Codes, Control*, vol. III, rev. edn (Routledge & Kegan Paul, 1977), to which I shall return.

5 Rorty, *Identities of Persons*, p. 313.

6 Erving Goffmann, *The Presentation of Self in Everyday Life* (Doubleday/Penguin, 1969).

7 I take much of the strictly moral philosophy which follows in definition of individuals from Peter Strawson, *Individuals* (Oxford University Press, 1963), although he is interested in individuals in a more metaphysical sense as well as a technical category.

8 I adjust the title of Thomas Nagel's fine book, *The Possibility of Altruism* (Oxford University Press, 1970), where Nagel indeed argues for its necessity.

9 I am aware that a number of contemporary human scientists, notably Michel Foucault and Jacques Derrida in Paris, oppose what they see as this preposterously bourgeois 'metaphysics of presence' and propose its superannuation. See Foucault's *The Order of Things* (Tavistock, 1970), and Derrida's *Of Grammatology* (John Hopkins University Press, 1976). My nursery riposte would be, 'Man may no longer be our subject, but only men and women can write the new history.'

10 See Robert Darnton's *The Business of Enlightenment: The Publishing History of the Encyclopédie, 1775–1880* (Harvard University Press, 1980).

11 Such as Alec Nove sketches out, in *The Economics of Feasible Socialism* (Allen & Unwin, 1983).

12 Conservatism of a realist kind is illicitly extended into conservatism of a political kind in his essay on these matters by Antony Flew, *Sociology, Equality and Education* (Macmillan, 1976).

13 This is a propositional form of Anthony Giddens's 'Theory of Structuration', as advanced in his *Profiles and Critiques in Social Theory* (Macmillan, 1982) and fully expounded in his *The Constitution of Society* (Basil Blackwell, 1984).

14 Mary Douglas, *Purity and Danger: An Analysis of the Concepts of Pollution and Taboo*, rev. edn (Routledge & Kegan Paul, 1969).

15 Basil Bernstein, *Class, Codes, Control*, vol. I (Routledge & Kegan Paul, 1971), and vol. III. See especially the introduction to volume I, where he describes his first encounter with Durkheim.

16 I simplify drastically here. For the hard argument, see Stefan Körner, *Experience and Theory: An Essay in the Philosophy of Science* (Routledge & Kegan Paul, 1966).

17 As before, I rely extensively on Max Black, *Models and Metaphors* (Cornell University Press, 1962).

18 Memorably indemnified by Ernest Gellner, in his attack on Oxford philosophy in *Words and Things* (Penguin, 1959).

19 For sorting which terms, see the classic exposition in Lionel Trilling's *Sincerity and Authenticity* (Oxford University Press, 1972).

20 In his classic, but often impenetrable study of these processes: Pierre Bourdieu with J.-C. Passeron, *Reproduction in Education, Society and Culture*, translated by R. Nice. (Sage Books, 1977).

CHAPTER 5   ACCESS AND PRESTIGE

1 Jerome Bruner, 'Culture and cognitive growth', in his collection of essays, *The Relevance of Education* (Allen & Unwin, 1972).

2 Bernstein has been rebuked for too much following a Durkheimean or fixed view of the social order, thus underestimating the drive and friction which a more Marxizing model would have provided. He replied to his critics with the concluding essay in *Class, Codes, Control*, vol. III (Routledge & Kegan Paul, 1977), 'Education and the systems of production', adapting his classification and framing analysis in order to correlate classroom practice, economic buoyancy or decline, and method of production.

3 Following Jorge Larrain, in *The Concept of Ideology*, (Hutchinson, 1979).

4 There is a useful short history of the word in John Plamenatz, *Ideology* (Macmillan, 1971).

5 Here referred to in T.J. Arthur's edition (Lawrence & Wishart, 1970).

6 Clifford Geertz suggest the two terms, in 'Ideology as cultural system', an essay in his book, *The Interpretation of Cultures* (Hutchinson, 1975).

7 As has been pointed out, Marxism took essential parts of its structure of theodicy from Christianity. See Denys Turner's powerful attempt to turn Marxism back into Christianity, *Marxism and Christianity* (Basil Blackwell, 1983).

8 The best first guide in a large bibliography is Perry Anderson's, in a commemorative issue of *New Left Review*, numbers 100–1. See also James Joll, *Gramsci* (Fontana, 1980). But Gramsci was writing for an untheoretic audience, and the best place to learn about him is in the original. See Antonio Gramsci, *Selections from the Prison Notebooks*, edited by Quintin Hoare (Lawrence & Wishart, 1977).

9 In his novel, *A Painter of our Time* (Penguin, 1965), p. 64.

10 Notes for the study of which are provided in Karl Mannheim, *Essays in the Sociology of Knowledge* (Routledge & Kegan Paul, 1952),

11 Bernstein, 'Ritual in education', *Class, Codes, Control*, vol. III.

12 Originally, George Sampson's, in *English for the English* (1922), edited with an introduction by Denys Thompson (Cambridge University Press, 1970).

13 I borrow here and later from Steven Lukes's admirable monograph, *Power: A Radical View* (Macmillan, 1974).

14 I have in mind the most difficult parts of Pierre Bourdieu and J.-G. Passeron, *Reproduction in Education, Society and Culture* (Sage Books, 1977).

15 As in J.A. Hobson, *Imperialism*, 3rd rev. edn (Allen & Unwin).

CHAPTER 6   THE SOCIAL MOBILITY OF A SUBJECT

1 As quoted by Alasdair MacIntyre, in *Secularization and Moral Change* (Oxford University Press, 1967).

2 John Robinson, *Honest to God* (SCM Press, 1964).

3 In 'God and the theologians', collected by Alasdair MacIntyre, *Against the Self-Images of the Age* (Duckworth, 1971).

4 Edward Norman has tried to rebut the (largely Latin American) call for a politicized Christian ministry in his Reith Lectures, *Christianity and the World Order* (Oxford University Press, 1979). Peterhouse, Cambridge, is not, however, the most exemplary place from which to argue with such supreme unction for a restatement of a non-social, wholly individual doctrine of grace.

5 The best suggestions, very much under the influence of Robinsonian theology, come from Ninian Smart, *The Phenomenon of Religion* (Macmillan, 1973).

6 It will be noticed that these observations rest on Michel Foucault's historical diagnosis of the Surveillant Society in *Discipline and Punish* (Allen Lane/Penguin, 1977).

7 I once more borrow gratefully from MacIntyre's *After Virtue* (Duckworth, 1981) especially chapters 6 and 7.

8 MacIntyre, *After Virtue*, p. 25.

9 Ibid., p. 24.

10 Ibid., pp. 25–6.

11 Greatly as I honour Elizabeth Richardson's pioneering study of a school under the Tavistock lamp, I think it is open to these strictures. See her *The Teacher, the School and the Task of Management* (Heinemann Educational Books, 1973).

12 As Miloslav Djilas identified it as being in *The New Class* (Allen & Unwin, 1956).

13 As commended in Rudolf Bahro, *The Alternative in Eastern Europe* (New Left Books, 1978).

14 W.V.O. Quine, *Ontological Relativism* (Columbia University Press, 1969).

15 I can't go far into these matters, but what I am saying conflicts with some of the essays in the well-known anthology of P. Gardiner, *The Philosophy of History* (Oxford University Press, 1974). I take much from Roy Bhaskar, *The Possibility of Naturalism* (Harvester Press, 1979), although mine is a very different, much more Aristotelian naturalism.

16 See notes 28, 29 and 31 of chapter 3. The following should be added to this list: William Lovett, *William Lovett: His Life and Struggles* (1860; reprinted MacGibbon & Kee, 1967); Fred Kitchen, *Brother to the Ox* (Heinemann Educational Books, 1959: 1939); James Dawson Burn, *Autobiography of a Beggar Boy* (1855: now out of print); Thomas Frost, *Forty Years Recollections* (Tinsley, 1880).

17 Paul Scott's *Raj Quartet* 4 vols (Heinemann, 1967–75), now made celebrated by its fine rendering on Granada TV, is a striking revaluation of the meaning of the imperial occupation in its most dismal and neglectful years. Nadine Gordimer, in *A Guest of Honour* (Jonathan Cape, 1970; Penguin 1973) seeks impressively to characterize the post-imperial politics of any one of the former Central African Federation countries.

18 James Morris gives a full revaluation of the Empire in his three-volume *Pax Britannica*, rev. edn (Penguin, 1978).

19 The structure of the action is classically analysed by E.H. Carr, in *What is History?* (Macmillan/Penguin, 1961). The history from below may be said to start from Christoper Hill's books *Puritanism and Revolution* (Secker & Warburg, 1958); *The Century of Revolution* (Nelson, 1961); and the founding of the journal *Past and Present*.

20 Fernand Braudel, *The Mediterranean in the Age of Philip II*, 2 vols (Harper & Row/Collins, 1973).

21 W.G. Hoskins, *The Making of the English Landscape* (Hodder & Stoughton, 1955); *The Midland Peasant* (Macmillan, 1957).

22 Peter Laslett, *The World We Have Lost* (Methuen, 1965).

23 E.P. Thompson, *The Making of the English Working Class* (Gollancz, 1963; Penguin, 1968); Eric Hobsbawm, *Labouring Men: Studies in Labour History* (Weidenfeld & Nicolson, 1964) and, with Georges Rude, *Captain Swing* (Lawrence & Wishart, 1969).

24 Notably in the Ruskin College journal, *Socialist History Workshop*.

CHAPTER 7   CLASS AND CULTURE

1 A complacency whose etymology excludes perimeter countries, for instance in the Caribbean or the Middle East.

2 E. P. Thompson, *Writing by Candlelight* (Merlin Press, 1980), p.201.
3 The phrase is Anthony Giddens's, in his essential primer, *The Class Structure of the Advanced Societies* (Hutchinson, 1973).
4 Classically written by Michael Young, *The Rise of the Meritocracy* (Penguin, 1961). The author is now, symmetrically, Lord Young of the Social Democratic Party and Dartington.
5 This is a rather compressed malediction, expanded in chapter 9. Nietzsche, of course, took his own conclusions with such absolute seriousness that they took away his reason. His descendants, however, are rather less ascetically self-indulgent. See *Beyond Good and Evil* (Penguin edn, 1973).
6 Such books as, first and classically, Germaine Greer, *The Female Eunuch* (Paladin, 1971); Juliet Mitchell, *Woman's Estate* (Penguin, 1971); Sheila Rowbotham, *Woman's Consciousness, Man's World* (Penguin, 1973); Ann Oakley, *Sex, Gender, and Society* (Temple Smith, 1972) are all, in their way, educational handbooks.
7 Most simply, polemically and reductively in Marx, 'A Critique of the Gotha Programme' in *Selected Works* (Foreign Languages Publishing House, Moscow, 1972).
8 For example, Roger Dale, Geoff Esland and Madeleine Macdonald (eds), *Schooling and Capitalism*, second level Open University reader (Open University with Routledge & Kegan Paul, 1976). A. Hunt (ed.), *Class and Class Structure* (Lawrence & Wishart, 1977); Rachel Sharp, *Knowledge, Ideology and the Politics of Schooling* (Routledge & Kegan Paul, 1980); Stuart Hall et al. (eds) *Resistance through Ritual* (Hutchinson, 1976); Mark Levitas, *Marxist Perspectives in the Sociology of Education* (Routledge & Kegan Paul, 1974); and Henry Giroux, *Ideology, Culture and the Process of Schooling* (Falmer Press, 1980).
9 In, first, *Lenin and Philosophy* (New Left Books, 1971).
10 This formulation derives from Jurgen Habermas, *Knowledge and Human Interests* (Heinemann Educational Books, 1974).
11 Now known as the Structuralists: notably Claude Lévi-Strauss, Jacques Lacan, Lucien Goldmann, Roland Barthes, and Michel Foucault (q.v.).
12 Jacques Derrida, *Of Grammatology*, translated by J. Spivak (Johns Hopkins University Press, 1976).
13 Basil Bernstein, 'Education and the systems of production', in *Class, Codes, Control* vol. III, rev. edn (Routledge & Kegan Paul, 1977), and subsequently in 'The stability of pedagogic discourse', CORE 1984 (microfiche).
14 Samuel Bowles and Herbert Gintis, *Schooling in Capitalist America* (Routledge & Kegan Paul, 1976).

192 *Notes to pp. 117–121*

15 Paul Willis, *Learning to Labour* (Saxon House, 1977). The subtitle is *How Working Class Kids Get Working Class Jobs.*
16 In an endearing last chapter, he takes the unusual risk for an ethnographer of showing the subjects of his study how he explains their predicaments and occasion. It is no surprise that they think he's all wrong, and Willis is morally and intellectually too scrupulous to summon up the spectre of false consciousness.
17 As the authors accuse their primary-teacher subjects, in Rachel Sharp and Anthony Green, *Education and Social Control* (Routledge & Kegan Paul, 1975).
18 Nicos Poulantzas, *Political Power and Social Classes* (New Left Books, 1973), p. 86, italics in original.
19 Nicos Poulantzas, *Classes in Contemporary Capitalism* (New Left Books, 1975), p. 14.
20 Poulantzas, *Political Power and Social Classes*, p. 67.
21 Classically, in such more-or-less scientifically-administrative versions as that of one of the founders of anthropology, E. E. Evans-Pritchard, *Social Anthropology* (Cohen & West, 1951).
22 Or better 'Fortuna' as Machiavelli would have it. Relevantly enough, Machiavelli is enjoying a revival in current political thought, not least because of the centrality he ascribes to 'Fortuna' – translatable as a mixture of luck, unknowable destiny (as in, 'my lady Fortune') and chance, all of them terms excluded from slightly earlier handbooks of political economy on the confident planning of the globe. See Quentin Skinner, *Machiavelli* (Oxford University Press, 1981) and his paper, 'Machiavelli on the maintenance of liberty', *Politics* no. 18, 1983.
23 The first is E. P. Thompson's essay 'The peculiarities of the English', in *The Poverty of Theory* (Merlin Press, 1978). Thompson breaks open both the functionalists' view of class as stratification (as in geology) and class as abstract historical necessity (as in Marxism). He insists, in this essay and the anti-Althusserian title essay, on the intractability of history as lived experience, and class as part of this dense, enormous process. The second is the vast concluding section of Jean-Paul Sartre's *Critique de la Raison Dialectique* (Le Seuil, 1960) (quotations in my own translation). The best empirical inquires into class in Britain are J. A. Westergaard and H. Resler, *Class in a Capitalist Society: A Study of Contemporary Britain*, (Heinemann, 1975); and Peter Townsend, *Poverty in the United Kingdom* (Penguin, 1979).
24 I try to bring out the methodical significance of this quality of Thompson's in my *Radical Earnestness* (Martin Robertson, 1982).
25 Sartre, *Critique*, p. 561.

26 Starting with R.H. Tawney's *Equality*, now reissued with an introduction by Richard Titmuss (Allen & Unwin, 1964). The next major educational text was by Jean Floud and A. H. Halsey, *Social Class and Educational Opportunity* (Heinemann, 1959). Past inequality in university admission is fully documented in the Robbins Report, *Higher Education*, Command 2154 (HMSO, 1963); in primary schools by Brian Jackson, *Streaming: an Education System in Miniature* (Routledge & Kegan Paul, 1964). Up-to-date figures and arguments include John Goldthorpe, *Social Mobility and Class Structure in Modern Britain* (Clarendon Press, 1980), as well as, stirringly, David Hargreaves, *The Challenge of the Comprehensive School*(Routledge & Kegan Paul, 1982).For the most recent figures on class membership of University admission, see UCCA, *Statistical Supplement* 1984. For more general statistics, see Ivan Reid, *Social Class Differences in Britain* (2nd ed. Grant McIntyre, 1981).

27 Up to 90 per cent in some cases, over 70 per cent in all. See D. Morrison and D. McIntyre, *Teachers and Teaching* (Penguin, 1969). See also Sara Delamont, *Interaction in the Classroom*, 2nd edn (Methuen, 1983) for the instruments of analysis *and* quantification of such findings.

28 Bernstein's early typology is given much more detail and purchase in the modes of Martin Halliday's linquistic taxonomy by R.M. Coulthard and J.M. Sinclair, *Towards an Analysis of Discourse: the English Used by Teachers and Pupils* (Oxford University Press, 1975).

29 Foucault, *Discipline and Punish* (Allen Lane/Penguin, 1977),

30 Stuart Hall's phrase, in 'The great moving right show' (in Pluto Press, 1981). Stuart Hall with Martin Jacques (eds), *The Politics of Thatcherism* (Pluto Press, 1981).

31 Among others , by Michael Apple in *Ideology and Curriculum* (Routledge & Kegan Paul, 1979). The critique is provided with the instruments of analysis, however, by Basil Bernstein in his essay 'visible and invisible pedagogies', in *Class, Codes, Control*, vol. III.

32 Much advertised in Geoff Whitty and Mitchael Young (eds), *Explanations in the Politics of School Knowledge* (Nafferton Press, 1978).

33 Brian Jackson and Dennis Marsden, *Education and the Working Class* (Routledge & Kegan Paul, 1962).

34 Richard Hoggart, *The Uses of Literacy* (Chatto & Windus with Penguin, 1957).

35 Brian Jackson, *Working Class Community* (Routledge & Kegan Paul, 1966).

36 David Holbrook, *English for the Rejected* (Cambridge University Press, 1964).

37 John Newsom, *Half Our Future* (HMSO, 1963).

38 For example, Centre for Contemporary Cultural Studies, University of Birmingham, in *Unpopular Education* (Hutchinson, 1981).

39 Which is where Stephen Lukes confines it in *Power: A Radical View* (Macmillan, 1974). But see Anthony Giddens, *Profiles and Critiques in Social Theory* (Macmillan, 1982).

CHAPTER 8   WORK AND MEANING

1 The two criticisms appear in Claude Lévi-Strauss, *Structural Anthropology* (Allen Lane/Penguin, 1964), pp. 279 ff. E. E. Evans-Pritchard, *Social Anthropology* (Cohen & West, 1951).

2 It is horribly relevant to recall at this stage that the dreadful gate to the Nazi extermination camp at Auschwitz bore the slogan 'Arbeit ist Freiheit'.

3 *Capital*, vol. I (Foreign Languages Publishing House, Moscow, 1887) (1st English edition), p. 72.

4 Most notably, Paul Sraffa in *Production of Commodities by Means of Commodities* (Cambridge University Press, 1960).

5 It is a story well told by David Meakin in *Man and Work: Literature and Culture in Industrial Society* (Methuen, 1976). A different history, in which 'capitalism' is substituted for 'industrialism' is famously told by Raymond Williams in his classic *Culture and Society: 1780–1950* (Chatto & Windus, 1957), Penguin, 1958).

6 Hannah Arendt, *The Human Condition* (Anchor Doubleday, 1959).

7 Max Weber, *The Protestant Ethic and the Spirit of Capitalism*, translated by Talcott Parsons (Allen & Unwin, 1948). R. H. Tawney, alone in England in taking up Weber in the 1920s, went on to document in detail the displacement of older Christian views of usury by capitalists: see *Religion and the Rise of Capitalism* (John Murray, 1926). Latterly, Albert Hirschmann has advanced the crucial ideological victory of the political economy as doctrine to the eighteenth century, in *The Passions and the Interests: Political Arguments for Capitalism before its Triumph*, (Princeton University Press, 1977).

8 The particular consequences of Calvinism for the pioneers who founded New England and were the intellectual originators of American capitalism are boldly drawn by Henry Bamford Parkes in *The American Experience* (Knopf, 1947).

9 This is to repeat Michel Foucault's radically determinist thesis in all his work, from *Madness and Civilisation* (1967) to his most recent essay available in English, *The History of Sexuality*, vol. I (Allen Lane/Penguin, 1979).

10 For a short history, see F. L. Carsten, *Revolution in Central Europe 1918–1919* (Oxford University Press, 1972).

11 In what follows I rely on Peter and Brigitte Berger's schematic structures for the analysis of the contemporary self. See *The Homeless Mind: Modernization and Consciousness* (Penguin, 1973).

12 It is called, in translation, *Economy and Society* (Routledge & Kegan Paul, 1962). Anyone inclined to take Weber lightly must also read 'Politics as a vocation', in *From Max Weber*, edited by H.H. Gerth and C.W. Mills (Routledge & Kegan Paul, 1948).

13 This is a well-known reversal much discussed in the anthropology of pre-industrial peoples, amongst whom the time is told by what they are doing, both for the days and seasons. See the discussion of time in John Beattie, *Other Cultures* (Cohen & West, 1964), and Clifford Geertz on 'Person, time, and conduct in Bali', in *The Interpretation of Cultures* (Hutchinson, 1975).

14 Particularly as written by Noam Chomsky in *American Power and the New Mandarins* (Chatto & Windus/Penguin, 1969).

15 E.P. Thompson 'Time, work-discipline, and industrial capitalism', *Past and Present*, no. 38 (1968).

16 For example, James Britton et al., *Schools Council Examination Bulletin: Multiple Marking* (Schools Council, 1966), and also *The Development of Writing Abilities* (Macmillan, 1975)

17 The statistical axiom of regression to the mean has never been part of their education.

18 See Harry Braverman, *Labour and Monopoly Capital* (Monthly Review Press, 1974).

19 As Peter Herbst would have it, in *Theoreticism and Critical Inquiry*, forthcoming.

20 I recognize that my politics at this point have a distinctly Oakeshottian timbre, but in my view these anti-technicist, humanly specific and experiential learnings can find as perfectly good a home on my Left as his Right. See Michael Oakeshott, *On Human Conduct* (Oxford University Press, 1975).

21 Andrew Harrison's useful phrase, from *Making and Thinking* (Harvester Press, 1978).

CHAPTER 9   VALUES AND THE FUTURE

1 See especially his last, lapidary work, *The New Leviathan*, (Clarendon Press, 1942).

2 Michael Rutter et al. *15,000 Hours: Secondary Schools and Their Effects on Children* (Open Books, 1979).

3 Taken from Krishan Humar, 'Holding the middle ground', in James Curran, Michael Gurevitch, and Janet Wollacott. (eds), *Mass Communication and Society* (Edward Arnold for the Open University, 1977).

4 The meaning of the word is most subtly entertained by Harold Bloom, in *A Map of Misreading* (Oxford University Press, New York, 1975).

5 I take the categories, for my very different purpose, from Charles Taylor's now canonical paper 'Interpretation and the sciences of man', first published in *Journal of Metaphysics* (January 1971); but see Roger Beehler and Alan Drengson, *The Philosophy of Society* (Methuen, 1979). This paper and all those by him on the same subject are now collected by Charles Taylor, in his *Philosophy and the Human Sciences*, (vols. 2, Cambridge University Press, 1985).

6 There is an important contemporary inclination to proceed in planning to the remorseless spatialization of time itself, thus subjecting it to the utilitarian calculus by which all values are numerically convertible. See Joel Whitebrook, 'Saving the subject: modernity and the problem of the autonomous individual', *Telos* (USA), vol. 50 (1981), pp. 79–102.

7 And see controversially definitive account in Derek Parfit, *Reasons and Persons* (Clarendon Press, 1984).

8 For a useful summary, see R. W. Connell et al. *Making the Difference: Schools, Families, and Social Division* (Allen & Unwin, 1982).

9 An anti-utilitarian point expounded by Stuart Hampshire in the title essay to his *Morality and Pessimism* (Oxford University Press, 1976).

10 Starting with the famous Club of Rome report, *The Limits to Growth* (Rome, 1972), and going on via the special issue of *The Ecologist, Blueprint for Survival* (January 1972), to Amartya Sen, *On Economic Inequality* (Clarendon Press, 1973), to Geoffrey Barraclough's famous trio of papers in the *New York Review* 'The End of an Era', 27 June 1974; 'The Great World Crisis', 23 January 1975; 'Wealth and Power: the Politics of Food and Oil', 7 August 1975.

11 The same sort of point is made on behalf of the English working class by Anthony Crosland, in *Socialism Now* (Jonathan Cape, 1974), part I.

CHAPTER 10   THE LANGUAGE OF POLITICS IN THE CONVERSATION OF
CLASSROOMS

1 In, for example, Anthony Arblaster and Steven Lukes (eds), *The Good Society* (Macmillan, 1969); Bernard Williams, *Ethics and the Limits of Philosophy* (Fontana, 1985);Alasdair MacIntyre, *After Virtue: A Study in Moral Theory* (Duckworth, 1981). See also the summary of these tendencies in Richard Bernstein, *The Restructuring of Social and Political Theory* (Hutchinson, 1979), and *Beyond Objectivism and Relativism* (Basil Blackwell, 1983).

2 Fred Hirsch, *The Social Limits to Growth* (Allen & Unwin, 1976).

3 If for instance the European Community were to put even so modest a proposal as the Brandt Report into effect.

4 Two such honourable mentions are called for: Michael Banton, *The Coloured Quarter*, (Jonathan Cape, 1955) and *Racial Minorities* (Fontana, 1973); and John Rex, especially in *Race Relations in Sociological Theory* (Weidenfeld & Nicolson, 1970). See also the excellent collection of essays published by the collective authorship of the Centre for Contemporary Cultural Studies, University of Birmingham, as *The Empire Strikes Back* (Hutchinson, 1982).

5 It is very fully tested and criticized by Bernard Williams in 'The truth of relativism', *Moral Luck* (Cambridge University Press, 1981).

6 See Thomas S. Kuhn. *The Structure of Scientific Revolutions* (Chicago University Press, 1972); and John Ziman, *Public Knowledge* (Cambridge University Press, 1976). See also Marcel Detienne, *L'Invention de la Mythologie* (Gallimard, 1981).

7 I am entirely unimpressed by Martin Wiener's argument, in *British Culture and the Decline of the Industrial Spirit* (Cambridge University Press, 1981) that technology was defeated by the genteel culturalists of the Ruskin commando.

8 In, respectively, Carl Hempel, *Aspects of Scientific Explanation* (Free Press, 1965); and Ernest Nagel, *The Structure of Science* (Harcourt Brace, 1961).

9 As summarized and contested by J.J.C. Smart and Bernard Williams, in *Utilitarianism: For and Against* (Cambridge University Press, 1973).

10 That is to say I acknowledge the justice of criticism in such television studies as *Bad New* and *Really Bad News*, Glasgow Media Group (Routledge & Kegan Paul, 1976 and 1979); Philip Schlesinger, *Putting 'Reality' Together* (Constable, 1978); John Fiske and John Hartley, *Reading Tevevision* (Methuen, 1978); Len Masterman, *Teaching About Television* (Macmillan, 1980).

11 I look for support in this statement to Nicholas Garnham, 'Contribution to a political economy of mass communication', *Media, Culture and Society*, vol. 1. (1979). Garnham, emphasizing the play of both liberalism and control in the cultural industries, vigorously repudiates the arguments from Marxism particularly found in *Screen* that everything on television is a form of ideological control: this latter is the Dave Spart view of history.

12 For a devastatingly comical account of which, see David Stove, *Popper and After: Four Modern Irrationalists* (Pergamon Press, 1982).

13 Jurgen Habermas, *Legitimation Crisis* (Heinemann Educational Books, 1975), part III.

14 See John Dunn, *Political Obligation in its Historical Context*

(Cambridge University Press, 1980), pp.243–300.

15 These are what Raymond Williams calls the agents of 'Plan X' in the concluding chapter, 'Resources for a journey of hope', in his *Towards 2000* (Chatto & Windus, 1983).

16 Bernard Williams's introduction to Isaiah Berlin, *Concepts and Categories: Philosophical Essays* (Hogarth Press, 1978), p.xviii.

17 This, I take it, is what Gramsci meant when he identified the forms of education as the perfectly proper site of political work for the revolutionary. See Antonio Gramsci, *The Modern Prince* (Lawrence & Wishart, 1957). His, of course, is hardly a Marxist, much more a latter-day Fabian's position, communicated with a proper urgency.

18 Taken from Stuart Hall, 'Encoding/decoding', in Stuart Hall et al. (eds), *Culture, Media, Language* (Hutchinson, 1978).

19 I am not trying to privilege ideas over materials, only to claim that the two are mutually embedded. The philosophic issues are a good deal knottier than this allows, of course; see J.L. Austin, 'Are there a priori concepts?', in J.O. Urmson and G.J. Warnock (eds), *Philosophical Papers* (Oxford University Press, 1961).

20 Or as Charles Taylor puts it, in 'Interpretation and the sciences of man', *Journal of Metaphysics* (January 1971), p.179: collected in his *Philosophy and the Human Sciences*, 2 vols. (Cambridge University Press 1985), 'We have to admit that intersubjective social reality has to be partly defined in terms of meanings; that meanings as subjective are not just in causal interaction with a social reality made up of brute data, but that as intersubjective they are constitutive of this reality.'

21 Paul Hirst, *Knowledge and the Curriculum* (Routledge & Kegan Paul, 1975); and F. Phenix, *Realms of Meanings* (McGraw-Hill, 1964); also HM Inspectorate in *Framework for the Curriculum* (HMSO, 1981), criticized by John White *et al; No, Minister: a Critique* (University of London Institute of Education, 1981).

22 For an exculpation of Plato, see Iris Murdoch, *The Fire and the Sun: Why Plato Banished the Artists* (Clarendon Press, 1977).

23 John Fowles, *The French Lieutenant's Woman* (Jonathan Cape, 1969), p.387.

24 As classically propounded by J.S. Mill, and revised for the cold war by Isaiah Berlin, in *Four Essays on Liberty* (Clarendon Press, 1961).

25 I owe this suggestion to Peter Herbst.

26 I owe much in these remarks to Basil Bernstein's habitual generosity with his ideas, and his gift of some during conversation.

27 I have in mind Pierre Bourdieu's well-known use of the phrase in his *Outline of a Theory of Practice* (Cambridge University Press, 1978).

28 David Hargreaves, 'What teaching does to teachers', *New Society* (9 March 1978), subsequently elaborated in his *The Challenge of the Comprehensive School* (Routledge & Kegan Paul, 1982).

29 For a history of that discourse, see John Passmore, *The Perfectibility of Man* (Duckworth, 1970).
30 Perhaps with this short list of recent books to hand: Alex Nove, *The Economics of Feasible Socialism* (Allen & Unwin, 1983); Gavin Kitching, *Rethinking Socialism* (Methuen, 1983), John Dunn, *The Politics of Socialism* (Cambridge University Press, 1984). See particularly, however, Charles Taylor's essay-sketch of the benign future, 'The politics of the steady state, in Colin Crouch and Fred Inglis (eds). *Morality and the Left*, a special issue of *New Universities Quarterly* (April 1978).
31 2 Timothy 3:1–2.
32 In a sadly unique example, he might look for help in Mike Cooley, *Architect or Bee: The Human Technology Relationship*, edited by S. Cooley (Langley Technical Services, 1980).
33 The phrase was first T.H. Green's, in his *Prolegomena to Ethics*, subsequently published in R.L. Nettleship's edition of his *Works* (Longmans Green, 1911). See also Inglis, *Radical Earnestness* (Martin Robertson, 1982).

Bibliography

Althusser, Louis. *Lenin and Philosophy*. New Left Books, 1971

Anderson, Perry. 'Components of the national culture'. *New Left Review*, vol. 50, 1968; reprinted in *Student Power*, edited by Alexander Cockburn and Robin Blackburn, Penguin, 1969.

—— 'The antinomies of Antonio Gramsci', *New Left Review*, vol 100–1, 1977.

—— *Arguments within English Marxism*. New Left Books/Verso Books, 1980.

Apple, Michael. *Ideology and Curriculum*. Routledge & Kegan Paul, 1979.

—— *Education and Power*. Routledge & Kegan Paul, 1981.

Arblaster, Anthony and Lukes, Steven (eds). *The Good Society*. Macmillan, 1969.

Arendt, Hannah. *The Human Condition*. Anchor Doubleday, 1959.

Austin, J.L. 'Are there a priori concepts?' *Philosophical Papers*, edited by J.O. Urinson and G.J. Warnock. Oxford University Press, 1961.

Bahro, Rudolf. *The Alternative in Eastern Europe*. New Left Books, 1978.

Banton, Michael. *The Coloured Quarter*. Jonathan Cape, 1955.

—— *Racial Minorities*. Fontana/Collins, 1973.

Barraclough, Geoffrey. 'The end of an era', *New York Review*, 27 June 1974.

—— 'The great world crisis', *New York Review*, 23 January 1975.

—— 'Wealth and power: the politics of food and oil', *New York Review*, 7 August 1975.

—— *From Agadir to Armageddon: Anatomy of a Crisis*. Weidenfeld & Nicolson, 1982.

Beattie, John. *Other Cultures*. Cohen & West, 1964.

Beehler, Roger and Drengson, Alan. *The Philosophy of Society*. Methuen, 1979.

Berger, John. *A Painter of Our Time*. Secker & Warburg, 1962; Penguin, 1965.

Berger, Peter and Brigitte. *The Homeless Mind: Modernization and Consciousness*. Penguin, 1973.

Berlin, Isaiah. *Four Essays on Liberty*. Clarendon Press, 1961.
—— *Concepts and Categories: Philosophical Essays*, with an introduction by Bernard Williams. Hogarth Press, 1978.
Bernstein, Basil. *Class, Codes, Control*, vol. I and (rev. edn) vol. III, Routledge & Kegan Paul, 1971 and 1977. *CORE* 1984 (Microfiche)
Bernstein, Richard. *The Restructuring of Social and Political Theory*. Hutchinson, 1979.
—— *Beyond Objectivism and Relativism: Science, Hermeneutics, and Praxis*. Basil Blackwell, 1983.
Bhaskar, Roy. *The Possibility of Naturalism*. Harvester Press, 1979.
Black, Max. *Models and Metaphors*. Cornell University Press, 1962.
Bloom, Harold. *A Map of Misreading*. Oxford University Press, New York, 1975.
Bolgar, R. R. *The Classical Heritage and its Beneficiaries*. Cambridge University Press, 1954.
Bowles, Samuel and Gintis, Herbert. *Schooling in Capitalist America*. Routledge & Kegan Paul, 1976.
Bourdieu, Pierre. *Outline of a Theory of Practice*, translated by Richard Nice. Cambridge University Press, 1978.
—— with Passeron, J.G. *Reproduction in Education, Society and Culture*, translated by R. Nice. Sage Books, 1977.
Braudel, Fernand. *The Mediterranean in the Age of Philip II*. Harper & Row/Collins, 1973.
Braverman, Harry. *Labour and Monopoly Capital: the Degradation of Work in the Twentieth Century*. Monthly Review Press, 1974.
Brittain, Vera. *The Testament of Youth*. Gollancz, 1942; Pan, 1980; Virago, 1984.
Britton, James et al. *Schools Council Examinations Bulletin: Multiple Marking*. Schools Council, 1966.
—— *The Development of Writing Abilities*. Macmillan, 1975.
Bruner, Jerome. *The Relevance of Education*. Allen & Unwin, 1972.
Burn, James Dawson. *Autobiography of a Beggar Boy*. London, 1855.
Carr, E. H. *What is History?* Macmillan/Penguin, 1961.
Carsten, F. L. *Revolution in Central Europe 1918–1919*. Oxford University Press, 1972.
Centre for Contemporary Cultural Studies, University of Birmingham. *Unpopular Education*. Hutchinson, 1981.
—— *The Empire Strikes Back*. Hutchinson, 1982.
Chomsky, Noam. *American Power and the New Mandarins*. Chatto & Windus with Penguin, 1969.
Club of Rome. *The Limits to Growth*. Rome, 1972.
Collingwood, R. G. *Speculum Mentis, or The Map of Knowledge*. Clarendon Press, 1924.

—— *An Autobiography*, Clarendon Press, 1939; reissued, with an introduction by Stephen Toulmin. Oxford University Press, 1981.

—— *The New Leviathan*. Clarendon Press, 1942.

—— *The Idea of History*, edited by T.M. Knox. Clarendon Press, 1946.

Collini, Stefan, Winch, Donald and Burrow, John. *That Noble Science of Politics: A Study in Nineteenth Century Intellectual History*. Cambridge University Press, 1983.

Connell, R.W. et al. *Making the Difference: Schools, Families, and Social Division*. Allen & Unwin, 1982.

Cooley, Mike. *Architect or Bee: the Human/Technology Relationship*, edited by Sue Cooley. Langley Technical Services, 1980.

Coulthard, R. M. and Sinclair, J. M. *Towards an Analysis of Discourse: the English Used by Teachers and Pupils*. Oxford University Press, 1975.

Crosland, Anthony. *Socialism Now*. Jonathan Cape, 1974.

Crouch, Colin and Inglis, Fred (eds). *Morality and the Left*, a special edition of *New Universities Quarterly*, vol 32, no. 2, April 1978.

Dale, Roger, Esland, Geoff and Macdonald, Madeleine. *Schooling and Capitalism*. Open University with Routledge & Kegan Paul, 1976.

Darnton, Robert. *The Business of Enlightenment: A Publishing History of the Encyclopédie 1775–1800*. Harvard University Press, 1980.

Delamont, Sara. *Interaction in the Classroom*, 2nd edn, Methuen, 1983.

Derrida, Jacques. *Of Grammatology*, translated by J. Spivak. Johns Hopkins University Press, 1976.

Detienne, Marcel. *L'Invention de la Mythologie*. Gallimard, 1981.

Djilas, Miloslav. *The New Class*. Allen & Unwin, 1956.

Douglas, Mary. *Purity and Danger: an Analysis of the Concepts of Pollution and Taboo*, rev. edn, Routledge & Kegan Paul, 1969.

Dunn, John. *Western Political Theory in the Face of the Future*. Cambridge University Press, 1979.

—— *Political Obligation in its Historical Context*. Cambridge University Press, 1980.

—— *The Politics of Socialism*. Cambridge University Press, 1984.

Ecologist, The. Blueprint for Survival. January 1972.

Eliot, T.S. *Collected Poems and Plays*. Faber & Faber, 1976.

Elliott, J.H. *The Revolt of the Catalans: A Study in the Decline of Spain*. Cambridge University Press, 1963.

Evans-Pritchard, E.E. *Social Anthropology*. Cohen & West, 1951.

Fiske, John and Hartley, John. *Reading Television*. Methuen, 1978.

Flew, Antony. *Sociology, Equality, and Education*. Macmillan, 1976.

Floud, Jean and Halsey, A.H. *Social Class and Educational Opportunity*. Heinemann, 1959.

Foucault, Michel. *Madness and Civilisation*. Tavistock Publications, 1967.

—— *The Order of Things*. Tavistock Publications, 1970.

—— *Discipline and Punish: the Birth of the Prison*. Allen Lane/Penguin, 1977.

—— *The History of Sexuality*, vol. 1. Allen Lane Penguin, 1979.

Fowles, John. *The French Lieutenant's Woman*. Jonathan Cape, 1969.

Frost, Thomas. *Forty Years of Recollections*. Tinsley, 1880.

Gardiner, P. *The Philosophy of History*. Oxford University Press, 1974.

Garnham, Nicholas. 'Contribution to a political economy of mass communications'. *Culture, Media, Society*. vol. 1, no. 2, 1979.

Geertz, Clifford. *The Interpretation of Cultures*. Hutchinson, 1975.

Gellner, Ernest. *Words and Things*. Penguin, 1959.

Geuss, Raymond. *The Idea of a Critical Theory: Habermas and the Frankfurt School*. Cambridge University Press, 1981.

Giddens, Anthony. *The Class Structure of the Advanced Societies*. Hutchinson, 1973.

—— *Profiles and Critiques in Social Theory*. Macmillan, 1982.

—— *The Constitution of Society*. Basil Blackwell, 1984.

Giroux, Henry. *Ideology, Culture and the Process of Schooling*. Falmer Press, 1980.

Glasgow Media Group. *Bad News*. Routledge & Kegan Paul, 1976.

—— *Really Bad News*, Routledge & Kegan Paul, 1979.

Goffmann, Erving. *The Presentation of Self in Everyday Life*. Doubleday/Penguin, 1969.

Goldthorpe, John. *Social Mobility and Class Structure in Modern Britain*. Clarendon Press, 1980.

Gordimer, Nadine. *A Guest of Honour*. Jonathan Cape, 1970; Penguin, 1973.

Gramsci, Antonio. *The Modern Prince*. Lawrence & Wishart, 1957.

—— *Selections from The Prison Notebooks*, edited by Quintin Hoare. Lawrence & Wishart, 1977.

Green, T. H. *Works*, edited by R. L. Nettleship. Longmans Green, 1911.

Greer, Germaine. *The Female Eunuch*. Paladin, 1971.

Grene, Marjorie. *The Knower and the Known*. Faber & Faber, 1965.

Habermas, Jurgen. *Knowledge and Human Interests*. Heinemann Educational Books, 1974.

—— *Legitimation Crisis*. Heinemann Educational Books, 1975.

Hall, Stuart, et al. *Resistance through Ritual*. Hutchinson, 1976.

Hall, Stuart. 'Encoding/decoding', in Stuart Hall et al. (eds) *Culture, Media, Language*. Hutchinson, 1978.

—— with Jacques, Martin (eds) *The Politics of Thatcherism*. Pluto Press, 1981.

Hampshire, Stuart. *Morality and Pessimism*. Oxford University Press, 1976.

—— and Kolakowski, Leszek (eds) *The Socialist Idea*. Weidenfeld & Nicolson, 1974.

Hargreaves, David. 'What teaching does to teachers', *New Society*, 9 March 1978.

—— *The Challenge of the Comprehensive School*. Routledge & Kegan Paul, 1982.

Harrison, Andrew. *Making and Thinking*. Harvester Press, 1978.

Hegel, J.W.F. *The Philosophy of History*.

Heidegger, Martin. *Basic Writings: from 'Being and Time' to the 'Task of Thinking'*, edited by David Krell. Harper & Row, 1977.

H.M. Inspectorate. *Framework for the Curriculum*. HMSO, 1981.

Hempel, Carl. *Aspects of Scientific Explanation*. Free Press, 1965.

Herbst, Peter. *Theoreticism and Critical Inquiry*. Forthcoming.

Hill, Christopher. *Puritanism and Revolution*. Secker & Warburg, 1958.

—— *The Century of Revolution*. Nelson, 1961.

Hirsch, Fred. *Social Limits to Growth*. Allen & Unwin, 1976.

Hirschmann, Albert. *The Passions and the Interests: Political Arguments for Capitalism before its Triumph*. Princeton University Press, 1977.

Hirst, Paul. *Knowledge and the Curriculum*. Routledge & Kegan Paul, 1975.

Hobsbawm, Eric. *Labouring Men: Studies in Labour History*. Weidenfeld & Nicolson, 1964.

—— with Rudé, Georges. *Captain Swing*. Lawrence & Wishart, 1969.

—— and Ranger, Terence (eds). *The Invention of Tradition*. Cambridge University Press, 1983.

Hobson, J.A. *Imperialism*, 3rd rev. edn, Allen & Unwin, 1937.

Hofstadter, Douglas. *Gödel, Escher, Bach: an Eternal Golden Braid*. Harvester Press, 1979.

Hoggart, Richard. *The Uses of Literacy*. Chatto & Windus with Penguin, 1957.

Holbrook, David. *English for the Rejected*. Cambridge University Press, 1964.

Hoskins, W.G. *The Making of the English Landscape*. Hodder & Stoughton, 1955.

—— *The Midland Peasant*. Macmillan, 1957.

Humphries, S. *Hooligans or Rebels?* Basil Blackwell, 1981.

Hunt, A. (ed.) *Class and Class Structure*. Lawrence & Wishart, 1977.

Inglis, Fred. *Ideology and the Imagination*. Cambridge University Press, 1975.

—— *The Promise of Happiness: Value and Meaning in Children's Fiction*. Cambridge University Press, 1981.

—— *Radical Earnestness: English Social Theory 1880–1980*. Martin Robertson, 1982.

Jackson, Brian. *Streaming: an Education System in Miniature*. Routledge & Kegan Paul, 1964.
—— *Working-Class Community*. Routledge & Kegan Paul, 1966.
—— and Marsden, Dennis. *Education and the Working Class*, Routledge & Kegan Paul, 1962.
Jacobson, Dan. *The Story of the Stories*. Secker & Warburg, 1982.
Jameson, Storm. *Journey from the North*, 2 vols. Collins/Harvill, 1969; Virago, 1983.
Jennings, Paul. *The Jenguin Pennings*. Penguin, 1962.
Joll, James. *Gramsci*. Fontana, 1980.
Keating, Peter (ed.) *The Victorian Prophets*. Fontana, 1978.
Kitchen, Fred. *Brother to the Ox*. Heinemann Educational Books, 1959.
Kitching, Gavin. *Rethinking Socialism: a Theory for a Better Practice*. Methuen, 1983.
Körner, Stefan. *Experience and Theory: An Essay in the Philosophy of Science*. Routledge & Kegan Paul, 1966.
—— *Categorial Frameworks*. Basil Blackwell, 1970.
Kuhn, Thomas S. *The Structure of Scientific Revolutions*. Chicago University Press, 1962.
Kumar, Krishan. 'Holding the middle ground', in James Curran (ed.) *Mass Communication and Society*. Edward Arnold for Open University, 1977.
Larrain, Jorge. *The Concept of Ideology*. Hutchinson, 1979.
Laslett, Peter. *The World We Have Lost*. Methuen, 1965.
Leavis, F.R. *The Great Tradition*. Chatto & Windus, 1948.
Lévi-Strauss, Claude. *Structural Anthropology*. Allen Lane, Penguin, 1964.
Levitas, Mark. *Marxist Perspectives in the Sociology of Education*. Routledge & Kegan Paul, 1974.
Lovett, William. *William Lovett: His Life and Struggles* (1860). MacGibbon and Kee, 1967.
Lukes, Steven. *Power: a Radical View*. Macmillan, 1974.
MacIntyre, Alasdair. *Secularization and Moral Change*. Oxford, 1967.
—— *Against the Self-Images of the Age*. Duckworth, 1971.
—— *After Virtue: A Study in Moral Theory*. Duckworth, 1981.
Maclure, Stuart. *Educational Documents: England and Wales 1816–1968*. rev. edn, Methuen, 1969.
Mannheim, Karl. *Essays in the Sociology of Knowledge*. Routledge & Kegan Paul, 1952.
Marx, Karl. *Capital*, vol. I. Foreign Languages Publishing House, Moscow, 1887 and 1958.
—— *The German Ideology* (with Friedrich Engels, 1848), edited by T.J. Arthur. Lawrence & Wishart, 1970.

—— *Selected Works*. Foreign Languages Publishing House, Moscow, 1972.

—— *Selected Writings*, edited by D. McLellan. Oxford University Press, 1977.

Masterman, Len. *Teaching about Television*. Macmillan, 1980.

Meakin, David. *Man and Work: Literature and Culture in Industrial Society*. Methuen, 1976.

Mitchell, Juliet. *Woman's Estate*. Penguin, 1971.

Mitchison, Naomi. *You May Well Ask: A Memoir 1920–1940*. Gollancz, 1979.

Morris, James. *Pax Britannica*, 3 vols, rev. edn. Penguin, 1978.

Morris, William. *Political Writings*, edited by A. L. Morton. Lawrence & Wishart, 1973.

Morrison, D. and McIntyre, D. *Teachers and Teaching*. Penguin, 1969.

Mphahlele, Ezekiel. *Down Second Avenue*. Faber & Faber, 1956.

Muir, Edwin. *Autobiography*. Hogarth Press, 1954; Methuen, 1968.

—— *Collected Poems*. Faber & Faber, 1960.

Murdoch, Iris. *The Fire and the Sun: Why Plato Banished the Artists*. Clarendon Press, 1977.

Musgrove, Frank. *Patterns of Power and Authority in English Education*. Routledge & Kegan Paul, 1969.

Nagel, Ernest. *The Structure of Science*. Harcourt Brace, 1961.

Nagel, Thomas. *The Possibility of Altruism*. Oxford University Press, 1970.

Nairn, Tom. *The Break-up of Britain*. New Left Books, 1978.

Needham, Joseph and Ronan, Colin. *Science and Civilization in China*. Abridged edn, Cambridge University Press, 1978.

Newsom, John. *Half our Future*. HMSO 1963.

Nietzsche, Friedrich. *Beyond Good and Evil* (1886). Penguin, 1973.

Norman, Edward. *Christianity and the World Order*. Oxford University Press, 1979.

Nove, Alec. *The Economics of Feasible Socialism*. Allen & Unwin, 1983.

Oakeshott, Michael. *On Human Conduct*. Oxford University Press, 1975.

Oakley, Ann. *Sex, Gender, and Society*. Temple Smith, 1972.

Ortony, Andrew (ed.) *Metaphor and Thought*. Cambridge University Press, 1979.

Parfit, Derek. 'Lewis, Perry and what matters', in Amelie Rorty, *Identities of Persons*. University of California Press, 1976.

—— *Reasons and Persons*. Clarendon Press, 1984.

Parkes, Henry Bamford. *The American Experience*. Knopf, 1947.

Passmore, John. *The Perfectibility of Man*. Duckworth, 1970.

Phenix, F. *Realms of Meaning: a Philosophy of Curriculum*. McGraw-Hill, 1964.

Plamenatz, John. *Ideology*. Macmillan, 1971.

Popper, Karl. *The Logic of Scientific Discovery*. Hutchinson, 1959.

Postgate, Raymond. *The Good Food Guide 1965–66*. Consumers' Association with Cassell, 1965.

Poulantzas, Nicos. *Political Power and Social Classes*. New Left Books, 1973.

—— *Classes in Contemporary Capitalism*. New Left Books, 1975.

Quine, W.V.O. *Ontological Relativism*. Columbia University Press, 1969.

Reid, Ivan. *Social Class Differences in Britian*. 2nd edn. Grant McIntyre, 1981.

Rex, John. *Race Relations in Sociological Theory*. Weidenfeld & Nicolson, 1970.

Richardson, Elizabeth. *The Teacher, the School and the Task of Management*. Heinemann Educational Books, 1973.

Ricoeur, Paul. *The Rule of Metaphor.* Routledge & Kegan Paul, 1979.

Robbins Report. *Higher Education*. HMSO, 1963.

Roberts, M.B.V. *Biology: a Functional Approach*. Nelson, 1971.

Robinson, John. *Honest to God*. SCM Press, 1962.

Rorty, Amelie. *Identities of Persons*. University of California Press, 1976.

Rorty, Richard. *Philosophy and the Mirror of Nature*. Basil Blackwell, 1981.

Rowbotham, Sheila. *Woman's Consciousness, Man's World*. Penguin, 1973.

Rutter, Michael, et al. *15,000 Hours: Secondary Schools and Their Effects on Children*. Open Books, 1979.

Sampson, George. *English for the English* (1922), edited by Denys Thompson. Cambridge University Press, 1970.

Sartre, Jean-Paul. *Critique de la Raison Dialectique*. La Seuil, 1960.

—— *Critique of Dialectical Reason*, translated by Alan Sheridan-Smith. New Left Books, 1976.

Saussure, Fernand. *Course in General Linguistics*. edited by Charles Bally and Albert Sechehaye. McGraw-Hill/Collins, 1974.

Schlesinger, Philip. *Putting 'Reality' Together: the BBC and the Presentation of News*. Constable, 1978.

Scott, Paul. *The Raj Quartet*, 4 vols. Heinemann, 1967–75.

Scruton, Roger. *The Meaning of Conservatism*. Penguin, 1980.

Sen, Amartya. *On Economic Inequality*. Clarendon Press, 1973.

Sharp, Rachel. *Knowledge, Ideology, and the Politics of Schooling*. Routledge & Kegan Paul, 1980.

—— and Green, Anthony. *Education and Social Control*. Routledge & Kegan Paul, 1975.

Sharratt, Bernard. *Reading Relations: the Structures of Literary Production – a Text/Book*. Harvester Press, 1982.

Skinner, Quentin. *Machiavelli*. Oxford University Press, 1981.
—— 'Machiavelli on the maintenance of liberty', *Politics*, no. 18, 1983.
Smart, J. J. C. and Williams, Bernard. *Utilitarianism: For and Against*. Cambridge University Press, 1973.
Smart, Ninian. *The Phenomenon of Religion*. Macmillan, 1973.
Somerville, Alexander. *The Autobiography of a Working Man* (1848). MacGibbon & Kee, 1967.
Sraffa, Paul. *Production of Commodities by Means of Commodities*. Cambridge University Press, 1960.
Stove, David. *Popper and After: Four Modern Irrationalists*. Pergamon Press, 1982.
Strawson, Peter. *Individuals*. Oxford University Press, 1963.
Tawney, R. H. *Religion and the Rise of Capitalism*. John Murray, 1926.
—— *Equality*, edited with an introduction by Richard Titmuss. Allen & Unwin, 1964.
Taylor, Charles, 'Interpretation and the sciences of man'. *Journal of Metaphysics*, January 1971.
—— 'The politics of the steady state', in Colin Crouch and Fred Inglis (eds), *Morality and the Left*, special issue of *New Universities Quarterly*, vol. 32, no. 2, April 1978.
—— *Hegel and Modern Society*. Cambridge University Press, 1979.
—— *Philosophical Papers*, 2 vols. Cambridge University Press, 1985.
Thompson, E.P. *The Making of the English Working Class*. Gollancz, 1963; Penguin, 1968.
—— *The Poverty of Theory*. Merlin Press, 1968.
—— 'Time, work-discipline and industrial capitalism', *Past and Present*, vol. 38, 1968.
—— *Writing by Candlelight*. Merlin Press, 1980.
Townsend, Peter. *Poverty in the United Kingdom*. Penguin, 1979.
Trilling, Lionel. *Sincerity and Authenticity*. Oxford University Press, 1972.
Turner, Denys. *Marxism and Christianity*. Basil Blackwell, 1983.
Universities Central Council on Admissions. *21st Annual Report 1982–3, Statistical Supplement*, UCCA, 1984.
Watson, James. *The Double Helix*. Weidenfeld & Nicolson, 1967.
Weber, Max. *The Theory of Social and Economic Organisations*.
—— *The Protestant Ethic and the Spirit of Capitalism*, translated by Talcott Parsons. Allen & Unwin, 1948.
—— *From Max Weber*, edited with an introduction by H. H. Gerth and C. Wright Mills. Routledge & Kegan Paul, 1948.
—— *Economy and Society*. Routledge & Kegan Paul, 1962.
Westergaard, J.A. and Resler, H. *Class in a Capitalist Society: A Study of Contemporary Britain*. Heinemann, 1975.

White, John et al. *No, Minister: a Critique.* University of London Institute of Education, 1981.

Whitebrook, Joel. 'Saving the subject: modernity and the problem of the autonomous individual'. *Telos*, vol. 50, 1981.

Whitehead, A. N. *Science and the Modern World.* Cambridge University Press, 1938.

Whitty, Geoff and Young, Michael (eds) *Explanations in the Politics of School Knowledge.* Nafferton Press, 1978.

Wiener, Martin. *British Culture and the Decline of the Industrial Spirit.* Cambridge University Press, 1981.

Williams, Bernard. *Moral Luck.* Cambridge University Press, 1981.

—— *Ethics and the Limits of Philosophy.* Fontana, 1985.

Williams, Raymond. *Culture and Society 1780–1950.* Chatto & Windus, 1957; Penguin, 1958.

—— *Drama in a Dramatised Society.* Cambridge University Press, 1975; collected in *Writing in Society*, Verso Books, 1983.

—— *Towards 2000.* Chatto & Windus, 1983.

Willis, Paul. *Learning to Labour: How Working Class Kids get Working Class Jobs.* Saxon House, 1977.

Young, M.F.D. (ed.). *Knowledge and Control.* Routledge & Kegan Paul, 1972.

Young, Michael. *The Rise of the Meritocracy.* Penguin, 1961.

Ziman, John. *Public Knowledge.* Cambridge University Press, 1972.

—— *The Force of Knowledge.* Cambridge University Press, 1976.

Index

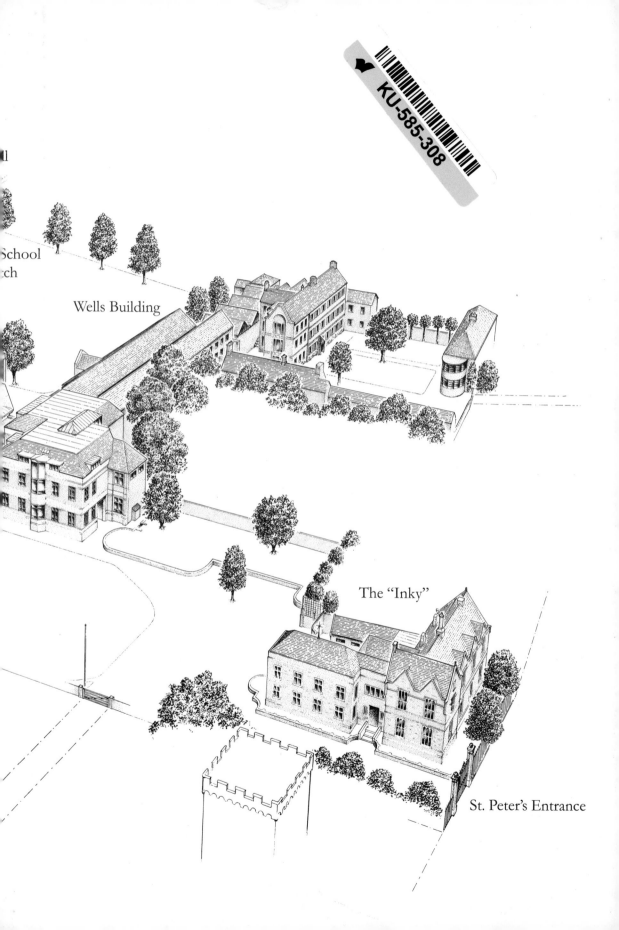

School
ch

Wells Building

The "Inky"

St. Peter's Entrance

Bedford School

A History

1552 – 2002

ALSO BY MICHAEL DE-LA-NOY

Elgar: The Man
Denton Welch: The Making of a Writer
The Honours System
Acting as Friends: The Story of the Samaritans
Eddy: The Life of Edward Sackville-West
Michael Ramsey: A Portrait
Windsor Castle: Past and Present
Exploring Oxford
The Church of England: A Portrait
The Queen Behind the Throne
The King Who Never Was: The Story of Frederick, Prince of Wales
Mervyn Stockwood: A Lonely Life

SUTTON POCKET BIOGRAPHIES

Scott of the Antarctic
George IV

EDITED

The Journals of Denton Welch
The Collected Short Writings of Denton Welch

BEDFORD
SCHOOL

A History
1552–2002

Michael De-la-Noy

BEDFORD

1999

This edition first published in 1999 by
Bedford School
De Parys Avenue, Bedford MK40 2TU

ISBN 0 9536685 0 9

SET, PRINTED AND BOUND IN GREAT BRITAIN BY
SMITH SETTLE LTD ILKLEY ROAD OTLEY WEST YORKSHIRE LS21 3JP

Contents

In loving memory of
Jeremy Somerville Snaith
1934 – 1993
The first Bedford School boy I met
'Look what the wind's blown in,' he said

List of Plates

Acknowledgements

I
t is a singular honour to be invited to write the history of your own school, and for that unlooked for distinction I have to thank the Head Master, Dr Philip Evans. I do so with a deep sense of gratitude, because I cannot pretend that I enjoyed my school days; yet through my acquaintance with Dr Evans, his staff and his pupils I have come to realise how relatively unhappy my childhood probably was, how much more prosaic my adult life would have been had my school days been in any way idyllic, and how much kinder, more courteous and less self-conscious I might have been as a boy had I enjoyed the privilege of being a pupil at Bedford today.

I must make it plain that although I have been accorded every conceivable assistance in my research, no one has attempted to influence what I have written, least of all the Head Master or the Governors. On the contrary, I have been accorded carte blanche to go where I wanted and talk to whom I pleased; the archives, too, far more extensive than I had anticipated in view of the fire of 1979 (they were safely stored at the time at 37 De Parys Avenue), were placed at my unrestricted disposal. For better or worse, this account is merely an attempt at objectivity by one reasonably disinterested outsider. I say outsider although I was at Bedford School; I mean outsider in the sense that I share few of the values of the vast majority of boys who have been to Bedford (I would not be a writer if I did), and if that fact predominates in what I have written, then I have failed. For it was never my intention to present a partisan view either of the public school system or of Bedford School, merely to recount, as honestly, accurately and entertainingly as I could, the 450 years of the school's history.

I have been welcomed into their studies and homes by many boys and masters, and Old Bedfordians have talked or written to me about their schooldays. And it is impossible to list the names of everyone whom I would wish to thank: monitors, junior boys undertaking drills, teaching and non-teaching staff. Conspicuously, however, two boys at Bedford, Adam Collett and Peter Burov-Monk, have burrowed industriously on my behalf in the archives, and John Sylvester, secretary of the Old Bedfordians Club, has responded with charm and patience to countless queries. Dr David Heald has made available much material and personal reminiscence in addition to sanctioning reproduction of extracts from his school memoirs. And to the following I am also especially grateful, for information, hospitality or help of one kind or another: The Rt. Hon Paddy Ashdown, MP, Miss Patricia Bell, the Reverend William and Mrs Brown, Mr Michael Brunson, Sir Michael Burton, Miss Pamela Clark (deputy registrar of the Royal Archives), Mr Philip Byam Cook, Mr John Eyre, the Rt Reverend David Farmbrough, Mrs Audrey Foote, Mr John Fowles, Mrs D. Grahame (secretary of the Victoria Cross and George Cross Association), Sir James & Lady Hennessy, Professor Fred Inglis, Mr Ian Jones, Mr Richard Lindley, the Rt Hon Lord Naseby (formerly Michael Morris, chairman of the School Governors), Sir Peter Parker, Mrs Frances Partridge, Mr Chris Pickford (Bedfordshire County archivist), Mr James Sewell (Corporation of London archivist), Professor Quentin Skinner, Mr Krishnan Srinivasan, Mr Andrew Underwood (Bedford Modern School archivist) and Mr Desmond Wigan (Clerk of the Harpur Trust).

My path at the school has been smoothed by, among many others, the Bursar, Lt Col. Howard Culley, the Director of Sport and Activities, Mr Tim Machin, the Director of Music, Mr Andrew Morris, the Head Master's secretary, Mrs Judy Kemp, and the school clerk, Mr Chris Shoyer. The help bestowed in countless ways by the Director of Studies, Mr Richard Miller, has been absolutely crucial and unremittingly enthusiastic and generous.

Michael De-la-Noy
Hove, 1998

Author's Note

In the time available between this book being commissioned and its publication it has not been possible for me to consult every scrap of original source material. Such a distinguished and prolific author as Christopher Hibbert took five years to research and write his 1997 history of Radley College, and Radley was only founded in 1847; had I enjoyed the same time span, publication would have post-dated the school's 450th anniversary. For early information I have therefore relied fairly heavily, in addition to material in the school archives, on a previous history of the school covering the years up to and including the Great War (*A History of Bedford School*, 1925), left uncompleted by John Sargeaunt at the time of his death in 1923 and rounded off (but without an index) by Ernest Hockliffe, and upon a history of the Harpur Trust by the late Joyce Godber, at one time Bedfordshire County Archivist. I think it is fair to say, however, that most people today would find Sargeaunt's account somewhat pedestrian, written in the scholarly and uncritical manner of a man of his generation, brought up at a time when authoritarianism was taken for granted and even the mildest unfavourable comments on the great were left to the up and coming upstart Lytton Strachey. And factually his early chapters did not find favour with Miss Godber, being marred, she thought, 'by insufficient historical understanding and by ignorance of the [Harpur] Trust'. At the same time, her own valuable contribution to research, *The Harpur Trust: 1552–1973*, is not easy to follow chronologically, and cannot be entirely relied upon for accuracy: 'Sir Graham White' for Mr Claude Grahame-White, for example.

I have also consulted an unpublished account of the Old Bedfordians Club compiled by Arthur Nightall, and of course a large number of issues of the school magazine, the *Ousel*; but by no means every issue. The fact is that each time you open a copy of the *Ousel* some item of interest strikes you, and my choice of material has been highly subjective. There is, after all, a limit to the length of any book, and had I included information on every subject and every person ever involved in the history of Bedford School I should still be writing well into the twenty-first century. Many tempting byways have therefore had to be resisted. I could easily have devoted an entire chapter to sport, another to music, and inevitably there will be readers with particular hobbyhorses of their own who will find my selection and handling of some events and achievements unsatisfactory. But it is the task of every biographer (and this is a biography — of a school) to select and distil, and hopefully to produce at least a recognisable microcosm.

Problems inevitably arise when different sources offer variations in the spelling of Head Masters' names, their dates, and even the dates of Acts of Parliament, although such variations, relating to a time when spelling was wildly inconsistent, records were often not kept up-to-date and methods of calculating time were in flux should not worry any but the most hopelessly pedantic. I had intended, for the sake of consistency, to follow previous research carried out by the school, but it turns out the school are not happy that every Head Master has yet been correctly identified, and there are even variations in school literature about dates for the opening of buildings. So if inconsistencies or errors appear they do so because a unanimity of agreement has been found impossible. I only hope the inconsistencies remain fairly trivial and the errors of fact minimal. At least at the last minute I was restrained by Dr Evans, a valuable proofreader inter alia, from repeating the *Dictionary of National Biography*'s assertion that Francis White was born 'probably in 1564'. Had that been the case he would, at thirteen, have been the youngest Head Master ever appointed.

I should also make it clear that this is an account of only one Harpur Trust School. Both Bedford Modern School and the Trust already have their histories, and I scarcely allude at all to the girls' schools within the Harpur Trust. Indeed, I only refer to the work of the Harpur Trust in so far as it has affected Bedford School, and then in no great detail; to have attempted a broader canvas would have been outside my remit and, I dare say, my ability.

M De-la-N.

Glossary

AFC	Air Force Cross
CB	Companion of the Order of the Bath
DCM	Distinguished Conduct Medal
DFC	Distinguished Flying Cross
DFM	Distinguished Flying Medal
DSC	Distinguished Service Cross
DSM	Distinguished Service Medal
DSO	Distinguished Service Order
KBE	Knight Commander of the Order of the British Empire
KCB	Knight Commander of the Order of the Bath
KCMG	Knight Commander of the Order of St Michael and St George
LVO	Lieutenant of the Royal Victorian Order
MC	Military Cross
MM	Military Medal
OBE	Officer of the Order of the British Empire
VC	Victoria Cross

DOMUS PATER Harperiae
Honos Tuus sit incola;
Tu porticus caelestibus
Praesidiis circumsede.

Impubes usque tu manus
Huc ventitantes respice;
Et inter mundi semitas
Pedes securos dirige.

Infirma verbo pectora
Rectoque cultu robora;
Cibum caelestem porrige
Et mala procul abige.

Ut omni mane gratiam
Tuam precentur cum fide
Et corde grato vesperi
Laudes tuas concelebrent.

Deo Patri sit gloria
Eiusque soli Filio,
Sanctissimo cum Spiritu,
Et nunc et in perpetuum.

Henry Le Mesurier, 1861

ONE

An Eagle Displayed

1552–1811

T HE REIGN of that unfortunate child Edward VI was one of the
shortest in English history. It lasted only half a dozen years, the boy
king dying in 1553, at the age of sixteen. Yet despite the nervous
energy consumed by religious and political upheavals inherited from
the previous reign and brewing up for the next, Edward's rule was remarkable
for the birth it gave to so many schools. In the space of sixteen months as
many as sixteen grammar schools were licensed by letters patent. Bedford was
one.

Letters patent enable a sovereign to confer rights or privileges without
recourse to parliamentary legislation. In the case of Bedford, town and gown
were indissolubly linked by letters patent permitting the Corporation to receive
endowments in order to support a school. Hence Bedford School's legal life,
so to speak, began at Ely, on 15 August 1552, when letters patent were granted
to 'the Mayor, Bailiffs, Burgesses and Commonalty of the Town of Bedford,'
granting them the right to 'erect, make, found and establish a free and perpetual Grammar School … for the education, institution and instruction of
Boys and Youths in Grammar, Literature and good Manners.'

The boys and youths were to be taught by a Master and an usher appointed
by the Warden and Fellows of 'the College of the Blessed Mary of Winton in
Oxford, commonly called New College.'[1] And as well as being granted permission to receive endowments with which to run the school the Corporation
were told they might provide, out of endowments, dowries for 'poor maids'
and alms for the poor. Much contention was to arise as a result.

Edward VI had been born into an age not only of acute political danger for
courtiers and clergy but of almost unprecedented intellectual excitement. His
father's first archbishop of Canterbury, William Warham, had been a friend of

the fastidious Dutch humanist Erasmus, who declared on arriving at Windsor Castle that he found the place more like a house of the muses than a Court. Edward's tutor, Sir Anthony Cooke, had daughters as learned as he, one of whom became the mother of Francis Bacon. Roger Ascham, tutor to the king's younger sister, Elizabeth, was a Fellow of St John's College, Cambridge and one of the leading educationalists of his day, and Elizabeth was to become one of the best educated monarchs ever to ascend the throne.

Edward had also been born into an age when survivors grew up quickly. But even allowing for the fact that as a very young boy he was well aware of his regal responsibilities, assumed on his accession and coronation in 1547 when he was only ten, he was old for his years. He would have known that since the death of his father, Henry VIII, funds intended for the furtherance of school and university education, funds that should have been accruing to the crown, were being creamed off by rapacious ministers. And listening attentively to a sermon preached in December 1550 by the Master of St John's College, Cambridge the king received a jolt. Clearly intent on impressing a boy of thirteen, and not too concerned that he happened to be his sovereign, the preacher denounced those who had 'craftily conveyed much from the King, from learning, from poverty, and from all the commonwealth, unto their own private advantage'. And he added, speaking directly to the royal youth, 'You that are in authority look upon it; for if you wink at such matters, God will scoule upon you'. The winking stopped, as did the pilfering, and letters patent began to flow.

Edward may not personally have instigated the creation of any new scholastic foundation, in the way that Henry VI had been responsible, in 1440, for Eton College (it was the Mayor and Burgesses of Bedford who were to petition the king for permission to establish a school in their town), but he most certainly approved of the general trend towards widening secular educational opportunities, especially in the wake of his father's destruction of so many seats of monastic learning. Appalling ill-health exacerbated by incompetent doctors (they eventually managed to poison him) ensured that Edward's life would never be a long or a happy one; he was said to be so solemn that he only ever laughed once. But he knew what he was doing, and his seal, affixed to the letters patent granted at Ely, just a year before his death, was no rubber stamp. Without the legality of those letters patent there would have been no future endowments, and King Edward VI can surely be regarded as Bedford School's first, and by birth most illustrious, benefactor.[2]

Reading the letters patent one could be forgiven for receiving the impression there had never previously been a school in Bedford. There had, of course, tiny though the town had always been, but to pretend that 'Bedford School' predates the granting of the letters is a bit like suggesting some sort of building must always have stood on the site of a great Elizabethan mansion. It probably had but it may only have been a mud hut. But a rudimentary school had almost certainly sheltered under the wing of St Paul's Church since the Domesday Survey of 1086, when the town was spelt Bedeford. St Paul's was at that time a collegiate church, maintained by secular canons who would have been perfectly competent to instruct Bedford's youngsters in Latin, writing and ecclesiastical history; they would most probably have known Aelfric's Latin grammar and his Latin–English glossary, and the pupils may also have been aided in their studies by a grammar for schoolboys composed by Thomas Linacre, one of Thomas More's mentors and tutor to Arthur, Prince of Wales. Management of the school would have been the responsibility of the archdeacon of Bedford, not, in the Middle Ages, a priest but a perpetual deacon, someone engaged in administration rather than pastoral work. In about 1166 the clergy of St Paul's became canons regular, subject to the Religious rule, and they moved to a priory at Newnham, on the banks of the Ouse, a mile or so to the east of the town centre, built for them by Simon de Beauchamp, the owner of Bedford Castle.

It is often said that little is known about the school between the years 1166 and 1540, the year that Newnham Priory was suppressed and the monks quietly dispersed. The truth is that nothing is known. It is unlikely, however, that the boys were taught at the priory, for the monks did not belong to an enclosed order, and they would have been free, for at least 280 years, to carry on their educational work somewhere in the town — but where we shall probably never know. What we do know is that by 1447 there was a Scolestreet (later Mill Lane and now Mill Street), and obviously at some point between 1166 and 1447 it was in Scolestreet, sometimes later spelt Scole Lane or Schole Lane, that the medieval school came to rest.[3]

And in 1548, eight years after the suppression of Newnham Priory, we find Edmund Greene (variously spelt Green or Grene), a Fellow of New College, Oxford, teaching in Scolestreet. Without any scholastic monks left in the town the school had been in a precarious situation, and it is perfectly possible that between 1540 and 1548 it actually closed down. There had been hints of an endowment to set up the school on a permanent basis, and it was quite obviously Greene's four years of satisfactory teaching that served as the impetus for the Corporation to seek letters patent. There is no evidence to explain who actually appointed Greene, but his connection with New College certainly explains why, in the letters patent of 1552, the Warden and Fellows of New College were nominated to appoint a Master and usher. Edmund Greene is officially recognised as Bedford School's first Head Master and he fully deserves the distinction, remaining as Master for a quarter of a century.[4]

Whoever was responsible for Greene's appointment, and for petitioning for the involvement of New College, placed Bedford scholars in the mainstream of educational development. New College had been founded by William of Wykeham as early as 1379; three years later he established the first great English public school, Winchester, whose boys he always intended should proceed to his own Oxford college.[5] He said his desire was to produce 'men of great learning, faithful to the Church of God and to the king and realm.' He became Lord Chancellor and bishop of Winchester, and was, said the fourteenth century historian Jean Froissart, 'a priest so much in favour with the king of England [Edward III] that everything was done by him and nothing was done without him.' Like Bedford, and a good many other schools, Winchester College had enjoyed monastic origins long before the date of its official foundation.

An inscription recalling Bedford's ecclesiastical roots adorns the Great Hall, where the Upper School assembles for prayers and notices. Those boys who have been attending during Latin lessons will know that the school was founded 'in this town by monks in ancient times.' The Latin inscription further recalls that the school was 'endowed and renewed thereafter by Sir William Harper, Knight, and Dame Alice his wife.' The name of Alice, who today we would address as Lady Harper, is commemorated in the Dame Alice Harpur School for Girls, one of four schools now administered by the Harpur Trust.[6]

'The monks in ancient times' would not have had many boys in their charge. Apart from the castle, built about 1100 and demolished in 1224, there was no private residence in Bedford of any size before Elizabethan times, and although by 1414 Bedford had a royal duke — John of Lancaster, third son of Henry IV — the town was for many years no more than a modest cluster of houses centred round the bridge (and the castle, while it stood — on a site just to the east of the Swan Hotel). Had there been any citizens with pretensions to upper class status they would have had their children educated at home by a tutor. Even by the time Sir William Harper appeared on the scene — he was born in 1497, possibly in Biddenham, more likely in Bedford — the town was only growing in size and importance very slowly, and Harper was a perfect example of an ambitious, quick-witted sixteenth century provincial boy who would not have hesitated to gravitate to the metropolis.[7]

That said, there is scant evidence for the early life of William Harper. That he attended the school established at least since 1447 in Mill Street can scarcely be doubted, for there was no other, and no other circumstance can explain his later desire to rehouse the school and then bestow gifts of land upon it. And it may well have been Harper who was instrumental in Edmund Greene's appointment as Master. He probably left Bedford when he was about sixteen to seek his fortune in London, and what we know for sure is that in 1533, when he was thirty-six years old, he was admitted as a freeman of the Merchant Taylors' Company — so it was quite natural that in 1561 he should help in the founding of Merchant Taylors' School. In 1547, at the advanced age of fifty, he married a widow, Alice, by whom he acquired a stepdaughter. He served for a year as treasurer of St Bartholomew's Hospital, became Master of his livery company and in 1553 he was chosen by the City Aldermen for the Ward of Bridge Without. He transferred to Dowgate Ward three years later and remained an Alderman until his death in 1574.

Merchant Taylors' owned a substantial house in Lombard Street, bequeathed to them for the use of members likely to reach the highest municipal office, and into the house in Lombard Street Harper duly moved. He served as sheriff for the year 1556–7, and in 1561 he reached the zenith of his City career when he was elected Lord Mayor. He celebrated the event, on 29 October, by laying on an expensive river pageant, 'with the althermen in ther skarlett, and all the craftes of London in ther leverey … and grett shutyng of gunes and trump-ettes blohyng.'[8] In February the following year he was knighted by Queen Elizabeth, and as duty now dictated, rather in the manner of Sir John Falstaff, five months later he was busy raising a band of soldiers for service in Normandy.

Bedford's eagle, emblazoned on so many blazers, bookbindings and letter-headings, has its origins in Harper's knighthood, for to commemorate his rise up the social ladder, in 1561 he was granted a coat of arms, to wit: 'Azure, on a fess between three eagles displayed or, a fret between two martlets of the first.' The eagle crops up again on Sir William's crest: 'Upon a crescent or, charged with a fret between two martlets azure, an eagle displayed of the last.'

Four years after Edmund Greene's arrival in Bedford, and to coincide with the granting of letters patent in 1552, Harper provided the Mill Street school with new premises in St Paul's Square: a two-storeyed building for the boys and the first usher, Robert Elbone, and an adjacent house for the Master, Edmund Greene. He also began to accumulate leases of land to the west of Bedford, presumably with the intention of ensuring an income for the school. But it was not until 1564, by which time Greene had been in his post sixteen years, that Harper purchased from the Queen's physician four parcels of grazing land in the parish of St Andrew's, Holborn. Even then, another mysterious two years were to elapse before Harper and his wife actually assigned the Holborn lands to Bedford Corporation. This they did by means of a Deed of Gift dated 22

April 1566, made 'Betwene the Mayre Baylefes Burgesses and commonaltye of the towne of Bedford in the countye of Bedford on thone partye And Syr wyllyam Harpar knyghte Alderman of the citye of London and dame Alyce his wyffe on the other partye.' There was little conformity of spelling in Tudor times, and it was often not even consistent within the space of one sentence. But in conformity with the royal letters patent the Master and usher were to be 'sustained' and the school continued for ever; funds were to be provided 'ffor the maryage of pore maydes of the sayd towne and for porre chylders ther to be nurrysshed and enformed'; and any 'resydue or superfluytye' was to be distributed 'in almes to the poore of the sayd towne.'

The purchase price of the Holborn plots had been £180 for thirteen acres and one rood, or in other words, 13.25 acres, and their initial rental value came to the princely sum of £12 per annum.[9] Situated just to the north of the currently inhabited area of London, St Andrew's already contained a few scattered houses, and William Harper had doubtless envisaged further domestic expansion, and hence a gradual increase in rents. And indeed, before long the land was bringing in an income of £40 a year. In the aftermath of the great fire of London, a speculative builder by the name of Nicholas Barbon was hot in pursuit of lucrative building plots in the neighbourhood of Holborn, and by the end of the nineteenth century, by which time all Harper's land had been built on, the Harpur Trust was in receipt of some £14,000 a year. Even if Harper could never have foreseen the eventual extent of commercial property in Holborn for which the Harpur Trust would be responsible, his shrewd investment has placed thousands of men, women and children in his debt. With good reason, he is, after Edward VI, commemorated as Bedford School's most notable benefactor.

In his philanthropic endeavours William Harper was very much a man of his time, but by no means a pioneer. One needs to recall that during the fifteenth and sixteenth centuries some 800 grammar schools were set up. Sir William Sevenoaks, Lord Mayor of London in 1418, had been a foundling, taking his name from the town in Kent where he was nursed back to life, and in 1432 he repaid his debt to society by endowing Sevenoaks Grammar School. Stockport Grammar School was left £17 a year in 1484 by a Lord Mayor and goldsmith, Sir Edmund Shae. John Percival, in whose house in Lombard Street William Harper lived, had founded a grammar school, in 1502, in Macclesfield. Within only a decade, St Paul's in London had been established by the Dean of St Paul's, John Colet.

But a large number of famous schools post-date Bedford: Oundle by four years, Repton by five. Harrow was not founded until 1571, Charterhouse not until 1611. In 1567 Rugby, later to be regarded as the archetypal Victorian public school, was established by yet another childless City merchant, Lawrence Sheriff, and in 1874, having trained James Surtees Phillpotts, Rugby was to provide Bedford with one of its great Head Masters.

Alice Harper died in 1569, and was buried in her parish church, St Mary Woolnoth. A year later Sir William Harper married again. His second wife was Margaret Lethers, a lady, it seems, of determined disposition; when Harper died it took the Merchant Taylors' Company eighteen months to repossess the house in Lombard Street, and without quoting the source of his information, writing in 1856 James Wyatt says she was 'neither just nor generous'.[10] In 1573 Harper drew up his last Will and Testament, leaving instructions for his burial at St Paul's, Bedford.[11] He died on 27 February 1574, aged seventy-seven, leaving behind him a large legacy of goodwill. When a contemporary who almost certainly knew him, William Jaggard, came to write *A View of All the Lord Mayors* in 1601 he recorded of Sir William Harper that 'manye excellent deedes of charity proceeded from this goodly knight, which are not yet gathered'.

In 1573 Edmund Greene was succeeded by William Smyth (possibly Smythe; in 1581 he became a canon of Lincoln), and in 1577 Francis White took over. Born at Eaton Socon, where his father was vicar, and educated at St Neots Grammar School, White may already have been familiar with the neighbourhood, and after resigning in 1587 he went on to enjoy a fairly spectacular ecclesiastical career, collecting no fewer than three bishoprics. It has, until now, always been said that prior to James Phillpotts only one Head Master (Matthew Priaulx) was a layman. This is not so, for it was not until the year after White left Bedford that he was ordained priest. In 1622 he was installed as dean of Carlisle, being consecrated bishop of the diocese in 1626. Two years later he was elected bishop of Norwich, and in an age that willfully accepted pluralities on a breathtaking scale, in 1631 he was elected bishop of Ely. When he died in 1638, most unusually for a Head Master of Bedford School, he was buried in St Paul's Cathedral.

White was succeeded as Master by someone called Chambers. And that is all we know about him. He was replaced in 1597 by Richard Butcher, but there is uncertainty as to how long Butcher remained.[12] Hence it is also not known exactly in which year Henry Whitaker (or possibly Whiteacre) became Master, but what is certain is that for the first decade of the seventeenth century, which saw the end of the Tudor dynasty William Harper had served, the Master was a Fellow of New College called Robert Barker. During his tenure of office Bedford Corporation voted to form a committee of two or three 'learned men' to 'oversee the school', and 'take trial and proof of the schoolmaster, his ability, aptness and diligence'.

This was in clear breach of the letters patent; in addition to laying upon New College a duty to nominate the Master and usher, the letters had appointed New College as Visitors. And it graphically illustrates the basic flaw in the letters. While New College were too far off to exercise effective control they were expected to whistle up competent teachers when they thought the salaries being offered by the Corporation, who had been charged by the letters patent with responsibility for paying the Master and usher, were too low; when Bedford Corporation thought they had been saddled with inferior teachers they felt frustrated by their lack of power to supervise.

Thanks to the Tudor historian and cartographer John Speed we have a very accurate idea how the town of Bedford looked when Robert Barker arrived; the school (spelt schole) was even pinpointed in St Paul's Square in his map of Bedfordshire, drawn about 1600.[13] Speed was born c. 1552, and, by another coincidence, before commencing his brilliant career as a cartographer he followed in William Harper's footsteps by becoming a Freeman of the Merchant Taylors' Company. He died in London in 1629, the father of eighteen children. What is plain from his map are the very limited boundaries of Bedford: St Peter's Church at the northern extremity, St John's at the southern; and from east to west the town just reached from Caudwell Abbey to St Loyes. Mill Lane is clearly shown, as are two other original thoroughfares, still in existence today, Duck Lane (now Duck Mill Lane) and Lurke Lane (now Lurke Street). As one would expect, houses lined the High Street, but much of the town between the criss-cross of streets consisted of orchards, meadowland and fields of barley.

In 1610 Barker was succeeded by another Fellow of New College, Daniel Gardener (perhaps Gardner), and 15 years later Gardener was joined as usher by a Cambridge graduate, the Reverend Giles James. Mr James might have stepped straight out of the pages of *Nicholas Nickleby*, for he proved to be the forerunner of Mr Squeers of Dotheboys Hall. If he bothered to get out of bed at all he did not do so before nine in the morning. And on the rare occasions when he turned up for work he immediately set about beating his pupils, so that the streets were said to resound 'with the yells and sodaine outcries' of the boys. If he did not happen to have a cane about his person, that was no problem; he resorted to hitting the boys with his fists.

The inspiration for Wackford Squeers was to be a criminal sadist by the name of William Shaw, who kept a school in Yorkshire called Bowes Academy and dispatched no fewer than twenty-five of his pupils to the village churchyard. But by Dickens's day violence against schoolboys was no novelty; Bedford School's Giles James once 'so mangled a boy in his mouth and throat' the school doctor thought the lad was going to die. James even set about the Master, and ended up in court, the Mayor of Bedford binding him over to be of good behaviour. James had obtained the curacy of Clapham with which to supplement his annual salary of £10 (the Master received £20 a year) so he was quite well off as well as a little mad, and decided to get his revenge by initiating criminal charges against the Master.

Daniel Gardener seems to have dealt most incompetently with the whole affair. Instead of asking New College to dismiss the wretched usher, or undertaking the task himself, he begged the Corporation to do the deed. In this they obliged, although they had no business to, and as soon as James had been sacked he appealed to New College, whose Warden and Fellows knew nothing of his outrageous conduct; they were merely incensed that the Corporation should have taken it upon themselves to dismiss an employee of the school, and promptly reinstated him. But relations remained surprisingly cordial, the Warden, when writing to the Corporation telling them not to interfere with the usher, beginning his letter, 'Good Mr Mayor', and signing off, 'Your loving friends the Warden and Fellowes.' The Warden, elected in 1617, was Robert Pinck, a great friend and supporter of Archbishop Laud, who was addressed from Bedford as 'The Right Worshipful Mr Doctor Pincke'. Having presided over a decline in school numbers entirely due to his failure to report on his usher earlier, Gardener hung on until 1636, withdrawing eventually to the tranquil vicarage of Godmanchester, near Huntingdon.

Things were not at first much improved by Gardener's retirement. He was succeeded by a young clergyman called William Varney, who managed to secure the living of St Peter's, where he spent more time than he did at the school. Within six years of Varney's arrival civil war had broken out (Charles I raised his standard at Nottingham on 22 August 1642), and it so happened that Varney took the royalist side. In 1656, seven years after the execution of the king, Varney declined to swear allegiance to the Lord Protector, Oliver Cromwell, and was ejected from his parish; he lost the Mastership of the school as well, and was replaced, for four years, by an enterprising New College Fellow called George Butler. It was the young and enthusiastic Butler who laid the very earliest foundations of boarding at Bedford, attracting to the school the sons of clergy and country gentry living too far afield to make a daily trek on foot or by pony. These early boarders lodged with the usher, and began to gain places at Cambridge colleges, an indication that standards of teaching were rising along with an increase of boys on the school roll. This brief period of expansion and success was cut short, however, in 1660; with the restoration of the monarchy and the arrival in England of Charles II from his exile in France the useless William Varney demanded his jobs back. He was as idle on his return as he had been in the past, but it looked as though things might pick up again when, in 1663, he died.

An 'able and sedulous' person was required to replace Varney, the Corporation told New College. Unfortunately, they chose John Allanson, one of the College chaplains who was also a chaplain to the Fleet. He seems to have preferred life afloat to life on shore, and hired a clerk, Daniel Langhorne, to act as surrogate Master, deigning to spend just four weeks in Bedford during the two years of life remaining to him. Aware in 1665 that a wiser appointment was required, New College broke with tradition by alighting on a Wykehamist who, instead of going up to New College, had graduated at University College, situated in the High Street and probably the second oldest college in Oxford. He was John Butler, who had already gained experience of teaching in a school of his own.

Butler's seven-year stint as Master coincided with a period when one of the town's most illustrious sons, John Bunyan (born in fact at Elstow, in 1628), was imprisoned in Bedford's County Jail, on the corner of the High Street and Silver Street. So strong a hold on the town did Bunyan's evangelical Christianity take that Mill Street eventually became host to a string of nonconformist chapels, Bunyan having begun his *Pilgrim's Progress* during a second term of imprisonment in the Stone House Prison on Bedford Bridge. With Butler's arrival the Corporation also began to see no reason why income from the Holborn endowment — by the middle of the seventeenth century it amounted to about £50 a year — should not start to benefit the town as well as the school. And why not? Both the letters patent and Sir William and Lady Harper's Deed of Gift had included provision for wedding portions and help for the poor. When arguments arose, as from now on they frequently did, they were concerned not with the legality of income going to charity but with the proportions in which the income from Holborn should be distributed. But during Butler's time, at any rate, disagreements did not entirely deflect the school from its educational purposes; a boy by the name of Samuel Bentham entered St John's College, Cambridge in 1670, and Valentine Cotton and John Harding went up to Peterhouse, Cambridge as 'poor scholars'. Peterhouse seems to have been a favourite college with Bedford boys; nine entered between 1685 and 1701.

But another century and a half was to pass before the school was set on anything like an even keel, and the more one explores the early history of inappropriate appointments, lack of adequate funding and antediluvian accommodation the more one wonders the school survived at all. It is also not surprising it lost so much ground to its contemporaries, failing almost entirely to attract any social cachet. To some extent this can be attributed to Bedford's geographical position. Winchester occupied the seat of England's ancient treasure house, adjacent to a great cathedral; Westminster was in London itself, Harrow almost so and Eton was so close to Windsor Castle that at one time Eton College and St George's Chapel shared the same choir. In the longer term, Bedford never benefited from an immediate acquisition, as a modern school like Stowe was lucky enough to do (or Radley, who took over Radley Hall), of an architecturally beautiful compound, not that this is always an advantage; in 1998 the fabric of Stowe House was found to be crumbling away. And when eventually Bedford was compelled to vacate its one Georgian building it was nobody's fault that it did so only to move into a purpose-built Victorian edifice, a building that entirely belied 340 years of the school's existence.

One of the strangest appointments as Master was made in 1672, when John Longworth arrived in Bedford. He was permitted to retain his Fellowship at New College and also became vicar of the nearby village of Oakley. This in itself was not so unusual; he would have needed the extra stipend to supplement his inadequate pay as Master. But in 1677 he set sail for America, resigning his Oakley living but not his post at the school, and for four years the grammar school was allowed to drift without anyone at the helm. Longworth was eventually replaced, in 1681, by a rather dubious New College Fellow called William Willis. In his early history of the school, John Sargeaunt, head of school 1875–6 and the first Old Bedfordian to become president of the Oxford Union, is eloquently reticent, as were so many Victorians, on the subject of Mr Willis's shortcomings. Apparently he began well, but soon his early promise tailed off. 'It seems probable,' Sargeaunt writes, 'that Bacchus at least, if not also a less reputable deity, was an object of his worship.'[14]

Whatever his predilection, for the bottle or boys, or both, within two years William Willis had gone, to be succeeded by Nicholas Aspinall, a celibate Cambridge clergyman who declined, perhaps in the wake of a scandal concerning Willis, to be bothered with boarders, but apparently did his work 'much to the general satisfaction'. With news from America that the absentee Longworth had died, Aspinall was confirmed as Master, and like so many potentially insolvent clergymen he proceeded to acquire pluralities, spending a disproportionate amount of his time preparing sermons, which in his day were expected to be preached at considerable length. Yet he was also said to attend to the school 'even to the prejudice of his own health'. This may have been a slight exaggeration, for few schoolmasters or clerics have been known to die of overwork, and it so happens that Mr Aspinall lived to be seventy — attested 'the best friend he ever had' by his usher, Benjamin Rogers.

Aspinall was Master for a quarter of a century, and he and his boys — in his heyday they numbered twenty-six — lived through stirring times; the Glorious Revolution of 1688, which settled once and for all the Divine Right of Kings and the supremacy of the Church of England, Marlborough's great victories against the French, the death, in 1714, of the last Stuart monarch and the succession of the House of Hanover. Boys taught by Aspinall entered Trinity College, Cambridge and Corpus Christi, Oxford, but one cannot say that when he ceased to be Master in 1718 Aspinall left the school in very good shape. Serious competition had arisen from two quarters. A private tutor called Benjamin Chesterton had set up business in the town; and an enterprising private boarding school in Aspley Guise, some dozen miles to the south-west of Bedford, was beginning to syphon off some of the town's more affluent boys. Perhaps having heard of these developments, a Fellow of New College described as 'a man of reputed ability' declined the offer of the Mastership, almost certainly, as things turned out, to the detriment of the school.

The job went instead to another New College Fellow, Matthew Priaulx, who arrived in Bedford only to find the school locked and barred. Eventually the usher smuggled him in through a back door. The explanation for this bizarre state of affairs was that, quite improperly, the Corporation had decided that in future they would appoint the Master. They refused to pay Priaulx's salary, appointed a Master of their own, and set him up in the Town Hall as a rival to Priaulx, who continued to teach in the grammar school. The situation was akin to the Church's experiment with two popes, one in Rome and one in Avignon. New College and Bedford, still only a market town with a population of about 2,000, were on a collision course. In 1724 the Lord Chancellor ruled that only Bedford children were to be educated free, which was calculated to discourage boarders, and in 1731 Priaulx reported that his usher 'never had but two boarders'. Four years later, ever optimistic, he said there were 'daily prospects of additions'. By the time of Priaulx's mercifully early death in 1739 the number of boys was down to three.

It was in 1725, finally out of patience with the Corporation, and out of pocket, having paid the Master's salary themselves for the past seven years, that New College took the Corporation to court. When the case was heard on 21 July it settled a number of contentious issues: the Warden and Fellows were confirmed in their right to appoint the Master and usher; salaries were to be paid by the Corporation, the Master to receive £30 a year; and after salaries had been paid and the Master's house repaired, the school was due to receive one-third of the remaining funds, the poor one-third and one-third was to be set aside to provide marriage portions.

One reason the numbers of pupils slumped to an all-time low in Priaulx's day was because he took his duties as Master in a very light-hearted manner. He had taken care to marry a woman with money of her own, into whose capital he dipped from time to time in order, he said, 'to keep himself as a gentleman, healthy and clean'. He was proud to announce that when he taught, he taught young gentlemen, but his time for teaching was in short supply; thanks to the bishop of Lincoln and the chancellor of the diocese of Peterborough he became proctor in both their ecclesiastical courts, but his most extraordinary achievement, considering the manner of his arrival, was to end up as town clerk of Bedford.

He found time, however, for various rows with his ushers. One year, on the mayor's feast day, Priaulx decreed a holiday but the usher coerced the boys into school, whereupon Priaulx paid off the usher and released the boys. There were at this time two classes, the Master taking the upper class, the usher the lower. But teaching was not of the highest standard. Priaulx himself admitted that all his class did was catechize nouns and pronouns eight hours every day. But when it came to husbanding the school's financial resources, the Corporation cannot be said to have set a good example either. Rents from the Harpers' gift now amounted to £150 a year, and civic worthies felt obliged to go on expense account sprees to the capital to sample for themselves the delights of Holborn. In 1733 seven members of the Corporation put in a bill for £40 19s 8d — as much as the Master's annual salary. The episode must have been broadcast far and wide for Oliver Goldsmith recalled it to mind 40 years later when he wrote *She Stoops to Conquer*.[15]

'What's here?' Marlow enquires of Hastings. 'For the first course; for the second course; for the desert [sic]. The devil, Sir, do you think we have brought down the whole Joiners Company, or the Corporation of Bedford, to eat up such a supper? Two or three little things, clean and comfortable, will do.'

Despite the court case of 1725, by 1739 all was sweetness and light once again between Bedford Corporation and New College, the Corporation entreating the Warden and Fellows to send them 'two worthy and fitting men' to serve as Master and usher, at the same time conferring the freedom of the borough on four of the Fellows. As Master, the college selected a newly ordained Fellow, twenty-three-year-old George Bridle, a person 'who is as fitted and capable to teach and instruct your children as either the College or I may venture to say that the University could produce,' the Warden assured the Corporation. As usher they chose William Bowles. But Bowles never set foot in Bedford. Bridle popped the usher's salary into his own pocket, and when he had the audacity to complain that it was paid late, he was told not to make 'such trivial complaints and peevish applications'. Slowly it dawned on even the dimmest townsfolk that no usher had been seen in Bedford for quite a number of years; moreover, Mr Bridle remained a resident Fellow of New College. The saga of Mr Bridle's Mastership becomes odder the more one delves into it. Bowles was well aware that Bridle was making off with his salary, of which he had no need; he was to become a canon of Salisbury. And the school remained without an usher until 1755 when Edward Towersey arrived. Yet despite the pressing attractions of Oxford and St Mary's, Bedford, during Bridle's thirty-four years as Master major developments occurred, the mayor himself being satisfied that 'no one doubts Mr Bridle's abilities'.

In 1747 there were only eleven boys. Fourteen years later a writing school, precursor of the English School, the Commercial School and eventually Bedford Modern School, was established.[16] School began at seven in the morning and continued until five in the afternoon. The Master and usher were allocated two half-holidays a week, and it has been estimated that the teaching staff put in thirty hours a week, the boys forty-two.[17] These hours were scarcely excessive, but as the curriculum was so limited the boys might have gone mad with monotony had they spent any longer at their lessons.

The eighteenth century Bow Street magistrate Henry Fielding has a character in a novel, *The Adventures of Joseph Andrews*, declare that public schools were 'the nurseries of all vice and immorality', and for many years many were. But compared to their contemporaries at Eton or Westminster, Bedford boys seem on the whole to have got off lightly, perhaps because Bedford has remained predominantly a day school. And even in Hanovarian England, which was endemically corrupt, many more children who lived at home were loved than were treated harshly. It was not until the twentieth century, as a pitiful record of endless beatings for trivial offences held in the school archives testify, that some of the evil results of bestowing unbridled power rather than benign authority on schoolboys permeated Bedford. At a time when Eton and Rugby boys were being flogged to within an inch of their lives and nearly roasted alive, Bedford Grammar School boys had little more to complain about than being taught by rote and receiving the odd cuff round the ear from some of the more belligerent teachers. The poet Southey wrote of a friend removed from Charterhouse towards the end of the eighteenth century 'because he was almost literally killed there by the devilish cruelty of the boys; they used to lay him before the fire till he was scorched'. Boys died in boxing matches; the chapel register at Eton records Edward Cockburn, in 1730, 'murdered by Thomas Dalton, his Schoolfellow.'[18]

The most spectacular improvement in Bridle's time was architectural. Until 1760 the Harpur estate was worth no more than £150 a year. Now many of the leases fell in, renewals were negotiated, and by the end of the century income exceeded £6,000. Harper's original endowment of £12 per annum was becoming big business, and an Act of Parliament of 1764 created trustees to take care of the finances; they included, in addition to thirteen aldermen and thirteen members of the common council, representatives of the Bedford clergy and laity. The mayor was to act as chairman, and it was the 1764 Act which effectively created the Harpur Trust, alternatively known as the Bedford Charity. Today the Trust is composed of twenty-nine Governors.

With the trustees relatively awash with money the Master's salary was raised to a realistic £200 a year, the usher's to £100. The trustees were obliged to find an additional member of staff for the newly established writing school, and his salary was fixed at £60 a year. After an initial three-month hiccup, George Jackson, a schoolmaster at Highgate, arrived to teach reading, writing and arithmetic, which would have been a good deal more useful to the majority of Bedford boys than Greek and Latin, and he remained until his death in 1803. By the time Jackson had acquired an assistant — in 1775 — the Master, George Bridle, could fairly be described as Bedford's Head Master rather than Master, and from now on the facilities and the staff were to increase in range and numbers at such a rate that accommodation could never keep abreast of demands made upon it.

It has to be remembered that until the middle of the eighteenth century the school was still making do with the Tudor buildings erected by William Harper; they were by now 200 years old, cramped, cold and in a bad state of repair. The Act of 1764 obliged the trustees to do something about it, and improvements were carried out in three stages, culminating in 1776 with two new houses in Horne Lane for the usher and writing master. Five years previously, £800 had been spent on a new house for the Master, whose former lodgings had caused him to have 'a continued cold'. But the first building operation was a renovation, in 1767, of the original school building; the result, still to be seen today and regarded by Sir Nikolaus Pevsner as 'the only Georgian public building of interest in the county', is a handsome, well proportioned classical building faced with Portland stone.[19]

Even before the restoration work had begun, Benjamin Palmer of Bedford Row in Holborn was commissioned to sculpt a statue of Sir William Harper, to stand in a niche above the front door. No one had the least idea what Harper had looked like and Palmer, or whoever it was who actually carried out the work, added stupidity to ignorance by depicting a sixteenth century Lord Mayor in eighteenth century garb. An equal absurdity was the erection by the trustees in the chancel of St Paul's Church, opposite the school, of 'a statuary medal', as Palmer's bill described it, 'where the said Sir William Harper and

Dame Alice his wife lie interred'. Dame Alice is no more interred in St Paul's than is Queen Anne. But statue and monument were duly installed on 2 July 1768, at a cost of £219 15s.

While it is easy to deride the early trustees for some of the silly things they did it is only right to record that in 1767 they furnished Bedford Grammar School with a very stylish building, protected by elegant iron railings. Imposing carriage gates to the left of the house led to the garden, and the new school was immediately considered worth drawing and etching.

The man who hoped to succeed Bridle was James Woodforde, aged thirty-three and a curate in Somerset, whose *Diary of a Country Parson* has become a classic. On hearing that 'the third best thing in the gift of New College', the headmastership of Bedford Grammar School, was vacant, he made enquiries, and on 1 September 1773 he recorded, '… a new built house with an exceeding handsome garden — 50 guineas paid the Master every quarter — Fuel, Candles, and all kinds of expenses about the house and gardens paid for the Master and no taxes whatever …. Upon the whole I like it very well, and I believe I shall accept it, if it comes to me'. Alas it did not, or a wonderful record of Bedford School might have filled the pages of Parson Woodforde's diary for the next thirty years. In the event he became a Fellow of New College later that year (he had been a scholar in 1759), and in 1774 he was presented to the College living of Weston in Norfolk, the parish he continued to nurture until his death on New Year's Day 1803.

There is no evidence that James Woodforde was ever seriously considered for the vacant Mastership. On 4 October he did set out for Oxford, but only to discover that the man chosen to succeed Bridle had turned out to be the Head Master of Thame School, the Reverend John Hooke (or Hook), a Fellow of New College since 1757. He was not a great success. In 1796, despite fine new facilities, he only had sixteen boys, a mere increase of four on the dozen he had inherited; by the time he died, in 1810, at the age of seventy-one, he bequeathed to his successor eleven pupils.[20] He had not been ably supported by his usher, Charles Abbot, who held at least two incumbencies and neglected his school duties as a result. Abbot had been usher for twenty-three years; now he was anxious to be promoted. But the Mayor of Bedford thought otherwise. He was himself an Oxford man and he wanted a Head Master who was 'zealous, ardent and indefatigable'. Abbot was none of these, as was made plain to the Warden and Fellows of New College when the mayor, the town clerk and the Rector of St Peter's travelled to Oxford to discuss the matter. (Sometimes the Warden of New College, who certainly stayed at the Swan in 1718, made the forty mile journey to Bedford on unmade roads.)

Meeting on 26 November 1810, the trustees of the Bedford Charity recorded that 'the children of the inhabitants [of Bedford], instead of having a Classical Education gratis, are in fact sent to other schools at a considerable expense to the parents'. And it did not escape their notice that whereas the Head Master of Bedford was receiving £200 a year, and the Head Master of Rugby only £113 6s 8d, 'that school is admirably conducted and flourishes whilst the school of this foundation for the want of a proper system of education is nearly useless'. It was a damning indictment of past mismanagement by staff, New College and the pre-1764 Bedford Charity Corporation officials. A new Head Master was to be asked to draw up a plan of campaign.

The man chosen for the urgent task was a clerical gentleman by the name of John Brereton, son of the vicar of the very parish in Holborn, St Andrew's, whose plots of land had been given to Bedford Grammar School by William Harper. Educated at Winchester and New College, Dr Brereton had previously taught at Blundell's, founded in 1604. He is the first Head Master whose likeness has come down to us, his portrait having been painted in 1833 by Samuel Lane. Brereton believed himself to be the heir to an extinct barony; otherwise he was eminently sane, and his arrival, achievements and perseverance were to prove crucial.

TWO

Steak and Porter

1811–1874

J OHN BRERETON'S most radical proposal was to take boarders into his house 'as Masters of other schools are universally permitted to do', a permission, he explained, 'which tended more than any other circumstance' to the high reputation in which other public schools were held. Rugby had recently been given permission by the Lord Chancellor to accommodate boarders; so had Harrow, by consent of the Master of the Rolls. Brereton's policy of taking boarders into his own house a decade into the nineteenth century really marks the beginnings of Bedford as a boarding school, destined towards the end of the twentieth century to attract boys from countries around the world. But although by 1820 almost half of Brereton's 84 boys were boarders, true to Sir William Harper's original intentions Bedford Grammar School continued during most of his time to cater primarily, as it still does, for day boys, the present proportion in the Upper School being roughly in the ratio of two boarders to every five day boys. (Local boys are not precluded from boarding, however, and some enjoy school life so much they persuade their parents to allow them to board.)

A public school usually requires to be seriously isolated in order to open its doors exclusively to boarders and there was never any likelihood of Bedford doing that. One of the disadvantages of a mixture of boarders and day boys is that day boys, even though they form a majority, may be made to feel inferior to those boys for whom school unremittingly encompasses two-thirds of their adolescent years. There is an intimacy inevitably associated with boarding house life denied to boys dispersed by the last bell, and a sense of inferiority among day boys, when it used to occur, was largely the result of a misplaced sense of superiority emanating from the boarders, whose prep was supervised, who ate together, shared dormitories, fagged, and were disciplined by a set of house rules and traditions which were never applicable to day boys. This feeling of superiority may in fact have been some sort of compensation for what until recent years were unquestionably the rigours of boarding school life: inadequate food and heating and a far greater chance of being caned.

Dr Brereton lost no time in becoming both Head Master and housemaster, for while income from the Bedford Charity was being diverted to provide dowries for 'poor maidens' both he and the school were woefully short of funds. Hence an income from boarding fees was to be welcomed. He had his stables and coach house converted into 'an eating room', to enable him 'for his own advantage and emolument to board and accommodate youths to be educated in the Grammar School together with the children of inhabitants.' Today it is possible to board at Bedford from the age of seven; it sounds as though Brereton's youths were rather older, although the expression seems to have been applied to boys no older than eleven.

The school year was divided into two terms, with two holidays of six weeks each. In an age when no schoolboy would own a watch, punctuality was not as easy to enforce as it later became, and on 26 November 1810 the trustees had noted that 'it being absolutely necessary for the regulations of the hours of the Grammar and English Schools that a clock be procured and placed in some conspicuous position, resolved that, as a new clock is wanted at St Paul's Church, the sum of 130 guineas be advanced to the parish in aid of purchasing a new clock to be fixed in the tower of St Paul's Church.' In case they still failed to notice the time, the boys were summoned to their lessons by the bell of St Paul's, said by 1857 to have been 'worn out in the service of the Trustees'. Prayers were read before early school, which in summer began at 7am and in winter at 8am. There was a half-holiday on Thursday and Saturday, and major saints' days were observed as a whole holiday. In addition, a new rule enabled Brereton to grant 'occasional remission from business' entirely at his own discretion. It would be surprising if there was not an extra half-holiday in the summer of 1815 to celebrate Wellington's defeat of Napoleon at Waterloo.

Monitors were appointed from among the senior boys, the first head of school recorded, in 1815, being seventeen-year-old Thomas Pearse. He may well have had a younger brother, H Pearse, who was head of school eight years later. Being head of school was no sinecure; when the circuit judge arrived in town to dispense justice the head of school had to welcome him with a letter in Latin. The monitors were armed with a cane, a custom that persisted into the second half of the twentieth century, and had instructions to administer two strokes to any boy who arrived late. Dr Brereton, by no means a brutal man judged by the standards of his time, devised his own ritual for caning. If a monitor was by the door when a boy arrived late, the miscreant was caned standing up; otherwise the 'victim', John Sargeaunt tells us, 'was followed to his seat and caned where he sat'. [1]

It was a commonly held assumption throughout previous centuries that no boy could be induced to learn without being regularly thrashed, a belief potently carried over into the nineteenth century by Dr Thomas Arnold, whose brief but bloodstained reign at Rugby — his canes were weighted with lead — did so much to set the pattern of middle class public school education in the nineteenth century, and even the twentieth. Arnold's approach may have been distorted by the fact that at Rugby, where he was appointed Head Master in 1827, at the age of thirty-two, he inherited a tradition of rampant drunkenness (not that boys at Eton and Winchester were any less addicted to wine and spirits), but he had a long list of cardinal schoolboy sins: profligacy in any form, lying, cruelty, disobedience, idleness. In his misguided attempts to eradicate what he saw as the inherently disordered nature of boys he became, despite having been a happy, affectionate, exuberant boy at Winchester, on occasions an exceptionally cruel man, once very nearly killing a delicate child with eighteen strokes of the cane. The boy was off sick for two days, and on his return to the classroom Arnold accused him of malingering. Thomas Arnold had a good deal to answer for; in 1913 his great-grandson, Edward Selwyn, became a more than usually incompetent Master of Marlborough.

Fagging, compulsory games, a broadening of the curriculum to embrace science alongside the classics, all hallmarks of the Victorian public school, can be traced in some measure to Arnold. His testimonial predicted that he would 'change the face of education all through the Public Schools of England'. If he did not achieve this object single-handedly his influence was profound. Despite spasmodic attacks on fagging in the press in the mid-nineteenth century, the custom persisted at Bedford well into the second half of the twentieth century; rugby football became compulsory at Bedford under Dr Brereton; and Brereton hired masters to teach drawing, French and mathematics.

Ultimately Arnold placed his faith, however, not in compulsory games but in compulsory religion — another hallmark of the public schools up to the present time. He became a mentor to senior boys, perhaps the first famous Head Master to form that sort of relationship, but he enrolled the senior boys in his crusade to expunge the wickedness of the younger ones. He was also ahead of his time in encouraging the supervision of boys by masters, and while inevitably this became equated with an unhealthy intrusion into privacy, it has to be remembered, when assessing Arnold's puritanical reforming zeal, that he entered the public school arena at a time when schools like Eton and Westminster were virtually run by the boys themselves, where atrociously dangerous bullying and unbridled sexual licence were the order of the day, and things could only get better, which, little by little, eventually they did. But it is ironic that a humourless disciplinarian like Thomas Arnold, whose arrogance was such that he was cordially detested by many parents, should have received so many plaudits while humbler men like Brereton beavered away with little recognition or reward. Nevertheless, without the pervasive influence of Arnold, much distorted by the publication, in 1857, of that illusory romance *Tom Brown's Schooldays* (in five years it sold 28,000 copies), many of the expanding schools like Bedford might have gone down the path of corruption epitomised, at their lowest ebb, by establishments like Westminster and Rugby.

Brereton actually arrived in St Paul's Square with his first boarders in tow. One came from as far afield as Devonshire, perhaps already known to Brereton from his time at Blundell's. As usher he had inherited Charles Abbot, to whom he offered four guineas a year for every boy he taught. Abbot said he wanted five. This was agreed, plus permission to take boarders himself into his own house, but none turned up. Nevertheless by 1816 Brereton had forty-one boys in the school, and the death of Abbot in 1817 relieved him of a tiresome colleague. Disappointed by his own failure to attract boarders, Abbot had informed Brereton's boarders that Bedford was a day school and they had no business to be lodging with the Head Master. He then refused to teach them. He had been better employed on botany; in 1798 Abbot published his *Flora Bedfordiensis*, and after his death part of his valuable library was purchased by John Higgins of Turvey Abbey. A man of numerous parts, Abbot had become an Oxford doctor of divinity in 1802, wrote a poem on the death of Nelson and published a collection of exceptionally tedious sermons.

Happier days lay ahead, for the Head Master's brother, Thomas Brereton, succeeded Abbot as usher, the last 'assistant master' to use the title usher until it was resurrected in 1979 for the Vice-Master, as a purely honorific title. He carried out the necessary alterations to his house and soon he too was a housemaster, remaining at the Grammar School fifteen years and earning the description 'assiduous, exemplary and effective'. Standards of education and boarding must have been high, for annual boarding fees, which included laundry and the ministrations of the writing master, came to fifty-five guineas. There was also an entrance fee of five guineas, and for an extra four guineas a year the boys could avail themselves of dancing lessons. Parents were asked to provide six towels for their sons, who were allowed an astonishing three changes of linen every week (boys in Sanderson's after the Second World War only had one). An even more enlightened attraction was provided by Dr Brereton. If a boy at Rugby — or indeed at Westminster or Shrewsbury — wanted a bed to himself he had to pay an extra fee, whereas Brereton assured his boarders' parents that each boy 'would be accommodated with a single bed'. Many amenities are offered today that were not available in Brereton's time, but the provision of single beds is one most people take for granted! What Bedford boys no longer enjoy, as Dr Brereton's boarders did, is a steak and a glass of porter for breakfast, porter being a heavy dark brown beer brewed from charred malt. But Brereton's porter was in fact a safe alternative to impure water rather than an unmerited luxury.

The basic reason why, in the eighteenth century, it had been common for boys to share a bed was to prevent them from freezing to death. At Charterhouse pupils were automatically assigned two to a bed, although it seems that at Eton the boys had some say in the matter, those preferring to sleep alone being allowed to do so. A letter written in 1758 by an apparently satisfied parent, Lady Caroline Fox, explained, 'The present way of settling is that Stephen and William are to lie together. Ophaly a bed to himself in the same room, and Charles in a little one by them; for neither Ophaly nor Charles like to have bedfellows; besides, they kick off the clothes so that other boys don't like to lie with them, and I'm told Stephen and William agree mighty well.'[2]

Until the end of the eighteenth century a single bed always entailed an extra charge; a single bed and a single room at Rugby in 1793, an amazing two-fold luxury, cost six guineas a year. Apart from the pressing matter of warmth, two other factors came into play, one physical and one financial. Two hundred years ago boys reached puberty later than they do today, and in consequence they tended to be smaller. And if each boy wanted a single bed more space had to be found for dormitory accommodation, or fewer boys could be admitted. In the early years of the nineteenth century Thackeray had his own bed at Charterhouse but only because it had been squeezed between two others so that he was obliged to clamber in from the bottom. Christ's Hospital, who were not well off, did nevertheless cut down on the number of boarders so that they could all have a bed to themselves, but it was not until the headmastership of Benjamin Kennedy (1836-66) that at Shrewsbury, originally situated in cramped conditions in the town, all the boys were given single beds, and then there was a resultant drop in the numbers of boarders, and hence a drop in income. At Harrow boys shared a bed until 1805. By providing a single bed for every Bedford boy in 1811 Dr Brereton was in the first wave of enlightened innovators.

Such spare cash as Brereton's trustees had accumulated after financing assorted town charities — in 1828 there were over twenty — and creating suitable accommodation for the new boarders was spent, two years after Brereton's arrival, on the purchase of a playground. It cost £688 17s and remained in use for eighty years. Children of this period were adept at inventing their own games and playing in the street, but the purchase in 1813 of a plot of land on which a crude form of hockey could be played marked the start of

Bedford's commitment to organised sports. Soon cricket and football were being played on Goldington Green, elementary soccer providing an opportunity for a disorganised rough and tumble without any serious rules, anyone who cared to do so charging on to the field and taking a kick at the ball, or another boy.

In 1820 a committee was appointed 'to revise the system of Education in the Grammar School', and they were able to inform the trustees that Dr Brereton had promised 'the utmost attention should be paid to boys in teaching them Grammar, English Composition, Arithmetic, Algebra, Geometry, Geography, the use of Terrestrial Globes and Planetarium, Practical Mensuration, Land Surveying and the French Language'. In consequence, the school acquired its first French teacher, J F Dupont, but French was only an optional extra, M Dupont turning up for two hours two evenings a week and being paid a nominal retainer of £30 a year.

By 1820 Dr Brereton, who taught the grammar school boys on the first floor, had become fed up with the noise made by pupils in the writing school, who occupied the ground floor. He said he required extra space for his own expanding educational establishment anyway, and proposed that the writing school should be rehoused. To this end the trustees had been buying up property in what was then called Angel Street, but Brereton had to wait another fourteen years for the writing school to take wing. The trustees were well advised to snap up property as it became available as near as possible to the original school site, for the town was now expanding fast. 'Land in and near the town has of late been much sought after, for building purposes', a local solicitor, R B Hankin, was writing in 1828. Plots, he said, were fetching from £200 to £300 an acre. [3]

According to Mr Hankin, it was the Grammar School itself, 'combined with the advantages of a respectable neighbourhood', which had rendered 'the town of Bedford a desirable place of residence for families, since parents, whilst conscious that their children are receiving a sound classical education, have the pleasing satisfaction of noticing their improvement from time to time, and watching over their moral and religious conduct.' He also thought it worth remarking that Bedford had 'ever kept pace with the improvements of the age, as its public institutions, buildings, and streets fully evince'.

There was a grain market held every Saturday, 'when the Sandy Gardeners attend with vegetables'. On Mondays pigs were brought in for sale at a market on the south side of the bridge. There were eight fairs a year, 'principally for cattle'. The town 'is neatly built,' Mr Hankin reported, 'and contains many handsome residences; the principal streets have lately been Macadamized, [the town] having been previously ill paved; its foot ways are flagged, and it is lighted and watched, and is kept particularly clean by the poor men from the

House of Industry.' There was 'no particular manufactory, the poor being employed principally in making lace and straw plat.' By 1821 the population of Bedford had grown to 5,466, and the Leeds Mail Coach thought it worthwhile making a stop in the town.

A map drawn to coincide with a survey carried out in 1841 shows a developing residential area stretching to the west as far as Union Street. The north side of Tavistock Street was well built upon, too. Once Harpur Street crossed Dame Alice Street it soon led off northwards into the countryside, however, and there was still no development to the east beyond Newnham Street. Although a certain amount of grazing land was still preserved in the centre of the town, increasingly the High Street, Silver Street, St Loyes and the southern side of St Peter's Street were becoming clustered with houses.

It was between 1833-36 that Bedford acquired its most prestigious public building. In response to an Act of Parliament of 1826, separating the writing school from the Grammar School, Edward Blore, who had already worked for the duke of Bedford at Woburn, and in 1847 was to provide additional accom- modation for Queen Victoria's expanding family at Buckingham Palace, was commissioned to construct new school premises facing on to the west side of what became known as Harpur Street. With its imposing central tower and elegant mock Gothic facade, it became home eventually for Bedford Modern School, until, in 1974, like the Grammar School in 1891, they were compelled, for reasons of space, to move to the north of the town. Now at least in command of the entire school building in St Paul's Square, Brereton may nevertheless have gasped at the cost; £13,731 for the new building, while the Grammar School regarded themselves as almost permanently starved of funds.

One of the new assistant masters now appointed to the Grammar School was a mathematician, the Reverend Edward Swann. He was joined, in 1832, by another cleric, Henry Le Mesurier. There is nothing strange in the numbers of clergymen who taught at Bedford; until 1854 it was not possible to teach at Oxford without assenting to the Thirty-Nine Articles, and no university post could be obtained unless a don was in holy orders (deacon's orders would do), so that scholarship, education and the Church all marched hand-in-hand. Dr Brereton was not only a priest and a headmaster but a classical scholar, an amateur archaeologist and a Fellow of both the Society of Antiquaries and the Royal Geographical Society. He studied astronomy, and was presented with a telescope by 'the ladies of Bedford'. Music was another source of recreation, and he was a patron of the Old Philharmonic Society. To send his boys off in jolly mood for the Christmas holidays he would lay on a fireworks display.

In Brereton's first year the trustees had been fussing about the provision of a proper box in which to keep the candles. By the winter of 1813 he was requesting the installation of gas. We can get closer to Brereton than to any of his predecessors. One of his pupils described him as 'a dapper little figure' with a 'round face like a bulldog'. He was said to walk fast, swinging a stick, and always to wear a double-breasted swallow-tailed coat, knee breeches, black silk stockings and a ruffled shirt front. [4] As with schoolboys, there was at this time no uniform daytime attire for Anglican clergy.

One of Brereton's most successful pupils, a boarder in his own house, was a boy called Henry Hawkins, who later, as Lord Brampton, sat as a tender-hearted judge, always recalling the effect it had had upon him of watching from the school window, in 1830, the body of a teenager, hanged for setting fire to a stack of corn, being carted home from St Paul's Square by his parents. (The last public hanging in Bedford, in 1868, was actually attended by Bedford Grammar School boys.) But probably Brereton's most famous old boy was a contemporary of Brampton, the great constitutional jurist Lord Farnborough, better known to posterity as Sir Thomas Erskine May, the name by which he made his reputation as an expert on constitutional history and parliamentary procedure.[5] Born in 1815, he entered the Grammar School when he was eleven, as a private pupil, according to the *Dictionary of National Biography*, leaving at the age of sixteen. He was made KCB in 1866 and served as Clerk of the House of Commons from 1871-86, the year of his death. In 1885 he had been sworn a privy councillor, and lived to enjoy his peerage for less than a month. This exceptionally famous Old Bedfordian was kept waiting over a century before he had a sufficiently distinguished building named after him, the Prep School's Erskine May Hall, opened in 1994.

There has never been any shortage at Bedford of boys with initiative, and two of Brereton's pupils, Foster Barnham Zincke, for nearly fifty years a parish priest in Suffolk and appointed chaplain-in-ordinary to Queen Victoria, and his equally splendidly named friend Warrington Wilkinson Smyth, at the Grammar School from 1827-35, embarked on what they claimed was the first recorded expedition of the Ouse, travelling 700 miles in three weeks. Smyth was the son of an admiral, which may have helped, became a geologist and in 1887 received a knighthood. His second brother, Charles Piazzi Smyth, left the Grammar School at the age of seventeen, landed a job immediately as an assistant at the South African Royal Observatory, and in 1845 was appointed Astronomer Royal for Scotland. There was a third boy in this talented family, Henry, who entered the school in 1843, served in the Crimean War, and became a General, a KCMG and Governor of Malta.

In June 1840 the Grammar School acquired the services of a twenty-seven-year-old drawing master whose reputation as an artist has not been fully acknowledged. Bradford Rudge had been born in Coventry in 1813, the son of

Edward Rudge, art master at Rugby, and it was at Rugby that Bradford was educated. When he was fourteen he was at the top of his class, and he seems to have left school by the age of sixteen. It is unclear why he migrated to Bedford, in 1835, by which time he was already married to his first wife, Martha, by whom he had a short-lived child, Emma, baptised and buried at Holy Trinity, Bedford in 1842.

It was after Bradford Rudge had been earning his living for five years executing lithographs of Bedfordshire views, and giving private drawing lessons for five shillings an hour, that he was hired by the Commercial School, as the writing school had been known since about 1820, to teach drawing, at a salary of £75 a year. Not long afterwards the Fellows of New College decided that 'the introduction of instruction in Drawing into the Grammar School would be highly beneficial to boys', and Rudge was able to add a further £40 a year to his income.

In 1845 Rudge drew a famous record of the *Bedford Times* coach outside the Swan on its last journey, and his oil painting of the Chequers Inn at Turvey can be seen at the Cecil Higgins Art Gallery. He frequently exhibited at the Royal Academy, and in 1881 he entered seven paintings at the annual Bedford Art Exhibition, being awarded the Mayoress of Bedford's prize in 1884. When he died the following year, at the age of seventy-two, the *Bedfordshire Mercury* recalled him as a 'rigid master, but in dealing with boys with talents for drawing he was admirably adapted to bring out the best that was in them'. Martha Rudge died in 1856 (she is buried at St Peter's), and Rudge remarried some years later. His second wife, Sarah Fereday, bore him a girl, Catherine, who was baptised at St Peter's Church in 1867, the family having removed to Goldington Road, and it was at St Peter's, where he had been churchwarden nine years, that Bradford Rudge's funeral service took place. His drawing of the Georgian school building in St Paul's Square is one of the most charming ever executed.

A young boy who studied at Bedford for two years towards the end of Brereton's time (he later moved to Harrow), and in 1920 lent his name to Burnaby boarding house, was Lt Col Frederick Gustavus Burnaby. Born in Bedford in 1842, he became, quite literally, a giant of a man. He stood 6ft 4 ins tall and his chest measurement was 46 ins. Commonly regarded as the strongest man in Europe, he was said to have carried a small pony under his arm. He became the classic nineteenth century man of action, an intrepid traveller, an authority on ballooning, a voluminous author, a correspondent for *The Times* and a courageous cavalry officer. And that was not all. The colonel was a linguist of renown, speaking fluent French, German, Italian, Spanish and Russian, and getting by on his travels in Turkish and Arabic. His dashing deeds were cut short in 1885, however, when he was mortally wounded at the relief of Khartoum. His biography, written by Thomas Wright, was published in 1908, and in addition to having a house and a road named after him, Colonel Burnaby is commemorated by a window in St Peter's Church, his father, the Reverend Gustavus Burnaby, having been Rector.

Dr Brereton's time at Bedford was dogged by two religious controversies. On his arrival in 1811 he had taken over, among his half dozen pupils, a Jewish boy, Nathan Joseph, admitted by his predecessor, John Hooke. But in 1817 doubts arose about the rights of Jewish children, and the Lord Chancellor, Lord Eldon, was asked to adjudicate on the question whether Jews might be admitted to any of the Bedford schools. In 1819, after a 'very *expensive* as well as extensive suit'[6], Lord Eldon delivered himself of the opinion that 'Jew boys' were not admissible to the Grammar School because he did not think that 'if the school consisted partly of Jew boys and partly of Christians the two systems could go together'. It was his duty, he said, to recollect that Christianity was the law of the land, and from this dubious proposition he drew the conclusion that as Christianity was taught in the Grammar School, Jews should not be admitted. He appeared to be relating Christianity solely with Anglicanism, for it was only the Anglican faith that was taught; and while it is true that since the Second Act of Supremacy of 1559 the Church of England has been known as a Church 'by law established', what that means has never been precisely defined, and nowhere is the Church of England's right to exist, as opposed to its mode of operation, enshrined in legislation. Brereton's own objection to Master Joseph, or to those Jewish boys who followed him, had not been based on religious prejudice but on the absence of Jewish boys from school on Saturday, the Jewish Sabbath. Jews were eventually readmitted in 1847 and future generations have dealt with the problem of religious observance by very properly exempting Jews from attendance at any Anglican service.

It was in 1843 that the other religious controversy was stirred up, by Isaac Lockwood, the incumbent of St Mary's. Doubtless recalling that in Oxford every don was obliged to profess allegiance to the Church of England, Mr Lockwood asked the trustees to insist that every master engaged by either the Grammar or the future Modern School should be an Anglican. In a town as famous for its Nonconformist traditions as Bedford, this was a particularly crass method of antagonising local people. Already the Commercial School was employing five Nonconformists. Were they to be sacked? Were Roman Catholics to be banned as well? Or humanists? A public meeting was called in protest, and Lockwood's resolution was defeated.

But then to Brereton's dismay a series of letters appeared in the *Northampton Herald* (it was not until 1845 that the *Bedfordshire Times* was launched) defending

Lockwood's position. They were even reissued as a pamphlet, cumbersomely — and misleadingly — titled *Are all Teachers? or Should Dissenters Teach in Church Endowments?* The author was Brereton's mathematics master, Edward Swann. No Harpur school was a 'Church endowment', but this absurd idea was nothing compared to the intemperance of Mr Swann's attack on Dissenters in general. 'To treat Dissenters with forbearance may be our duty,' he wrote, 'but it is not a treatment to which they can lay claim. It is like exchanging compliments with a man who is breaking into your house.' Great damage was done by Swann to the reputation of the Grammar School, but at least its doors remained open to those boys whose families preferred to worship in chapel rather than in church.

Instead of fussing about religious affiliations, what the trustees themselves had been far more concerned to discover was whether the boys were illegitimate. In 1830 they had decreed that 'all persons who shall in future come to settle in the town and be desirous of sending a child to be educated in any of the Schools, to deliver to the Clerk of the Trust previous to admission a certificate of the parents' marriage and also a certificate of the child's baptism or other sufficient evidence of its legitimacy and of the identity of the parents described in the said certificate.' What they would have made of a nation a quarter of whose families, at the end of the twentieth century, have only one parent one can scarcely imagine. But reference to 'persons who shall in future come to settle in the town' provides interesting early evidence of the migration to Bedford encouraged by its schools. By the time Dr Brereton retired (in 1855) the population of the town had swollen to 11,500, of whom 7,000 had been born elsewhere.

It has been suggested that Dr Brereton clung to office too long — for forty-four strenuous years — but he was a dogged man, determined to do his best for Bedford Grammar School. Within sixteen years of his appointment the first printed school list recorded ninety-five boys. He reached his peak in 1849 with 187 boys. In 1848 he wrote to the trustees asking for more accommodation and more teaching help. 'Had I not given up my hall for one of the Masters the last ten years to instruct his classes,' he told them, ' it would have been impossible to give that instruction. There is an actual provision for seventy-two boys and the numbers are now 128 in the Lower School Room.' Constantly irked by the largess bestowed on the luxuriously accommodated writing school, he added, 'I do not wish to draw any invidious distinction when I call your attention to the state of the other Schools, but in them ample room has been provided with a due supply of masters when required.' [7]

Despite the levy of substantial school fees, the cost of providing materials was a constant headache, and in 1850 it was decided to charge parents a deposit of one guinea 'as security… for the fair use of the books by each boy entering the Lower School Room and two guineas for each boy entering the Upper School Room.' But despite all the problems, academic attainment took large strides under Brereton. By the end of 1851 a warrant had been received from Queen Victoria, by now in the fourteenth year of her long reign, 'granting the privilege to the Trustees of the Bedford Charity empowering them to give Certificates to the candidates from Bedford Grammar School for degrees in Art and Laws at the London University.'

Brereton's last years saw a decline both in the numbers of boys attending his school and in his own health and powers. The two may not have been disconnected. By 1852 pupils had fallen from 187 three years before to 158, and by the following year to 129. In 1855 he could only hand over to his successor a roll call of 113. But these fluctuations in fortune do not seem so very reprehensible compared to Westminster's performance, where during the quarter century prior to 1846 numbers had slumped from 300 to 90. Repton was once reduced to one pupil; when Edward Thring arrived at Uppingham in 1853 he found only twenty-eight boys, and in 1798 a newly appointed Head Master at Shrewsbury found just two. Provision was made for Brereton's successor to receive £300 a year, the usher, now known as the second master, £200. Thirty boarders were allocated to the Head Master's house, twenty to the second master's and ten each to the houses of two assistant masters. The year 1855, by which time he was seventy-three, saw Brereton retire from the headmastership, and four years later an Old Bedfordian who had the patronage of a living in Kent enabled him to become a county parson. He died on 6 September 1862, at the age of eighty.

Brereton managed to increase the full-time staff from two on his arrival to seven by the time he left, and although he never complained of his own unappreciated and under-paid workload, it must have been galling for him to discover his maths master Le Mesurier maintaining fourteen servants by dint of private coaching and a curacy, presumably one that was richly endowed. Brereton trained one of his staff so well he became dean of Manchester, a diocese created in 1847, and he educated some very distinguished boys. Before Brereton arrived, Bedford Grammar School had been run for 259 years by eighteen Head Masters, serving on average just under fifteen years each. He stuck to it for forty-four years, longer by far than any other Bedford School Head Master before or since. His great achievements were to increase dramatically, and until near the end maintain, the numbers of boys; to place boarding at Bedford on a firm footing; and in both respects to establish foundations for the school's ultimate expansion and survival. He must surely rate as Bedford's first great Head Master.

Bedford's next Head Master, who remained for nineteen years, Frederick Fanshawe, was very much a man of his time, conservative, High Tory, dedicated to learning without being an imaginative teacher, a stern moralist. Brereton had felt at home in Regency England. Fanshawe was a Victorian. When he took his First Class degree at Balliol in Humaner Letters in 1841 Queen Victoria was twenty-two and had been on the throne four years. They were exact contemporaries. He was also unnervingly well-connected, more suited perhaps to Westminster than to a grammar school in a small provincial town. He himself had been educated at Winchester. His father was a General, as was his maternal grandfather, the famous Peninsular War campaigner Sir Hew Whitefoord Dalrymple. He chose for his wife the daughter of another General, Sir Frederick Goldfinch. He often gave the impression of being a military disciplinarian himself.

Frederick Fanshawe moved on from Balliol to Exeter College, Oxford to become a Fellow and tutor, having of course first been ordained. Not being a Fellow of New College, he must nevertheless have come to the attention of the Warden and his colleagues (Oxford was an intimate and close-knit community where everybody knew everybody else's business), for he was the don they did not hesitate to select to replace Dr Brereton when the trustees wrote asking for 'a man who, as a teacher, is fully up to the times, and will constantly advance with the improvement of the age'. They thought the curriculum of the Grammar School 'much too narrow', and that Natural Philosophy, Modern Languages and English Literature should be taught alongside Latin and Greek. 'We want,' they insisted, 'a man as a master who, like the late Dr Arnold, can rule and yet be loved, securing the cordial co-operation of every assistant and the ready obedience of every pupil by making all feel personally interested in the work, and who can discourage every vice by showing that he himself attaches due importance to all the virtues and diligently cultivates them as a means not only of usefulness but of happiness.'

It is interesting that the pernicious shade of Dr Arnold had come to influence the mental processes of Bedford townsfolk in such a positive manner. Arnold had been dead thirteen years but was already a legend, the patron saint of public schools. What should not be misinterpreted in the trustees' rather wooden demands is their reference to discouraging 'every vice'. There is no reason to suppose that the boys Mr Fanshawe was being summoned to inculcate with 'all the virtues' were more prone to 'vice' than any other perfectly normal boys. The vices Dr Arnold regarded as so vicious — lying, cruelty and so on — would have been the ones the trustees also had in mind.

Unworldly, as any young man might be who had spent the whole of his short life in the cloistered confines of Oxford, Fanshawe almost certainly failed to investigate the situation in Bedford before he accepted the job, and immediately discovered that his new masters, the trustees, were full of grandiose rhetoric but were too tight-fisted to enable expansion to take place — just as Dr Brereton had discovered. By December 1856 Fanshawe was lamenting that the school had received no help at all. 'I have done all that I possibly can with the existing staff,' he told New College. 'The new masters are all hard at work; and yet it is quite impossible that we can do the work as it ought to be done without more help.' He wanted to be able to superintend the work of the whole school, yet, he explained, 'My own time is so thoroughly taken up with my own class that I can only occasionally in a superficial way have a lesson of another class.' New College supported him in principle, but failed to persuade the trustees to supply the funds to finance extra staff — yet they were urging the provision of lectures in astronomy and, for those boys destined for careers in civil or mechanical engineering, more time to be devoted 'to the art of drawing'.

Whether Fanshawe was by nature a bully or early on became depressed by the miniature scale on which the Grammar School, now 300 years old, was developing, and took his frustration out on his pupils, it is hard to say; probably both. John Sargeaunt tells us that sometimes he would lose his temper and box the ears of stupid or idle boys.[8] Sargeaunt even goes as far as to question Fanshawe's scholarship. Nevertheless one of his boys, John Scott, who became a county court judge, gained a Triple First. Certainly of English Literature Fanshawe knew little and in some respects cared less; a man who declines to mention Milton's name because of the poet's politics cannot be taken too seriously. And he had an unfortunate propensity to dismiss the very existence of Cambridge University, a snobbish affectation that can have done little for the self-esteem of boys clever enough to have been accepted for Cambridge colleges.

Much in Fanshawe's favour was his dislike of the cane, although we are told that he did use it 'as a corrective for bad language, and for anything that savoured of impurity',[9] 'impurity', as opposed to vice, denoting some sexual act. But there was scarcely any need for the Head Master to raise his hand; the second master he had inherited from Dr Brereton, Henry Le Mesurier, was happy to administer all the chastisement any man or boy might consider sufficient. Although he often behaved like a rampaging bull, Le Mesurier was in fact the kind of ill-tempered eccentric whom schoolboys rather enjoy, as long as they manage to dodge the books he hurls about or the cane indiscriminately wielded. It seems that an uninspired rendition of Macbeth's soliloquy on the dagger could send Le Mesurier into a frenzy of physical or verbal abuse. At least he never resorted to sarcasm, the least effective form of teaching and the one boys resent most; given the least excuse, like Giles James he simply lashed out with his fists, and as he grew older, in appearance more than ever like a grizzly bear without any teeth, so his bellows became almost incoherent, and the comical effect of his undirected rage balanced the well-merited fear he inspired.

Whereas Fanshawe, who appears to have remained disgracefully oblivious of the reign of terror being waged within his school, was High Church in a vaguely Tractarian sort of way, Le Mesurier seems to have attended services at St Paul's, a church on what today we would call the catholic wing of the Church of England, solely for the pleasure of rubbishing any liturgical practice that had even a whiff of Rome about it. John Sargeaunt tells us, 'He had a footstool made of two large blocks of wood one on top of the other. When a new curate advanced some then new-fangled High Church doctrine, he startled the congregation by kicking his footstool violently into its component parts and exclaiming, "Pooh! Pish! Pack of nonsense! Popish nonsense!"' [10]

Until this time the Bedford Grammar School boys had merely taken part in services at St Paul's as ordinary members of the congregation. They had no chapel of their own, and no Head Master could preach exclusively for them; no Head Master could preach at all without an invitation from the vicar. Fanshawe realised there was no hope of having a school chapel built, but he thought a service held for the school on Sunday afternoons would be the next best thing, and there exists a letter from Fanshawe dated 11 May 1857 setting out his reasons. It appears to be a round robin to all the parents, and its contents throw revealing light on his character, and the primary purpose for which he thought public schools existed; to bring boys to God.

Having been long deeply impressed with the importance of having a Chapel attached to every Public School, in which the Pupils might be able to assemble as one Congregation, and the Master might have the opportunity of specially addressing them as boys, and endeavouring to promote amongst them as a united body a high tone of religious feeling, I am glad to be able to inform you that I have obtained permission from the Vicar and Churchwardens of St Paul's for the use of the Chancel of that Church for an afternoon service for our school.

I have felt a conscientious obligation to endeavour to secure this as soon as I could venture with God's help to undertake the duty. I feel most strongly convinced that such Christian union amongst the boys as may thus be fostered will tend with God's blessing to strengthen religious principles and Christian character through life: and also that there will insensibly (sic) grow in the boys a feeling of religious gratitude to God for the Christian sympathy of their Master with them, and his endeavours to do what he can for their eternal welfare, however unequal he may be adequately to perform the task.

I therefore sincerely hope that the Parents of our boys will, as far as they conveniently can, arrange for their sons to come to their afternoon Service to St Paul's Church. Our Service will commence at 3 o'clock.

I have the honour to remain
Yours very faithfully
Frederick Fanshawe

It is a tribute to the fortitude and generous nature of Fanshawe's pupils that after forty tumultuous years Le Mesurier was presented with a silver salver and a cheque for 200 guineas, although one boy worked out that the subscription came to less than a halfpenny for every stroke of the cane the half-crazed old monster had inflicted.

There were compensations on the teaching staff. Dr Brereton's son Charles had been appointed assistant classics master, and was a particular favourite with the boys, generally regarded as handsome despite an aquiline nose and 'somewhat thin brown hair'. One of his pupils described him as 'refined and dignified to a degree', able to inspire the boys 'with love of order and method', being particularly skilled at teaching Greek grammar. [11] But like most masters of his generation — and like many before and since — Charles Brereton was much addicted to the cane, using it not for official punishment but as a teaching tool, imagining that the fear of physical pain would induce a boy to learn. He combined his duties at the Grammar School with an assistant curacy at St Mary's Church, until in 1869 he resigned in order to take over as incumbent. His successor, John Lee, left in 1875 to become Head Master of Barnet Grammar School, an early instance, of which there were to be many, of a Bedford School teacher moving on to a headmastership. Le Mesurier's successor as second master, W E Bolland, became Head Master of the Worcester Cathedral Choir School.

The year 1859, only his fourth in office, witnessed one of the most momentous events in Fanshawe's headmastership, a full-scale riot. It followed confusion over the allocation of a shared cricket pitch, both the Grammar and Commercial boys turning up the same afternoon. Outnumbered by about four to one, a dozen Grammar School boys beat a judicious retreat, the Modern School boys, as we should call them from 1877 onwards, pelting their rivals with stones. But on St Peter's Green the Grammar School, led by a future cleric, A L Foulkes, decided to make a stand, Foulkes wresting a stick from one of his opponents and felling a Commercial boy called Clarke — 'Nobby', needless to say. This reversal of fortunes prompted some of the town's artisans, no doubt fathers of the boys at the Commercial School, to retaliate, and only the timely intervention of the Rector of St Peter's prevented Foulkes from being lynched before the police arrived to march him off.

Who should at that moment drive by but Foulkes's Head Master, who was roundly set upon by a crowd in the High Street when he asked what was happening. Fanshawe apparently rescued Foulkes from the clutches of the police and hustled him to safety in a nearby house, which was promptly besieged. So the police sent for a magistrate to read the Riot Act. This had no effect whatsoever, and the anger of the crowd was only dampened by a fortuitous thunder storm. After many years of retelling, the saga of the riot has acquired a number of variations, one having Fanshawe escape by scaling a garden wall and jumping down into Lurke Lane. [12] Another version of events alleges that the police escorted Foulkes to the school, where he spent the night in the Head Master's observatory, built by Dr Brereton, making his escape next day by river and eventually being given sanctuary by some relatives of Fanshawe who lived in Leicestershire. If only half of this is true, Fanshawe seems to have behaved with rash if creditable loyalty towards the boy, for it is further said that when a police officer arrived to serve a warrant on Foulkes for his arrest, Fanshawe's footman slammed the gates of the playground in the policeman's face. On Foulkes's eventual return to Bedford, Fanshawe escorted him to a solicitor's office, and Foulkes always maintained it was when the townspeople discovered that he was with the solicitor that the siege and subsequent dramatic flight took place. At all events, Foulkes duly ended up in court, and was fined £5.

In 1855 Fanshawe had actually threatened to resign over the trustees' reluctance to provide him with adequate accommodation, a threat they could not afford to let him carry out; it would have made finding a replacement too difficult. But it still required an equally unwelcome threat to take the matter to the Charity Commissioners, established by parliament in 1853, before the erection of an extension to the school building was begun in 1858. Fanshawe acquired three additional classrooms, a tower and a large hall, premises opened with some ceremony on 17 April 1861, the occasion being marked by the singing of a new school hymn, *Domus Pater*, written by the volatile but versatile Henry Le Mesurier. Within the tower was hung a bell, rung in future (from a room which served as a school office) by the porter, John Chamberlain. Thus were laid the origins of the present Bell Room.

Fanshawe was now enabled to expand his curriculum and to increase the number of boys — from 104 in 1861 to 204 five years later. But his trustees were still not off the hook. The conduct of a number of public and grammar schools came under official scrutiny in 1866, the Taunton Commission being allocated eight schools to examine, among them Tonbridge, Christ's Hospital, Dulwich College and Bedford. The commissioner assigned to visit Bedford was Mr R S Wright. He noted that 130 of Mr Fanshawe's 194 boys learned French, 83 mathematics, but that no one was being taught any history. So far as the distribution of Trust income was concerned, he concluded the payment of marriage portions had become an anachronism; indeed, he found the use of part of Harper's endowment for purposes other than education illustrated the 'unrestrained application of local and indiscriminate lavishness', words which, when published in 1868, came as a shock to the trustees and a much needed tonic to Mr Fanshawe. Save for some of the almshouses the trustees had been supporting, the Commission recommended the abolition of all expenditure on welfare, and with the restitution to the school of funds hitherto diverted by the trustees to their own pet charities, Mr Fanshawe found himself, by Christmas 1871, able to cater for 285 pupils, by far the largest number the school had yet attained. Even now, however, space remained absurdly inadequate.

The major upshot of the Taunton Commission's investigations was a requirement for the Bedford Charity to be radically reconstituted, and in 1873 the Endowed Schools Act reduced the number of trustees from fifty-one to twenty-seven. The Universities of Cambridge and London were each to supply one trustee, New College two. The lord lieutenant and the local members of parliament were drafted in as ex-officio governors. The mayor and corporation remained pivotal, but from now on a continuity in chairmanship became possible. As the Lord Chancellor was to appoint a representative, endless law suits became a thing of the past. What had now been set up was a pattern of governorship altered from time to time over the years as necessity has dictated, but in essence still adhered to.

It was while all this was going on that the fifty-seven-year-old Italian patriot Giuseppe Garibaldi, at the time possibly the most fabled man in the world, made his 1864 barnstorming tour of England. He was received by the Prince of Wales and the archbishop of Canterbury; workmen, it was said, cheered him until they were hoarse, women fainted at the sight of him. In short, he was the pop idol of his day, and his breathless itinerary took in Bedford, for he was anxious to visit the Britannia Works to inspect a new steam plough. Knowing he was to dine at Cliveden and the Reform Club, to meet the Foreign Secretary and receive the Freedom of the City of London, he arrived with a suitable selection of presents for his hosts. Among these pre-packed gifts was at least one portrait, painted in 1861 by an Italian by the name of A Pio, and as the Mayor and Corporation would have turned out to greet Garibaldi on his visit to the town it is a reasonable assumption the Mayor was presented with Pio's painting. How else did it drift into the hands of the Harpur Trust? Having been cleaned it now hangs in a corridor at Bedford School, next to Phillpotts's chair of state, an interesting memento of a brief visit to the town of a nineteenth century international hero.

At Uppingham, in 1869, an embryo meeting of what became the Head Masters' Conference was held. Frederick Fanshawe was invited to attend but was unable to do so until the following year. Meetings were held at irregular intervals to begin with, so that Fanshawe only attended once again, in 1873, at Winchester. There were just four more meetings before the turn of the century, in 1886, 1890, 1894 and 1900, Bedford being represented at all of them.

Some of the school's present societies saw their origins in Fanshawe's time. By 1868 there was a flourishing choir, and an orchestra of apparently eight players, but it is difficult to imagine what they played; a limited range of chamber works, presumably. Duets and part songs were popular, as was the music of Mendelssohn, the darling of the Victorians. The Debating Society dates from 1873, although the early motions smacked more of the history classroom than the debating chamber: Was the use of eating utensils common among the Ancient Romans? Was Francis the author of the Letters of Junius? Was the use of sign-boards common among the Romans? In fact, before the nature of a debating society was fully grasped it seems that meetings were at times taken as an opportunity for the reading of a paper on some literary or scientific subject.

Despite his scholastic and emotional drawbacks, Frederick Fanshawe was a Head Master who fought tenaciously for the school, and eventually achieved some expansion of space and a considerable rise in the number of boys. His was an incumbency that bridged two clearly demarcated periods of the school's history, paving the way for the great explosion that was to occur under his successor, an explosion of enthusiasm and faith in the future that might never have occurred had it not been for Fanshawe's rather dull but determined personality. He was a man with high ideals but perhaps a rather blinkered perspective on the world, of which, beyond the walls of academe, he knew very little. He had to battle far harder than he should have done with unsympathetic trustees, and under the circumstances he did rather well. He retired in 1874, dying only two years later. His memorial, as he had wished it to be, was the Fanshawe Divinity prize, awarded for the first time in 1876.

Edward VI, the school's most illustrious benefactor, painted by
an unknown artist *c.* 1547, when the king would have been ten,
the age at which he succeeded to the throne
By courtesy of the National Portrait Gallery, London

The original school house in St Paul's Square, refaced in 1767,
drawn by Bradford Rudge, art master at Bedford 1840–85
Photograph: Jerome Watson

St Paul's Church, Bedford, where Sir William Harper is buried
Photograph: the author

James Surtees Phillpotts, the dynamic Victorian Head Master who vastly increased the numbers of boys at the Grammar School and in 1891 moved the school to its present site

THE OUSEL,

The Journal of the Bedford Grammar School,

INCLUDING (ON THIS OCCASION) A BOOK OF WORDS FOR THE SPEECHES.

No. 1.]	JUNE 15TH, 1876.	[PRICE SIXPENCE.

EVERY great institution has produced its *vates sacer*. Our "holy bard" is the *Ousel*. We know its wings are but of wax, and do not mean like Icarus to soar too near the sun and fall

VITREO DATURUS NOMINA RIVO.

It is said that no representative government can be higher in character than those it represents, and we are not presumptuous enough to wish to be so. We have not, therefore, aimed at producing a Literary Magazine, but a journal which shall be a fair representative of the various interests of the School. Nevertheless, we wish to represent the School at its best, and we hope we shall get sufficient support to enable us to maintain a literary section.

WE wish the School to speak through us, and not we to the School. Therefore, we wish for contributions

I.

Where Dundagil breasts the wave,
 Cliff and island castle-crowned,
Where the giant billows rave,
 Piercing barriers iron-bound,
 Stands a bare and aged tower
 Silent as with mystic power.

II.

Never sounds o'er Blackpit steep
 Merry tune of chiming bell,
Bottreaux never to the deep
 Can its joys or sorrows tell;
 Silent as with mystic power
 Stands that bare and aged tower.

III.

Yet when all is hushed in sleep
 And the main is halcyon calm
I have heard that from the deep
 Steals a soft and wavy charm:

Top left Frederick Fanshawe, Head Master 1855–74
Top right The Reverend Septimus Phillpotts, school chaplain and brother of James Phillpotts
Below The first issue of the *Ousel*, founded by James Phillpotts two years after he became Head Master

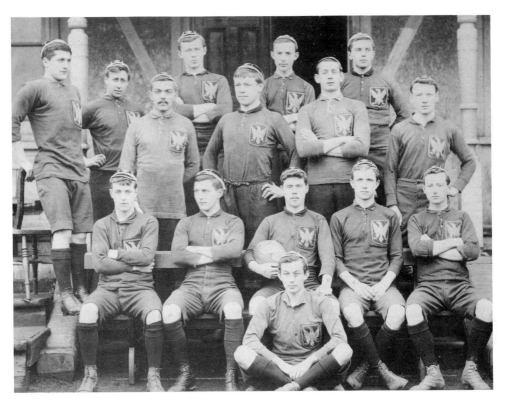

Top They don't make Rugby XVs as burly as this any more. In 1890, adorned with enormous eagles, for some reason this Bedford team was recorded by a Brighton photographer, A. H. Fry

Below Form IV3, photographed in June 1895, four years after the school had moved to its present premises. Some wore Eton collars, some wing collars. Many sported gold watch chains. At this time boys even came to school in sailor suits

43

In 1913 an Old Boy, Claude Grahame-White, caused great excitement by landing his
aeroplane on the school playing field. The photographer was Noel Carrington,
one of three brothers of the Bloomsbury artist Dora Carrington who
were educated at Bedford School

Opposite Jim Lambert, one of about 450 Old Bedfordians who were killed in the
First World War. On the back of his photograph has been inscribed:
'Gave his life for his country on the night of All Saints Day,
or early morn of All Souls Day 1915'

45

John King, Head Master 1903–10

Reginald Carter, Head Master 1910–28

THREE

The Chief

1874–1884

With the arrival in 1874 of James Surtees Phillpotts (he was appointed on 20 October 1874 and took over the reins the following January) Bedford School acquired its second great Head Master. Recognised as a colossus in his own day, Phillpotts became known as The Chief. He was not however the only Head Master to be known as Chief. John King may have been; Reginald Carter certainly was — as was a young man of thirty-seven who arrived from Charterhouse as Head Master in 1928, Humfrey Grose-Hodge. But it was as Chief, not The Chief, that for twenty-three years Grose-Hodge was universally known. How this came about is a mystery, and to one old lady who had known Phillpotts well it came as a considerable surprise. Her name was Lady Carter, and she was the widow of an Indian Army General. She lived in Glebe Road in a house stuffed with Indian bamboo furniture, where one day she was dispensing afternoon tea to a fifteen-year-old boarder, who happened, in the course of conversation, to refer to Grose-Hodge as Chief.

'Chief?' she enquired. 'Who *do* you mean?'

'The Head Master,' the boy replied.

'Good heavens, child,' said Lady Carter. 'Mr Grose-Hodge isn't Chief. *Phillpotts* was the Chief.'

In passing, the memory of one of Lady Carter's sons, Major 'Toddy' Carter, is worth recalling, both for his amusing eccentricity and extraordinary kindness. He was a bachelor Old Bedfordian who lived with his aged mother, and was himself, by the late 1940s, well past middle age. He walked with a limp, and wobbled precariously through the school grounds on a bicycle with a wicker basket. On this uncertain machine he propelled himself to chapel every Sunday, arriving late and breathless. Still wearing his bicycle clips he would stomp his noisy way up the aisle to take his place at the back of the Ashburnham block. He may well have suffered from asthma, for to the weekly delight of every boy within earshot he heartily wheezed his way through the service, always, during the responses, half a sentence behind the rest of the congregation.

The same boy who had been to tea with Lady Carter nursed a youthful ambition to be a writer, and one day he spotted a large and very old-fashioned typewriter in the window of a second-hand shop. The price was £5, far more than he could afford, so he plucked up his courage to ask Major Carter for a loan. The next day the Major came flying by on his grid, as a bicycle was known at Bedford, and with a cheery wave produced the necessary fiver. (Another Bedford School expression which appears to have dropped out of usage is shag, meaning a drill; as has shent. If your bicycle was one of the vintage variety — there was an old man dressed in oily dungarees who sold highly unreliable second-hand bicycles for five shillings in a narrow passageway off St Cuthbert's Street — you were said to possess a shent grid.)

The original Chief was only the third Head Master of Bedford not to have been in holy orders, and the first not appointed by New College. His vocation was to be a schoolmaster, not a priest, and as he never taught in Oxford there was no need for him to be ordained. But he was the son of an archdeacon and the grandson of a formidable bishop, Henry Phillpotts of Exeter. Consecrated at Lambeth Palace in 1831, Bishop Phillpotts immediately showed his High Tory principles by voting against the Reform Bill, and he had his episcopal palace attacked for his pains. When not locked in theological arguments with his fellow bishops, liturgical disputes kept him almost permanently at loggerheads with his parochial clergy. In 1839 Lord Melbourne had wanted Lord Wriothesley Russell, a half-brother of Melbourne's political colleague Lord John Russell, to have the deanery of Exeter, and on 9 January he wrote to Lord John to tell him the diocese needed 'a man of the firmest character and the greatest ability to cope with that devil of a bishop, who inspires more terror than ever Satan did'. The famous Anglican wit Sydney Smith once remarked that he had to believe in the Apostolic Succession because there was no other way of explaining the descent of the Bishop of Exeter from Judas Iscariot. The father of fourteen children, Henry Phillpotts clung to office until he was 91 and blind, dying in 1869 just nine days after most reluctantly resigning his see.

James Phillpotts, the bishop's grandson, was born on 18 July 1839. Educated at Winchester and New College, Oxford, he took a First Class degree in Classical Moderations when he was twenty-one and a Second Class in the Final Schools of Humaner Letters two years later. He was instantly snapped up as an assistant master by Rugby, where he taught for a dozen years before being invited, at the age of thirty-five, to become Head Master of Bedford Grammar School. Here he remained, with his wife Marian Hadfield, whom he had married in 1868, and their two sons and three daughters, until his retirement in 1903. Those twenty-eight years changed the face of Bedford School beyond recognition; they may even have ensured its survival.

It was an era that produced impressive headmasters; Edward Thring of Uppingham, Edward Benson, first Head Master of Wellington College, Frederick Temple of Rugby, Benson and Temple each becoming archbishop of Canterbury. And Arnold's influence at Rugby remained potent. In 1860 a new foundation, Clifton College, three of whose boys became Head Masters of Bedford, took a huge risk by appointing as their first Head Master John Percival, a twenty-eight-year-old assistant master at Rugby. His example must have been one to inspire James Phillpotts, for by the time Percival resigned in 1879 (he returned to Rugby as Head Master and ended up bishop of Hereford) Clifton was already one of the largest schools in England, with 680 boys and 50 masters. [1]

By the Easter term of 1875 Phillpotts had 270 pupils; by Christmas 1888, 804. He had inherited seven classrooms, two of them very small, and a shortage of teachers meant that each master had two classes, dividing his time between them. Greek and Latin still remained the mainstay of the curriculum, however inappropriate a classical education might have been for any particular boy. Arithmetic was adequately taught; English and History, as today in so many schools, inadequately. Facilities for organised games remained rudimentary. Phillpotts himself was not only a scholar but an able sportsman, on a single day winning the Oxford University Mile and then coming third in the steeplechase. He rowed in his college Four, and no photograph of Phillpotts can leave anyone in doubt about his powerful physique. He had the bearded face and beautiful head of a man imbued with wisdom and knowledge, two attributes that do not always go together, and a mind peculiarly open to innovation and liberalism. Not every distinguished classical scholar has lent his name for over a century to an English prize, for it was in February 1884 that parents endowed the Phillpotts English Literature prize in honour of the school list reaching 500 boys for the first time.

One of Phillpotts's instant reforms sounds too trivial to mention, except that it shows how commonsensical he could be. He abolished the practice of opening up for work at 7am, for the frontiers of the town were expanding, many boys had further to walk to school than in the past, and he wanted other boys to be able to come in from surrounding villages by train — not, however, an infallible method of ensuring punctuality. In the 1940s there was a boy who came to school by train and never appeared on time, even though school did not begin until 9am. On entering the classroom he would explain, like a parrot, 'I'm sorry I'm late, the train was late', and just as frequently his entry was greeted by a chorus from the class: *'I'm sorry I'm late, the train was late.'* Phillpotts in fact divided morning school into five periods of three-quarters of an hour each, rightly realising that 45 minutes without a break was as long as most boys can concentrate on one subject without losing interest. He also provided generous breaks between school lessons, the commencement of just two afternoon periods being postponed until 4pm.[2]

The very year that Phillpotts arrived so also did a little boy of nine, Charles Greene; his father lived in Bedford, and Greene remained at the Grammar School for ten years. It was perhaps only because in 1910 Charles Greene was appointed Head Master of Berkhamstead School, and decided to have his son Graham educated at Berkhamstead, that Bedford missed the distinction of claiming as an old boy one of the greatest novelists of the twentieth century. A boy destined to be an even more renowned headmaster than Greene, and an Old Bedfordian who returned on several occasions to preach in the school chapel, arrived in 1878 at the age of eleven. He was Hubert Burge, who became successively Head Master of Repton and Winchester, and in 1911 was consecrated bishop of Southwark, being translated in 1919 to Oxford. He was appointed Clerk of the Closet, and died in office in 1925 at the age of sixty-three.

Phillpotts would not have been a classic Victorian as well as a classicist had he not appreciated the long-term importance of science, and within six months he had engaged Arthur Talbot to teach chemistry and Mechanical Science; his is a name that will ring a bell with boys who have boarded at Talbot's in De Parys Avenue. The room behind the statue of Sir William Harper was fitted up as a science laboratory and lecture room, and Mr Talbot, who knew what he was about, asked for a fume cupboard constructed of non-combustible materials; the Governors, who did not, said wood would be all right, and it was not long before there was an almighty explosion. Talbot was such an inspiring teacher that in summer boys cheerfully turned up on a voluntary basis at six in the morning, paying an extra guinea a term to cover the cost of practical work. It was another three years before science was taught at St Paul's, Talbot and Phillpotts being pioneers, and in 1895 Talbot was busy experimenting with X-rays within a year of their discovery.

One of Mr Talbot's successors at 27 De Parys Avenue (Talbot built the house himself and was the first housemaster) was John Renwick, for thirty-one years a mathematics master and known to generations of boys as Junk, for they conveniently preferred to think of him as 'Mr Rennet', rennet being an ingredient of junket. Junk Renwick joined the staff in 1919, when he was thirty-four, and his being a bachelor well into middle age did not prevent him having two boarding houses, Merton when it was the Paulo-Pontine house at 14 De Parys Avenue, from 1931-36, and Talbot's (formerly Hedgehope) from 1936-45. Junk Renwick had an exceptional memory, and was reputed to be able to complete *The Times* crossword in the time it takes most people to spread the marmalade on their toast. He was also said to savour a glass of port in his study after lunch. One hot summer's afternoon the class he was due to take sat bolt upright as his entry was expected, and then, in unison, began to sway very gently from side to side. 'Oh dear,' said Mr Renwick, clasping his forehead, 'I'm afraid I don't feel very well. I shall have to go home and lie down.'

Having been elected an honorary Old Bedfordian in 1941 Junk Renwick served as Master of the OB Masonic Lodge, founded on 22 June 1925. The Lodge is a member of the Public Schools' Lodges Council, which at present consists of 32 schools. They meet in London, and each year a festival is held in one of the schools; in 1984 Bedford acted as host, and following that year's festival a cheque for £570 was handed over to the school as a contribution to the cost of the new Audio Visual Room. Members of staff as disparate as Dr William Probert-Jones, Director of Music, and Sgt Major Blincow of the CCF have in the past been members.

By good fortune, in 1875 a former brewery with a small parcel of land standing to the east of the school playground came on the market, and on 29 May the school snapped it up for £2,600. The brewery itself was knocked down, 'thus at once doubling the area of the play-ground and providing temporary class-rooms, and giving space for the erection of workshops'.[3] Recalling the event in a resumé of the school's history prepared after Phillpotts had been Head Master 17 years, an anonymous contributor wrote, 'It should be noted that the Headmaster has always attached great importance to physical training and to handicraft. This, after all, is only a return to old Greek notions; and it is well to remember that the results of Greek education have never been excelled. There be some who doubt if they have ever been equalled — in modern times.'[4]

Within a year a fairly elementary carpentry shop had been incorporated, a small forge was added, and part-time instructors in metal work were engaged. Ever eager to put his 'Greek notions' into practice, on 22 April 1877 Phillpotts laid the foundation stone for a fives court and gymnasium. (Radley claim to be the first public school to have had a gym, built in 1860.) The cost was met by parents, masters and old boys, and by the following year these new opportunities for physical training were in use, but whether the boys ran naked round the gymnasium, as their Greek forerunners would have done, may be doubted.

There was in fact a whirlwind of activity. Literary and Natural History Societies were founded in October 1876; a Drawing and Sketching Society and a Bicycle Club followed a year later. In 1878 a Shakespeare Society was formed. At Christmas that year, which witnessed particularly severe weather (the Ouse froze over), an enormous Art and Science Exhibition was organised, crowds apparently flocking in 'day after day, night after night'.[5] Phillpotts has a reasonable claim to have founded a school library, initially by suggesting that on leaving, boys should present a book to the school, rather as Eton boys present their housemaster with a portrait. In the event, more books were given by masters and old boys than by boys as a leaving present, but a gift of £100 in 1877 from the 9th duke of Bedford must have helped to fill the shelves, possibly by as many as 400 volumes. The previous year Phillpotts had founded the *Ousel*, the title for the school magazine having, it is said, been hit upon by himself. But whether he had in mind the European blackbird, sometimes known as the ousel, or the River Ouzel, which joins the Great Ouse at Newport Pagnell, no one knows. He was so taken by the name that when he retired to Tonbridge Wells he did so to a house he called The Ousels.

The first issue was dated 15 June 1876, and cost sixpence. In 1894 an assistant master, Henry Cross, took editorial charge, and in October 1895 a rival magazine, the *Magpie*, was launched, which was odd, as Cross was editor of that as well. The *Magpie* folded after eight issues, but not before its weekly appearances had prompted the *Ousel* to go weekly as well. One wonders what game Mr Cross was up to. Since then the *Ousel* has appeared in a number of different formats, with varying regularity and very variable degrees of professionalism; today it is a corporate effort, appears three times a year, strives to be a paper of record, and in recent times has attained an extremely high standard of production.

One purpose of the *Ousel* is to keep Old Bedfordians abreast of school activities and their own progress in the world, and an early example can be traced of how its title caught the imagination of an Old Bedfordian at the school under Brereton, from 1863-73, Canon William Johnson. Johnson was diverted from a career in the Indian Civil Service by an appeal he had heard at Oxford for recruits to the Universities' Mission to Central Africa, an Anglican group supported also by Cambridge, Durham and Trinity College, Dublin, and a direct outcome of David Livingstone's adventures. He was ordained deacon in Zanzibar in 1876, was priested two years later, and during his missionary and exploratory work in Africa he underwent extreme privation, illness and danger, even temporarily losing his sight. In 1884 he returned to England to raise funds for a steamer, and this he named *The Ousel*. He translated the entire Bible into Chinyanja, and in 1896 he was appointed archdeacon of Nyasa. His heroic achievements were recognised by an honorary Fellowship of University College and an honorary Oxford doctorate of divinity. He died in 1928 at the age of seventy-five.

In June 1880 the school hall was enlarged, by means of a 25 ft extension, and thus were provided two new classrooms on the ground floor and two in the gallery. The next year a preparatory department was installed in rooms near the Castle Brewery, Phillpotts cycling over every day, much as his contemporaries had taken to using bicycles in Oxford, to see that all was well. In October 1882 the old Corn Exchange was rented, to provide another eight classrooms. But these were temporary measures. By the summer of that year there were 400 boys in the school, and drastic measures were required. An entirely new block of eleven classrooms was built on the old brewery site, and known as the Cowper Buildings they were opened on 21 October 1884 by Earl Cowper (a title that is now extinct), Lord Lieutenant of Bedfordshire and hence an ex-officio Governor of the school.

Buildings, societies, games, clubs: there were not many pies in which Phillpotts did not dip a finger. He had initiated a School Speech Day in 1877, during the course of which Act III Scene I of *King John* was performed, together with a selection from *Cyclope and Euripides*, which would have been enjoyed by the staff and boys alike; three assistant masters were graduates of Oxford, eight of Cambridge, all of whom would have been steeped in the classics, and it was not until 1884 there was a head of school (General Sir Walter Braithwaite) who was not on the classical side. Even before his gymnasium had been built, Phillpotts had laid the foundations of one of the school's most popular and enduring entertainments, the annual Assault-at-Arms. At the conclusion of the open air sports day on 18 April 1877, 'a troop of a dozen boys performed various exercises on the horizontal and parallel bars under the guidance of Sgt J H Campbell, the Instructor'[6]. The first official Assault-at-Arms was held in the School Hall on 13 April 1881, 'when boxing and singlestick are first mentioned', singlestick being a form of one-handed fighting or fencing with a wooden stick or sword. The *Ousel* said, 'We must not close an account of this novel entertainment without thanking Mr Vie for so kindly coming forward to assist in accompanying on the piano'. Later generations of Old Bedfordians will remember the strains year after year of Schubert's incidental music to *Rosamunde* as twentieth century athletes went flying through the air in immaculately pressed white trousers and singlets to exhibit their prowess on wooden horse and bars.

Fussing a bit like a mother hen, in 1880 Phillpotts was writing to parents to say, 'There is a good deal of measles about the Town, and I should be glad if Parents would keep any boy at home who has not had measles and has any symptoms of a cold: eg running at the nose, eyes watering, sneezing, sore throat or cough'. A decade later he regretted to have to tell parents the 'Sanitorium Fee of 3/6 a Term' had proved to be insufficient. He needed an extra '1s 6d per boy per Term'. Twelve months later he was warning parents about mild cases of scarlet fever in the town and offering to let boys go home a week early for the Christmas holiday.

On quite a different subject, when it was discovered that 'for the last week or more an itinerant photograph seller' had been 'vending his wares in the town' it appears that Phillpotts was again kept fully informed, and approved a plan of action. For 'many of the photographs were of an indecent character. Having sold some of these to a few boys in the principal school in Bedford, the senior monitors (it is said with leave of the headmaster) told the dealer on Wednesday that if he came down to the school boathouse he would probably do a roaring trade'. On his arrival, the boys chucked him in the river. [7]

This was no more than Phillpotts would have expected. Of parents seeking a place for their sons in his school, he made stringent enquiries about the boys' truthfulness, industry, obedience and above all their 'General Conduct and moral tone'. He made it plain that 'all bad language and ungentlemanly conduct was forbidden'. Smoking was 'absolutely forbidden'. Nor were boys to carry firearms or catapults. They were never to lounge in the street, and strictly off limits were public houses, billiard rooms and race meetings, although Phillpotts himself was not averse to horses, on occasion making straight for a meet of the local hunt the minute midday prayers were ended.

When it came to punishing those who transgressed school rules, the Head Master wrote out instructions for the guidance of his staff. No assistant master might hit a boy on his head or face, or box his ears. If a master administered corporal punishment he was to do so only with a cane, not in anger but only after deliberation, the punishment was to be entered in the school diary the next morning, and no more than two cuts were permitted. These were liberal regulations by any standard. He had advice too when it came to writing half-term reports. 'Some masters,' he noted, 'write excellent reports showing a real understanding of the boys' good and weak points and sympathy as well'. But 'Other masters make boys out all black with no relief'. It was a curious fact, he wrote, 'that the Masters who are the most successful in managing their forms give the best character to their boys'.

Phillpotts was no mean psychologist. He told his staff to remember that 'blaming boys before others often leads to exhibition of temper which might be avoided by speaking when alone. Troublesome boys may have independence of character. Very good boys may lack it.' A boy who was 'not quick' need not be characterised as 'dull and stupid'.

The provision of organised sporting activities was a part of Phillpotts's scheme for placing his grammar school on a footing to compete with Rugby, who by 1879 had nine fives courts, two pavilions, cricket pitches, a gym and a swimming bath; Rugby, of course, was the place where he had trained and to whose ethos he was so strongly attracted. He was keen that Bedford should compete with other equally well-established and illustrious schools; The Leys, in Cambridge, for example. Form and house games came first, but in 1881 a cricket match was played against Merchant Taylors'. (The first recorded inter-school cricket match was played in 1796 between Eton and Westminster.) Of thirty-one school matches played before 1912, twenty-four were won and only four lost.[8] In 1882 the school played against Dulwich; that was the year the Head Master had purchased a cricket field from someone called Mrs Orr. In November 1883 (a little late in the season) a cricket pavilion was presented to the school; by 1887 Bedford was taking on St Paul's.

Competition, both against other schools and within the school itself, informed the new culture. Boys were frog-marched to the Town Baths, just above Chetham's Boat Yard, to learn to swim so that house swimming races could be organised. Phillpotts no doubt considered it vital in any case that boys taking part in rowing should be able to swim. He had only been Head Master two years when the 1st IV won the Junior Fours in the Bedford Regatta. In 1878 the 1st IV won the public schools race and in 1879 both the Junior Fours and the Public Schools Fours. By 1880 the 1st IV were achieving success at Henley. Cups were again carried off at Henley and the Bedford Regatta in 1881, and it was clear that Bedford was well on the way to becoming a school renowned for its rowing, with a steady succession of Bedford boys gaining rowing Blues at university.

There was by this time a vast empire, and officers and civil servants were re-quired to run it. The way to teach boys to strive for future success was to set them against one another — in friendly rivalry, of course. In order to involve day boys in the competitive side of the school, Phillpotts aligned the school houses with boarding houses. Thus a boy who lived in the Ashburnham area of Bed-ford, and was enrolled in Ashburnham House, would have an affinity with boys in the Ashburnham boarding house, which came to be Sanderson's. Soon there were six school houses: Ashburnham, Bromham, Crescent, St Paul's, St Peter's and Pontines — 'across the Bridge'. St Paul's and Pontines merged to become Paulo-Pontine, and St Cuthbert's was added. House recitation competitions were instituted in March 1879; in February 1888 house choir competitions began.

Immensely energetic himself, Phillpotts saw no reason why others, younger than he, should not work off some surplus energy, and before long he had boys drilling during their mid-morning break. A drum and fife band was formed, and soon the school was being marched to Goldington Green for crypto-military manoeuvres. Monitors acted as NCOs, and enjoyed themselves strutting about and shouting orders. But it was not until May 1887 that a school cadet corps was officially formed, just in time to train a generation of boys to take part in the Boer War. In fact, about 150 Old Bedfordians did so, twenty-two of them losing their lives.[9] By the turn of the century, schools and youth clubs throughout the country were preparing their boys for a European conflict that seemed increasingly inevitable, and somewhat ahead of schedule, Bedford, together with Sherborne, Haileybury, St Paul's and Bradford, went off to the first ever Public School Camp, held in 1889 near Wantage. The summer of 1914 was to find 10,000 public schoolboys in camp.

Apart from taking a leading role in drilling, the monitors appointed by Phillpotts (there were nineteen, one in charge of each form) had very specific rules regarding their conduct and duties. They were selected by the Head Master 'on grounds of character, influence and discretion', and it was made plain that entry to the Sixth Form did not automatically guarantee selection. As the average age of the monitors was eighteen we must assume that a number of boys were now staying on until at least the age of nineteen. In order to encourage an appreciation of the hierarchical nature of the society they were being trained to serve, monitors were graded into half a dozen classes: junior options, senior options, sub-monitors, pro-monitors, full monitors and moni-tors. At the apex of this pyramid was the head of school, who alone was permitted to inflict corporal punishment. And no punishment was to be handed out by him without the other monitors meeting to discuss the matter, in order to 'enforce tradition by careful hearing of a case as training for the younger monitors'.

If the monitors decided a boy deserved punishment the defendant could still appeal to the Head Master. These safeguards against indiscriminate caning of boys by boys were remarkably enlightened for the time, and fell away in the next century, when, until caning was abolished altogether, in 1987, house and school monitors let fly with their canes whenever they felt like it. Nevertheless there was trouble in 1879 when the head of school was taken to court by the father of a boy to whom he had administered five strokes of the cane — certainly an excessive caning for a boy to administer. Doubtless desiring to support the status quo, as most lay magistrates are prone to do, the justices found in favour of the head boy.

Phillpotts had a particularly soft spot for small boys, who were said to respond eagerly 'to his brisk and vivacious call'. And the monitors were especially charged with keeping a fraternal eye on the younger boys. 'Each one does his best,' Phillpotts said when addressing the school in 1884, 'not only for the organisation of games but also to prevent bullying, which in a large school is apt to creep into practice. Anyone who thinks of his own school days can remember how much of the happiness of his life was taken away by thoughtless ill-treatment by the older ones, but in this school there is the feeling that every little boy should find himself here in another home where there is an opening for a happy career amid the general influences of the warm affection and good feeling of those around him.' He added, 'If this has been realised here it is due not only to the masters and monitors but also to a noble succession of heads of the school,' at which point his oration was interrupted by cheers. (Boys were much given to cheering in the past. John Keate, the legendary nineteenth century Head Master of Eton, was frequently cheered by the boys he had soundly thrashed.)

On 15 June 1874, just four months before Phillpotts's appointment as Head Master of Bedford Grammar School, Disraeli pronounced in the House of Commons, 'Upon the education of the people of this country the fate of this country depends.' No serious minded mid-Victorian would have argued against that proposition, but it was a far cry from the eighteenth century belief that an entire grammar school could quite adequately be taught in one large hall, from an era when the concept of a written examination had never crossed anybody's mind. Many men in authority in Phillpotts's youth had no academic qualifications to speak of. John Scott, the future Lord Chancellor (he became Lord Eldon), was examined in 1770 for an Oxford degree in Hebrew and History.

'What is the Hebrew for the place of a skull?' he was asked.

'Golgotha.'

'And who founded University College?'

Believing it wise to stick to the myth, Scott replied, 'King Alfred.'

'Very well, Sir,' he was told by the examiner, 'you are competent for your degree.'

It was not just the growth of Britain's empire that was demanding properly educated administrators; the worlds of commerce and engineering were in competition with German expansionism, and as the empire came to engulf a fifth of the world's surface so the Anglican Church needed clergy to carry the doctrines of Lambeth to every corner of the globe, even, eventually, to the frozen wastes of the Arctic. An ever more heavily mechanised army and navy required officers capable of doing more than ride to hounds and pass the port. Boys had to be taught in a more tutorial fashion than before, which meant smaller classes and more classrooms. The recruitment and proper remuneration of competent and well qualified masters had become a *sine qua non*.

It was against this background that Phillpotts found it quite intolerable that a master who had been teaching in 1878 in the Old Brewery buildings should be asked, in 1882, to remove his boys and their textbooks to a temporary building on the old playground — and to repair later that year to the Castle Rooms, only to be moved on to the old Corn Exchange. The meanderings of this particular class eventually took them to the Cowper Buildings, back to the Corn Exchange, to a room in the public library and to St Peter's Rectory. It was all very well 'special committees' being appointed to report on accommodation, one such concluding in November 1884 that a) additional accommodation was needed, that b) additional accommodation should be provided at once for 300 boys, and that c) to fix a limit 'to number of boys' was undesirable. One inspired suggestion was to build on the playground — but then where would the boys play? An even dottier idea was to erect an extra floor on the eighteenth century school building. With 586 boys in the school at Christmas 1884 Phillpotts began to envisage the possibility of an eventual school population of 1,000 (only Eton, Marlborough and Cheltenham were now larger than Bedford), and he realised that there was only one thing to be done, for the school to abandon its present accommodation and to move, lock, stock and barrel.

FOUR

A Regular Parade of Admirals

1884–1903

O N 31 AUGUST 1883 the *Daily News* reported that Bedford was rapidly becoming the metropolis of education in England, which explains why James Phillpotts had come under ever increasing pressure to find additional accommodation for his growing school. And one cause of expansion at this time was what we might call the Anglo-Indian factor. Many professional and service families who wanted a good education for their sons could not afford expensive education, and the attractions of Bedford as a town were both domestic — there was a river, an abundance of pleasant parks, recreational amenities and practically no industry — and educational; the Grammar and Modern Schools were both good and inexpensive. Local families, however hard up, had pride in their appearance. Most days the High Street almost took on the atmosphere of an Italian resort, Bedford residents parading their clothes and themselves, anxious to see and be seen. There was an air of quiet gentility, of Victorian respectability, that greatly appealed to people sometimes born, often bred, in India, people accustomed to commodious houses and plenty of servants who were now looking for somewhere to settle in England.

A glowing description of the attractions on offer was painted in *Bedford in 1888*, published by the *Bedfordshire Times*.

[The] High Street affords clear evidence of the giant-like strides of trade and enterprise in Bedford. In the principal streets of the town it may almost be said that not a shop is to be got for love or money. The handsome new business premises that are constantly erected, the palatial shopfronts that are ever being inserted, the frequent employment of the decorator's art, the enlargements and renovations, together with the stagnation in the Bankruptcy Court so far as Bedford is concerned, and the numerous retired tradesmen whose villa residences adorn the suburbs, all betoken great commercial activity.

59

Bedford in 1888 was proud to boast that Socialists in the town were 'few in number'. Nor was Bedford, as yet, polluted by the presence of 'any Anarchists, Vegetarians, Mormons or Shakers'.

Patricia Bell, who has made a study of Anglo-Indian Bedford, has written: 'Bedford as a centre in England for Anglo-Indians — those English families whose working years were spent aboard in India or the services — was at its most typical in the years between 1880 and the outbreak of the Great War ... the great jump came after the reorganisation of the Harpur Trust secondary schools in 1873, and the Anglo-Indian ascendancy lasted until 1914.'[1] A brochure produced in 1913 remarked that 'society in Bedford is just what Anglo-Indians have been accustomed to', and a boy at school in Bedford during the heyday of the Anglo-Indian ascendancy recalled that out of his class of thirty, seventeen boys had been born in India. [2]

There were indications of what might be going to happen as early as 1822, when a Royal Naval officer, Captain G B Trollope, arrived in Bedford with the express purpose of entrusting the education of his brood of six young sons to Dr Brereton. Such early settlers tended to favour The Crescent, begun in 1826, near Holy Trinity Church. The census of 1871 reveals a retired major general at No 4 The Crescent. His neighbour at No 8 was a major in the Bengal Medical Service, whose wife and three children had all been born in the East Indies. Such was the scramble for places at the Grammar School that the vicar of Elstow was granted a licence to live outside his parish — in The Crescent — because until 1873 a day boy and his family had to live within the borough.[3]

Clerical vocations have not been in short supply among Bedford School boys, who have provided bishops for such diverse dioceses as Bombay, Blomfontein, Ely, the Falkland Islands, Liverpool, Gloucester and Chota. One of Phillpotts's Old Bedfordians, John Gregg, born in 1873, became archbishop of Dublin and then archbishop of Armagh and Primate of All Ireland, being made a Companion of Honour in 1957. Nor have the diplomatic service or the overseas civil service lacked Old Bedfordians, anxious to serve in India, Japan, Burma, Korea, Rhodesia ... But those who have achieved high office in the Church and diplomacy must be well outnumbered by those who have attained seniority in the armed forces, a feat that would not of course have come about had it not been for two world wars. Nevertheless the Anglo-Indian connection and the attraction for Bedford boys of a military career (under Phillpotts the school specifically educated boys for Woolwich and Sandhurst) seem to be linked. Between 1880 and 1891, thirty-eight Grammar School boys entered Woolwich, and forty-five went to Sandhurst. Others opted for the Senior Service or the fledgling airforce, and some did rather well. General Sir Cyril Deverell, at school under Phillpotts from 1887-93, was appointed Chief of the

Imperial General Staff in 1935 and was shortly afterwards promoted Field Marshal. In the same year, Air Chief Marshal Sir Cyril Newall, at school a little later than Deverell (from 1897-1903), was placed in charge of the RAF. He became Governor General of New Zealand and was admitted to the Order of Merit.

Since 1877 Queen Victoria had been Empress of India, and Empire was the theme of an address delivered by the Mayor of Bedford at Speech Day on 5 July 1888, when he launched what was in effect a publicity drive to attract yet more boys to the Grammar School. Addressing the Lord Mayor of London, who had been escorted in a carriage procession from the Midland Station to the Corn Exchange, he said Bedford was sending back to London 'a hundred-fold more than London sent to Bedford, in well-educated young men and women who could help to make the future greatness of the Empire'.[4] He hoped that London 'might send down its youth to be educated at Bedford and Bedford would promise to send them back well-formed young men and women, well-developed, well-educated and good-mannered,' fit, in effect, for the export trade to the Empire.

The local MP, Samuel Whitbread, spelt out, if in somewhat convoluted language, the current plan of campaign. 'We felt,' he said, 'there was an opening for a grand national benefit if we should establish a grammar school which should be within the means of that numerous body of public servants who have passed their lives at home and abroad in the public service, and alas in cases of many, their silver is apt to deteriorate to copper before it gets home. I yet think that we were conferring in that manner not only benefit upon this town but a great benefit to the nation.'

The late-Victorian development to the west of Kimbolton Road, enshrining the names of various saints, chosen it seems more or less at random (St Andrew's Road, St Michael's Road, St Augustine's, St George's), was a direct result of the influx of Anglo-Indians, rather fewer than 100,000 of whose kindred spirits — soldiers and administrators — were keeping in thrall two hundred and fifty million Indians. The daughter of one such family, Beryl Irving, whose parents had come in search of 'good and cheap education', left an account of her Bedford childhood. 'Our houses,' she wrote, 'were large enough to accommodate an Edwardian number of young, and under their gables the Anglo-Indians were trying to make ends meet with dignity. We were of those English families who had served their country in India in one way or another, but chiefly in the army. Our houses were crammed with Benares tables, strings of little carved elephants, placid Buddhas and malevolent gods. Our mothers made good curries.'[5]

At the turn of the century the curate-in-charge of St Andrew's noted, 'The congregation at St Andrew's is very largely composed of persons who have lived in India or the colonies. Last Whitsunday, for example, both the clergy who officiated were ex-Indian chaplains. The Lessons were read by an ex-Indian officer of police, and of the six gentlemen who collected the alms, four had spent long periods of service in India and Ceylon.'

The Indian influence lingered long after Phillpotts's headmastership. 'As late as the twenties you invited friends to "tiffin" rather than to lunch; you said you were going down to "the bazaar" when you were going shopping in the High Street.' [6] Washing remained 'dhobi', a tailor was a 'derzi'. By around 1890 the Anglo-Indians had taken over the High Street promenade. 'Every morning between 11 and 12.30 there was a regular parade of admirals, generals, colonels and other officers with their ladies up and down High Street between the Swan and St Peter's; and never was there such a doffing of hats and caps and so much bowing and saluting as friends and acquaintances met one another.' [7]

In 1902 the borough programme for the coronation of Edward VII confirmed that 'The rapid growth of Bedford during the last two decades... has been due mainly to the success of the Harpur Schools. As most of the scholars must reside with their parents, there has been a large demand for a good class of villa residence. This demand has been met by the creation of new suburbs in all directions.'

The numbers of houses in Bedford increased from 3,614 in 1871 to 8,893 in 1911, the population from 16,581 in 1871 to 39,185 forty years later. One Anglo-Indian settler recorded: 'The society in Bedford is just what Anglo-Indians have been accustomed to, and therefore what they want ... Paterfamilias have no difficulty about finding kindred spirits to play golf, bridge or row.' [8] In other words, the more that Bedford had to offer to Anglo-Indian families the greater numbers of such families would settle in Bedford, and the greater the influence the colonial stamp of mind would have upon the school.

For many centuries St Peter's Church had owned glebe land stretching as far north as Park Avenue. A man of extraordinary foresight, Phillpotts had his eye on this land as early as 1881, when he recommended to the school Governors that they purchase a large rectangular plot representing something like half the present main school playing field. They declined to take his advice and allowed the land to slip into other hands. When in October 1882 it again came on the market, Phillpotts snapped it up himself, managing to persuade the Governors to pay £2,783 10s for it thirteen months later. A second slice of land, more or less where today the Pavilion stands, was purchased in June 1884 for £450.

The decisive event that enabled Phillpotts to uproot the school was the purchase on 27 August 1887 for £4,800 of seven and a half acres of glebe land, an area which in due course became the heart of the school estate. Four days later St Peter's Rectory, which stood at that time in St Peter's Street to the east of the church, was secured. This cost a further £2,000, and the old rectory became the site of the school's new preparatory department, known to generations of boys as the Inky. With some 17 acres secured over a nail-biting period of five years it was at last feasible to draw up plans for a new school building to be erected more or less in the centre of the estate — a little to the south of centre in point of fact, immediately opposite Glebe Road; Burnaby Road did not as yet exist. In May 1891, five months before the new building was opened, Phillpotts made his fifth purchase, a stretch of land which continued his first 8.5 acre plot of playing fields as far north as Park Avenue itself.

For any architect, the new school would have been a prestigious commission, and there was no shortage of plans submitted for the consideration of yet another 'special committee'. Basil Champneys, who had designed the Cowper Buildings, believed he could produce a workable structure for £15,000, which was wildly optimistic, but Phillpotts, driven perhaps by understandable impatience, declared himself impressed. The Governors however had their doubts, and the London School Board's architect was called in to adjudicate. He did not believe the sort of accommodation needed could be provided at such a low cost, and thought at least another £5,000 would have to be found. So E C Robins was invited to submit plans with a budget of £20,000. Robins's designs were finally accepted, but only after he had pointed out that an additional £5,000 would be required for roads.

Cautious as ever, the Governors had refused to sign an architectural contract until they were satisfied that funds were available. The old school building was expected to bring in £8,500 (it was sold to the Corporation and became the Town Hall); other Harpur Trust property to be disposed of was valued at £5,500, and the Governors said they were in possession of a similar sum in stock. After months of delay, Phillpotts launched a building appeal, contributing £500 himself, a not inconsiderable sum for a headmaster to find in 1888. The duke of Bedford and Samuel Whitbread chipped in with £1,000 each, and within a week Phillpotts had raised over £7,000.

The foundation stone was laid, by Samuel Whitbread, chairman of the Governors as well as Bedford's MP, on 17 October 1889, the year in which, by a happy coincidence, the *Public Schools Year Book* was first published. It contained the names of thirty-six schools, one of which was Bedford. Accommodation was to be provided for 1,026 boys, but how such a precise, some might say arbitrary, figure was arrived at we do not know. It took two years to complete the building, which from the first was described as being in the Tudor style, a flight of architectural fancy, surely. It turned out to be what we should call Victorian Gothic, its most striking feature being an enormous central hall 102 ft 6 in long, 50 ft wide and rising 51 ft 6 in, with first and second floor galleries on the south and west sides of the hall and classrooms off the galleries. It would not have occurred to any Victorian architect that the impressive emptiness of the upper reaches of the hall was a magnificent waste of space.

There were no central doors as there are today, only the present entrances from the east and west ends of the building. Neither was there a central staircase; boys clattered their noisy way up flagged staircases at either end of the building, which over the years became dangerously worn. There were 42 classrooms all told, ranged on the south, east and west sides of the building; the unlit northern facade faced the main playing fields, but with no outlook from ground level. The Head Master's study was located in the same position as today, at the north-west corner, and the internal door of his study was reached down a passage behind the platform at the west end of the hall. The Bell Room was at the west end, with easy access to the Head Master's study; the masters' commonroom, a companion room to the Head Master's, was at the north-east corner.

Every mod con was incorporated. The Hall, lobbies and corridors were to be 'warmed by hot water on the low pressure system', two boilers being fixed in the basement, 'and therefrom flow three circulating pipes which pass round the hall in a chamber provided below the floor, and from these pipes connections are made with the radiators fixed about the building'. Ventilation of the Hall was 'obtained by means of four sets of Bunsen burners in the extract shafts and twists, and has been so calculated as to ensure the air being completely changed every twenty minutes'.

As for the classrooms, they were to be warmed by Boyd's Hygiastic ventilating stoves, 'being an open fire-place with hot-air chambers through which the air passes, being admitted into the room through an ornamental grating in the centre of the tiled over-mantle; the passage of the air is regulated by valves. To each room a separate extract shaft is provided, fitted with Bunsen burners and Boyd's wall-face ventilators, fixed near the ceiling, while fresh air is admitted by two Tobin's Tubes. Cross ventilation has been secured by fanlights on the hall side of the rooms, and over the doors.' [9]

The school building was opened with appropriate pomp and ceremony on 29 October 1891 by the 10th duke of Bedford. The whole town seems to have participated, decorating the High Street and lining the processional route from St Paul's Square, a Volunteer Corps band leading the boys, of whom there were now just over 800, making Bedford, *The Times* reported, very nearly the largest public school. The Governors, the Mayor and Corporation, the Lord Lieutenant and a good many Old Boys brought up the rear. Most of the boys watched the opening ceremony from the galleries, parents and those who had contributed being allocated chairs in the body of the Hall; it was into these galleries that in later years Inky and Lower School boys crowded on the first day of term. The choir, wearing Eton collars, arrayed themselves at the back of the platform. Phillpotts was enthroned in a gigantic chair of state, still in the possession of the school; the music master, P H Diemer, was seated at a grand piano.

The school hymn was sung, and the duke declared the building open. Phillpotts chose for his Lesson the passage 'Let us now praise famous men', and his brother, the Reverend Septimus Phillpotts, who was school chaplain, and was said to know Horace and Virgil by heart, read the prayers. The head of school, F T Duhan, did his stuff by asking for an extra half-holiday. And so the boys and masters dispersed to the old buildings once again, where they saw out the Christmas term. The first day of school in 1892 was 22 January, and that was the day the new building was first occupied. Even then lessons were disturbed by the sound of carpenters finishing off internal fittings.

On the afternoon of the opening ceremony the school 1st XV played the Old Bedfordians, and were beaten 'after a very even game'. Fortuitously, the Old Bedfordians Club (spelt variously in the past Bedfordian and Bedfordians', but in 1935 regularised as Bedfordians) had been founded in the last hectic weeks while the new school building was being prepared for its unveiling; on 23 August 1891, following an exploratory meeting in December the previous year attended by some 40 OBs. A provisional committee consisting of five former heads of school was formed, one of whom was Hubert Burge; another, William Surtees, head of school 1889-90, also became a bishop — of Crediton. The first honorary secretary was Henry Cross, at the school from 1873-84. He and his brothers, who attended Bedford as day boys as well, were typical examples of the Anglo-Indian connection. Their father, Lt. Colonel William Cross, had served with the 38th Madras Regiment, and he and his wife Isabel settled at No. 2 Goldington Road. It is a salutary reminder of the health hazards in Victorian England to discover that the eldest boy, William, who had attained the Sixth Form, died in 1877 at the age of 18 from some fever or other, quite possibly typhoid. Henry was a brilliant all-rounder; having won a classical scholarship to Hertford College, Oxford, in 1888 he rowed for his University.

It was in 1890 (four years before taking over the *Ousel)* that Henry Cross returned to Bedford, to take charge of the mercantile class. Incensed, as was everyone in England, not least Queen Victoria, by the death at Khartoum in 1885 of General Gordon, in the summer of 1898 Cross managed to get himself accredited to the *Manchester Guardian*, obtained leave of absence from Phill-potts until October, and set sail for the Sudan to report on Kitchener's belated relief expedition. He was present at the Battle of Omdurman, and died 18 days later, on 20 September, of enteric fever. When the school cricket pavilion was enlarged and re-sited in 1899 it was named the Cross Memorial Pavilion.

The first dinner organised by Old Bedfordians by way of a reunion predated the Club by 19 years. It was held at the Swan Hotel in Bedford, in 1872, when about 60 people turned up. The first London dinner took place in 1883 at the Holborn Restaurant, when the redoubtable Colonel Frederick Burnaby was in the chair, and the first overseas 'dinner' predated the Club as well, being held in 1886, although it was not exactly a salubrious affair. There were just two OBs present, one of whom, W P Braithwaite, reported to the *Ousel*, 'The usual toasts were drunk, though liquor was somewhat scarce and the place not altogether to be desired; it was at Hman Anig, Upper Burma ... just after we had attacked and taken the place, and the bullets were still occasionally whizzing about.' The menu had consisted of bully beef. A dinner at the Swan in 1891 sounds rather more appetising: mock turtle soup, cod, beef Tournedos, turkey, saddle of mutton, pheasant, trifle and fruit. When ten OBs mustered for dinner at the Royal Hotel, Durban in 1905 they seem to have had no difficulty consuming a ten-course menu.

As the school entered the last decade of the nineteenth century its academic structure seems light-years away from anything we would encounter, or even comprehend, today. There was a prep school, catering for about eighty boys aged between eight and ten. Then there was a junior school for boys between ten and thirteen, of whom there were some 190. In the Upper School there were two departments. One, the classical, is easy enough to grasp; this consisted of about 190 boys in upper and middle forms. And then there was a department called the Civil and Military. This was the department entered by boys destined for a military career, and included about 110 boys between the ages of twelve and fifteen in a junior and civil section; there were some 190 boys in upper and middle forms, and another forty or so in what was called the Mercantile and London class. No fewer than seventeen masters taught classics, twelve modern languages, thirteen mathematics and one arithmetic. Science remained in its infancy; there was one chemistry teacher and two who took physics and natural philosophy. One master taught botany; one or two took drawing and painting.

Since 1880, 276 Oxford and Cambridge Higher Certificates had been awarded, with 165 distinctions, and since 1884, 234 Lower Certificates had been obtained, with 470 distinctions. Within the past decade, 44 open scholarships had been won at Oxford and Cambridge. There were two leaving exhibitions on offer each year, one of £70, the other of £60, and within the school a variety of prizes to be competed for in addition to the Fanshawe

Divinity Prize and the Phillpotts English Literature prizes. The Warden and Fellows of New College presented an annual prize for Classical Composition; there were prizes for Engineering and for something called Sanitary Science.

As it had been the express purpose of the Civil and Military department to prepare boys for entry to Woolwich and Sandhurst, once the school began celebrating Empire Day, every 24 May, there was never any shortage of heavily decorated Old Bedfordians to take the salute. Two brothers became, respectively, a rear admiral and an air chief marshal. One year the admiral, Sir Robert Burnett, appeared on the playing field. Sedately inspecting the cadet corps, he paused before one unsuspecting innocent and enquired, 'Is your father an Old Bedfordian?'

It occurred to the boy, for the first time in his life, he actually had no idea where his father had been to school.

'No, Sir,' he replied.

'Tell him from me,' said Admiral Burnett, 'I'm sorry for him!'

One use to which the Great Hall was put very early on was as a venue for the delivery of lectures, and the task of engaging outside speakers was undertaken by Arthur Talbot, the pioneering chemist. Before sailing, in July 1901, on his first Antarctic expedition, Robert Scott had been to Norway to pick the brains of an experienced explorer, Fridtjof Nansen, and Nansen came to Bedford School to lecture. So did Sir Ernest Shackleton, who had been to the Antarctic with Scott in 1901, and in 1908 had himself got to within ninety-seven miles of the South Pole. When news reached England in 1912 of Scott's catastrophic return march from the Pole he became a posthumous national hero, and lectures on exploration were a sell-out; at Bedford both Nansen and Shackleton attracted audiences of 2,000. In December 1903 Albert Armitage, Scott's second-in-command on his first expedition, was invited to lecture.

One of the Great Hall lectures was given by Mr Talbot himself, on the erudite subject of Rontgen Rays, as X-rays were originally called. An admission charge of 1s (5p in modern currency) was made, the proceeds going towards the cost of new workshops. The Hall was utilised for Speech Days, concerts and plays (in April 1902 *Little Dick Whittington* was put on three nights running), and for the Assault-at-Arms, for which, in 1900, carriages were to be ordered for 9.30pm. Invitations to Speech Day on 7 July 1898 had suggested carriages at 5.15pm. The reason many events that took place in the Great Hall had a price tag attached was to sponsor one new project after another. And some of the titles of early lectures had a peculiarly patronising ring. The Reverend L B Butcher on India: Its Folk and Faiths, for instance. Later on, pioneering film shows — what Grose-Hodge would announce as 'an exhibition of motion pictures' — would be held, and when the film broke down, as it frequently did, one of the masters would improvise on the piano to keep the audience happy.

Four Fives courts, two open and two covered, came into play in 1892, but by far the most important development following the opening of the main building was the construction of a new prep school. The old St Peter's Rectory was demolished, and the Inky arose on its site, the nickname referring not to the state of the boys' hands but standing as an abbreviation for Incubator. In January 1894 the age of admission to the prep department had been lowered to seven, in the hope that local parents would be encouraged to enter their boys at Bedford at the age that other prep schools had been creaming them off. Looking at the new building today, opened in 1899, it is difficult to imagine it only cost £2,694 19s. The Inky was supplied with Head Masters of its own, one of whom, Donald Palmer, Head Master 1959-75, devoted his entire thirty-nine-year career to the Inky. Mistresses as well as masters came to play an inspired part in the teaching of prep school boys. Lyn Harman, for example, retired in 1978 after teaching in the Inky for forty-two years. Phyllis Siller, who was presented to Princess Margaret during her visit to the school in 1952 and retired the next year (she died in 1970), became deputy head of the prep school, working under a particularly sympathetic Head Master, Tom Snow (he served from 1933-59). In 1944 Mr Snow wrote in his report on one ten-year-old, 'His fortnightly reports have not been good enough, with their references to disobedience, slowness to settle and so on. But he is so pleasant about it that it is difficult to be angry with him!' To which Humfrey Grose-Hodge appended a warning note: 'Yes, but he will not be able to get away with it indefinitely!'

Born in 1899, an early Inky boy, Harold Abrahams, was to achieve fame as the subject of the film *Chariots of Fire*. He joined the Inky in September 1908, spent one term in the Upper School, and in 1913 he entered St Paul's, moving on a year later to Repton. Between 1920-23 he represented Cambridge against Oxford in athletics, winning eight events in all, and ran for Great Britain in the Olympics in 1920 and again in 1924, the year he won the 100 metres. He died in 1978. Another sportsman to whom the Inky can lay claim — but only just — is the golfer and *Sunday Times* journalist Henry Longhurst, whose sojourn lasted one term. Born in 1909, Longhurst, who lived at Bromham, spent the Easter term of 1916 in Form I5, but left for health reasons, and eventually entered Charterhouse. In 1930 he captained the Cambridge University golf team, and wrote a dozen books, including an autobiography titled *My Life and Soft Times*. He too died in 1978.

It was about the time that Phillpotts was making up his mind to move the school that he enrolled one of his most dazzling pupils; Hector Munro, better known as the short story writer Saki. Munro was born in Burma in 1870, where his father was Inspector General of Police. His mother died young and his grandmother lived in Devon, so it is a reasonable assumption that Munro was a boarder. He began his career as a political satirist on the *Westminster Gazette*, served as a correspondent for the *Morning Post* in Russia and France, and published his first volume of short stories in 1904. (Perhaps his best known book, published in 1912, was *The Unbearable Bassington*; a collected edition of his works came out in 1963.) 'You can't expect a boy to be depraved until he's been to a good school,' he wrote in *The Baker's Dozen*. Having refused a commission, H H Munro became a sergeant in the 22nd Royal Fusiliers, and was killed near Beaumont Hamel on 14 November 1916. He was forty-six, having enlisted at a far older age than he ever need have done.

And in 1901 Phillpotts acquired another writer every bit as brilliant as Saki. He was Hesketh Pearson, whose parents were among those who had moved to Bedford in search of a good school they could afford. Born on 20 February 1887, Pearson was initially sent to Orkney House School in Clapham Road, where he endured 'five years of helpless misery' at the hands of the Head Master, a man he described as 'a flagello-maniac'. [10] The Pearson family lived at 31 Shakespeare Road (renumbered to 53), and when he was 14 he entered Bedford Grammar School. He came to believe that most schoolmasters were idiots, and like many writers, he did badly scholastically, refusing to learn anything that did not engage his interest. (His contemporary, Osbert Sitwell, destined to write the most original autobiography of his generation, refused to pay attention to any subject at school other than history.) With Dr Johnson, Pearson believed that 'all intellectual improvement arises from leisure'.

He had to admit, however, that out of the thirty or so masters he encountered, two called forth his 'liking and gratitude'. The first form master he had, R W Rice, who played cricket for Gloucestershire, failed to encourage him to memorize Scott, but a master called Rolfe, 'a strict person whom I never much liked', did at least stimulate an interest in historical novels. When it came to mathematics, Pearson distinguished himself by scoring nought in an Algebra paper. He says that Rolfe's whole life was his work (which is true of many dedicated schoolmasters), but there was apparently no laughter in his classroom. 'All of us were frightened of him. He had dark red hair and a longish pointed red moustache, and sometimes looked extremely severe. Rigid discipline reigned during lessons, and inattention invariably resulted in a caning.'

It was at school that Hesketh Pearson's interest was aroused in Charles II, whose biography he was to write in 1960. ' The Whig historians,' he explained in his autobiography, 'in trying to whitewash that strangely unattractive figure William III, did their best to blackwash Charles II, but the worse they made him appear the more I liked him; and when we had to write an essay on the theme, mine erred on the side of hero-worship.'

Like many creative pupils, Hesketh Pearson took far more interest in the masters than in the lessons they tried to teach, and he was destined to become one of the most distinguished biographers of his time, perhaps of the twentieth century. [11] He says that Phillpotts fascinated him. 'As he strode on to the platform for prayers in the hall, with his long grey beard, flowing gown and mortar board, he looked like Zeus or Jupiter or any Old Testament prophet.

'Occasionally he treated us to what we called a pi-jaw, which I chiefly liked because it went on for half an hour and practically eliminated the first morning lesson.' He thought that Phillpotts was equal to any situation, and remembered that 'when one morning the citizens of Bedford formed a procession to the school, accompanied by a band, to demand that the boys be given a holiday because Mafeking had been relieved … the big central door was opened, the hall was quickly packed with patriots, the boys were sent up to the galleries, and the old Chief delivered an impromptu harangue, received with yells of delight. He then stooped down from the platform, shook hands vigorously with a thousand or more townsmen, freed us for the day, and probably spent the rest of it having his arm massaged.'

Hesketh Pearson was initially a day boy in Paulo-Pontine, but for his last four terms he became a boarder at Merton House in Kimbolton Road, 'being the last house but one before the fields and hedgerows started'. He says he was fairly happy there, 'as happy as I could ever be in a state of restricted liberty'. His housemaster was H W Barnes, affectionately known as Podgy. Pearson alleges it was Barnes who named his boarding house after his Oxford college, but he may have been mistaken. An article in the *Ousel* for 4 April 1945 states the name Merton was chosen by a previous housemaster, the Reverend W E Bolland, in 1872. Podgy later took holy orders and became a school chaplain, and Pearson regarded him as 'the nicest and most sensible master I ever met'.

Hesketh Pearson left school in the summer of 1905, with, he says, 'small Latin, less Greek, no mathematics, an almost pathological hatred of punishment and cruelty, a violent objection to routine, and a firm disbelief in compulsory education.' It was therefore quite a bold move on the part of William Brown (Head Master 1955-75) to invite Pearson as his guest of honour at Speech Day in July 1962. In a 'humorous and entertaining speech' in which he recalled his nought for Algebra Pearson said that in fact the Head Master's invitation had been very subtle. 'It must have occurred to him,' he told the assembled boys and parents, 'that I could be exhibited as a horrible example of one whose footsteps should on no account be followed.' But then he added, 'It means that if a fellow with such a disgraceful school record can be honoured in this fashion, there is hope for everybody!' In his entry in *Who's Who* Hesketh Pearson recorded that he wasted two years in a City shipping office before going on the stage in 1911, and he must be one of the very few Old Bedfordians ever seriously to have contemplated making his living in the theatre, although Christopher Jefferson, at school 1983-94, seems set to have a fine stage career. When war broke out Pearson joined the army as a private, was commissioned in the field and mentioned in dispatches. It was not until 1931 that he commenced the career for which he was obviously destined, that of a biographer, writing lives, among many others, of Darwin, Sydney Smith, Bernard Shaw, Walter Scott, Beerbohm Tree, Shakespeare, Conan Doyle, Charles Dickens, Disraeli, W S Gilbert and Oscar Wilde. He died on 6 April 1964.

Phillpotts was not around to appreciate the evidence of Pearson's talents, but he would have known about and been proud of the early academic attainments of another of his pupils who entered the school in 1895. Gilbert Campion, born in Simla in 1882, took a Double First at Hertford College, Oxford, and like his fellow Old Bedfordian Thomas Erskine May he entered the service of the House of Commons and became a highly respected constitutional historian, editing the 14th and 15th editions of May's Parliamentary Practice. He was raised to the peerage as Lord Campion in 1950, dying eight years later.

A rather strange photograph was taken in the Great Hall some time between 1892 and 1903, showing the hall packed with boys and Phillpotts in his chair of state sitting in front of them, apparently looking up at the platform. What was happening on the platform is anybody's guess; quite possibly a drama presentation. But in the hopes of making a lot of money, someone made a wild guess as to the identity of a boy in the second row. Believing him to be Oscar Wilde, in 1998 they sent the photograph to Bonhams, where it was expected to make £900. No one at Bonhams identified the setting (Wilde was educated at Portora School, Eniskillen), but at the last minute they had doubts as to whether the boy was Wilde, and the photograph was withdrawn. Wilde was thirty-seven in January 1892, the earliest possible dating of the photograph, a little elderly for a schoolboy, perhaps. And by April 1895 he was in prison. Although he did undertake lecture tours, there is not a shred of evidence that he ever paid a visit to Bedford; had he done so, he would surely have been on the platform anyway, not in the audience.

The road that Bedford had travelled under Phillpotts may be gauged by an 1880-1902 survey of the 'sixty-four leading public schools' undertaken by Professor J R de S Honey of the University of Rhodesia. In an article in *The Victorian Public School*, edited by Brian Simon and Ian Bradley, Professor Honey concluded that twenty-one schools would have been happy to associate with Bedford, the distance between schools being a factor. They included Charterhouse, Clifton, Dulwich, Eton, Haileybury, Harrow, Marlborough, Repton, Rugby, St Paul's, Tonbridge, Uppingham, Wellington, Westminster and Winchester.

As if agreeing to bow out with the old century, Queen Victoria quietly breathed her last on 22 January 1901, and on 2 February the school, still without its own chapel, attended a service in St Paul's Church, 'In Commemoration of Her Late Majesty Queen Victoria of blessed and glorious memory'. The following year, still only aged 63 but looking, and no doubt feeling, older, Phillpotts decided the time had come to step down, and on 10 December 1902 he wrote to the Governors, addressing them as My Lords and Gentlemen, to inform them of his decision. He appeared in the Great Hall for the last time at 7.30am on 2 April 1903, when the school gave him three cheers 'with great heartiness'. His portrait, painted by Arthur Hacker, was exhibited at the 1906 Royal Academy. He enjoyed a long retirement, dying on 16 October 1930 at the age of ninety-one , the year the Phillpotts Gates were hung in Burnaby Road in celebration of his ninetieth birthday.

FIVE

The Man in his Flying Machine

1903–1915

To FOLLOW a great man in any office is never an enviable task, but Phillpotts's successor, John Edward King, born in 1858, was no stop-gap, even if he sensibly saw his job to be primarily one of consolidation. He was already an experienced headmaster, which may be why he was preferred to a Rugby applicant, Frank Fletcher, who became Master of Marlborough. Educated at Clifton, King had been a Fellow and tutor of Lincoln College, Oxford, and had served his apprenticeship as a schoolmaster at St Paul's before being appointed High Master of the academically renowned Manchester Grammar School. By the end of his career he was to have held three headmasterships.

As a demonstration of practical leadership, one of King's first moves was to take personal charge of the cadet corps. Since its formation in 1887 its numbers had slumped to a mere 90. He assumed the rank of major, went into summer camp with the boys, and saw a school rifle team gain eighth place out of forty-two public schools competing for the Ashburton Shield at Bisley in 1904. Some of the names of the rifle team bear testimony to the early cosmopolitan nature of the school; one of the cadets was called Van Cuylenberg, while a sergeant was named Glünicke. Dressed in pillbox hats tilted at a rakish angle, with a band under their chin, members of the corps bore an unmistakable resemblance to hotel bellhops, and looked extremely smart. Fortunately, as he had opted for uniform, King was clean-shaven, in stark contrast to his predecessor, although at least seven of his staff still sported beards, and nearly all had a moustache. In fact, for an Edwardian headmaster King was unusually youthful and good-looking.

He was a modern man in many ways, seemingly well attuned to the new century. One of his early innovations was to found an engineering course. The

73

Fitting Shop, as it was called, encompassed carpentry, a saddlery shop and facilities for moulding and casting. There was already an astronomical observatory attached, there were 'screw-cutting and wood-turning lathes, boring and shaving machines, benches with vices for fitting'. In these workshops, an illustrated brochure explained, the boys received 'an excellent training for engineering and Colonial careers'.

The same promotional literature assured readers that the 'beautiful apparatus in the glass cases' in the Physical Laboratory excited 'the admiration of every visitor'. The Laboratory was fully equipped 'with air-pumps, spectroscopes, experimental electrical and other apparatus'. There was a darkroom, 'wireless telegraphy apparatus', and a lecture theatre to accommodate 200 boys. One hundred and twenty students at a time could attend lectures in the Chemical Laboratory, where fifty boys could simultaneously carry out practical work, 'each boy having his own drawer and cupboard for apparatus.' Instruction was in the hands of 'an unusually well-qualified staff'. [1]

In 1905 Dr. King had a small handbook printed, marked 'Private. For the use of Masters only', and in it the Engineering Department is listed alongside the Classical and Civil and Military Sides. But one should no longer conclude that a boy on the Classical side was undergoing a stultifying diet of Greek and Latin; he was also taught English, French or German, mathematics and science. Work on the Civil and Military Side comprised mathematics, French, German, Latin, English, drawing and science. Boys in the new Engineering Department studied English and one foreign language. Every form, 'where possible', went to the gymnasium 'at least one period per week'. The prep school boys were expected to master Elementary French, singing and Nature Study in addition to English, Arithmetic, Elementary History and 'Geography of the British Isles'.

What later became known as the Great Hall was at this time called the Large Hall, and here the school assembled each morning for prayers at 9am. There were five morning periods with a break of only fifteen minutes, at 11.15am. Masters were reminded it was important that punctuality 'should be strictly observed', and those masters who had free periods were also reminded they 'should not leave the School buildings without notification at the Bell Room'.

When it came to writing reports on their pupils, masters were told they should be candid 'but should avoid expression or comment, eg *dull, stupid, hopeless*, likely to give unnecessary pain to parents, who may have to read them in India'. Such phrases as '*never attends, makes no progress, does no work*' were 'apt to throw side-lights on the Master as well as on the boy'. Companions, reading, interests, disposition, manners, temper, tone as well as work were 'all matters upon which the insight of the Master can be of useful guidance to the Parents'.

But masters were warned that when writing to parents to be careful 'to say nothing that commits the authorities of the School'.

As for corporal punishment, King more or less endorsed the code of practice laid down by Phillpotts. No assistant master was to strike a boy on the head or the face, or box his ears, '(whether the punishment is meant seriously or not)'. No master was to administer more than three strokes of the cane, candidly referred to as 'cuts'. Boys might be held in detention on Saturday afternoons, from 2.30pm to 4pm in the Summer term and between 4pm and 5.30pm in the Easter and 'Xmas' terms. It was meant as a punishment for 'persistent idleness and negligence'. King very sensibly disapproved of a boy being made to write out lines. They should have 'useful work set to them,' he told his staff, for writing was 'injured by long impositions'. He was a humane man, if strict. He thought that when a master was minded to order a boy to attend extra school at seven in the morning discretion should be exercised in the case of 'delicate boys or boys who live at a distance from the school, especially in the winter months'. And in the case of young or delicate boys, homework might be remitted. But 'extreme idleness and serious breaches of School rules and such misconduct as dishonesty in work, lying, indecency should be reported to the Head Master to be dealt with by him.'

It seems also that John King, like Phillpotts, was endowed with common-sensical qualities of a kind that serve any master well in his long-term relation-ships with boys. Hesketh Pearson was one of the less orthodox spirits King had inherited from Phillpotts, and in his autobiography Pearson recounts his entanglement with a clerical master named Massey, 'Called "Pot" on account of his belly'.

He lost his temper easily, his small reddish beard bristled with wrath, and like all fat little men in that condition he looked funny. An answer I gave to one of his questions annoyed him, and he trembled with rage, which made me laugh. Insensate with fury, he picked up an ink bottle and threw it at my head. I caught it neatly and threw it back, catching him on the belly, where it broke and deluged him with ink. He was so utterly confounded that he remained for several seconds with his mouth open, staring at me as if he could not believe his senses. Gradually he became conscious of what had happened, said nothing at the time, but at the end of the lesson took me down to report my behaviour to the headmaster ... He listened to Pot's account and then asked what I had to say. I simply explained that I had made a good catch, returned it, and could not be blamed for Mr Massey's failure in the field. King sent me out of the room, had a heart-to-heart talk with Pot, and I heard no more about it. From that moment I had complete confidence in the new 'head', who was conspicuously fair.

Having sorted out the cadet corps and the need to introduce engineering to the curriculum, King turned his attention, to some extent because he was forced to do so, to the provision of a school chapel. His arrival coincided with a decision by the vicar and churchwardens of St Paul's to discontinue making provision for school services — most probably because the school was now just too big. On 16 December 1903 King presided over 'a large influential meeting, representative of parents, friends and Old Boys,' who came to the conclusion 'that the only satisfactory course now open was to raise a building appropriated to the corporate worship of the School, such as was possessed by the great majority of English Public Schools.' [2]

The meeting was told that the Governors 'were fully in sympathy with the project' but that provision of a school chapel 'did not fall within their powers,' and 'no help was to be expected from the Harper Trust' (sic). Voluntary subscriptions seemed to be the answer. Indeed, a 'provisional appeal' had already been launched. The site proposed was 'the ground offered for the purpose by the Headmaster at the end of Pemberley Lane adjoining the School Field,' and it was further suggested that the chapel 'should be built of a size sufficient to accommodate 700 persons and of a character in harmony with the School Buildings.'

A meeting held on 19 July 1904 decided that no building operations were to be started until £5,000 had been promised, and that some firm decisions about a design should be made by Michaelmas — in other words, within the next ten weeks. But progress was painfully slow. By July 1905 no more than £4,329 had been raised. But a meeting convened for 7 April 1906 was able to discuss plans submitted by a London architect, G F Bodley, 'one of the first architects of the day' the two honorary secretaries of the School Chapel Fund assured potential supporters. Bodley had costed the chapel at £7,000. Samuel Whitbread had promised a generous £500, but gifts of ten shillings, of which there were a good many, were unlikely to purchase many bricks.

It is not easy today to appreciate how relatively cramped the school site was prior to 1906. On the eastern side the boundary followed a right of way which now leads to the chapel, behind the science block, and from the science block due north to Park Avenue. There were, at this time, three houses on the east side of Pemberly Avenue (as it was then spelt), and three on the west, at the very top. There were, however, eight proposed building plots on the west side, extending from Pemberley Crescent very nearly as far as Phillpotts. In addition, between Pemberley Avenue and flush with the school playing field was the Pemberly Estate. A substantial house stood at the north end of the gardens, and these consisted of a tennis court, hothouses, a fruit and kitchen garden, another tennis lawn and a paddock with stables which stood almost adjoining what is now the Science Building. When all this land and property came on the market in October 1906 King put in a successful bid for it, paying £8,250 and almost doubling the area available for playing fields, thus ensuring for the school not only far more privacy than it had ever expected to enjoy but a perfect setting for his chapel. [3]

Bodley had been told — on 23 February 1905 — that a delegation from Bedford had paid a visit to the chapel he had designed at Queen's College, Cambridge, which they had admired, and he was asked to imitate the Queen's College arrangement by positioning seats facing inwards, that is to say, facing north and south — a common enough practice, surely, in college chapels. Having inspected the proposed site, on the south-west corner of Pemberley Avenue, Bodley discovered it lay on a clay fault, and on 19 November 1906 he informed the school that the foundations would have to go down an additional fifteen feet, which would 'cause an extra of £650 over the original estimate'. It was eventually realised that the best way to obtain the cash was to form a non-profit making Bedford Grammar School Chapel Society, with the purpose of raising £4,000 worth of 4 per cent debentures at par, and the sum was pledged by means of attracting eighty £50 subscriptions.

Old Bedfordians, headed by the Bishop of Bombay, got busy collecting money in Lower Bengal and the Punjab, and a fine row broke out between the Old Bedfordians Club and the architect over an east window; Bodley was against having one, preferring that an eastern reredos should be lit by windows on the north and south. The OBs were adamant, and eventually the chapel acquired a very fine triptych reredos as well as stained glass in memory of OBs killed in South Africa. No one could have imagined at this stage that one day panelled walls behind the pews (the chapel had chairs to start with) would be adorned with the names and regimental badges of Old Bedfordians killed in two world wars. The foundation stone, at the east end, was laid on 18 May 1907 by Lord St John of Bletsoe, whose barony, appropriately enough, was an ancient Tudor creation, dating from 1559. Fourteen months later, on 11 July 1908, the Bishop of Ely, Bedford then being in his diocese, turned up to dedicate the chapel. (It was on 30 March 1914 that the archdeaconry of Bedford was transferred to the diocese of St Albans.) Embellished by many gifts from masters and Old Boys, the chapel, in its very prominent position on the school estate, stands in a way as John King's enduring monument. But in different ways it commemorates many people. David Mitchell, who entered the school in 1973, was to become one of its most promising but unfulfilled talents. Head of Burnaby, captain of Rugby, head of school in his last year, 1985, he died in a motor accident on 28 June 1986, aged twenty. A flower bed on the south side of the steps leading to the west door has become the resting place for his ashes.

On 24 July 1909 a bronze Memorial Tablet, now in the school archives, was dedicated by Bishop Edward Hodges, Rector of St Cuthbert's and an assistant bishop in the Ely diocese. It contained the names of the twenty-two Old Bedfordians who had died in the Boer War, together with one killed, in 1898, at Tirah, one in China in 1900, and Henry Cross, the war correspondent who had died in the Sudan in 1898. Hodges, born in 1849, had been consecrated bishop of Travancore and Cochin in the south-west tip of India and between 1904 and his retirement in 1924 he had the unusual distinction of serving as an assistant bishop in no fewer than three English dioceses — Durham, Ely and St Albans. From 1910-24 he was archdeacon of Bedford.

Lieutenant General the Rt Hon Sir Arthur Paget, C-in-C Eastern Command, who had rolled up with two aides-de-camp, unveiled the Memorial, the bishop dedicated it, and the congregation remained standing while the director of music gave a rendition on the organ of Chopin's Funeral March. A second Tablet, since destroyed, was then unveiled in the Great Hall, which included also the names of Captain Bray, Captain Morris and Lieutenant Skinner, RN, but scant details about their deaths; these occurred between 1901 and 1905. What is interesting about the Boer War casualties is that nine of them had died from disease and only eight held commissioned rank; one had been a sergeant, one a corporal, one a lance-corporal and ten were troopers. When addressing the school, General Paget had a special thought for the half dozen Old Bedfordians who had died in South Africa from wounds. In a splendid flight of jingoistic fantasy he said it was a satisfaction to a soldier to know that if he found himself dangerously wounded, that though his body might lie in an unknown grave, his name would be left, not to be a fleeting memory gone in a few years, but to be handed down as long as the tablets remained on the walls.

Dr King discovered ten boarding houses in operation when he arrived, not all of them full, and he contrived to have two of them closed down so that the others might take a share of the boys displaced and run at a profit. Fees in 1900 varied between £79 a year for a boy under ten to £89 a year for a boy over sixteen. The houses have a complicated history, sometimes, when moving about, taking their original name with them, sometimes having their name altered in honour of some master or Old Bedfordian. Merton House, for example (which no longer exists), began life in Horne Lane, moved to Kimbolton Road, later to 7 Pemberley Avenue and finally came to rest in De Parys Avenue.

Glanyrafon — the house by the river — was in Newnham Road, not far from the Embankment. Before being closed altogether it had the indignity in 1950 of being renamed Kirkman's, ostensibly to honour the memory of a maths teacher at the school from 1893-1919, J P Kirkman, housemaster of Glanyrafon from 1906-15, although cynics supposed the person really being remembered was his son, General Sir Sidney Kirkman, at school from 1910-14 and in 1946 elected president of the Old Bedfordians Club. Houses which, like Merton and Glanyrafon, no longer exist include Copthill in Bromham Road, Oaklands in Kimbolton Road and Westfield in Linden Road. In 1939 Ashfield in Rothsay Place became Sanderson's, in honour of a classical sixth master, H K StJ Sanderson, housemaster from 1910-25; Hertford House in De Parys Avenue became a hotel. As if with the intention of driving an historian completely dotty, Glanyrafon was renamed Kirkman's, transferred, as Kirkman's, to a house in De Parys Avenue, now the home of the Bedford School Study Centre, and when the boys in Kirkman's moved to the old Farrar's, their house became Phillpotts.

One of the most gifted and versatile pupils at Bedford under John King's tuition was Henry Grierson. He arrived in 1901, at the age of ten, and left in 1910, the same year as King. His skills on the piano were only matched by those on the rugby pitch and cricket field; on one memorable occasion he scored a century against Dulwich. At Pembroke College, Cambridge Grierson won his cricket Blue, and after the Great War he captained Bedfordshire CCC, played rugger for Bedford, Leicester, Rosslyn Park and the Barbarians, became a county squash player and a proficient golfer and angler. It was in 1935, while watching a cricket match at Bedford School, that he conceived the idea of forming an 'over forty' cricket club (he was by then forty-four himself), and in 1937 the first two Forty Club matches were played, against Bedford and Wellingborough. Grierson died in 1972, having inaugurated the second largest private cricket club in the world. [4]

In 1910 John King was asked by his old school, Clifton, to return as Head Master, an offer he found irresistible. But before his departure he became embroiled in legal proceedings concerning a boy discovered reading an unauthorised book in class. The boy had been taken to see the Head Master, who ordered a caning. Upon hearing sentence pronounced, the boy did a bunk. King wrote to his mother to say that unless her son returned to face the music he would be expelled. Mama dug in her heels, said her son would not return if it meant being beaten, and appealed to the Governors. She must have been an exceptionally foolish woman to have imagined the Governors would not support their Head Master over such a trivial case of school discipline, and when they declined to take sides in the dispute she instituted legal proceedings. Incredibly, the case was heard at Bedford Assize by the Lord Chief Justice. Sitting without a jury, he found in favour of the school, and the mother landed herself with a bill for costs, said to have amounted to £600. [5]

Dr King eventually retired to Chilton Polden in Somerset, dying in 1939 at the age of eighty. He left £200 to the school, and a legacy of descendants; three grandsons were educated at Bedford, and in 1932 his second son returned to the school to teach.

Reginald Carter, chosen to succeed King at the age of forty-two, had followed a very similar path; Clifton College as a boy, a Fellowship at Lincoln and a previous headmastership, in his case, since 1902, the Rectorship of Edinburgh Academy. A scholar of Balliol, with immaculate Classical credentials (a First Class degree and the Gaisford Greek Prose prize), Carter was also — like Phillpotts — a sportsman, but more unusually for Bedford, a Head Master dedicated to the arts, painting and musicianship being his own particular gifts. He can, in fact, be credited with the first stirrings of a musical tradition at Bedford, which floundered somewhat in later years until revived with gusto under two inspired musical directors, Ted Amos and Andrew Morris. In Carter's time there was a Musical Society with a membership of about 240. Each June they performed a concert in conjunction with a school play, and they put on another concert in November. Carter played in the orchestra, and within a year of his arrival the Society had staged a production of *Judas Maccabaeus*. Haydn's *Creation* was performed in 1912 and in 1921 Handel's *Acis and Galatea*. In 1917, fired no doubt by patriotic fervour, the school sang Elgar's *Caractacus*, a cantata based on the life of a British chieftain who is supposed to have roamed the Malvern Hills. It was an idea suggested to Elgar by his mother, first performed at Leeds in 1898, and dedicated to Queen Victoria.

Some idea of the age of rapidly expanding technology and mechanical invention that coincided with Carter's years at Bedford — they were to last until 1928 — can be gained by trying to imagine the excitement when in 1913 a thirty-four-year-old Old Bedfordian, Claude Grahame-White (born in 1879, he was at Bedford 1892-96), landed in his aeroplane on the school playing field. Grahame-White, an aeronautical engineer, was the first Englishman to be granted a certificate of proficiency as an aviator. He went on to win many flying prizes and to write extensively on aeronautics, and his firm, the Grahame-White Aviation Company, became proprietors of the London Aerodrome, then situated at Hendon.

On the evening of 23 July 1913, according to a report in the *Ousel*, 'all Bedford was roused to excitement by the appearance of a monoplane over the town, and its descent upon the School Field, which was soon filled by crowds of sightseers. On stepping out of his driving seat, Mr Grahame-White was welcomed by the Head Master [presumably Carter had been forewarned of the visit], and the machine was wheeled to the back of the School, where it was left for the night ... The next morning it was visited where it stood, under guard of two of Bedford's stalwart policemen, by many interested scholars, who arrived unusually early for School that morning.'

It would have been the first aeroplane many of the boys had ever seen, at close quarters at any rate, and at mid-morning they were treated to a talk from

Grahame-White in the Great Hall. He then took off, flew three times over the town and again landed on the playing field. 'He had no sooner alighted than he was caught up on the shoulders of a crowd of boys and carried into the School.' From photographs of his plane, taken outside the school buildings, it resembled nothing so much as a Heath Robinson contraption of flimsy paper and string, but it must have been rather more sturdy than that, and for the boys, with the Great War and the advance in mechanisation that it was to foster only a year distant, their encounter with the intrepid airman and his innovative flying machine placed them at the very frontiers of the twentieth century.

Grahame-White may have been one of Bedford's first intrepid airmen but certainly not its last. In 1933 Lt Col Stewart Blacker, at school 1903-5, piloted by the Marquess of Clydesdale, heir to the Duke of Hamilton, flew in an open cockpit over Mount Everest. The epic flight was as controversial as it was dangerous, some people actually accusing Blacker of blasphemy. As he later wrote himself, 'Lots of good people thought that to look down on the virgin summit of the highest mountain in the world was somehow the act of a Peeping Tom.'

Colonel Blacker had originally been educated in Dublin, and entered Bedford in 1903, when he was already sixteen, an unusual occurrence at the time. The family moved into 26 Lansdowne Road, and two years later Blacker passed into Sandhurst. He was commissioned in the Indian Army; hence it was from Purnea in Northern India that he set out in a Westland biplane on 4 April 1933, with the aim, successfully accomplished, of bringing back the first pictures ever taken of the summit of Everest. Neither man nor machine were designed for flying at such an altitude, and there was every likelihood the plane would crash or the airmen asphyxiate — or very probably, both. The cold must have been absolutely intense, yet Colonel Blacker managed to take a stunning series of photographs, the camera itself having been adapted to work at high altitude. It was to be another nineteen years before Mount Everest was conquered from the ground.

The guest of honour at Speech Day in 1914 was none other than Field Marshal Earl Roberts, a holder of the Victoria Cross since he was a twenty-five-year-old subaltern; he won the decoration in 1858, just two years after it had been instituted, leading a cavalry charge at Khudaganj. According to a report in the *Bedfordshire Times*, the Field Marshal 'bore his years and honours with the alertness and activity of a boy,' and one of the boys to whom Lord Roberts presented a succession of books was P Liesching, who walked off with no fewer than five prizes: the Fanshawe Divinity prize, the New College prizes for Latin Prose and Latin Verse, the Earl Cowper English Verse prize and the Sanderson's prize for Greek Iambics. Roberts did not miss the opportunity of reminding the boys of 'their duty to their country and to the great Empire of which we are so proud,' nor of calling for the formation of a 'National Army.' And he beseeched his young listeners to 'have character' and to be 'gentlemen in every sense. And, mark you, when I say gentlemen, I do not mean gentlemen by birth, but a gentleman by nature — a man who is fearless, morally and physically, truthful and honest, upright and straightforward, pure and clean in mind and body, cherishing a manly independence, but at the same time respectful to all in authority, and kindly and considerate to everyone who is associated with him.'

Trotting out every cliché in the book in a speech worthy of Baden-Powell, Lord Roberts was encouraging the school to stiffen its sinews and summon up its blood on 27 July, and just eight days later the country was at war. On 14 November the old Field Marshal, aged 82, died; his visit to Bedford must have been among his very last engagements.

There was no Speech Day the following year; perhaps by the summer of 1915 it was felt inappropriate to mount a festive occasion of any sort. With the outbreak of hostilities on 4 August 1914 the gymnasium was taken over by the Bedfordshire Yeomanry, still devoted to their horses (many English commanders believed the war would be decided by cavalry), and later the 4th Seaforths moved in, sleeping in the Great Hall while awaiting embarkation. The Engineering Workshops, so providentially established by John King, began to turn out parts for submarines, and eventually manufactured 13lb shells. Allotments were cultivated by each school house, chestnuts, apparently used in the manufacture of munitions[6], were harvested (during the Second World War they were fed to pigs, some of the animals being kept at Farrar's), and boys assisted on nearby farms. House collections raised over £754 for a Public Schools Hospital Fund. Masters in those days still remained on the elderly side, and most were too old for military service, but the younger members of staff were soon answering the call for volunteers. Those who served with the colours included the OTC sergeant major, the gym instructor and the school porter.

A member of staff who arrived in 1913, aged twenty-six, the Reverend Henry Perry, who later had a boarding house (Merton, when it was in De Parys Avenue), and became Head Master of the Lower School and an honorary canon of St Albans, was seconded almost straight away as an army chaplain. He remained at the school thirty-four years, retiring in 1947 to Turvey as parish priest. Perry was a founder of the Quadrangular Tournament, an annual boxing and fencing competition (long since discontinued) between Bedford, Eton, Haileybury and Dulwich, first held in 1921. It was said that his own strength was such that if he caned a boy he was instructed to do so left-handed and back-handed lest he slice the lad in half (this story may, however, only be apocryphal). Like so many clergy, he lived to a good age, dying in 1969 aged eighty-two. A basically indolent man, devoid of any apparent semblance of spirituality, he used to preach on the existence of God, the proof of which, he claimed, lay in the way that each year a spring bulb would open up.

There was no Quadrangular Tournament in 1927, but between 1921 and 1962 Eton won the boxing outright just five times (in 1960 they drew with Dulwich, and in 1949 their place was taken in the Tournament by Felsted); Haileybury only won three times, drawing with Bedford in 1932 and with Dulwich the following year; Dulwich pulled off eight outright wins, drawing with Haileybury in 1933 and with Eton in 1960; and Bedford notched up 22 outright victories, sharing a tie with Haileybury in 1932. But at fencing, Eton consistently outshone all their rivals, winning the foils on 24 occasions and the sabres 25 times (in the sabres, between 1926 and 1942, they were unbeaten). In the foils, Haileybury managed to draw with Dulwich in 1945 and to win outright the following year, but they never won the sabres at all. Dulwich achieved 10 outright wins in the foils, drawing with Haileybury in 1943, and in the sabres they scored a respectable 14 outright wins and two draws with Eton, in 1951 and 1958. Bedford won the foils half a dozen times and the sabres on only four occasions. Was Bedford's superior showing in the boxing ring, and Eton's at fencing, a matter of brawn over breeding, and vice versa? Boxing, now generally frowned upon, was a blood-letting 'sport' in which generations of boys pranced round the ring destroying one another's brain cells in order to gain points for their house. But one year word got round that enthusiasm was waning and a campaign of emotional blackmail was launched. No matter that you had never boxed before, boys were told, if you go into the ring and lose you will still have gained a point for your house, and we promise that novices will only be pitted against fellow novices.

A boy who fell for this call to esprit de corps and became a dubious volunteer ran round the playing fields to lose weight in the hope of only having to box someone small, and took a crash course in nimble footwork from a particular friend in his house called Napper. 'Keep your guard up and you'll be all right,' Napper assured him. Unfortunately the boy was particularly right-handed, and found it hard to keep his right hand up as a guard and to strike out with his left. So things were looking decidedly grim when he clambered into the ring only to find in the opposite corner a member of the school boxing team. Meeson had recently lain low several peers of the realm from Eton, showed no mercy on this occasion either, and came leaping across the ring, both arms flailing. The astonished novice, striving not to lose too much blood on behalf of Ashburnham, stepped aside and Meeson landed flat on his face.

For one incredible moment Napper's pupil thought he must be winning. But the tumble had only served to inflame the sporting instincts of Meeson, and the next few seconds were taken up by Meeson regaining an upright position and then going for the kill. Suddenly Jack Carlton, later housemaster of Sanderson's, was frantically banging the gong. 'Well done,' he said, ' but I think you're a little outclassed.'

It was in the midst of war that the Governors, after perusing Brereton's first school list of 1816, and noticing it was headed Schola Bedfordiensis, decided to drop the word Grammar from Bedford School, on the somewhat spurious grounds that in Brereton's time the school was called Bedford School, and all they were doing was reverting to nineteenth century usage. It would surely be more accurate to suggest that Brereton (designated Archididascalus; his usher, Abbot, was Pedagogus) thought there was no appropriate rendition into Latin of the word Grammar in the context of the English educational system, and that the Governors were motivated by snobbery; if they thought they were in some vague way enhancing the status of the school they were at the same time in danger of appearing to reject much of its history, even its royal origins.

The briefest possible explanation appeared in the *Ousel* for 19 May 1917. 'During the Easter holidays the Governors decided that the name of the school should henceforward be "Bedford School", the word "Grammar" — a survival, in our case, of an ancient and honourable title, which has, of recent years, generally depreciated in meaning — being permanently dropped as giving a false impression to those not intimate with the school. The change,' this rather clumsily worded announcement concluded, 'has been cordially welcomed'.

In 1930 R. F. Walker won the Colts Pole Vault with a leap of 8 ft 3 ins
Photograph: Sport and General

Above In 1933 the Prince of Wales, later Edward VIII, paid a visit to the school, arriving late but as usual charming all those he met. With him is a youthful Humfrey Grose-Hodge, recently arrived from Charterhouse as Head Master
Below The oak sapling presented by Adolf Hitler at the 1938 Olympics in Berlin to the Old Bedfordian sculler Jack Beresford is planted close to the Phillpotts Gates. The boys with bare knees were in the Inky, those with long grey trousers were in the Lower School, and the boys in blue jackets were in the Upper School
Photographs: Central Press

86

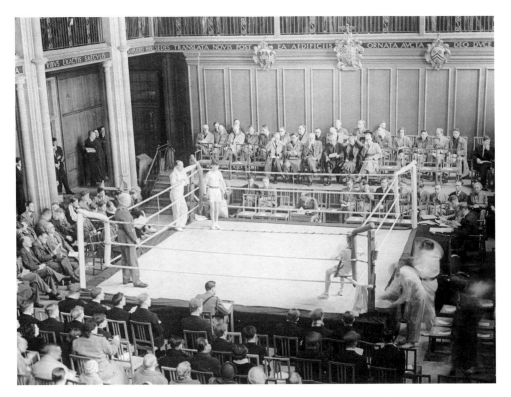

Above The annual Quadrangular Tournament between Bedford, Dulwich, Eton, and
Haileybury was taken so seriously the Head Master, Humfrey Grose-Hodge,
wore his gown for the event. The memorial chairs were
all lost in the fire of 1979
Below Phyllis Sillar, for many years a devoted teacher of the Inky boys. She served as
deputy head of the preparatory school when Tom Snow
was Head Master

The author, aged eight, second from the left in the top row, in his first year at Nash's.
Seated on the ground on the left is Jeremy Snaith, the first Bedford School boy
the author ever met. He became one of his closest friends

Opposite top A legendary teacher in the Inky, Miss Lyn Harman, who retired in 1978
after forty-two years. Lower School boys in Farrar's used to fantasise
that she would marry their house tutor, Bernard Pybus,
but she disappointed them

Below Dr William Probert-Jones, Director of Music from 1937–57

A galaxy of top brass entertain Field Marshal Montgomery in 1946. On the Field Marshal's
right is Sir Richard Wells, Bt, chairman of the Harpur Trust, and on his left
Sir Edward Crowe, president of the Old Bedfordians Club. Second
from the right is the Head Master, Humfrey Grose-Hodge,
talking to Lt General Sir Sydney Kirkman

Opposite top Standing on your hands was child's play if you had Sgt Major Jackson to
hold your ankles. He was drill instructor at the school for thirty-two years

Below Major General Henry Foote, VC, CB, DSO, one of four Old Bedfordians
who have been awarded the Victoria Cross

The open air swimming pool, since built over to accomodate the new sports complex.

SIX

Conspicuous Bravery

1915–1928

IT MAY NEVER be ascertained for certain how many Old Bedfordians served in the First World War, nor how many died. Sargeaunt gives the number who served as 2,318, a total of 448 being either killed instantly or dying of wounds, and a further 375 being wounded but surviving. There are however 454 names of boys believed killed recorded on the north wall of the Memorial Hall, representing six more deaths than Sargeaunt has accounted for. Having carried out their own research, Beryl and Stuart Blythe, who live in Kempston, believe that four names appear on the Memorial Hall roll of honour that should not be there, and that seventeen names have been omitted. If that is so, the numbers who died come to 467. They have written: 'Mistakes seem to have occurred when there was more than one brother killed ... One man went on the board when his cousin should have been listed.' They believe an officer in the Royal Irish Rifles was mistaken for an Old Bedfordian. [1]

If a round figure of 460 deaths is agreed — or any figure, come to that — it must have represented a heartbreaking experience for Carter and all those other masters who had taught the boys, only to hear that they had been blown to bits on the Somme; and for those boys who had been at school with them and had lost their friends so young. Many who returned were scarred for life, physically and mentally. Many would never speak of their experience. Among those killed were a son and a nephew of the Chief.

The numbers of decorations won by Old Bedfordians was impressive. One-hundred and twenty-eight DSOs were awarded in addition to a DSO and two bars and five DSOs and one bar. One OB received the MC and bar, and a further 207 the MC. Six boys won the DSC, three the DFC, three the AFC, six the DSC, three the DCM and five the MM, indicating that eight of those decorated were not commissioned. Those who inevitably brought upon their

93

school the greatest renown were an astonishing three recipients of the Victoria Cross.

The first to be awarded, posthumously and after some unavoidable delay, went to Sub Lieutenant Arthur Walderne St Clair Tisdall, killed in action at Gallipoli on 6 May 1915. It was not until spring of the following year that it was announced the King had been graciously pleased to approve the award of the VC to Tisdall 'in recognition of his most conspicuous bravery and devotion to duty'. (It is for Conspicuous Bravery — nothing less — that the Victoria Cross is awarded.) On 25 April Tisdall had led several sorties on to the beach to rescue men under heavy fire. 'I have been through much since August 1914,' one witness testified, 'but I sincerely assure you that I have never seen more daring and gallant things performed by any man.' A naval surgeon recorded that he had occasion to visit the beach from which Walderne Tisdall rescued so many wounded men, and 'heard it constantly expressed that he bore a charmed life as he waded up to his neck in the sea, pushing in front of him a boatload of wounded ... Tisdall was a man who had absolutely conquered fear ... It is a great honour at last to be able to pay a humble tribute to the memory of a very gallant gentleman ... His work of magnificent self-devotion (sic) was performed under a perfect hail of pom-pom, machine-gun and rifle fire at almost point-blank range.'

Tisdall's chaplain wrote to his parents to say, 'There is a rumour here that he is to be mentioned for the Victoria Cross, as he rescued men three times under heavy fire, at the risk of his own life. He was a charming companion, a great scholar and an excellent officer, loved by his men.'

Walderne Tisdall was 24 when he was killed, just eleven days after performing the deeds for which he was awarded the Victoria Cross. He had been a golden boy. Born in Bombay in 1890, he was at Bedford 1900-9, 'a boy of remarkable ability and promise all through his school career,' according to his second Head Master, John King.[2] He became a monitor, and won the New College Latin Verse prize, the Earl Cowper English Essay prize, the Senior Eames Divinity prize (his father had been a missionary in India), the Phillpotts English Literature prize, the Head Master's Greek Prose prize, the Fanshawe Divinity prize and the New College Latin Prose prize. From the Classical Sixth he went up to Trinity College, Cambridge where he was elected to a Major Classical Scholarship. Among his academic achievements at Cambridge was the award of the Chancellor's Gold Medal, and that was on top of gaining a Double First.

Walderne Tisdall was a contemporary of Dora Carrington (born in 1893), the unlikely lover, among others, of Lytton Strachey, and the unwilling wife of Ralph Partridge; hence an intimate in every sense of the Bloomsbury Group.

Carrington's family moved to Bedford in 1902, and Dora was educated at the High School; her brothers, Samuel, Teddy (killed in 1916) and Noel, mentioned in dispatches and later a distinguished editor at Allen Lane (he commissioned their Puffin books), all entered Bedford in 1903 and would have been known to Tisdall. When a book in his memory was published in 1916 Carrington, who went on to train as an artist, provided an early sketch of the main school building.

One of the men under Tisdall's command wrote home to say, 'You would see it in the papers about our dear officer "going down", Mr Tisdall. He was one of England's bravest men. All his men about cried when he went because all the boys thought the world of him.' He was buried by the men who loved him, close to the spot where he fell. But he has a memorial at his father's church, St George's in Deal. His brother, John Tisdall, at Bedford 1901-13, was killed in 1916 at Guillemont.

Second Lieutenant Montague Moore of the Hampshire Regiment won his Victoria Cross on 20 August 1917 at a spot known as Tower Hamlets, east of Ypres. As befitted his gallant deeds, he gloried in the full name of Montague Shadworth Seymour Moore. He was only twenty when he was commended for 'most conspicuous bravery in operations necessitating a fresh attack on a final objective which had not been captured'. Dashing forward at the head of some seventy men, Moore arrived at his objective, a mere 500 yards further on, with only a sergeant and four men left alive. 'Nothing daunted, he at once bombed a large dug-out and took twenty-eight prisoners, two machine guns and a light field gun.' Throughout the night, now aided by reinforcements, Moore repelled German bombing attacks, and in the morning he beat off a succession of counter attacks. He held his post under continual shell fire for thirty-six hours, until his comrades, originally numbering six officers and 130 men, had been reduced to ten men in addition to himself. It was amazing that his was not a posthumous VC. He eventually withdrew with his wounded 'under cover of a thick mist'. His citation concluded: 'As an example of dashing gallantry and cool determination this young officer's exploit would be difficult to surpass'. Moore eventually reached the rank of major, and after the war he became a Game Warden. He died in 1966, and his ashes were scattered in a Game Park in Kenya.

It was the same year, 1917, that Major George Campbell Wheeler (he was promoted to Lieut Colonel) won the Victoria Cross with the 9th Gurkha Rifles at Shurman, on the River Tigris in Mesopotamia. At school, Wheeler had played half-back, distinguishing himself in the last minute of a match against Dulwich in 1897 by breaking away to score the winning try by jumping clean over the Dulwich full-back. According to the *Ousel* No 876 for 1970, 'This dangerous feat was also accomplished by W W Vassall in the Merchant Taylors' match seven years later'. With a Gurkha officer and eight men, Wheeler rushed an enemy trench 'under heavy bombing, rifle, machine-gun and artillery fire'. Having been counter-attacked 'he led a charge with another officer and three men', and although receiving a severe head wound from a bayonet he managed to disperse the enemy.

An extraordinary list of coincidences link George Wheeler of Bedford School, whose decoration and medals are now in the National Army Museum, with his namesake at Bedford Modern School. He too was a major, his Christian name was George, both were born overseas, both were members of the Indian Army, and Bedford Modern School's George Wheeler, like Bedford's, won his Victoria Cross in Mesopotamia, although two years earlier.[3]

Some of the grief felt by other ranks in the Great War when their junior officers were killed can be attributed to the class system still so firmly in place; boys from impoverished homes expected to draw the short straw throughout their lives, and healthy, handsome, well-fed young men from public schools and country houses seemed to them like gods, the perpetual inheritors of wealth and privilege born to take care of lesser mortals like tenants and servants. Something of the common soldier's feeling of security was destroyed when the peer's eldest son was struck down. By 1939 that sense of dependence, which generated unconditional love, had largely been wiped out.

Typical of the feelings of Old Bedfordians who mourned friends was an inscription written on the back of a photograph of Jim Lambert: 'Gave his life for his country on the night of All Saints Day, or early morn of All Souls Day 1915'. There was another boy called Denzil Heriz-Smith, who was at Bedford for ten years. He played for the 1st XV, was captain of the gym and a member of the shooting VIII. In 1913 he was made head of school and in 1914 he received the Tarbutt Prize, for being the best all-round boy. His actual trophy? A silver cigarette box, now in the possession of the school. He served with the 6th Bn the Northamptonshire Regiment, and died from severe wounds received on 17 February 1917; he was twenty-three. Between 1910-13 he kept a diary, now in the school archives, and hundreds of his school and army letters have been preserved. One of the most ironic discoveries from his diary is that in 1912 he supported, but lost, a motion in the Debating Society worded as follows: 'In the opinion of this House modern warfare would, if conducted on a large scale, be so disastrous that it is necessary to settle all disputes by arbitration'. He was a friend of Jim Lambert, to whom he wrote from the trenches, 'Their snipers are very good indeed. You put up your head for a mere second in daylight and that is that. Holly, in your company, did it with fatal results. I think they must use clipped bullets for they make a horrid mess of anyone they hit.' In the spring of 1998 a party of Bedford boys went to visit Denzil's grave. 'As we paid our respects,' one of them wrote in the June 1998 issue of the *Ousel*, 'a silence enveloped the group, broken only by bird song. For me, this was the most moving and harrowing experience of the trip.'

Another First World War Old Bedfordian of heroic stature was C D Booker, at school 1912-15, who died in August 1918 at the age of twenty-one, saving the life of another young, and inexperienced, pilot. Both were attacked by 10 Fokker biplanes, and it was recorded that 'his first thoughts went to his new pilot and he successfully drove five Fokkers from his tail. He then dealt with the remaining five, shooting down three before being downed by the remaining two. He died a gallant death, the bravest of all.' Booker had previously shot down 29 enemy aircraft, and been awarded the DSC and the French Croix de Guerre. When his decorations and medals were auctioned in 1997 they made £6,200.

On 27 June 1918, with four months of hostilities still to be dragged out, a visit was paid to the school by George V and Queen Mary, the King in Field Marshal's field uniform. They had come, in effect, to thank the school for its contribution to a war the outcome of which looked set to preserve their throne. They arrived at Bedford by train, and after lunch they drove to the Burnaby Road entrance to the school. Wounded soldiers, to whom the King later spoke, were given seats near the pavilion, and the King inspected a contingent of the OTC. After a march past the King and Queen repaired to the Great Hall, where they were entertained by renditions of three school songs, *Bedford by the River, Play the Game, Bedford* and a *Boating Song*. The King congratulated the school 'on the splendid record of its members, past and present' who were serving and had served in the war. 'Many of the OTC,' he said, 'which I see before me, and which I wish to congratulate on its smart appearance on parade just now, will be joining the army at a moment of the greatest gravity in the history of this country. I feel sure you will emulate the deeds of those who have gone before you and help to maintain the high standard of the British Army, which never stood higher than it does today.' Not surprisingly, loud cheers greeted His Majesty's announcement that he had asked the Head Master to grant not an extra half-holiday but an extra week's holiday.

It was in 1918 that the OTC was joined by a former Grenadier Guards sergeant major, Joseph Blincow. Until his retirement thirty-six years later his sayings and mannerisms became part of Bedford School folklore. 'Close the door, boy, there's a draft!' he would bellow in the open air swimming pool. No love was lost between Mr Blincow and an Old Bedfordian housemaster, Harry Mackay (head of school 1920-21, Harry Mac, as he was always known, would have trained under Blincow). Harry Mac was a talented musician, who composed what he called dotty ditties to accelerate the appreciation of French grammar. On Wednesday afternoons Mr Blincow would be drilling a squad beneath Harry Mac's window. Up would shoot the window, and the order would be given, 'Right boys, dotty ditties. Drown the sergeant major, boys! Drown the sergeant major!'

Somehow it always transpired that on Field Days Mr Blincow would position himself in a field liberally endowed with cowpats — and not just because of his bovine name; it was in fact pronounced with a silent 'w'. And somehow he never knew they were there. Without a twitch of a muscle a line of innocent-looking boys in corps uniform would watch as the sergeant major determinedly walked backwards, straight into a large and particularly squashy cowpat, his immaculately blancoed gaiters no longer his pride and joy.

Upon the eccentricities of Harry Mac himself an entire chapter could be devoted. A lifelong bachelor of a variety now extinct, Harry Mac became a greatly loved housemaster of Sanderson's, where, until he gave up the house in 1949, he provided a home for his aged mother; it was commonly rumoured that Harry Mac employed the old lady to pedal a Pennyfarthing in the basement attached to a generator, thus economising on electricity bills. He would commence saying Grace as he came downstairs and finish just after sitting down. Kippers, served not infrequently for breakfast, he referred to as rich denizens of the deep seas. 'Imperial food, boys, imperial food,' he would announce, 'rich denizens of the deep seas.' He loved a scrummage in the classroom, and if a boy misbehaved Harry Mac would quite often give the others permission to administer rough justice. 'Beat him up, boys, beat him up,' he would say, and when he tried to restore order the boys all pretended not to hear. Kitted out with a pair of field glasses, rather than walk round the room to inspect written work he would tell the boys to hold up their exercise books for inspection through his binoculars.

On one occasion a member of Harry Mac's class laid a booby trap for another boy, a pile of books on top of the door. Unfortunately, Harry Mac came in first and received a thud on the head. Halfway through the class he sent the offender on some pretext to the Bell Room. When the boy returned, the contents of several boxes of chalk cascaded on to him from the top of the door. He liked fun and was an extremely kind man; he actually liked boys, which not all masters do. While touch judging (he was in too much pain to play) his appendix burst and he developed peritonitis, and such was the crudity of surgery in 1920 he very nearly died. When in 1948 one of his boarders was diagnosed with appendicitis he sat on the boy's bed in conspiratorial mood. 'Now listen to me, boy,' he said. 'Whatever you do, don't let matron give you any syrup of figs. They gave me syrup of figs and my appendix burst.' As soon as the boy had been driven to hospital, Harry Mac followed with a basket of fruit.

It was strange that Harry Mac matured into such an amusing and tolerant man (the only failing in boys he found hard to forgive was bad manners) for discipline when he was at school was becoming more than ever the responsibility of the monitors, who were given more freedom than ever before to brandish their canes. The punishment book for the Christmas term of 1919 makes depressing reading. For repeated ragging at games a boy received three cuts. Four boys received four cuts each for 'creating a disturbance with fireworks in the streets after lock-up'. But 'letting off stink bombs' only merited three cuts. A boy who had broken a window with a stone received five strokes of the cane, two more than masters were permitted to administer. Some of the boys certainly seem to have behaved badly. For breaking chairs at a concert the culprit received three strokes. 'Insubordination to an option' rated two cuts; for bullying a smaller boy, two boys got three cuts each. In 1920 a boy was caned for 'persistently and deliberately wearing soft and coloured collars.' How could one wear a soft coloured collar other than deliberately? For 'indecent behaviour at a meeting of the Scientific Society' four boys received four cuts each. That's sixteen swipes of the cane, and we are not even told what the monitors thought 'indecent behaviour', a highly subjective term, amounted to.

A merciful mystery also surrounds the activities of three boys who only got one cut each 'for using the wrong latrines for the wrong purpose'. Forging a master's signature for leave off games was deemed to deserve 'four of the best'. So did firing an airgun. But being out after lock-up 'twice with a tweed cap on' earned the unhappy youth five cuts.

And so it goes on, a long and incredibly dreary litany of trivia. For 'consistently wearing a sports coat' a boy received two strokes of the cane. Being five minutes late for house runs was an offence punishable by a monitor. So was 'rushing along the corridors and through the swing doors to public danger'. Boys who rode through the Glebe Road gates, were rude to monitors or spoke during prayers could all expect to bend over and be beaten. Smoking was heavily frowned upon; two boys caught smoking in Russell Park received five cuts each, and even a boy who was with them but not actually smoking received three. It was rough and ready arbitrary justice, meted out on behalf of the Head Master by boys often acting like insufferable prigs.

'Wearing loud socks': three cuts.

'For staying in water in baths after bell had rung': two cuts.

'For most unsporting behaviour during a house match': three cuts.

'Walking on school flowerbeds': three cuts.

'For taking a valve out of someone's bike tyre': three cuts.

A boy was caned in 1924 for insulting a master — but not by the master. Another was caned for riding a motorbike. Someone guilty of 'improper behaviour in the gym' got away with one stroke of the cane, but for spitting in the gym another naughty boy received two strokes. Breaking a goal post earned the miscreant three strokes. The whole thing was a lottery. Telling lies, 'wearing chocolate-coloured flannel bags on Sunday', 'wearing a grey tie', 'kicking a master's door', going to the pictures, stealing books; all these offences were dealt with by monitors. Three boys were stupid enough to write their own names on a lavatory wall, and each received three cuts.

Sometimes the offences were vaguely worded. 'Constant failure to look at house notice board' begs the question what constant means. 'Cutting swimming and causing considerable trouble' is equally ambiguous. What is very evident from this period is the fear of sex, in all its manifestations. 'The association of Boys with Girls this term has caused me much anxiety,' R U F Kynaston noted in 1935. 'Nothing serious has occurred but I would warn future Heads of the school that this is a matter which needs constant and careful watching since it can lead to grave consequences.' Six cuts, exorbitant at any time, were administered to a boy 'for being continually in the company of girls'. In 1926 a boy received four strokes of the cane for 'walking up and down the High Street on Sunday afternoon with girls'. R D Stewart, head of school in 1927, might have done better to tone down his sanctimoniousness and brush up on his punctuation when he recorded beating another boy for 'Dirty talk and bullying a boy who older than himself is however very much weaker'.

They saw themselves as Sir Galahads, these muscle-bound monitors, lashing out left and right in defence of morality. The very same day, Stewart had felt obliged to administer three cuts to another boy for 'dirty talk and disgusting language'. But the prize entry in the punishment book must surely go to 'Posting a libelous notice to the detriment of two monitors in a public place'. Or should it? One really is spoilt for choice. In 1930 a boy received three cuts 'for sitting on a fence with a girl on a Sunday afternoon'. Would Monday have been all right? The boy who had transgressed in this heinous fashion bore a well-known Bedford name, that of Inskip, and clearly Inskip was an incorrigible womaniser; shortly afterwards he received another three cuts for 'holding a long conversation with some girls in Russell Park'. As the conversation had been a long one we must envisage a couple of monitors secreted in the bushes with a stopwatch. 'OK, Inskip,' they snarl, leaping from their place of concealment. 'Your time's up. That's eight and a half minutes conversation. You know school rules only permit seven.'

Like capital punishment, corporal punishment had no discernible deterrent effect whatsoever. Boys continued to make 'insulting remarks in a loud voice about Goodall in the nets' (1929, three cuts); even 'to wear plus-fours during term-time' (1932). But to be fair to the senior boys, they were largely following the dictates of their elders and betters. In 1919 Reginald Carter had a new handbook for masters printed, and its contents were still, in essence, the product of a Victorian mind. 'Rowdiness,' he reminded his colleagues, 'unnecessary talking, noisy entrance into, or departure from a room, keeping hands in the pockets in a Master's presence, slovenliness of person are all examples of bad manners on the part of boys: so also are badly written and unrevised exercises, careless preparation and the like. Never allow bad manners to pass unchecked. Like an ill weed they grow apace.'

On the subject of punishment he wrote, 'The less punishment the better', and then promptly reined himself in, adding, 'When punishment is necessary, it should be rigorously exacted.' Masters were still restricted to three cuts of the cane, while monitors were permitted six. 'Boys guilty of serious offences,' Carter wrote, 'such as extreme idleness, dishonesty in work, serious and deliberate falsehood, indecency, and boys who have been caned twice during a term by a Master *should be reported to the Head Master*.' In Notes on Work, Carter provided handy suggestions for short essays. They included a description of the King's chauffeur on the drive from Balmoral to Buckingham Palace. Never mind that the journey was made by train.

By this time, of course, the original Holborn estate purchased by Sir William Harper was thoroughly built upon, and many of its poor inhabitants were paying rent which went towards keeping down the fees of Bedford School boys. In 1921 it only cost £18 a year to send a boy under ten to Bedford as a day boy; over twelve, and his parents had to find £30 a year. The most expensive fees for boarders were £129 a year. In 1924 a nine-day OTC camp at Tidworth cost £1 10s. Life for the well-off was incredibly cheap and servants were still two-a-penny. But for working class families, the aftermath of the war often meant grinding poverty. It was very much in keeping with the times that Bedford, like other schools in a similar situation, was to open a club, in Holborn, to provide recreational and educational facilities for the sons of such families. And it was to Carter's credit that as early as 1913 he suggested such a club. The war intervened, but he came back to the idea in 1920, when he encouraged a group of Old Bedfordians to set up the Holborn Boys' Club, generally known as Bedford House. For the first eight years it had premises at 9 Sandland Street, and for the next two years it was housed at 12 Lambs' Conduit Street. Boys were admitted from the age of ten and some remained members until they were nineteen. By 1933 it was necessary to appoint a full-time warden, Brian Rendell. The boys boxed and fenced against the school, and the School and Bedford House Scout Troops went into summer camp together. Discussions on current affairs were held; some very ambitious drama productions (*The Moon is Down* by John Steinbeck, for instance) were staged.

By 1936 the club could muster sixty boys between the ages of 10-13$\frac{1}{2}$ (the Minors), thirty between 13$\frac{1}{2}$-15$\frac{1}{2}$ (the Juniors) and sixty-five between 15$\frac{1}{2}$-19 (the Seniors). They were paid a visit on 9 March 1938 by the Duke of Gloucester, in his capacity as president of the National Association of Boys' Clubs. A year later, at the outbreak of war, two of the club's somewhat over-enthusiastic lads, aged fifteen and sixteen, attempted to enlist. Serious disaster struck on the night of 12 May 1941 when Bedford House fell victim to the last of the mass fire-raids on London; a string of incendiary bombs fell on Lambs' Conduit Street, six of them on the club. With immense courage, three boys on fire watch tried to tackle the flames and had to be restrained by police from re-entering the building, which was gutted. During the course of this raid, some five-sixths of Harpur Trust property was destroyed.

For the next six years Bedford House shared the premises of the Tonbridge Boys' Club, near St Pancras Station (their land had been given to them by the Skinners' Company), but even here they were not entirely safe; on 10 February 1945, just as everyone thought the war was drawing to a close, a V2 rocket fell only 100 yards from the club premises, blowing out nearly every window.

In 1946 two surplus government huts, one made of wood, the other of steel, were purchased and transported to the bombed site of 9 Emerald Street, and here Bedford House made do for the next ten years. The temporary premises were thought grand enough to be opened by Field Marshal Viscount Montgomery, on 10 April 1947, but by 1949 membership of the club was down to fifty, which no doubt reflected the gradual increase in recreational and other amenities being supplied elsewhere; it may also have reflected the increasing restlessness of London youths, whose horizons were beginning to expand. In 1950 'juvenile gangsterism' [4] spread from the Islington area to Holborn, and a good deal of intimidation prevented boys from entering their premises. Better street lighting was provided, and the police offered to patrol the neighbourhood of the club more often. High-rise office blocks and flats began to take the place of terraced streets, and areas like Holborn gradually lost their community spirit.

Both the school and the Old Bedfordians Club had provided fraternal as well as financial assistance, and in 1954 Bedford School boys began spending visits lasting two nights, when they were 'also shown over typical secondary modern schools'. [5] It was rather a case of public schoolboys learning how the other half live. And increasingly, working class boys resented being entertained by toffs, for egalitarianism was beginning to erode the pre-war acceptance of class divisions. In 1954 the Harpur Trust had to bail the club out to the tune of £400, and by 1956 it was becoming apparent that in many ways it had outlived its original purpose; membership was now down to forty. Yet the following year the huts, pretty well worn out, were abandoned, and on 23 September

1957 the club took possession of well-equipped brand-new premises, receiving a visit on 3 December that year from the Duke of Edinburgh, patron of the London Federation of Boys' Clubs. The writing was on the wall, however, for such philanthropic enterprises, contemporary with the days when every Bedford School boy collected either for the Missions to Seamen or the Waifs and Strays. The Holborn Boys' Club has long since ceased to exist, and after 30 years as Warden, Brian Rendell died in an old people's home in Minehead in 1983, at the age of eighty-two.

With the Great War fresh in his mind, and Bedford House established, Reginald Carter next turned to the question of providing a fitting and permanent memorial to those Old Bedfordians who had died. At the annual general meeting of the Old Bedfordians Club on 24 July 1921 it was decided that a letter should be sent to all OBs, canvassing their views about a possible Memorial Hall, containing the names of the fallen, or perhaps something less expensive, like a war memorial or a statue. By July 1923 the executive committee had proposals for a Memorial Hall incorporating a library and a museum, for by now £6,200 had been collected. An Old Bedfordian and a pupil of Edwin Lutyens, Oswald Milne, was consulted, and he reported that a two-storey building linked to the main school by means of a covered way, containing a ground-floor library and a first-floor hall, could be built for £7,000. Milne went on to stamp his imprint across the school estate, designing the open air swimming pool, the gym and much of the Science Block.

On 26 July 1925, at the conclusion of OB Week, the foundation stone of the Memorial Hall, due to be built at the west end of the school, on a north-south axis, was laid by an Old Bedfordian, Lieut General Sir Walter Braithwaite. Sixty members of the OTC (ten from each school house) formed a guard of honour. In his speech, General Braithwaite almost exactly replicated figures produced by Sargeaunt, citing 2,318 OBs as having served in the war, of whom, he said, 450 (two more than Sargeaunt) had been killed and 375 wounded. The covered way was built at an additional cost of £856; General Braithwaite invited Prince Henry (in 1928 created Duke of Gloucester), the 26-year-old third son of George V and Queen Mary and the first member of the royal family to have been sent to school, to open the Memorial Hall; and this, on 26 July 1926, he duly did. After attending a civic reception at the Town Hall the prince arrived in his dashing 10th Royal Hussars uniform (too young to have served in the war, he had had the misfortune in 1900 of being selected as a godson for the Kaiser), and among those presented to him was Carter's predecessor as Head Master, John King.

Lunch was served in the gymnasium, and afterwards the Memorial Hall was dedicated by an Old Bedfordian, John Gregg, then archbishop of Dublin. Few present could have dreamed that one day the south wall of the upstairs hall would be engraved with the names of boys killed in a second world war. Over the door of the hall, for many years used for morning assembly by the Lower School and for meetings of the Debating Society, was inscribed one word: Remember. The hall now contains a three volume Book of Remembrance; papers, including the *China Review*, are provided; and the ground floor library contains some 13,000 volumes.

It was still felt that the Memorial Hall lacked an outward visible symbol of heroism, and eventually a bronze statue of St George was commissioned, at a cost of £750, and placed in a niche on the north wall. It was unveiled on 29 July 1928 by General Braithwaite. (A niche on the north wall of the main school building, possibly intended by Phillpotts as a home for the Town Hall statue of Sir William Harper, remains empty to this day.)

Carter's time at Bedford saw a steady erection or acquisition of new premises. £1,170 was spent on tennis courts in 1912. In 1921 the Harpur Trust purchased Georgian buildings at the east end of St Peter's Street, from 1802 until 1914 a girls' Moravian school. The cost was £3,000. Renamed the Howard Building in honour of Geoffrey Howard, at that time chairman of the Harpur Trust, it was used for many years not only to provide facilities for music and art but as a dining room and changing room for day boys who lived too far away to go home in the middle of the day.

A year later it was decided the old Chetham's boat yard would no longer suffice for the expanding rowing activities of the school, and new boat houses to accommodate Bedford Modern School, Bedford School and the Town Boat Club were built. To help defray the school's share of the cost, £3,000 was raised at a bazaar, a considerable sum at the time. Since before the turn of the century Bedford had raced annually against Shrewsbury (founded the same year as Bedford), alternately on the Ouse and the Severn, both crews notching up an equal number of wins. The school was by now accustomed to competing in the Ladies' Plate at Henley, but its most famous years as a rowing school still lay ahead.

Only two years before his departure, Reginald Carter placed the school firmly in his debt by establishing the Bedford School Trust; on 9 July 1926. The Trust is now a registered charity, entirely under the control of the school, with a total portfolio of about £2 million. Thus each year Carter's original scheme may bring in an income of anywhere between £40,000 and £50,000. Much of this income is used to provide scholarships and bursaries, but the trustees have discretion to make grants for furniture and equipment or, for example, to benefit the Musical Instrument Fund. Bequests of £100,000 are not unknown, and a major benefactor of the Bedford School Trust is the Gilbert Cook

Scholarship Fund, established by his family in memory of John Gilbert Cook, at Bedford 1922-29. The clock on the north-east elevation of the Recreation Centre was presented in his memory.

The Gilbert Cook Scholarship Fund within the Bedford School Trust is now substantial, and the school has reason to be grateful to Philip Byam-Cook, the brother of Gilbert Cook, and the Hedley Foundation for their generous support. Gilbert Cook Scholarships are intended to reward all-round excellence, and many boarders, in particular, have repaid their debt to the Gilbert Cook Scholarship Fund by enhanced performances academically, in cultural activities and in sport.

An inspired appointment Carter made in 1924 was to the Bell Room, although some of the credit should go to his predecessor. In 1907 John King took on a Bell Room boy on two weeks' trial. His name was Ernest Bull. In 1924 Carter confirmed Bull as chief clerk. He was to remain in office over half a century, retiring in 1962, when the school gave him a standing ovation and a farewell luncheon in the Memorial Hall, the Head Master (William Brown) declaring an extra half-holiday. Ernest Bull quite simply devoted his entire life to Bedford School, cycling round the grounds, most reluctantly taking an annual summer holiday in Hove, ceaselessly refreshing his memory. As boys filed out of chapel he recited to himself their names — and not only their names but, if they were Old Bedfordians, their father's as well, and sometimes their grandfather's, reminding himself at the same time of their houses and colours and scholastic achievements. Twice a year, when the honours list was published, by 11am Mr Bull had the name of every OB in the list, their years at school and their school achievements, ringed and written up for collection by a *Bedfordshire Times* reporter. It is no exaggeration in the case of Ernest Bull to say that he became an institution, and no disrespect to those who have followed him to suggest that he was both unique and irreplaceable. He only lived to enjoy a brief retirement, dying on 14 September 1964. Three days later his funeral procession wended its way from Kimbolton Road through the school grounds and down De Parys Avenue to St Peter's Church, following the route Mr Bull had taken three or four times a day on his way to and from the Bell Room for fifty-five years.

SEVEN

The Test of an Educated Man

1928–1935

B Y 1928 Reginald Carter was sixty, no great age for a Head Master, but after eighteen years in the post, with all the strain imposed by the Great War, he decided to retire. In the way that the chapel stands as a physical monument to the efforts of John King, so the Memorial Hall is a fitting reminder of Carter's time. Before he left he sat for a portrait by Gunning King, an artist suggested by himself, a commission that cost a modest £150. He died on 20 August 1936, at the age of sixty-eight.

Carter's thirty-seven-year-old successor, Humfrey Grose-Hodge, straddled two entirely different worlds. Born in 1891, well within the reign of Queen Victoria, he remained at Bedford until the commencement of the second half of the twentieth century, almost into the reign of Elizabeth II, and like Carter he had to endure the disruption, not to mention distress, of a world war. In many ways, Grose-Hodge's headmastership was a dramatic period in the history of the school. A crucial building programme careered ahead and scholastic excellence competed with athletic. During the 1936-7 season Bedford won every inter-school cricket and football match, and in 1938 the captain of cricket scored over 1,000 runs, including 200 not out in a school match. 1936-7 saw a record number of State Scholarships awarded and 1937-8 witnessed a record number of University Scholarships. The main building was severely damaged by what could have proved a catastrophic fire. The Lower School was inaugurated. And royalty now seemed quite incapable of keeping away.

That would not have displeased Grose-Hodge, who was nothing if not a snob. But like every aspect of his personality, he carried off his snobbery with panache. Much more importantly, he was an intellectual. But he placed both academic work and sport on an equal footing, and without pretence to any personal interest in sport he believed implicitly in its value, turning out in all weathers if not to cheer the 1st XV at least to patrol the touchline, accompanied, as he was wherever he went, by a beautiful white Pyrenean mountain dog.

Humfrey Grose-Hodge, the son of an honorary canon of Birmingham, was educated at Marlborough and Pembroke College, Cambridge, where he took a First Class degree in the Classical Tripos. In 1913 he was president of the Union. Before settling for a career as a schoolmaster he served in the Indian Civil Service, as an assistant magistrate in Bengal, so that he would have felt quite at home with the Anglo-Indian tradition at Bedford. From 1920 until he arrived at Bedford in 1928 he was Classical Sixth Form master at Charterhouse. When he first took over he used to apologise for looking so young, but Head Masters far more youthful than he had been appointed. Geoffrey Fisher, later archbishop of Canterbury, was only twenty-eight when he became Head Master of Repton in 1915.

It took Grose-Hodge only a matter of months to decree that in future Bedford School boys would be uniformly dressed: a blue jacket and grey trousers and black shoes for everyone except monitors, who enjoyed the inestimable privilege of wearing brown shoes (today they sport coloured waistcoats as well). An absurd little cap had perched on the back of Bedford boys' heads since the nineteenth century but had not previously been compulsory. It had no peak to speak of, and instead of raising his cap to a master in the street, a boy would touch the badge with two fingers. No one has ever provided a plausible explanation for this unique headgear; one theory was that the cap purchased on your arrival in the Inky at the age of seven would last until you left at eighteen, for it did not matter how large your head grew, the cap was intended to stay on the back of it. Under Grose-Hodge, in summer boys could opt to wear a boater, those who had not swum the school pass being stigmatised by being compelled to wear a white button on their cap and a white band on their straw hat.

The introduction of a standard and compulsory uniform was a godsend to two town outfitters, J & A Beagley in St Peter's Street and Our Boys in Silver Street. They sold boring black ties for boys without school colours and large white eagles to adorn the blazers of the bloods. Inky boys wore short grey trousers and a grey double-breasted jacket, and when in 1935 the Lower School was hived off from the Upper School, Lower School boys wore a grey suit with long trousers.

Putting boys into uniform dress was somehow symbolic of Grose-Hodge's desire to give the school tone and dignity, which undoubtedly he did, partly through his own persona. Small in stature, he had an overawing presence — some would say, tinged with pomposity. What mattered was the sense of certitude, of security even, that emanated when he entered a room or mounted the platform; you really could have heard a pin drop. He adopted mannerisms that marked him out from all the other masters, many, in the early days, a good deal older than he. 'In the name of God, Amen!' he would snap from the pulpit when, as he did every term, he delivered a sermon in chapel. During prayers in the Great Hall he held a book over his face. He gave lectures on the miracles, providing rational explanations without destroying their spiritual significance, and unlike some of the more effete younger masters who joined the staff after the second world war and affected a fashionable agnosticism, he undoubtedly held revealed religion to be true, and believed it was perfectly feasible to compel boarders to attend chapel on Sunday, just as they were compelled to learn French and science during the week; you can always reject religion when you leave school, he would say, if you know what it is you're rejecting. Masters were told, in *Notes for the Use of Masters at Bedford School* drawn up by himself in 1946, 'meant for the information and guidance of young Masters who have recently joined the Staff', that it was 'part of every Master's duty — one of the conditions of his appointment — to attend Morning Prayers punctually at 9am if he is "in School" for the first period, and if for the last, to stay for prayers at 1 o'clock on half-holidays'.

Grose-Hodge may be said to have had a religious attitude towards education; certainly an enlightened one. 'The aim of education,' he told his staff, 'is to help boys, as they grow up, to attain the best of which they are capable; and it should be remembered that this objective is a different one in every case. What value his education has been to a boy will appear, not in boyhood but in manhood; for the final aim of the School is to produce not merely good schoolboys or even good citizens, but good men.' He went on to say, 'Technical efficiency is essential if a man is to earn his living in the world of to-day; but the quality which is needed if he is to enjoy a full and happy life is spiritual. Skill at games may be a source of enjoyment and good health, but it is second in value to the spirit in which the game is played. The test of an educated man is not what he knows, nor what he can do, but what he is. There is no competitive examination for entry into the Kingdom of Heaven.'

Grose-Hodge was twenty-three at the outbreak of the Great War. Whatever his reason, in 1914, for joining the Indian Civil Service rather than enlisting in the British Army, it was certainly not to avoid combat; in 1916 he was commissioned in the Indian Army Reserve of Officers, serving on the north-west frontier of India and Mesopotamia, in Palestine and in Syria before being invalided out of the Indian Civil Service in 1920. A natural cleavage to patriotism and religion was what differentiated Grose-Hodge and his contemporaries, those Old Bedfordians whose names were already inscribed in the Memorial Hall and the chapel, from modern men and women. Grose-Hodge survived into an alien age, and even by the time he became Head Master of Bedford School, cynicism and disillusion with post-war poverty and unemployment — there *was* no country fit for heroes to live in — had begun to sap the vitality of the nation's youth. A second call to arms in 1939 could not depend on volunteers alone, and by the time Grose-Hodge retired in 1951, blind faith in the established organs of government, the Tory Party, the law and the Church, was beginning to crumble. [1]

In a preface to his 1946 instructions to his staff, Grose-Hodge explained that they were not intended as a rigid and comprehensive code or to relieve a master of the responsibility of using his personal judgement in individual cases. 'They amount in many instances to "counsels of perfection", but it is felt that no other counsel is worth having.' So much for the stern and unapproachable martinet some people professed to see in Grose-Hodge. He understood a great deal about human nature, and in particular about boys, by whose pretensions to adult status he was not in the least taken in. 'A very high standard is demanded of Monitors,' he wrote. 'The idea that they are appointed "to see rules kept and not to keep them" is not to be tolerated ... Their responsibility is great, but it should be remembered that the oldest of them is little more than a child. They need help and will appreciate it if — but only if — it is tactfully given.' A 'child' whom Grose-Hodge installed as head of school in 1932 was William Brown, who matured sufficiently to be appointed Head Master twenty-three years later.

Grose-Hodge had a list of dictums, some of which are worth recalling:

'Boys' inability to express themselves on paper is often due to the incomplete and slipshod way in which they are allowed to speak.'

'Spelling and punctuation, grammar and syntax, equally with neatness and legibility, are as important in Mathematics and Science as they are in History and Language — accuracy of thought is often conditioned by power of accurate expression.'

'Boys will not use good English unless they read good English, and to this end they must be taught to use the Memorial Library.'

On matters of discipline, as early as 1 November 1930 Grose-Hodge was minuting in the Punishment Book, 'In case of an offender over sixteen years old, it is desirable that the matter should be referred to the Head Master'. He was as keen on good conduct from masters as he was from boys. 'Politeness, punctuality, neatness and cleanliness of dress and person can only be insisted upon by a Master who is punctilious in these respects himself,' he reminded members of the commonroom. 'A Master who has come to school unshaven cannot rebuke, as he should, a boy who has not washed his hands.' No master was to smoke during school hours, nor appear without a gown during the morning, in the presence of boys. Today, gowns are only worn in chapel or on the most formal occasions.

He reminded them that 'cases of dishonesty, bullying or indecency must invariably be sent to the Head Master with a written report', but he pleaded for 'wise handling' on the part of masters. Boys rarely cheat, he said, unless overworked, inadequately supervised, threatened with punishment or 'when obviously expected to do so'. He was the first Head Master of Bedford to have the courage at least to attempt a rational justification of caning, which he saw as a last resort. 'Caning may do much harm or much good', he believed, 'and should be used rarely but effectively. It is designed to check general or reiterated faults of any kind. A bad boy cannot be made into a good boy by hitting him, and if the cane were only a deterrent it is questionable whether its use would be justified. The object of caning is to compel a boy's attention, to impress upon him that his fault is serious and to break down his obduracy. Its value largely depends on what is said to him afterwards.'

Such sentiments may not be thought to hold much water today but they were fairly radical in 1946. It is interesting to record that all parks were officially out of bounds at this time, for Farrar's boys regularly paid visits to Bedford Park, just yards from their house, to buy ice creams and, in the harsh winter of 1947, to learn to skate on the frozen pond. Also off limits were Marks & Spencer, Woolworth's 'and other multiple stores', which did not entirely eliminate the temptation to shoplift; books disappeared from time to time from the shelves of Hockliffe's in the High Street. There was a general catch all rule relating to conduct: 'Any boy whose behaviour, manners, or even appearance are such as to bring discredit on the School at any time or place, will be regarded as having broken a School Rule'. Non-conformity was Grose-Hodge's bête noire. One day he noticed a boy wearing a tie pin. 'That, dear boy,' he said, 'is the kind of thing loud young men did in London in my day. Take it orff.' Today, boys are quite likely to turn up for school wearing a signet ring. Girls he pronounced 'gals'; gone was 'gorn'. He preferred a word with three syllables rather than one, and if it possessed a Latin root, so much the better; to find a word he could use with its origins in both Latin and Greek was very heaven. The thought of a boy munching a doughnut outside the school grounds was more than he could bear, and at prayers one morning he riveted the school by announcing it had been drawn to his attention that boys had been seen masticating in the street.

There are today relatively few Old Bedfordians on the academic staff, but their recruitment used to be quite common. An Old Bedfordian who returned to the school to teach French and German in 1927 rejoiced in the name of Alban Goderic Arthur Hodges. A casualty of the Great War (he had a leg blown off in Belgium in 1917 and was never out of pain), he typified a breed of eccentric masters who exerted immeasurable influence over a period of perhaps some twenty-five years. They are a breed now elbowed out of public school life by excessive conformity and a paranoid fear of scandal. It is a safe bet that until the day Mr Hodges retired in 1954 no boy ever knew what his Christian names were, but they knew his initials, and that was enough; he was always called Aga. Born in 1893, Aga had been a boarder from 1908-12 in Merton House. Before joining the 4th Bn the Northamptonshire Regiment in 1914, with whom he served in Gallipoli, he read theology at King's College, Cambridge, with the intention at the time of following in his father's footsteps by seeking ordination. He returned to King's after the war, fitted up with a wooden leg, and having taken a degree he went on to the Sorbonne and Heidelberg to improve his French and German. Like Harry Mac, Aga was a very kind man, and one of those masters easily led astray by boys who preferred to listen to anecdotes about the war than an exposition of French grammar. At the age of seventy-nine he published an autobiography, *Memoirs of an Old Balloonatic*,[2] living on for a further decade in a house on the Embankment, and then in a flat in Bushmead Avenue.

Why Aga Hodges never went ahead with ordination may have been due to his failure to grasp even the first fundamentals of orthodox theology. When Pater, as he always referred to his father, was himself a very great age and thinking of dying, an assistant curate from St Paul's went to see him, to administer Holy Communion. Pater being rather deaf, the curate shouted into his ear trumpet, 'I'm now going to say the General Confession', whereupon Aga leapt to his feet and exclaimed, 'The General Confession! Don't be ridiculous, Pater has never sinned in his life.'

It was not long before Humfrey Grose-Hodge was engaged in a skirmish with an Old Bedfordian whose name however has been hidden from posterity.[3] In November 1932 Grose-Hodge wrote to the secretary of the Old Bedfordians Club to complain that a young OB had let off a firework in one of the galleries of the Great Hall. He wished to be present at a meeting of the executive committee when the matter was discussed. The secretary told Grose-Hodge there was no need for him to appear, but he could come if he wished. He duly turned up, to report that he had received an anonymous letter giving the name of the culprit. Consequently he had interviewed the OB, and forbidden him to come on to the school premises until further notice. He asked the committee to take some form of disciplinary action.

After Grose-Hodge had left the meeting the committee 'discussed the matter exhaustively', and eventually resolved to write to the young man to tell him he ought to resign from the Club. Rather than be pushed, he decided to jump, and his membership fee, three guineas, was returned. Not long after-wards, Grose-Hodge again intervened in a matter of Club membership. Apparently an application had been received from a boy who joined the school in 1929 and had left in the middle of the summer term of 1933. Grose-Hodge would not recommend him for the Club, so the boy's mother had instructed a Bournemouth solicitor to write to complain. It transpired the boy had left because of ill-health, and Grose-Hodge backed down.

Humfrey Grose-Hodge took his relations with the Old Bedfordians Club seriously. On 9 May 1934 he wrote to the secretary to say, 'Once again I have received from you a complimentary ticket to the Old Bedfordian Dinner, and I feel the time has come to raise the question whether an Honorary Vice-President of the Club may not, and should not, pay for his own dinner. Speaking for myself, and I believe my fellow Vice-Presidents, I would much rather do so. Otherwise I eat an excellent dinner at the expense of many younger, and possibly more impecunious, young men. This request of mine raises another issue: is a Vice-President a member of the Club? If he is — and I should rather like to think I was — he should certainly pay for his own dinner. Perhaps you will be kind enough to bring this to the notice of the committee.' Such was the momentous nature of this communication that the committee deferred the matter for consideration at a later meeting.

It was during Grose-Hodge's early years at Bedford that many essential embellishments to the chapel were carried out. By the beginning of 1929 wrought iron pendants made by the boys had replaced the original rather commonplace chandeliers (in 1998 the pendants themselves were replaced by modern uplighters). Work was eventually completed on the carving of the pews, although when Grose-Hodge arrived some of the original chairs were still in use. There was an extraordinary practice of charging day boys and their parents to use the chapel, in order to pay off a deficit on the building costs, but the debt cannot have been very enormous; it was extinguished in 1930 when Septimus Phillpotts left the chapel a legacy of £200. Known, needless to say, as Seppy, Phillpotts had taken over Merton House when it moved to 39 Kimbolton Road in 1893, and his must have been a life fraught with difficulties. He suffered from a phobia which involves the fear of germs and dirt in general, so that he was forever washing his hands and was terrified of touching a door handle or even a towel.

The Great Hall, too, was only gradually being transformed from the plain brick of James Phillpotts's day to oak panelling, not completed on the ground floor until 1934, and in the top gallery until 1937. Three state chairs arrived in 1929, the Bedford Town arms in 1934, and those of New College, Oxford the following year. An entertainment laid on by the monitors paid for a fine octagonal electric clock in black and gold, which was positioned above the panelling on the north wall. A steady new supply of oak chairs with rush seats was replacing the old, unsightly cane and bentwood chairs. All these hard-earned gifts were to be destroyed in 1979.

In 1930 an open air swimming pool was constructed, with a tuck shop in a kiosk at one corner, on a site just south of the Memorial Hall, now occupied by the Recreation Centre, whose amenities include a heated pool. And on 29 October 1932 the foundation stone for a new Science Building, to replace ramshackle tin sheds (the gymnasium until now had been a tin shed too), was laid by an Old Bedfordian, W Langdon Brown, Regius Professor of Physic at Cambridge. Construction work must have been swiftly undertaken, for on 8 November the following year the most popular man in England, the thirty-nine-year-old Prince of Wales, came to the school, to undertake a general tour of inspection and specifically to view — but for some obscure reason not officially to declare open — the new science block.

A supplement to the *Ousel* produced at Christmas 1933 devoted nine pages of sycophantic eulogy to the visit, reporting that on the first day of the Christmas term 'A moment's disappointment may have been caused when the Head Master announced from the platform in the Hall… that there would be no opening ceremony [in connection with the new Science Building]; but it was succeeded by the highest pitch of enthusiasm when he added that all the new buildings, as well as the Laboratories, would be visited and inspected in the course of the term by no less a personage than His Royal Highness the Prince of Wales.'

In preparation for the great day, originally fixed for 24 October, 'every man and boy in the school knew his appointed place and how to get to it. The Guard of Honour had practised and practised until their chests looked almost pneumatic and their buttons, strained to the utmost, shone like suns.' At less than twenty-four hours notice, however, His Royal Highness the Prince of Wales postponed his visit, having taken to his bed with a chill. But only a fortnight later boys arrived for morning prayers 'dressed in their blue suits [until the mid-1990s blue suits were normally worn on Sunday] and — dare we add? — fresh from a more elaborate toilet than is deemed necessary on less auspicious occasions.' The prince was due at 'about 11.30am'. At 11.15am the guard of honour was drawn up. Half an hour later, and all too typically of the Prince of Wales, a message was received that he would be late. He had only landed at Henlow, a good thirteen miles away, at a quarter to twelve.

What the Prince of Wales lacked in punctuality and thoughtfulness for others he famously made up for in charm, and this he proceeded to lay on with practised royal diplomacy, chatting to Sgt Major Blincow about the Grenadier

Guards and asking questions about the portraits of former Head Masters. No one seemed the least put out when he entered the Science Block and said he thought it was the prep school. He showed considerable interest in the equipment, once he had grasped where he was, leaving behind him 'the impression of a practical mind and keen powers of observation, while everyone must have felt — the boys not least — the charm and ease of his manner in talking to them.'

By way of the workshops, the forge and the Inky, where he inspected a second guard of honour, this time formed by Boy Scouts, and where he received three cheers from boys 'yelling more loudly than anyone who did not know them would have thought possible', the prince made his way, accompanied by the head of school and captain of the 1st XV, to the new gymnasium, contemporary with the new Science Block. It had been erected immediately to the south of the swimming pool. 'Damned good' the observant royal visitor commented after watching a display of gymnastics. And so via the swimming pool the prince eventually arrived at the Memorial Hall, where he investigated the library and signed the visitors' book on the page his brother Prince Henry had used. Goodness knows what time it was by now (the tour of inspection could not have taken less than an hour, conceivably an hour and a half), but the next port of call, seemingly without a break for refreshments, was the Great Hall, where 'enthusiastic cheers from the assembled School expressed a welcome more unmistakable than any words: but there was a deep silence when His Royal Highness rose to speak.' No doubt having been tipped off by his long suffering private secretary, Sir Godfrey Thomas, that in 1918 the King had organised an extra week's holiday, Edward announced that 'the best way of commemorating this very happy visit of mine will be for you to have a longer holiday at Christmas', Grose-Hodge having agreed to delay the start of the Easter term by five days. The head of school, R V Symonds, brave boy, sang three verses of *Bedford by the River*, and the prince finally retired to the Head Master's study to smoke a pipe. Two years later he was king; by December 1936 he had abdicated and gone into exile. And on the day of the prince's accession, 21 January 1936 (not 1935, as the *Ousel* for June 1995 would have us believe), there was an amusing hiccup at morning assembly. Apparently Grose-Hodge opened the proceedings by standing to attention and announcing, 'The King is dead! Long live the King!' which was the cue for the director of music, James Denny (he taught at the school 1933-37), to strike up the national anthem on the piano, which he did with such vigour that the G string broke, 'going TWANG, twang, twang, twang … Partially stifled giggles, both by staff and boys, were quickly brought to an end by Denny who (with consummate skill) immediately started again, transposing into either F sharp or A flat.'

A very strange brochure had been produced for the visit of the Prince of Wales. Identical photographs of the Science Block and the Swimming Baths were reproduced on different pages. A photograph of the Phillpotts Gates was captioned 'Philpott', while a photograph of the Great Hall was mistakenly identified as the Memorial Hall. But the most bizarre feature was a page devoted to the British Union of Fascists. A display box, beneath a photograph of Oswald Mosley ranting, read: 'Join To-Day. For Particulars of Membership apply to the British Union of Fascists, 4 Bushmead Avenue, Bedford.' Headed Ich Dien, the Prince of Wales's own motto, the copy aimed to equate the prince's interest in the Empire with that of the British Union, while proudly proclaiming both its anti-democratic and anti-Semitic message: 'Years of useless conferences all over Europe have made our people sick to death of the party system. Politicians now entering parliament, and with the best intentions in the world, are at once crushed and swamped by the party machine — a machine so designed that nothing but chaos and ceaseless compromise can be the result of their deliberations.

'Fascism *knows* that the only way to end the present chaos of industrial depression, low wages and gross betrayal of Great Britain's interests by foreigners to foreigners, lies in the Corporate State.'

The brochure had been published by Frederick Kelsey of the Bedford Diary Office, 25 Waterloo Road, Bedford. Clearly no one at the school had bothered to check the proofs; how else, among other glaring errors, could the Inky have been called the Junior School? Perhaps Mr Kelsey had slipped in gratis the full-page advertisement on fascism. Although at this time many well intentioned people believed the only alternative to communism was fascism, looking back from the vantage point of the 1990s one's first reaction is that it almost beggars belief that Grose-Hodge could have sanctioned or condoned the photograph of Mosley and its accompanying editorial copy. But there was at the time — and it continued to be produced intermittently for the next thirty years — a radical alternative school magazine called *Mosaic*. And issues for the year 1933 were stiff with contributions arguing the pros and cons of fascism. In fact, even the most cursory glance at articles that appeared in *Mosaic* to coincide with the visit of the Prince of Wales reveals that sympathy with fascism was pretty rife in the school in 1933. And like so much else that goes on in public schools, this state of affairs reflected fairly accurately the mores of middle class society as a whole. Before that decade of shameful appeasement and political naïveté was over, Grose-Hodge was to harbour guests even more dubious than fascists.

If *Mosaic* was free of censorship in 1933, an issue produced in 1963, together with one of its editorial advisors, Fred Inglis, who had been hired in 1961 to teach English and coach the Colts (he was a Cambridge Rugby Blue), managed to stir up the wrath of an influential group of Old Bedfordians. Satire was very much in vogue (*Private Eye* had been launched in 1961), and having been taught by Leavis, Fred Inglis, who is now Professor of Cultural Studies at the University of Sheffield, veered towards what he calls today 'the genteel left'. He was young and full of enthusiasm, and was very naturally in sympathy with the radical aspirations of *Mosaic*, as were other highly respected teachers on the staff at the time; the head of English, Peter Stileman, later housemaster of Sanderson's, was an editorial advisor, and the head of History, John Eyre, contributed poems, as did a future Head Master, Michael Barlen. But in its Summer 1963 edition *Mosaic* went over the top, so far as the OB lobby was concerned, and they complained to the Head Master, William Brown, about some mildly satirical verse, sanctioned by Inglis and written by a young contributor, Andrew Berridge, on the shortcomings, among others, of the colonial secretary, Duncan Sandys — by now universally known as Sunken Glands, or the Headless Man, for he had allowed himself to be photographed in a somewhat compromising situation. The poem accused Sandys of adultery, and the school was terrified he might sue. Professor Inglis recalls, 'I was taken for a stroll round the school playing fields by Bill Brown, who after much deliberation said, "I think perhaps you had better leave". So I packed my bags and accepted a visiting Fellowship in America. Then some of the boys' parents went to Brown to tell him to keep me, so I was reinstated — but in fact I only stayed on until the end of the Christmas term. After all, I had my pride! Meanwhile, Brown ordered that all copies of the offending magazine should be withdrawn and handed to the school porter, who ceremoniously burned them in an incinerator!' Mr Brown could not have been too pleased to discover the January 1964 issue of *Mosaic* dedicated to F C Inglis.

Looking through the names of masters published in the 1933 brochure, it is interesting to see that two future Vice-Masters were on the staff, H Boys-Stones, housemaster of Burnaby, and V F D Lee — Spanner Lee; he was always threatening to tighten things up. Also in situ was a future Head Master, C M E Seaman. So was R H Keable, famous for continually saying, 'Now boys, watch the board while I go through it'. Harry Mac, fresh from Lincoln College, Oxford, was also in position, as was A H Cobby, who used to encourage his class, not entirely in jest, with an outsize ruler called William. When Cobby retired in 1954 his appreciation in the *Ousel* noted, 'For fools and bad manners he had no use whatever, and in encounters of this kind he sometimes found it difficult to control himself'. A I Dunn was already on the staff too — Daddy Dunn to countless boys who used to creep up behind him to snip mementos off his gown.

An Old Bedfordian who remembers Daddy Dunn very well is David Farmbrough, who was head of Farrar's in 1941. He moved to Talbot's the following year, and was confirmed in the school chapel in March 1943 by Michael Furse, then bishop of St Albans; he distinctly remembers his vocation to the priesthood being triggered by a visiting preacher, a vocation that was encouraged by one of the school chaplains, Douglas Melhuish. He duly trained at Westcott House, in Cambridge, and appropriately enough, in 1981 he was consecrated bishop of Bedford. Now retired, Bishop Farmbrough recalls that Daddy Dunn taught Latin and 'was extremely deaf. He was constantly being asked, "Please Sir, what is 'what' in Latin?" to which he invariably replied, "What's what?"' No wonder the bishop, who won the Phillpotts English Literature prize two years running, says that his Latin never recovered. [4]

Grose-Hodge made some innovative appointments. Although he had no formal qualifications, he appointed Guy Barton art master; after the war Barton went on to found the art department at Marlborough. In 1947 he chose as senior art master an exceptionally talented teacher and writer, W R Dalzell, who inspired a succession of boys for twenty-three years, passing on to those less well endowed as artists themselves a large measure of his own enthusiasm. He was knowledgeable about architecture and museums, and among the books he wrote were *Living Artists of the Eighteenth Century* and *The Shell Guide to the History of London*. But Dalzell was only one of a steady stream of distinguished art masters. Cecil Brown sculpted the Camel Corps 1914-18 War Memorial in London, and Leslie Cubitt-Beavis was responsible for a striking statue of Sir Thomas More, erected on the Embankment at Chelsea Old Church. No musician himself, in his last year Grose-Hodge took a calculated gamble by employing Ted Amos, who was to lift the musical achievements of the school to new heights.

As for Grose-Hodge's science block, an extension was opened in 1958 by an OB, W W S Robertson, more renowned for his passion for rowing than for science, the new wing being financed by a grant from the Industrial Fund for the Advancement of Scientific Education. Twenty-six years later the Secretary of State for Education and Science, Sir Keith Joseph, reopened the renovated physics and chemistry laboratories. Meanwhile, in 1934 gates at the Glebe Road entrance were hung, and new offices for the OTC were ready. The following year the sports pavilion was rebuilt.

On 8 October 1934 Grose-Hodge addressed the options in the lecture theatre, reminding them, according to a notebook kept by W D H Moore, head of school 1934-5 [5], of their responsibility 'as officers of the school' to 'report any cases of dishonesty, indecency and bullying'. The only 'unfortunate incident', Moore went on to record, was the sacking of a member of the 1st

XV; he had been out after lock-up in 'mufti'. Obviously the Head Master's admonition had been taken to heart, for shortly after his pep talk a boy who was both captain of boats and a pro-monitor was demoted, because, to keep up with his work, 'he cheated, and when he was discovered, lied to his form-master'. In 1936 another monitor was demoted to option for breaking out of the Sanitorium 'while suffering from mumps'.

Things were not looking too good among the hierarchy. C R D Danby, head of school 1936–7, thought that 'some of the monitors seemed to place pleasure before duty'. He recorded that 'a rather unfortunate incident' occurred during the last night of the school play. While wandering round the galleries he discovered a pro-monitor and an option smoking. (It is amusing to recollect that in the seventeenth century it was compulsory at Eton to smoke, because it was thought to ward off the plague; boys were beaten for not smoking.) But worse was to follow. Another monitor 'appeared in court for an offence against girls, which might almost be termed immoral, and the Head Master had no other option than to ask him to leave.' [6] And all this levity despite the fact that in 1935 a partition between the monitors' room and a waiting room had been demolished to provide the monitors with more spacious and comfortable accommodation. 'The advantage', Moore wrote in his report book, 'was that monitors have found it less necessary to let off steam as they did in the old cage-like room, which certainly made us feel like wild beasts on occasions.'

EIGHT

Hitler's Oak

1935–1945

IN 1935 Humfrey Grose-Hodge instituted a major restructuring on the academic side. He felt that boys not yet twelve were too young to be pitchforked from the Inky into the Upper School, so the Lower School was created for boys between 11½ and 13½.[1] Considering that for many years they were taught in the Upper School building, it is surprising how the Lower School managed to create its own identity, with their own Head Master (Canon Perry, who was succeeded by Noel Sutcliffe) and their own boarding houses. Few boys who had gone into long trousers and waved the Inky goodbye would have agreed that the Lower School was 'the senior half of our Preparatory Department'.[2] What it was in practice was a group of some 200 boys too old for the Inky, too young for the Upper School, who were being groomed for public school life in a more measured manner than would have been the case had they remained until 13½ in a prep school elsewhere. Generous donations of sporting trophies enabled the new Lower School houses to compete in football, cricket, boxing, sports, gymnastics, fives and swimming.

There had been a boarding house for juniors called Castleside — too far distant from the school to be practical for small boys. It was sold in 1930 and Redburn, on the corner of Rothsay Gardens and Newnham Street, was purchased and enlarged, with the aim of eventually housing senior boys. Today it is the boarding house twinned with Paulo-Pontine. In 1936 the school was able to purchase a pair of houses in Pemberley Avenue adjacent to the school playing fields, one of them, No 28, having been the home of an Old Bedfordian, the Reverend Charles Farrar. In 1879 he was head of school, and became an early historian of the Harpur Trust. A major extension, providing a playroom and two large dormitories, was added, and so Farrar's came into existence for the use of Lower School and some older Inky boarders. It is now a senior house, renamed Phillpotts, and is twinned with St Cuthbert's.

Under its housemaster Noel Sutcliffe — Sooty to the boys, on account of his swarthy complexion — life at Farrar's could be rather an exhausting business. Married to a delightful wife, with two beautiful little boys, he was not averse to weilding the cane on youngsters, nor to interrogating some of them, at the age of twelve, about sex. He was a man of restless energy, forever getting up house entertainments and organising handicrafts; construction of balsawood airplanes in the garage was almost compulsory. The *Farrar's Gazette* for Easter 1945 reported several sightings of the chapel ghost — a headless soldier dressed in an army greatcoat — and some of the boys tackled that most tricky of all poetic forms, the Limerick, with commendable success:

> There was a young man of Cologne
> Who rang up a friend on the phone.
> I am sorry to say
> There was some slight delay
> For the number he dialled was his own.

It is a tribute to the stamina of boys of eleven and twelve that at Farrar's they endured harsh treatment yet produced creative magazines and house plays. If Sutcliffe caught a boy talking in the dormitory after lights out he would send him to the locker room to choose the gym shoe with which he was to be chastised. A boy who actually ran away was caned on his return, without ever being asked the cause of his unhappiness. Two house tutors at Farrar's could not have been in greater contrast. One was a German refugee by the sinister name of Schulhof, a born bully who took the boys for walks by literally pulling them along by their ears. He was mercifully succeeded by a sweet-natured archetypical prep school master, Bernard Pybus, who had a small bed-sitting-room near the dormitories and read books to the boys, like *The Invisible Man*. The boys were also allowed to listen to two seminal BBC radio shows, *ITMA* and *Much Binding in the Marsh*. Mr Pybus owned a clock presented to him by a previous school which struck on the quarter with the chimes of different churches; he also possessed a gramophone on which, with the aid of fibre needles he clipped as one might a cigar, he played 78s of Webster Booth, leaving his door open so that the lush tenor would lull the boys to sleep. Mr Pybus used to cycle back to Farrar's in the company of his Inky colleague Lyn Harman, and some of the romantically inclined Lower School boarders convinced themselves it could only be a matter of weeks before wedding bells were chiming as well as the bells in Mr Pybus's clock. But they were doomed to disappointment.

It was Grose-Hodge's practice to visit the boarding houses once a term, and after dining with the housemaster to interview each boy, and discuss with him his school report. On one such occasion, at Farrar's, the boys thought one of their number had taken leave of his senses, for he announced, with appropriate bravado, that he intended asking Grose-Hodge for his autograph. Into Sutcliffe's study he marched, bold as brass, to be confronted with a lecture on one of the worst reports he had ever received. Not in the least abashed, the brazen boy produced his autograph book and invited an astonished Head Master to sign it. 'There,' said Grose-Hodge, handing back the book, 'I've done something for you, haven't I?'

'Yes, Sir.'

'Then do something for me. *Work!*'

It was in 1936 that further consideration was given to the needs of day boys, by the erection of a new building to the south of the Howard Building, to supplement changing and recreational facilities for boys living too far away from home to return at midday. From now on they were known as day boarders, and their new quarters were named the Craig Building, in honour of a former president of the OB Club and chairman of the Governors, Sir Maurice Craig. The same year a new boarding house was added, Nash's at 3 De Parys Avenue, especially for the youngest Inky boys. It had been the home of Dr Gifford Nash, father of two Old Bedfordians and medical officer to several boarding houses, and its garden opened directly on to the Inky playing field.

For very young boys, life at Nash's in its early days could prove a trial. Home-sickness was forbidden, and the housemaster, Mr Thomas, was not averse to beating a boy of eight who turned up late for tea. Today Nash's provides friendly classrooms, boys who would previously have gone to Nash's or Farrar's being accommodated in Eagle House, a purpose-built junior boarding house at 9 De Parys Avenue.

It is perhaps worth recapping on the current boarding house situation. Including Eagle House, opened in 1993, there are seven, six of which are senior houses, all six being linked to a school house: Sanderson's, in Rothsay Place (Ashburnham); Burnaby, in Burnaby Road (Bromham); Pemberley, in Pemberley Avenue (Crescent); Redburn, in Rothsay Gardens (Paulo-Pontine); Phillpotts, in Pemberley Avenue (St Cuthbert's); and Talbot's, in De Parys Avenue (St Peter's). In addition, there are now day houses with facilities for day boys, Crescent having the use of the Craig Building, for instance. Two day houses, for Bromham and St Cuthbert's, have been named after former Head Masters, Brown and Carter respectively.

Boarding houses were originally owned by the housemasters, but during the 1920s, as housemasters retired, Reginald Carter had been gradually buying them up for the school. Eventually they all came under the umbrella of the Boarding House Trust. And until the early 1990s the school adopted the extraordinary practice of collecting boarders' fees and, while retaining the boarding portion, passing on the boarders' tuition fees to the Harpur Trust. The Head Master who arrived in 1990, Philip Evans, abolished the Boarding House Trust, and the boarding houses are now run as part of the Harpur Trust. Hence there are savings in the auditing of accounts and the houses benefit from the financial resources of the Trust.

By 1936 it was becoming apparent to politicians whose heads were not firmly buried in the sand that Nazi Germany was preparing for expansionism, by peaceful annexation if possible, by force if need be. Hitler had already risen to power as Chancellor via a bloodbath. Yet so desperate was the rest of the world for peace that sportsmen were happy to converge on Berlin for the 1936 Olympics, an event put to major political advantage by the Nazi Party. Among them was an Old Bedfordian, Jack Beresford, possibly the greatest oarsman, certainly one of the greatest scullers, of all time. Born in 1899 and at Bedford School 1913-17, Beresford won a medal in every Olympic Games between 1920 and 1932, rowing in the single sculls at Antwerp, for which he won a silver medal, again in the single sculls at Paris, winning a gold medal. At Amsterdam in 1928, in the Eights, he won a silver medal, and a gold medal in 1932 at Los Angeles in the coxless Fours. These achievements were all in addition to the cups awarded to him at Henley, and the silver medal he won as a single sculler at the Empire Games in 1930, held in Ontario. Nothing if not versatile, Beresford, in the company of Leslie Southwood, who stroked, won the double sculls in Berlin, and was presented by Hitler with an oak sapling. This he duly handed over to Humfrey Grose-Hodge, decked out in gown and mortar board for the ceremony, and initially it was planted near the Phillpotts Gates. As events in Europe began to take a decided turn for the worse, such conspicuous evidence of German goodwill was quietly uprooted and replanted behind the gymnasium. Here it flourished until the plot was required for the present sports complex, when orders were given to have the alien tree cut down.

In September 1935 Hitler had stripped German Jews of their nationality, and on 7 March 1936 his troops had reoccupied the demilitarized zone of the Rhineland. So it may perhaps be thought, and not just with the benefit of hindsight, that the most extraordinary happening of 1936 was a visit to Bedford School from a contingent of the Hitler Youth. This astonishing event occurred on 28 November, when 'a party of young German men and women from Hanover visited the School and gave us a delightful entertainment, consisting of music, singing and dancing. They marched on to the platform in file and at a command from their leader, they turned their faces, brimming with health and vigour, upon their admiring audience. The men in brown shirts and black shorts, and the women in white blouses and dark skirts, they brought with them the atmosphere of modern Germany.' This ecstatic account, published in the *Ousel* on 16 December 1936, might have been written by that German master of propaganda, Joseph Goebbels, himself. They sang a cantata, a helpful note in the programme supplying a translation: 'All that is old and weak has to go. Farmer, worker and soldier are the pillars of the new realm. The flag is its symbol, is the sign of unity. We all follow it. With confidence we march into the future.' They might as well have added, 'into Czechoslovakia'. The leader of the Nazi visitors, Herr Helms, explained that all the songs with which they were happy to entertain the boys of Bedford School 'were the songs of Hitler Youth, and were all written by young Germans between the ages of twenty-two and twenty-seven'. Apparently an atmosphere of 'gaiety and merriment' pervaded the second half of the entertainment, 'just as patriotic zeal had characterised the first, and it was with great regret that, after an address of thanks in German by the Head of the School, we saw them leave the platform. They marched this time to the tune of the accordion, the strains of which were lost in the noise of enthusiastic applause.'

The visit of the Hitler Youth had in fact been organised by a teacher of German, Fritz Carling, an open admirer of Hitler; in his classroom he displayed swastikas and photographs of the Führer, and he even wore his hair in the manner of Hitler. Aga Hodges thought Carling a traitor even before the arrival of the Hitler Youth; and Grose-Hodge had incurred Aga's displeasure — to put it mildly — by handing over to Carling his German class. Grose-Hodge's tolerance, if not active encouragement, of Carling's pro-Nazi sympathies (the Hitler Youth visit would have been endorsed by Grose-Hodge) persuaded Aga that Grose-Hodge was not to be trusted, that in fact he too was a traitor. After serving under three Head Masters, Carter, Grose-Hodge and Clarence Seaman, Aga one day, in retirement, delivered his considered verdict on Grose-Hodge. 'When I think of Grose-Hodge,' he spluttered, 'I think of him with horror. And when I say horror' — his voice now on a par with any chapel choir treble — 'I mean *horror!*'

But the visit of the Hitler Youth would have been an occasion of especial gratification to an Old Bedfordian who entered the school in 1919 as Norman Wright. Having changed his name to Baillie-Stewart on the eve of joining the Seaforth Highlanders between the two world wars, Norman Baillie-Stewart achieved notoriety as the 'Officer in the Tower', the Tower in question being the oldest prison in England, the Tower of London, particularly reserved for traitors. According to an account of Baillie-Stewart's less than brilliant career, either as army officer, spy or — as he claimed — double agent, contributed to the *Ousel* in March 1997 by David Heald, Baillie-Stewart had 'his first brush' with MI5 in 1932, 'when he was arrested for allegedly selling secrets about

British army vehicles to a mysterious blonde German woman known as "Marie-Louise"'. It seems that he claimed the paltry £90 he received 'was in return for amorous favours rendered in a Berlin public park', but payment for transactions of this nature are more usually made by the man. And surely Baillie-Stewart was not short of the price of a hotel bedroom?

But the chances are his entire life was a web of deceit and invention. It was in 1933 that he was court martialled and sent to the Tower. On his release in 1937 he moved to Germany and applied for German citizenship, so his claim to have assisted Jews to escape can be taken with a very large pinch of salt indeed; you do not accept another country's nationality only to risk immediate execution, unless of course you really are a second Scarlet Pimpernel, and the only person who ever believed he was that was Baillie-Stewart himself.

By 1940 Baillie-Stewart was broadcasting pro-German propaganda to Britain, and when he was arrested in 1945 in Austria by American Counter-Intelligence he claimed in his defence that he was entitled to broadcast in the way he did as he was a naturalized German. Nevertheless it was planned to put him on trial for high treason, a charge the Attorney-General, Hartley Shawcross, thought, on reflection, might not stick, and he was lucky only to be found guilty of an infringement of wartime Defence Regulations and to go down for five years. On his release from prison he removed himself to Ireland, 'made a living selling Wild West stories', and all too appropriately died, in 1966, in a Dublin bar. 'Norman Ballie-Stewart, OB,' Dr Heald concludes, 'was a figure at once somewhat ridiculous and pathetic, but also in a way romantic and glamorous', which under the circumstances is a pretty generous verdict. Aga Hodges would have dubbed him a rotter.

Born in 1926, and according to a 1944 edition of the *Ousel* 'endowed with an unusually attractive personality and a natural dignity', a boy called John Fowles obtained a House Exhibition to Bedford in the Christmas term of 1939, when he was thirteen. For a future novelist he did well academically, gaining two Higher Certificates during three terms in the Sixth Form, although in 1974 he told *The Times* he had been 'in a cram class, and I think we were worked savagely hard. And there was the general shock of boarding school … the brutality. Not that it was worse than anywhere else. One was caned or beaten with a slipper regularly every month. I really hated it like poison.'

Fowles was in Burnaby, and at the age of fifteen he suffered what he has termed 'a sort of nervous breakdown', caused by 'not being able to cope'. He spent a term at home, and although he may have 'hated it like poison' in retrospect, on his return to school he received emotional and educational support from Aga Hodges and became captain of cricket, head of school, and an eager adolescent supporter of the status quo. But had he remained, in quieter and older reflection, an uncritical advocate of 'the public school system' he might never have written, as he did in 1969, *The French Lieutenant's Woman*, or fifteen years later *The Ebony Tower*. In 1989 John Fowles, who had been living a reclusive life for many years, suffered a stroke, and by 1998 he was making plans to ensure that after his death his home at Lyme Regis, the setting for *The French Lieutenant's Woman*, should become a retreat for writers. Equally distinguished as a man of letters, John Armstrong, at school 1920-29, became editor of the *Encyclopedia Britannica*. Robin Clarke (1944-55) was editor of the *New Scientist*, and in 1995 John Witherow, at school 1965-70, became editor of the *Sunday Times*.

By the time war broke out in 1939, doubtless to the surprise of those who had so recently applauded the Hitler Youth, Grose-Hodge, now aged forty-eight, was well into his stride as Head Master. Like Carter, he had to brace himself for the loss of boys he had taught (268 in the event), and with air raids even on Bedford a distinct possibility it was necessary to take precautions against enemy action. The ground floor rooms of boarding houses were reinforced with steel pillars, sandbags were filled and boys were instructed in fire drill. Soon sheep were discovered grazing on the playing fields, and shire horses arrived when it was time for haymaking. A Bedford School Pig Club was formed, and some eighty boys took instruction on the school field in tractor driving.

It was no time at all before Bedford was offering refuge to other schools. Victoria College in Jersey were forced to beat a hasty retreat, 44 of their boys being given accommodation by Bedford. In July 1940 boys from Rye Grammar School were evacuated to the town, and made use of Bedford's gymnasium, swimming pool, science laboratories and workshops; in 1945, back in their own premises, they invited Grose-Hodge to their Speech Day. The Victoria College boys were assimilated into Paulo-Pontine and retained a head boy of their own. They brought with them two masters and a prep school mistress, Victoria Aubrey, whose teaching career spanned some 60 years. It is more than likely that Grose-Hodge's hand was at work in framing a Latin plaque commemorating the wartime collaboration of Victoria College and Bedford School. Fixed to the east end of the Great Hall, it miraculously survived the fire of 1979, and can now be seen near the Head Master's study. It reads:

A barbaris domo expulsi
Ab humanis in alteram
recepti domum
nunc, ut victoriam
reddidit deus
hospites hospitibus
gratias agimus
Victoriae Collegii alumni

By this time the OTC had been renamed the Junior Training Corps, and according to the 1941 *Year Book* of the Old Bedfordians Club, members of the JTC had been 'mounting guard on the School buildings, ready to deal with any paratroopers that might land on the ground'. They were ready to pounce on them, perhaps, and wrap them up in their parachutes, but the boys would not have been issued with live ammunition. An Air Training branch of the JTC was formed, and no fewer than 17 masters were called up for military service. This meant that even the Upper School, previously an all-male preserve, had to fall back on recruiting female staff, among them two Oxford graduates, of Somerville and St Hilda's. The widow of an RAF pilot who became a biology mistress married Bob Symonds, coach of the 1st VIII and Harry Mac's successor as housemaster of Sanderson's.

Bishop David Farmbrough found conditions at Talbot's in September 1942 'pretty poor. Mice would come out into the commonroom when it was quiet during prep to scavenge for crumbs. Food was pretty sparse and basic. At the beginning of my time at Talbot's Renwick had a housekeeper — a somewhat unpleasant woman. Each week she used to ask a boy to take a parcel to the post office for her. After a time we became suspicious and daringly opened a parcel to find it contained our rations of butter, tea, bacon and so on, being sent to her sister. Renwick was told and sacked her. We all had one hot bath a week and a cold bath in the morning during my first year or two. One bath was filled and a monitor stood by to ensure everyone went through it.

'During air raids at night we had to go down into the changing rooms/ lavatories and sleep on mattresses on the floor … Among wartime chores was being taken by lorry during September and October out to local farms to help pick potatoes, and in school to help move grass from the playing field to a silo which was built where the dining halls now stand.'

Despite wartime privation — one pound of jam a month per person, tiny rations of meat, butter and sugar — senior boys retained sufficient energy for there to be no let up in the rituals of pre-war boarding house life. Bishop Farmbrough recalls, 'Fagging was still the normal thing, and the first year was quite tough. Any monitor could call "fag" at any time and the last fag to get to him had to take the chore he wanted done. We lived in the commonroom on the edge of our chairs waiting to leap up. We also had a personal fag master, and we had to clean his shoes, sport and JTC kit etc. There was quite a lot of slipper beating and caning. For caning by the Head of House the commonroom was cleared so that he had a good run at the victim.'[3] Bedford slang for a beating was a swishing; the number of swishes you received was the number of cuts or strokes.

A boy at Talbot's two years senior to David Farmbrough whom he would have known, although probably not well (two years difference in age in those days could act as a chasm when it came to friendships), was a future Liberal MP and life peer, Stephen Ross. Stephen was the son of an Old Bedfordian, Reginald Ross, at school from 1904-14, who served with the Rifle Brigade in the First World War and was awarded an MC (he died in 1970). Stephen was at Bedford from 1939-43, arriving from his London prep school with a 'very good character'. He became articled to a firm of chartered surveyors on the Isle of Wight, bought a small farm, became a county councillor and stood for parliament, unsuccessfully, in 1966 and again in 1970. His dogged determination to enter the House of Commons paid off in 1974 when he caused a sensation by overturning a Conservative majority of 17,000. He became Liberal Party defence spokesman, and with all-party support he steered the Housing (Homeless People) Bill through the Commons. His majority on the Isle of Wight gradually slipped back to realistic figures, but in 1983 he managed to retain the seat by 3,503 votes. His Tory opponent was the young Virginia Bottomley. Ross had backed David Steel as party leader after the dramatic resignation of Jeremy Thorpe, and on his retirement from the Commons in 1987 Steel recommended Stephen Ross for a peerage. He died in 1993, at the age of sixty-six.

A wartime evacuation to Bedford in 1941, to which the school was sworn to secrecy, was that of the BBC Symphony Orchestra. Having been bombed out of temporary premises in Bristol, one of the first cities to receive devastating air raids, both the BBC Symphony and Theatre Orchestras sought shelter in the Great Hall, from where a large number of broadcasts were made, under the batons of Adrian Boult, Clarence Raybould and Stanford Robinson. Prokofiev's score for *Alexander Nevsky* received its first performance at the school on 8 December 1941, conducted by Sir Adrian Boult, and with Peggy Ashcroft, Leon Quartermaine and Robert Donat taking part. Even the 1944 Promenade Concerts were transferred to the Great Hall, with a visit from Sir Henry Wood himself. Soloists who performed at Bedford included Harriet Cohen and Yehudi Menuhin, and a jig composed by the school's director of music, Dr William Probert-Jones, was performed on 28 February 1942 when the Symphony Orchestra laid on a private concert for the school. The summer of 1943 saw a visit from the distinguished music critic Edward Sackville-West, a war-time producer and music assistant at the BBC. A recording of Elgar's Second Symphony made in the Great Hall by Boult in the autumn of 1944 — it was a work with which Boult had been closely associated since giving a masterly performance in 1920 in the presence of Sir Edward and Lady Elgar — was acclaimed by Compton Mackenzie in the *Gramophone*, who wrote that he did not know 'a better piece of recording', as much a tribute to Phillpotts's architect as to the BBC Symphony Orchestra. In gratitude for wartime hospitality, on 20 July 1961 Sir Adrian Boult returned to open the music school.

Early in 1942 morning service was broadcast to Europe from the school chapel, Grose-Hodge giving an address. In the spring of 1944 the Head Master broadcast to Old Bedfordians on active service overseas, and in June the following year he gave a talk on the Home Service titled 'Shall I Become a Schoolmaster?' After the war, Grose-Hodge, who had published his best known book, *Roman Panorama*, in 1944, was invited to be an occasional contributor to the BBC Brains Trust.

The war saw two informal visits from royalty. On 10 June 1942 Queen Marie of Yugoslavia, who is buried at Windsor, dined with the Grose-Hodges at School House before attending a concert in aid of Yugoslav Week and a reception afterwards in the Head Master's study. The following morning the Queen made a tour of inspection, visiting the workshops, the gym, the swimming pool and the Memorial Hall, where she signed the Visitors' Book; as did the Duchess of Gloucester, on 9 February 1944, during a visit to inspect contingents of the Red Cross and St John's Ambulance in the Great Hall.

By now the war was taking its toll of Old Bedfordians, but not in such devastating numbers as in the Great War. A posthumous George Cross was awarded to Commander R F Jolly, at school 1907-14, and the George Medal was won by Major M E Smith (1925-35). A Major General in the Indian Army, H R Briggs, received two bars to his DSO (he had an MC as well), and six OBs received a bar to their DSO; in addition, forty-one OBs won the DSO. Fourteen OBs won the DSC, of whom three were awarded a bar. A midshipman in the Merchant Navy won the DSM. A chaplain to the New Zealand Forces, the Reverend F O Dawson, at school 1922-25, received the MC and bar, a very astonishing achievement for a non-combatant officer. Two other OBs won an MC and bar, and a further sixty-three the MC. Two non-commissioned OBs, both corporals, won the MM. Thirty-eight DFCs were awarded to OBs, four of whom won a bar. The DFM went to another non-commissioned OB, a flight sergeant, and five OBs were awarded the AFC. Two-hundred and seventy-four Old Bedfordians were mentioned in dispatches, and foreign orders and decorations were conferred on 41 OBs, by Belgium, France, Greece, Luxembourg, the Netherlands, Poland, Russia and the USA.

The greatest excitement of the war was the announcement in the *London Gazette* on 18 May 1944 that Lt Col Henry Foote, DSO, at school from 1918-23, had been awarded the Victoria Cross. It will come as no surprise to learn that the school was granted an extra half-holiday. Born on 5 December 1904 at Ishapur in Bengal, Foote was brought to England at the age of $2^1/2$ in the care of an Ayah, following the death of his mother when he was only fifteen months old. His father, a Royal Artillery officer, no doubt chose Bedford for his son because of its Anglo-Indian connections. He became a boarder at

Glanyrafon, a school monitor, head of his house and, in 1923, a recipient of the Tarbutt prize for being the best all-round boy of his year. Tarbutt Memorial prizes were also awarded to boys who by their own example had encouraged others to develop their talents. As with Heriz-Smith's cigarette box, the actual prize Foote was given might raise a few eyebrows today; it was a silver cigarette case.

Told by Reginald Carter that he had not a hope of passing the Army entrance examination, Foote gained 56th place out of some 500 candidates, and entered Sandhurst, where he applied to join the Royal Tank Corps, later the Royal Tank Regiment. His first posting was to the 3rd Battalion at Lydd in Kent, where tradition demanded that the subalterns put on a fancy dress show at the conclusion of a guest night. Foote unwisely chose the costume of a pantomime fairy, and was known throughout his distinguished army career as Fairy Foote.

By 1942 Foote held the acting rank of Lieutenant Colonel, and for 'outstanding gallantry and stern application to duty' at Sidi Suliman Bu Ali, on 4 June 1942, he had been awarded the DSO. His citation, signed by the commander of 32 Army Tank Brigade, who had witnessed Foote's heroism, explained that although Foote's tank had been blown up in a minefield he 'continued to direct the fight on his feet in the face of heavy machine gun fire from "dug in" infantry'. Ordered to go to the assistance of a unit in severe trouble, he proceeded to lead his own tanks on foot, 'and on arrival took command of all the tanks in the area. He stabilised the position and reorganised protection for our infantry ... his name was a byword amongst all the tank crews who feared for his personal safety as he was without a tank. I feel that it was his inspiration which saved the whole of our attacking force from being overrun by superior forces. He is,' the brigadier, who had himself been awarded the DSO and the MC, concluded, 'a very valiant officer'.

Foote's amazing bravery on that occasion was but a dress rehearsal for his actions covering the period 27 May-15 June the same year, for which, so soon afterwards, he won the Victoria Cross; the reason for the delay in the announcement of the award was because Foote, together with vital witnesses to his actions, had been taken prisoner, and it was only after he had escaped from an Italian camp that he heard about it — while listening to the wireless.

On 6 June 1942, during ferocious fighting against Rommel in the protracted battle of Gazala, Foote's tank was again knocked out, and while changing to another tank he was wounded in the neck. Regardless of pain and danger, he continued to lead his battalion from an exposed position on the outside of someone else's tank. That tank, in turn, was lost, so Foote did exactly what he had done before, carried on commanding and leading a tank battalion on foot, 'encouraging his men by his splendid example. By dusk,' this second citation went on, 'Lieutenant Colonel Foote, by his brilliant leadership, had defeated the enemy's attempt to encircle two of our Divisions.'

Six days later, Foote was ordered to delay the enemy tanks so that the Guards Brigade could be withdrawn. The first wave of British tanks having been destroyed, Foote 'reorganised the remaining tanks, going on foot from one tank to another to encourage the crews under intense artillery and anti-tank fire. As it was of vital importance that his battalion should not give ground, Lieutenant Colonel Foote placed his tank, which he had re-entered, in front of the others so that he could be plainly visible in the turret as an encouragement to the other crews, in spite of the tank being badly damaged by shell fire and all its guns rendered useless. By his magnificent example the corridor was kept open and the Brigade was able to march through.'

The citation for Foote's VC concluded: 'Lieutenant Colonel Foote was always at the crucial point at the right moment, and over a period of several days gave an example of outstanding courage and leadership which it would have been difficult to surpass. His name was a byword for bravery and leadership throughout the Brigade.'

A DSO is sometimes awarded to the colonel of a regiment or battalion in recognition of general and outstanding valour displayed by his entire unit. But not the VC. Foote's Victoria Cross was received for acts of individual and supreme courage of which legends are made. As is commonly the case with heroes, he was the most modest of men. He was promoted Major General in 1951 and appointed CB the following year. On 6 June 1962 he returned to the school to open a new miniature rifle range, and on 30 September 1986 he appeared on the BBC television programme *This Is Your Life*. From 1968 until his death in 1993 Foote served as vice-chairman of the Victoria Cross and George Cross Association, and asked to be buried in his parish churchyard, St Mary's, West Chiltington, in Sussex, as near as possible to a former rector, G H Woolley, who had won the VC in Belgium in 1915. His widow, Audrey Foote, has retained a set of the General's miniature decorations and medals but has presented his Victoria Cross, Distinguished Service Order, campaign medals and the insignia of the Companionship of the Order of the Bath to the Royal Tank Regiment.

A very odd set of coincidences marked the army career of General Foote and his Glanyrafon fag, a boy named Bill Liardet. Like Foote, Bill Liardet was really called Henry. He followed Foote into the Royal Tank Regiment, fought in the Western Desert, was awarded the DSO, appointed CB, also became a Major General, and, as if that was not enough, having been born two years later than his old fag master, he died two years after him.

It was ironic that after having been left alone by the Luftwaffe, and with only nine weeks left before the war in Europe was to come to an end, the main school building should have caught fire. On the evening of 28 February 1945 the roof was suddenly found to be well and truly alight. At the end of the day, more damage was caused by water than heat, but it took nine fire engines two hours to locate the seat of the blaze and finally to extinguish it. By the time the first fire engine arrived on the scene the beams supporting the roof of the south side were ablaze from end to end. It was of course already dark when the fire was spotted, and searchlights had to be trained on the roof to help direct the rescue operations. Had the flames spread to the roof of the Great Hall the entire building would almost certainly have been lost. As it was, fanned by a moderate west wind the fire, for which no cause was ever ascertained, swept in an inferno between the roof and the ceilings of every classroom in the top gallery.

Three monitors were the first on the scene, trying, even before the fire brigade had arrived, to locate the centre of the blaze. Soon boys from Burnaby were racing from their house to rescue chairs, tables and portraits from the Hall. They were joined by masters, other boys, parents and Old Bedfordians in a mad scramble to carry out papers from the Bell Room, books and furniture from the Head Master's study, libraries from classrooms, orchestral instruments and two grand pianos. And all the while gallons of water were cascading down the stairs, until Grose-Hodge's study and the Bell Room were flooded. After they had extinguished the flames, the firemen remained behind to help dam the flood with sandbags and to sweep away some of the water.

In the early hours of 1 March a monitor and 20 other boys turned up to arrange the furniture in the Great Hall, and at 9 o'clock prayers Grose-Hodge, who had been up all night, walked on to the platform as if nothing had happened. All non-academic activities continued uninterrupted; class work was suspended until the following Monday, until such time, in fact, as the Fifth and Sixth Forms had carried out salvage work. It was vital that all sodden material should be removed from the top gallery before the water it held could soak through to do more damage, and tons of debris were carried down in buckets by boys whose reward, from time to time, was the pleasure of hurling irreparably charred desks out of the windows. Damage to the structure of Phillpotts's building had been contained to just five classrooms and a large southern area of the roof, and anyone who had witnessed the intensity of the flames and the height to which they soared might well have attributed the final outcome to nothing less than a miracle. Tarpaulins covered the roof initially; scorched timbers had to be hacked away and loose tiles removed; and by the end of the summer holidays restoration work had been completed.

The school had broken up for Easter in the usual way, and was due to reassemble for the summer term on 8 May. Victory in Europe intervened, however, with the surrender on 4 May by the German High Command to General Montgomery of all German forces in north-west Germany, Denmark and Holland (the final capitulation was signed on 7 May), and term started on 10 May, with the school in festive mood.

On her visit to the school in 1952 to commemorate the 400th anniversary of its foundation Princess Margaret received a bouquet from an Inky boy, eight-year-old Nicholas Hubbard. On the right is the recently appointed Head Master, Clarence Seaman, and in the background the head of school, Anthony Stearns, and the Vice-Master, H. Boys-Stones

Photograph: Bedfordshire Times

136

After opening the new school dining halls in 1966, Queen Elizabeth the Queen Mother
enjoys afternoon tea with some of the senior boys
Photograph: Central Press

Opposite top In 1957 the Duke of Edinburgh paid a visit to the
Bedford School Holborn Boys Club
Photograph: Hornsey Journal

Below Sir Adrian Boult, whose BBC Symphony Orchestra broadcast from
Bedford School during the Second World War, returns
to rehearse the school orchestra
Photograph: F. Jewell-Harrison

Above An evocative view of the school
playing fields from the pavilion
Photograph: F. Jewell-Harrison

Right William Brown, so far the only Old
Bedfordian to have been appointed Head
Master. He served from 1955 to 1975

Above John Eyre, a charismatic theatre producer and history master revered by many famous Old Boys taught by him. His 1958 History VIth included, back row on the right, Quentin Skinner, destined to become Regius Professor of Modern History at Cambridge

Left Richard Roseveare, Vice-Master from 1973 to 1977, and for 15 years a popular housemaster of Redburn

Boys and masters stand aghast as an arson attack in 1979 guts the main school building
Photograph: Bedford County Press

Right The Great Hall of James Phillpotts's school building in the aftermath of the fire

The south front of the new school building dating from 1981, seen from the Prep School playing fields. On the left is the Recreation Centre, built at the same time; on the right, the dining halls, opened in 1966

NINE

Taught to the Highest Standards

1945–1952

THE WAR had resulted in extensive damage to property in Holborn, and until bomb damage was cleared away, sites levelled and new office blocks built, funds available from the Harpur endowment were drastically reduced. Income for 1938-9 had been £35,527; by October 1940 rent arrears had already reached £3,650. In July 1941 arrears of rent to the tune of £5,128 amounted to 14 per cent of potential income. By the time the rent roll had fallen in 1942-3 to £12,447 it had reverted to the levels of 1825-67.

In 1947 the Harpur Trust let land in Theobald's Road on a building lease, on which Adastral House and Lacon House were built, at a ground rent of £9,572. For a good many years opinion in the Trust was divided over the wisdom of selling the freehold. Voting in 1954 was to accept; at the next meeting the resolution was rescinded, but in 1962 the sale went through for £222,000. By this time, rents exceeded £60,000, and four years later they reached £100,000, a figure, thanks to the demand for office accommodation in Holborn, which by the next decade had exceeded £230,000. [1]

Holborn rents, or the lack of them, were not the only immediate post-war problem. A decision had to be made whether to apply for Government Direct Grant 'and with it, the new regulations, which would reduce the School once more to the status and functions of a local grammar school, or to reject the grant, raise the fees, and apply for recognition as an Independent School'. [2] By a majority decision, the Governors voted for Independence. The debate that raged throughout the country about Independence versus direct grant was largely one based on snobbery. West End audiences had fallen about during the course of a play on the subject, because an elementary school boy sent to a public school had disgraced himself by flushing a kipper down the lavatory. As

143

an Independent school, Bedford was committed to taking 10 per cent of elementary schoolboys; direct grant would have meant 50 per cent. An article in the 1939-45 *Supplement to the Ousel* did not mince words. 'This would, we believe, have changed the whole character of the School. The Board, or we should now say the Ministry, spoke of awarding fifty per cent of places in all Direct Grant schools. But whose places? Our School was full, we could not be fuller. If more boys came from Elementary Schools, fewer boys could come from Preparatory Schools, and very much (sic) fewer, incidentally, from our own Preparatory School. If places in the Lower School must be found for seventy-five elementary schoolboys every year instead of for fifteen, only another twenty-five or so would be left for our Preparatory School instead of the sixty or more places which it needed. To what school was it proposed that the remaining thirty-five members of our First Forms should be transferred?' As half the school's income would have come from the County Council it was concluded that as 'he who pays the piper calls the tune our income would have been safe, but our freedom would have gone'.

On 18 May 1945 Humfrey Grose-Hodge convened a meeting in the Great Hall, to which he invited 'the fathers and mothers' of all Bedford boys and High School girls to hear their views about Independence, for if the schools retained Independence fees would have to be raised. He took the opportunity of Speech Day on 28 June the following year to spell out his own position on the matter. He said he regarded the re-establishment of the school's independence as the most important event within living memory. As Grose-Hodge's own living memory went back, inter alia, to the defeat of Germany in 1918 that remark places in perspective the vehemence with which the battle over Independence had been waged. He said he was sorry that the issue had aroused opposition — or rather, that opposition had been aroused against Independence. But, he claimed, opposition had not come from those most nearly concerned. He had believed at the time that it was right for the school to remain Independent, he believed it even more strongly now, and he was confident that the future would prove it. 'You see,' he said, 'I personally believe in liberty. And as the school is fuller, and its waiting-lists are longer, than ever before it would appear that the general public, with whom, after all, the last word rests, believe in liberty too'.

The guest of honour invited to this Speech Day was the victor of another of the decisive battles of history, whose defeat of Rommel at El Alamain had restored British morale and turned around the tide of war in the Middle East. General Sir Bernard Montgomery, now ennobled as a viscount and with a Field Marshal's baton in his knapsack, arrived wearing battle dress, and told the school he had brought with him two books recently written by himself. One was the story of the Eighth Army from the time when he took command in Egypt in 1942. The other was the story of the armies which went to Normandy.

'A great many people today,' the Field Marshal explained, in a typical Monty staccato burst of egotism, 'write a great many books about these things. I won't say anything about that. All I would say is that these two books are true, and what is in them is factually accurate. They are not accessible to the general public, but I felt that I would like to present them to Bedford School as a small token of my esteem. I have written inside each one an inscription and I hope the books will be placed in the school library.'

After lunch the Field Marshal watched a cricket match, which 'started all in favour of the OBs, because owing to a mistake the School team (with the exception of the Farmer-Wrights) had lunch at home instead of in the Pavilion. The result of this was that those present had double rations.' ³ The score was 143 runs for eight wickets declared by the OBs, 64 runs for seven wickets knocked up by the school. Monty had tea at School House, according to a photograph caption in the *Ousel*; in the Pavilion, according to a report in the same issue. Perhaps he had two teas. At all events, he stayed on for the OB dinner that night held in the Great Hall; it was a major post-war reunion, and he was only one of two Field Marshals to attend, the other being an OB, Sir Cyril Deverell. Not to be outdone, the air force produced an Old Bedfordian Marshal of the Royal Air Force, Lord Newall. It seems the head of school, S Y Goudge, made 'one of the best speeches of the evening — brief, witty and admirably presented.'

It had not been too difficult for Grose-Hodge to induce Field Marshal Montgomery to attend Speech Day, for Monty held Bedford School in the highest regard. When he was appointed Chief of the Imperial General Staff at the conclusion of the war he had under him a team of thirteen high-ranking staff officers. No fewer than eight of them were Old Bedfordians: Brigadier E J B Buchanan (1907-10), Major General Sir Noel Holmes (1907-9), Major General H R Kerr (1909-14), Lieut General Sir Sidney Kirkman (1910-14), Major General L G Phillips (1906-10), Major General Sir Eustace Tickell (1905-11), General Sir Colville Wemyss (1900-9) and Lieut General F E W Simpson (1914-15). Simpson was later promoted General and knighted, and when he died in 1986 it was recalled that Montgomery, with whom Simpson had been closely associated for much of his service, had regarded him as the best staff officer he had ever met.

The school has produced so many distinguished service personnel it may seem invidious to highlight any, but certain names were mentioned in their day with bated breath. Marshal of the Royal Air Force Sir Thomas Pike, at school

1915-23, was Chief of the Air Staff at the same time that his elder brother, Lt General Sir William Pike, was Vice-Chief of the Imperial General Staff. In 1941 he was awarded the DFC and bar and crowned his career by serving as deputy supreme allied commander from 1963-67. He died in 1983 at the age of seventy-six. An Old Bedfordian Air Vice Marshal, and holder of the Air Force Cross, Sir Sefton Brancker (1891-94), died in the fire which destroyed the R101 at Beauvais in 1930, on its maiden flight to India. He was only fifty-three and for the past eight years had been Director of Civil Aviation at the Air Ministry. He had originally been commissioned from Woolwich in the Royal Artillery and in 1900 had been wounded and mentioned in dispatches in South Africa. Responsible for the first regular air service between London and Paris, until his untimely death Brancker had lived a charmed life, surviving two crash landings (one on the sea) and a motor accident in London in which he was injured.

One of the school's most famous sailors has to be Admiral of the Fleet Sir Michael Fanu, who entered the Inky in 1922 when he was nine, leaving to train at Dartmouth when he was fourteen. The family lived in Cornwall Road, so he only had a short walk to school, and in a speech he made some time after he had won the DSC in 1941 he recalled Bedford as populated always by god-like men, 'tall, athletic, virile, handsome and wearing enormous coloured scarves'. By the age of 31 he held the rank of Commander, and in 1968 he became First Sea Lord. Shortly before he was due to take up the appointment of Chief of the Defence Staff he contracted chronic lymphatic leukemia, and died at the age of fifty-seven. His biography, *Dry Ginger*, written by Richard Baker, appeared in 1977.

Another Old Bedfordian with outstanding gifts, Sir Pierson Dixon, had his life cut short, in 1965, at the age of sixty. Born in 1904, Pierson Dixon was at school 1916-23 and achieved one of the most prestigious diplomatic postings, as ambassador to Paris. He was a classical scholar, a novelist and a considerable sportsman. After the war he served as ambassador to Prague, and Sir Michael Burton's tenure of the Prague Embassy half a century later is a unique instance of two Old Bedfordians occupying the same embassy. Sir Pierson had accompanied Anthony Eden as principal private secretary to the wartime conferences at Yalta, Cairo, Quebec, Moscow and Potsdam, and in 1954 he succeeded Gladwyn Jebb as Permanent Representative at the United Nations. In 1950 he was Grose-Hodge's guest at Speech Day.

There was a fascinating postscript to Bedford's involvement in the second world war. A rash of adventure yarns included Eric Williams's *The Wooden Horse*, the tale of a daring escape from a prisoner of war camp in which one of the characters is called John Clinton. He was in reality an Old Bedfordian, Richard Codner, born in 1920 and at school from 1934-39. He was commissioned in the

Royal Artillery, captured in Tunisia, and was one of three prisoners of war to escape through a tunnel excavated while fellow prisoners diverted the attention of their German guards by taking exercise over a vaulting horse. After the escape, Codner was awarded the Military Cross, became assistant district officer in Tanjong Malim, and was killed in an ambush in Malaya in 1952.

Someone else who fought with great distinction during the war was John Durnford-Slater, destined for a military career after entering Wellington College at the age of thirteen. He was awarded the DSO and bar and by the age of only thirty-six he held the rank, in the Commandos, of brigadier. On leaving the army he looked around for suitable civilian employment, and joined the school as bursar. Naturally he also took charge of the CCF, but he found adjustment to civvy street a difficult one to make, and seems to have made little impression on those still alive who undoubtedly knew him. In 1953 he published his army memoirs, *Commando*, and following various bouts of emotional stress he very sadly committed suicide.

The immediate post-war years saw what the Boat Club's records describe as 'the start of a golden period'. The club was founded in 1860 by the Reverend J B Lee, the first race against Old Bedfordians taking place that year. By 1864 a school regatta had become a regular summer fixture, rowing being confined, between about 1867-90, to Fours. The school first appeared at Henley Regatta in 1879 in a new Fours event called the Public Schools' Challenge Cup, which Bedford succeeded in winning in 1881, beating Radley and Westminster. In 1931 the school entered the Ladies Plate, a trophy in the form of a ewer presented by the Ladies of Henley in 1846, losing to Monkton Coombe by a canvas in the quarter final. It was Princess Elizabeth who unwittingly opened up 'the golden period', a chapter of achievements which has never been surpassed. In 1946 she presented a new prize, the Princess Elizabeth Cup. It was an exciting time altogether, for there had been no regatta held at Henley since 1939, nor a regatta at Marlow during the war years.

At Marlow, in the 1946 Public Schools Race, the 2nd VIII beat St Edward's School, Oxford in their first heat and went on to win the trophy by defeating Radley by half a length. No doubt spurred on by the example of the 2nd VIII, two weeks later the 1st VIII, having entered for the first Princess Elizabeth Cup at Henley, beat a fast Cambridge crew, Christ's College, in their first race. Under very rough conditions following a violent thunderstorm they beat Eton in the second heat, and went on to defeat Radley in the final. Messages of congratulations poured in, including a sporting one from the Head Master of the Modern School, whose own 1st VIII had narrowly missed racing against Bedford in the final. 'It must be very gratifying,' he wrote, 'as it is unusual to bring off a double in the rowing world. Well done'.

The cup was presented by the princess herself, who was accompanied to the regatta by Princess Margaret, and the crew who were received by Princess Elizabeth got a rather closer view of her than they, and the rest of the school, had obtained on 14 February the previous year, when on a visit to the town the princess had driven into the school grounds through the Phillpotts Gates and straight out again through the Glebe Road Gates, just giving Humfrey Grose-Hodge time to raise his mortar board and call for three cheers. The princess's itinerary had in fact involved a reception in the morning at the Town Hall, lunch at the Swan and in the afternoon a visit to the Corn Exchange, where she took the salute at a Women's Land Army Rally. Rather than walk across from the Town Hall to the Swan she had driven up the High Street for the benefit of the town's people, and then up De Pary's Avenue and back to the Swan via Kimbolton Road — quite a detour.

Back at Henley in 1947, in the Princess Elizabeth Cup the 1st VIII met their old friendly rivals Shrewsbury in the final, and won. And in 1948 they pulled off a hat trick, beating Radley in the final. Three year later Bedford won the Princess Elizabeth Cup yet again, a triumphant achievement for their coach, Bob Symonds.

The 1946 1st VIII contained among its crew James Crowden, in his fifth and final year at the school. (Weighing in at 12 stone 3lb he was the heaviest boy in the boat.) The previous year he had been elected president of the Debating Society by thirty-three votes to twenty-two. The first thing he did was make an appeal for motions to be debated, and during his term of office the Society considered whether restrictions on the sale of drink and drugs were compatible with the rights of the individual; whether or not athletics played too important a part in modern education; whether the death penalty should be abolished; and whether civilisation had performed its task of civilising. Crowden was later to serve, for two years, as president of the Old Bedfordians Club. In 1970 he was pricked High Sheriff of Cambridgeshire, and in 1992 he was appointed Lord Lieutenant.

It was at another distinguished oarsman's funeral, on 10 June 1994, that James Crowden had the melancholy task of speaking. Michael Maltby, at school 1943-54, one of three brothers whose widowed mother had worked as matron at Sanderson's, had been killed in a disastrous helicopter crash which wiped out a large contingent of the Northern Ireland Intelligence Service. He had come into his own as an oarsman at Pembroke College, Cambridge, stroking the winning Cambridge crew in 1958 and becoming president of the University Boat Club the following year. He rowed in the first British crew to go to Russia since the Revolution, and while a master at Winchester he coached the 1st VIII.

Bedford School routine after the war had a distinct ring of déjà vu about it. In the summer of 1947 P E Barnes, head of school, was concerned about a wave of thefts during PT. He thought 'it rather pointed to someone in Talbot's but nothing concrete could be established'. The following year a monitor was 'deprived of his brown shoes' because he had been seen entering a café, and an option was dismissed because he had gone round boasting that he had attended a dance in St Neots. In April 1949 the school celebrated with a half-holiday when RSM Blincow was awarded the British Empire Medal. Half-holidays have been given for a variety of reasons, the best of all being stumbled upon when he was Head Master by William Brown; he ordered a half-holiday on 16 March 1956 'Because it is a lovely afternoon.'

Krishnan Srinivasan, who made a spectacular career as a diplomat, arrived in the Inky in 1947, at the age of ten. It is very remarkable that he recalls about his school days 'a great lack of fulfilment and under-achievement,' [4] for he became a Lower School option, an Upper School monitor and head of Sanderson's, winning his colours for boxing and cricket. His father was in the Indian Navy, and Srinivasan, who became his country's ambassador to the Netherlands and Foreign Secretary, and in 1995 was appointed deputy secretary-general to the Commonwealth Secretariat, has no recollection of any racial prejudice although he was one of only a handful of black or Asian boys at the time, and in 1951 he was the only overseas boy out of thirty-nine boys in Sanderson's. 'On the contrary,' he has said, 'I was an object of curiosity rather than prejudice, and I rather took advantage of that'. He was caned for being involved in a scrummage in the dormitory, swung a cane himself when he became a monitor, and remembers the brown shoes he wore 'with disgust'. At the age of 16 he renounced his Hindu religion and was baptised and confirmed in the school chapel. Although he thinks conditions at Sanderson's were 'very spartan' he had no hesitation in sending his own son to Bedford; but by that time something of a revolution had taken place. In 1996, in one senior boarding house alone, there were boys by the name of Songtavisin, Ahmad, Cheung Ng, Wu, Kawada, Damit, Katchi, Yakub, Muangsombut, Zain and Masri, and the school were employing auxiliary staff called Conte, Lepore, Martino, Sobek, Wisniewski and Salvatore. In the Prep School's Eagle House, in 1999, some half of the boys were from overseas.

Before the advent of communal dining halls, boarding houses were serviced by worthy women often disparagingly referred to by the boys as skivvies. There was a skivvy at Sanderson's who told the boys she had once been fabulously wealthy but had been fleeced by a fortune hunter. In an unpublished fragment of memoir, a boy who was in the house with this particular skivvy — and at the same time as Krishnan Srinivasan but three years his senior — has left a somewhat unappetising impression of life at Bedford as a boarder in the last years of Grose-Hodge's headmastership.

Hunger, cold and lack of privacy are my abiding memories of school. We slept in unheated dormitories with all the windows open, under two thin ex-army blankets. Without threepenny portions of chips, tipped into cone-shaped paper packets through which the fat oozed on to your fingers and then your handlebars, I doubt if I should have survived the hours between lunch and tea. For warmth we huddled, when the monitors allowed us to, in front of one intermittent coal fire in the commonroom, and when we were chucked out of there so that the tables could be laid for meals we congregated in the changing rooms, where at least the hot water pipes provided some degree of comfort.

There was only one study at Sanderson's, occupied by day by the head of the house and his deputy. The rest of us slept, worked and ate perpetually surrounded by the noise, distraction and intrusion of forty other boys, towards whom we were largely indifferent or actively hostile. I have always thought it particularly hard on anyone of my generation sent to prison who has not first been to a public school; inadequate and often uneatable food, mindless violence, carefully arranged discomfort, adherence to petty rules, inadequate sanitary arrangements and an insistence upon sometimes unbelievably stupid people being addressed as Sir were all endemic to school in my day, and prison should hold few terrors, and certainly no surprises, for any OB boarders over 50.[5]

There was felt to be something of a mystery about Grose-Hodge's decision to retire in 1951, just one year before the school was due to celebrate its 400th anniversary and Princess Margaret was scheduled to pay a visit; and had Grose-Hodge stayed on for those events, instead of landing a new Head Master in the middle of them in his first year, he would, in 1953, have clocked up his own quarter-century. It was generally understood he was diabetic, and had been advised by his doctor to go in 1951, when he would in any case be sixty, but sixty, at that time, would not have been a compulsory retirement age. Whatever the truth, he cannot have been too unwell in 1951, serving as a Governor of the Harpur Trust from 1956-61 and surviving retirement for a decade, although it is true that his last three years were clouded by pain and illness. He died, aged seventy, on 7 January 1962.

The school gave him what he had asked for, a watercolour by Paul Sandby, and in his farewell address he said how fortunate he was not only to have been happy at Bedford but to have known that he was happy. One can only hope that this was true. In so many ways he seemed an anachronism, more suited as Head Master to a smart, academically famous school like Winchester or Westminster. There were rumours, mainly spread by Aga Hodges, not the most reliable of witnesses where Grose-Hodge was concerned, that he had applied for other headmasterships. It is probably true to say that Grose-Hodge gave more to Bedford School than Bedford gave to Grose-Hodge. Despite the very hearty reputation it enjoyed in his time, he gave it dignity. When he arrived in 1928 there was no swimming pool and no proper gymnasium or science building; there was no regular school uniform. He presided over any occasion with a sureness of touch that marked him as a true professional. Although his meetings with boys tended to be conducted on the hoof, as he scurried from one engagement to another, he was a Head Master no boy ever forgot. 'Come along, dear boy, keep me company as far as such and such a place,' he would say to some scholar anxious for advice or information.

At bridge, as one might expect, he excelled, and according to an editorial in the *Ousel* for 10 March 1962 'he naturally expected to play most of the hands, and of course required absolute silence while he did so. Should his partner or an opponent unwarrantably take over for a hand, it afforded him an opportunity of talking authoritatively on some topic of the day. But as partner or opponent at any game he added greatly to its pleasure'.

Some of Grose-Hodge's remarks, delivered in a clippped, rather brusque, manner, seemed a bit pedantic. In reminding the school of a change in summer time he would advise them to wind their watches forward 11 hours rather than back one, in order not to damage the spring. 'The result, I am told, is the same,' a remark received with polite titters. Exhorting boys about to sit an exam, he would conclude, 'And now I wish you all what none of you should need, good luck'. He was fatherly in a paternalistic sort of way; no boy was confirmed without a private talk at School House. He seemed not so much aloof as lonely, his wife barely ever by his side. He walked everywhere; she rode a bicycle. Like Phillpotts, he had a brother who was also, for sixteen years, a master at the school, Geoffrey Grose-Hodge. They were an ill-fated family. Geoffrey died from a heart attack in class in 1952; one of his sons and his fiancée were killed in a car crash.

There was a ritual to be observed by boys who were leaving; they were expected to attend on Grose-Hodge in his study to say goodbye. To a boy who left the same term as he did, Grose-Hodge said, 'You've not been happy here, have you, dear boy?'

'No, Sir'.

'Believe me,' said Grose-Hodge, who had known the boy since he was eight, 'if there had been anything I could have done to have made you happier, I should have done it'.

It was a brave remark, to some extent an astonishing admission of failure, made, nonetheless, by a man who was without doubt a great Head Master, a verdict which surely deserves to stand notwithstanding Grose-Hodge's occasional, and rather surprising, lapses of judgement. He once announced that he intended reading a paper to the Mitre Club, who duly assembled at School

House, accompanied by four members of staff. They listened in something rather less than rapt attention to a dissertation on Robert Burton's 1621 worthy work the *Anatomy of Melancholy*, at the conclusion of which one of the masters, John Eyre, tried to open up a discussion by broadening the topic. Grose-Hodge appeared ill at ease, dismissed the boys, produced coffee for the four masters and said, 'Gentlemen, I have a confession to make. I know nothing about this subject whatsoever. The paper was written by my son'.

Grose-Hodge's character was nothing if not contradictory. To boys who achieved distinction at university he invariably wrote notes of congratulations, not always receiving the courtesy of a reply, and whilst it was probably not possible for any boy to be on intimate terms with him, he showed an unexpectedly pastoral side to his nature when in 1938 a family virtually destitute arrived at 25 St Augustine's Road; Mrs. Dorothy Parker and her two youngest sons, Alan and Peter. Her husband, an engineer, whose life was dogged by financial collapse, first in France, then Shanghai, was striving to re-establish himself in Africa; the boys, although cosmopolitan and bilingual, were a year behind with their education and there was no money to speak of. Yet Grose-Hodge admitted Alan and Peter as day boys, and when their eldest brother was killed flying with the RAF in 1940 Grose-Hodge was one of the first to offer Mrs Parker practical and emotional support.

Two other masters who took an interest in the family were Aga Hodges (perhaps because Peter, of whom he was particularly fond, had spent the first seven years of his life in France, the country to which Aga was emotionally drawn all his life) and Cyril Rhodes-Harrison, a Roman Catholic who eventually retired to Malta; he spotted in Peter an aspiring actor and recommended him for the role of Sir Toby Belch in *Twelfth Night*. It is a tribute to the support he received from Grose-Hodge in particular, as well as to his own outstanding abilities, that although Peter did not see his father for 10 years, and in 1944 was shattered by the death of his brother Alan whilst flying over Caen, he achieved, both at school and in later life, an enviably happy and successful career. Peter Parker, born in 1924 and fourteen when he entered Crescent, acquired his house colours for football, cricket, athletics, swimming and his favourite sport of all, boxing. He was a member of both the 1st XV and the 1st XI, and Grose-Hodge, who again went out of his way to care for Mrs Parker when Alan was killed, made him a monitor and agreed to his plea to be transferred from the Science Sixth to the History Sixth.

On leaving school in 1942, and while waiting to be called up, Peter Parker was billeted at Dulwich College and went each day to the London University's School of Oriental and African Studies to learn Japanese. It has stood him in good stead in business ever since. At the end of the war he was employed as an interpreter, and on demobilisation in 1947, aged twenty-three, he held the rank of major. From 1954-56 he was secretary of the Duke of Edinburgh's Study Conference on Human Problems of Industry, and was rewarded by the Queen in 1957 with the MVO, notwithstanding he had left the army a convinced left-winger, fighting the Bedford constituency in 1951 for Labour. (In 1985 Members of the Royal Victorian Order fourth class were converted retrospectively to Lieutenants.) Best remembered as chairman of the British Railways Board from 1976-83, Peter Parker was knighted in 1978, and in 1993 made KBE. He was at one time treasurer of Bedford House, and was invited as guest of honour to Speech Day by Ian Jones at a time when the school was being rebuilt after the fire of 1979. In 1989 he published his autobiography, *For Starters*, which contains practically no mention of his school days. Amazingly youthful in his seventies, Sir Peter Parker still radiates the charm and zest that enabled him to bounce out of Bedford burdened by impoverished parents and the loss of two brothers, but determined to shine on their behalf as well as his own. He has some adages which any boy intent on a career in business could do worse than memorize. 'Hire people cleverer than you are and delegate more than you think is good for you'. Another, even more apposite today: 'Learn one more language at least; it's never too late'.

Grose-Hodge's successor was a milder, more gentle person, Clarence Seaman. Born in 1908, he was already familiar with Bedford, and with responsibility. Educated at Christ's Hospital and St John's College, Oxford, he spent seven years — from 1932 to 1939 — as an assistant master at Bedford, and the next six years at Rugby. In 1945 he had been appointed Rector of The Edinburgh Academy. Someone who remembers being taken for a weekly divinity class when Seaman first taught at Bedford is Sir James Hennessy, who went straight into the Upper School in 1937, at the age of fourteen, as a Bromham day boy, boarding with an aunt in Linden Road. But his strongest recollection of his time at Bedford was of Grose-Hodge's early dynamic leadership. 'He was one of the best Head Masters you could have had, with gravitas,' he says. 'Everyone respected him. He wanted Bedford to become a leading public school'. [6]

James Hennessy, created KBE in 1982, is a good example of a boy of his time who did less than brilliantly at school but succeeded with distinction in later life. The most senior position he reached was junior option, and for a future diplomat his tuition in French from Aga Hodges left a good deal to be desired; he says that at school he learnt no French at all. In 1968 Hennessy entered the Prime Minister's Office, and from 1973 to 1976 he took on the unenviable role of High Commissioner to Uganda, keeping his bags permanently packed in case of the need to beat a hasty retreat from the unpredictable temper tantrums of the country's murderous despot Idi Amin. For 18 months he served as Governor of Belize and was agreeably surprised in 1982 to be invited to create the post of Chief Inspector of Prisons in England and Wales. From 1986-89 he served as president of the Old Bedfordians Club.

In 1951 Sir James Hennessy's divinity teacher, Clarence Seaman, took over a school with 964 pupils, a school steeped in sporting and athletic tradition, where boxing and rugger counted for more than academic achievements, and if Grose-Hodge had seemed an unlikely choice for such a school, what could one say about Seaman's appointment? Perhaps the Governors hoped he might bring some sense of refinement to Bedford. Both they and he were in for a shock. More than one sympathetic Old Bedfordian of the early 1950s believes that battling with Bedford's sometimes unruly mob of senior boys broke Mr Seaman's spirit, and within four years he had returned to his alma mater, where he spent fifteen years as a respected Head Master in altogether calmer waters. But he was only sixty-six when he died in 1974, after just four years of retirement, and all the indications are that he was never very strong physically; he may have been unwise to have taken on at Bedford what in many respects at that time resembled a rough house.

It would be quite misleading, however, to give the impression that the middle of the twentieth century was entirely an arid period at Bedford academically. As a healthy counter balance to the mania for sport there were, on the staff, at least two masters of distinction whose influence wrought untold benefit for boys who still hold their memories in deep respect. One was a classical scholar, Douglas Galbraith, who arrived in 1947, and put down such fertile roots that he remained on the staff for thirty-two years. His first task was to train up a succession of boys from the Classical Sixth fit to go to Oxford and Cambridge as Classical scholars and commoners. But there was scarcely a school society or function into which he did not throw his enthusiastic weight. The Mitre Club and the Debating Society benefited in particular from his open minded attitudes and generous fund of knowledge and anecdotes. Having served with the Royal Artillery during the war, he joined the JTC as a captain, and acted as chapel warden for nine years. He was briefly housemaster of Glanyrafon and for 15 years he looked after the day boarders. But outside the classroom the most outstanding achievements of this many faceted man were obtained on the towpath. Jangling with stopwatches, and recklessly careering along on his bike, he coached the 2nd VIII with such success that in 1963 he was elected to Leander for his services to rowing.

Galbraith's brother had died while at university, and the school became his entire life; he gave to its boys and masters not only legendary hospitality (he often took a table for Sunday lunch at the Swan) but quiet and unobtrusive financial support. He was in fact a rich man, and took pleasure in financing Hellenic cruises for the Sixth Form Classicists or in helping to purchase boats or effecting repairs to the chapel organ, and when he died in 1995 he bequeathed to the school a very considerable legacy, in addition to his home, No 2 Burnaby Road, now the school's medical centre. A boy who was taught by Galbraith, Michael Brunson, born in 1940 and now political editor of ITN, says, 'I left the school in 1958 and forty years on I hold the intellectual grounding that I received there as one of the greatest possible benefits I received from any source, more important, for example, than the benefits I gained from Oxford. I was very well taught at Bedford, to the highest standards, by the likes of Douglas Galbraith. But this was teaching in very small classes to the few who even dared to contemplate studying Latin and Greek to university entrance level, so it is perhaps hardly surprising that the standard was so high. But it has led me to hate intellectual sloppiness or laziness, in myself or others, ever since'. [7]

Michael Brunson's recollections of life at Bedford were not however all halcyon. 'What I think the school of the fifties disastrously lacked', he has written, 'was the care of the whole boy, especially if, like me, you happened to be a day boy, who first entered on a scholarship from Goldington Road Primary School! A "sink or swim" attitude pervaded the place. I survived, partly because I was bright, by participating in things like the Lower School Debating Society ... But I was an object of ridicule because I could not, or would not, play games ...

'Similarly, for someone like myself, with both parents at work, there were virtually no facilities at the place. Nowhere to have lunch, nowhere, apart from a desk which might or might not be available in the Memorial Library, to study. Frankly, if you weren't a full or day boarder at the time, you were, as far as the school's facilities were concerned, a bit of a damned nuisance'. [8]

A contemporary of Douglas Galbraith whose name is still recalled with gratitude by boys who benefited from his teaching both within and outside the classroom, and who happily is still alive, was the head of History, John Eyre. Indeed, in 1997 Paddy Ashdown, for eleven years leader of the Liberal Democrats, who became a boarder at Farrar's in 1952, chose John Eyre as his best teacher in an interview he gave to *The Times Educational Supplement*.[9] It was as a boy of eleven that Jeremy Ashdown waved goodbye to his parents at Belfast Docks and sailed alone for England. Still unaccompanied (his parents would probably have been reported to the police by some enterprising busybody today), he made his way to Lime Street Station, in Liverpool, 'the grimiest station I have ever seen', as he recalled in later life,[10] and from there he caught a train to Crewe. 'Ever since, I have had a panic about trains. I always imagined

I would miss the connection, and to this day I arrive at stations and airports hours early'. From Crewe young Ashdown made his way to Bletchley, where he changed again, for Bedford. By the time he had staggered to Farrar's to start his two years in the Lower School there seemed to be few further indignities in store, apart from a good deal of ragging about his broad Northern Irish accent. He was dubbed a 'bog Irishman' and saddled by the other boys with the nickname Paddy. Hence it was from Farrar's, in 1952, that the future leader of the Liberal Democrats, the Rt Hon Paddy Ashdown, emerged.

'Paddy' Ashdown's father, John Ashdown, had been head of Glanyrafon, and must have thought highly of the school to have dispatched his son on such a potentially hazardous journey. But Jeremy was following in an exceptionally long family tradition. Not only his father but his grandfather and his great-grandfather had been educated at Bedford, partly because of the school's connection with the Raj; John Ashdown was a colonel in the Indian Army.

Paddy soon got into scrapes in the Farrar's playroom, for he was by nature a rumbustuous and argumentative boy, who could never resist challenging someone else's opinion. In the Upper School — having been enrolled in St Cuthbert's he graduated to Kirkman's — his disputatious nature found full rein in the Debating Society. 'I was always in a minority', he recalls, 'and I suppose at school I would have been labelled a radical. I just liked airing contrary opinions'. Until 1967, when he was twenty-six, Paddy Ashdown supported the Labour Party, very probably because it was when he was sixteen that he first came under the influence of John Eyre, a master who did little to disguise his own left-wing views. It was Eyre who interested the previously somewhat philistine Ashdown in poetry, art and music. Until then Ashdown had behaved as 'a hearty boy in a pretty hearty school', gaining colours for rugby and athletics. In the Quadrangular Tournament he did his best to bloody a scion of the Bath family, but he admits he was not 'neat enough' to make a very good oarsman. But John Eyre invited him to poetry readings, and found a couple of not too demanding parts for him in productions of *Murder in the Cathedral* and *The Ascent of F6*.

Paddy Ashdown was one of those boys for whom at this time Bedford conspicuously catered, the late developer. No sooner made a school option by Mr Seaman than he disgraced himself and was demoted. But he ended up head of Kirkman's, and claims, with reasonable cause, to have been a reforming head of house, for never once did he cane another boy. This was innovative, for most senior boys caned simply to wreak revenge on the next generation. Ashdown had himself been caned, once, he confesses, for being 'excruciatingly rude' to a master. 'I loved the school', he says. 'It was right for me. I was difficult to teach, very undisciplined and very sporty, but the last two years were magical. John Eyre opened up a side of my personality I never knew existed. The school gave me the priceless gift of an enquiring mind. Of course, it also gave me an innate sense of my own superiority, but that got knocked out of me in the Royal Marines!'[11]

It was in 1983 that Paddy Ashdown was first returned to Westminster, as MP for Yeovil. He became leader of the Liberal Democrats in 1988 and a privy councillor a year later. In 1993 he returned to his Lower School boarding house, Farrar's, to unveil a plaque to commemorate its change of status to an Upper School house and its change of name to Phillpotts, the first house to be named after a Head Master. (In 1994 Phillpotts also had a new 1st VIII boat named after him.)

In his *Times Educational Supplement* interview, Paddy Ashdown recalled John Eyre as 'a tall, gaunt man, with fair, lanky hair', who 'came across as a sort of rebel. He was very different from the main body of teachers and I can remember wondering why on earth he had come to teach at a place like Bedford. I can't remember exactly how he taught; he just made all the literature live. He got us all very involved in critical analysis; A C Bradley on Shakespeare, and so on'.

Other boys influenced by Eyre include John Percival, a TV producer, Andrew McCulloch, the actor, Professor Robert Hewison, theatre critic of the *Sunday Times*, and Quentin Skinner, a Fellow of Christ's College, Cambridge and since 1996 Regius Professor of Modern History at the University. He entered the Inky as a boarder at Nash's in 1947, and remembers the house-master, Donald Palmer, with affection. Haunted in a friendly way by an exceptionally brilliant older brother, Quentin needed all his wits about him, but while a junior at Redburn he contracted TB from the matron, whom he remembers 'coughing all over the dining room table'. As a consequence, he very nearly died. His parents were abroad, but fortunately his guardian, an aunt, happened to be a doctor, and for six crucial months she nursed the ailing boy herself.

It was equally fortunate that before joining the Inky Quentin had spent a year at a kindergarten in Aberdeen, where it seems that children progressed academically a year ahead of their English counterparts, so after missing twelve months of schooling at Bedford he found himself, on his return, still level pegging with his contemporaries. In 1952 his mother returned to England from Africa, bought a house in St Edmund's Road, and Quentin continued his Bedford education as a day boy. Once in the Upper School he was recognised by John Eyre as a fellow intellectual; he acted as convenor of the Mitre Club and ended up in Eyre's very select History Sixth. Because he had failed an audition for the part of Ophelia, and Eyre thought that he might be disappointed, he also ended up lighting Eyre's production of *Hamlet*. He remembers John Eyre as 'an incandescent intellectual and wonderfully funny. He undoubtedly got me my scholarship to Caius, and taught in a very Socratic fashion, with enormous enthusiasm and by asking his pupils questions. He was a real intellectual, very widely informed'.

This was a time when it was not in the least fashionable to be clever, and rather than be considered a swot Quentin Skinner developed all-round talents; despite his near-fatal illness as a small boy he became a good long distance runner and captain of the Gym Club, his chosen sport in the gym being fencing. He was appointed a monitor, sang in the chapel choir until his voice broke (although not well enough to land the female lead in *Hamlet*) and played the violin ('but not well'). True to the republican principles instilled in him by John Eyre, Quentin Skinner is reliably reported as having declined the knight bachelorhood customarily offered to a regius professor. Lest it be thought there are no clever boys around today, or inspired teachers, it was announced in 1998 in the second issue of a recently launched *Newsletter* that Bradley Lord, deputy head of school, had 'managed an astonishing eleven A's in his GCSEs' and while continuing to study English, History, French and German had provisionally been accepted by New College, Oxford. But the *Newsletter* had not quite got the facts about Lord's 'astonishing' achievement correct. What he had amassed was a truly incredible total of eleven A *starred* Grades. Academically, Bradley Lord will remain for all time one of the most outstandingly brilliant boys ever to have passed through the school. He went on to gain four Grade As at A Level and indeed entered New College, to read Languages.

By general consent among the boys of Bradley Lord's generation whom he teaches, the head of English, Dr Richard Palmer, is considered a charismatic master who commands the respect and affection of his pupils. No doubt he is in line for a reunion lunch at the Reform somewhere around the year 2035. For in 1996 Richard Lindley, another TV presenter and reporter, who used to work on *Panorama*, organised a lunch at the Reform Club in Eyre's honour, and Paddy Ashdown recalls that 'Every one of his former pupils at the lunch — all now in pretty prominent positions in one field or another — recognised the huge impact he had made. The most amazing thing was that he could remember the parts every one of us had taken in the plays'.[12]

One of those who was produced in *Hamlet* by John Eyre was Michael Burton, who took the lead in 1954, at the age of seventeen. Fortunately for his future career as a diplomat, Michael was fluent in French and German, and when in 1955 he won the William Doncaster Scholarship in Modern Languages at Magdalen the school was given a half-holiday. He entered the Foreign Office in 1960, served in Dubai, Khartoum, Paris, Amman and Kuwait, and for six years held the post of Minister in Berlin, where on her state visit to the city in 1992 the Queen invested him as a Knight Commander of the Royal Victorian Order. He crowned his diplomatic career in 1994 by becoming ambassador to the Czech Republic. A contemporary of Michael Burton, Allan Ramsay, entered Sanderson's in 1951 at the age of fourteen, fencing, rowing and playing rugger for his house, and being chosen for the 1st XV and the 1st VIII. After National Service with the Dorset Regiment he too entered the Diplomatic Service, and was appointed to three embassies. He was ambassador to the Lebanon from 1988-90, the Sudan from 1990-91, and for the next four years he was ambassador to Morocco, being made KBE in 1992.

The production of school plays was undertaken on a rota basis by Cyril Rhodes-Harrison as well as John Eyre. *Macbeth* was produced in 1944 and again thirteen years later; *Julius Caesar*, a great favourite with schoolboys, was also put on twice in the Great Hall, in 1945 and 1964, and John Eyre mounted an open air production in modern dress, staged on the steps of the Pavilion. Lighter fare included productions of *She Stoops to Conquer*, *The Beggar's Opera* and, in 1953, *The Rivals*. In 1968 it cost £220 19s 5d to mount *The Jew of Malta*, a production which resulted in a net profit of £18 6s 1d, a rather more satisfactory outcome than in 1961, when all the ticket money for the school play was stolen. 'Perhaps we could get a wall-safe built into the Monitors Room' the head of school, K G M Benn, minuted. As in Shakespeare's day, all the female parts were played by boys, sometimes in an alarmingly alluring manner; it was not until quite recent times that it occurred to anyone to collaborate on theatrical productions with the Girls' High School, and any fraternisation between Bedford's boys and girls during term time used to be absurdly covert. Since 1996 girls from the Dame Alice Harpur School have attended Wednesday afternoon meetings of the CCF; the closest most boarders got to a girl in Grose-Hodge's day was on a Saturday afternoon at the decorous dancing classes held by Miss Nancy Harding, daughter of the school's old director of music, Dr H A Harding, who had taught from 1899 to 1926. They were gruesome occasions, cohorts of boarders smarming down their hair with brylcreme before arriving at Crofton House, and then eyeing the girls to see which, if any, they fancied. There was an annual school dance, from which boys would return in semi-disarray with tales of conquest to put Leporello's catalogue in the shade, but in truth, the most daring enterprise ever undertaken by a boy widely regarded as the Don Juan of his day was to take a girl to the Granada Cinema, strictly out of bounds, as were all cinemas, its restaurant more famous for the newly imported Italian cappuccino than its dress circle ever was for illicit sex.

TEN

Forty-four Rebels

1952–1979

In any 1st XI of famous Old Bedfordians the name of Archibald Martin would have to be included; in 1952 he received the Nobel Prize for Chemistry. Born in 1910, Dr Martin was at Bedford 1922-28, studying chemistry without the benefits of the new Science Building. After a period overseas he became a College Exhibitioner in Natural Sciences at Peterhouse, Cambridge, and in 1937 he was awarded a doctorate of philosophy for a thesis dealing with vitamin E. In 1950 he was elected a Fellow of the Royal Society. The research which earned him a Nobel Prize was work on chromatography, a method of chemical analysis, conducted at Cambridge and the Wool Industries Research Association's laboratories in Leeds. It was a fitting achievement to coincide with the 400th anniversary of the school's foundation.

The event was celebrated by a visit on Speech Day by Princess Margaret, still immensely glamorous and unspoilt by disappointments in love. And she did the school proud, arriving shortly after midday at the Burnaby Road entrance, asking for the summer holidays to be extended as the Head Master might 'think most fitting', attending a sherry party in Mr Seaman's study and then a luncheon in the Memorial Hall. In the afternoon she paid a visit to the Inky and planted a commemorative *Prunus*, and stopped off at the swimming pool to watch a light-hearted display of diving laid on by the Lower School. From there she moved on to view a cricket match for a few moments before taking tea in the Pavilion with the monitors. She tactfully took the opportunity to talk for some while with Humfrey Grose-Hodge, singled out by implication in his speech by Mr Seaman as one of the school's three great Head Masters. Seaman had linked his name with Brereton and Phillpotts — a judgement about which, interestingly enough, the present writer had not previously been aware.

161

Some impressions by Lower School boys recorded in the *Ousel* for 26 July 1952 make amusing reading. Referring, presumably, to Nicholas Hubbard, the prep school boy chosen to present the princess with a bouquet, a Lower School boy commented, 'He did a typical "Inky" bow'. But what an 'Inky bow' was he did not explain. Perhaps Hubbard bent from the waist instead of merely inclining his head, the Coburg bow imported by Prince Albert and practised by courtiers ever since. Another boy thought the princess was 'quite small and very pretty'. 'She has one of the nicest smiles I have ever seen' commented another.

In the summer term of 1954 the head of school was Howard Ward. He began his report for 21 June in suitably dramatic manner. 'The Summer Term 1954', he wrote, 'will never be forgotten by anyone who was at the school during it'.[1] According to a story in the *Sunday Dispatch* of 13 June, 'The Headmaster of Bedford — one of the oldest public schools in Britain — will decide this week what action to take against 45 boys who have admitted drinking at regular intervals in a local public house.

'Last week', the *Sunday Dispatch* continued, 'a housemaster found a packet of cigarettes in a boy's jacket. The boy admitted he had bought them in a public house.

'This was reported to Mr C M E Seaman, the headmaster.

'The following day, as the news got about, forty-four other boys went voluntarily to the amazed headmaster in large groups and confessed that they, too, had been drinking in a public house in Bedford town'. The housemaster — of Burnaby — was Owen Bevan, the inspired coach of the 1st XV.

Ward's report went on to say: '*For many years* boys had been in the habit of visiting public houses both in and out of the town although it was in fact against the rules. On away matches masters had turned a blind eye to it, but in Bedford of course it had been done on the quiet. One of the main reasons for it was that there was nowhere for boys to meet, for instance between about 5.30 and 6.30 or 6.15. They could go to a café in the town but that works out expensive after a while. Anyway, the fact remains that the Rose and Crown in Greyfriars Walk had become a meeting place for boarders. The question immediately springs to mind: why was it not checked in its early stages? The answer: Monitors were very much involved and the Head of the School did not know of it. Obviously it was kept from him as much as it was from the masters'.

Ward's contention that a head of school would not have been aware of what was going on scarcely bears examination; it sounds as if he would have been involved in pub crawls before he became head of school. Ward ignored the fact that to enter a public house would not only have been a breach of school rules but against the law. And his suggestion that visits to a café would cost more than visits to a pub may strike regular drinkers as an odd one. Odder still, for 'the Head of the School' he had originally written 'I did not know of it'. It is odd because this entry in his report book begins with a list of all the monitors and the senior and junior options, and beside his own name, the name of the deputy head of school, and thirteen out of twenty-one monitors, fourteen out of thirty-six senior options and sixteen out of sixty-eight junior options he had placed a cross, with the following explanation: 'X these monitors owned up. This sounds as though it reflects discredit on the others, but it is not intended to; if they were guilty but did not own up their consciences will prick them for a very long time. But I believe they are almost completely innocent of going into public houses'.

The *Sunday Dispatch* had been remarkably well informed. The grand total of boys who had apparently gone voluntarily to Seaman to 'own up' was indeed 44. But no one had asked them to. What they had done, in a hamfisted show of support for the Burnaby boy, A E Gent, who had been unfortunate enough to be caught with a packet of fags in his pocket, was to threaten the authority of the Head Master. 'You can't sack the lot of us', they were saying, 'so you can't sack Gent'.

But Ward provided his own explanation, both for Mr Bevan's actions and those of the boys most trusted by Mr Seaman. 'The first time I learnt of any trouble', he wrote, 'was on Wednesday, June 9th, when Gent — a monitor — was summoned to the Head Master. Mr Bevan had on the previous day searched through boys' jackets at the Boarding House while the CCF was on a Field Exercise at Stowe; he said he was looking to see what kinds of things a thief would find and want to take. In the first jacket he found a packet of cigarettes, in the second nothing, in the third another packet of cigarettes. He stopped then — "the percentage was too high!"'

'It transpired that Gent had bought the cigarettes in a public house at Tonbridge during the match the previous week. It now leaked out that the entire XI, bar one but including a remove-former, had visited the same pub. Unfortunately the Deputy Head of the School [W R Street] was Captain of the eleven. But before this information was known the word had got round that Gent was in serious trouble for something that the majority of seniors had done at some time or other. Therefore, as the newspaper cutting says, large numbers of boys trooped through to the Head Master to confess — so much so that the affair seemed farcical.

'Came the Exeat and a short breathing space.'

The affair may have seemed farcical to Ward, but to the Head Master it spelt mayhem. It might have been better had Mr Bevan dealt with the matter himself instead of handing over responsibility for a relatively trivial offence to the

Head Master. Gent having been summoned to see Mr Seaman, it might have been better still if his forty-four friends had supported their Head Master, and in consequence their school. But Ward seemed to imagine that by backing up Gent, he and his accomplices had done something fine and manly. All they had done in effect was turn morality on its head.

Once the school had reassembled, Mr Seaman held separate meetings with monitors and options, and even 'a meeting for masters which went on from 8.30 until 11. Conferences were also held with the governors'. This was scarcely surprising. The Head Master had been let down — over the years — by his staff, let down by his most senior boys, he was faced with a revolt, and the scandal had been fed to the national press. On 17 June (Black Thursday, according to the unrepentant Ward) Seaman addressed the school 'on the subject of monitorial duties which are more important than their privileges'. It was, thought Ward, 'a marvellous speech'. The fifteen monitors who had mistakenly 'confessed' because one of their colleagues had been found out doing something 'that the majority of seniors had done at some time of other', as though that was a lawful or logical reason why he should not be dealt with, were demoted, without 'any hopes of general reinstatement'. Seaman had been given no other choice, but the decision he took, and it was both brave and correct, left him with the entire Upper School system of self-regulation kicked from under him. 'All senior boarders who were involved were sacked without exception: Talbot's would have been in such a bad way owing to the demotions as all the "side-tables" had to go except one that the Head Master asked Mr Bourne [he had succeeded Junk Renwick] to leave Johnson as Head of the House. At Kirkman's the studies were emptied and other innocent senior boys brought into them. At Pemberley where No 1 study holds four boys the three senior boys were sacked but only one boy came into the study … At Burnaby the studies became store-rooms where former inhabitants could leave their things; no new blood was brought in … For once, Sanderson's was not too drastically involved as Morris was in the clear; all the options involved were sacked of course. The same applies to Redburn.

'At School, no new Head of the School was appointed but a triumvirate was set up of Allen, Howard and Harrison. Lessons were read in chapel as usual but options had to be brought in for the collection. No prayers were read by Mons at 9 o'clock assembly and all notices were read by the Head Master. The Head Master was not fetched into prayers but Mr Bull tipped him the wink when to come in — and he usually did it far too early'.

Not in the least abashed by his personal contribution to Seaman's tribulations, Ward went on to say he regarded his own demotion as being 'very harsh'. He thought the Head Master had several things that he held against him 'which caused him to demote me to the rank of plebeian'. And an impressive list of complaints it was too. Ward had failed to report boys sneaking off to a pub during a school play; he had failed to report plans for a mock wedding of a monitor in the Rose in the High Street, albeit on the first day of the Easter holiday; and, again during the holiday, he had issued invitations to a 'Bedford School Monitors Dance' without seeking permission. And Ward had the brass neck to add that he had been into a pub himself for a pint of bitter on a hot day and had 'given permission' to another monitor to go in too; given permission to a monitor to break a school rule!

'Future generations be warned', Ward concluded his report: 'This H.M. is as liable to take action over holiday activities as over those that happen during the term…But as is becoming more and more evident, Messrs Grose-Hodge and Seaman could not be more dissimilar in their attitudes to things like this'.

Little did he know that Grose-Hodge had regarded 'the oldest' of his monitors as 'little more than a child', nor that he had decreed that 'Any boy whose behaviour, manners, or even appearance are such as to bring discredit on the school at any time or place, will be regarded as having broken a School Rule'. The phrase 'any time or place' quite obviously includes conduct during holidays; no boy suddenly ceases to be a Bedford School boy because he is out of uniform.

The surprising upshot of this disgraceful occurrence was the ultimate reinstatement of all the monitors and options. Seaman congratulated the boys on 'the way they had borne their misfortune and assured them that the moment they were reinstated the whole incident would be forgotten. With regard to references, etc, in future life, this incident would NOT BE HELD AGAINST THEM, which I thought was very decent of the H.M.' Ward was among the first to be reinstated. 'After the 15th of July', he noted, 'everybody did their best to forget the whole unpleasant episode, particularly as they realised that there was a lot more to it than there seemed at first — there was the lack of facilities at school for providing boys with meeting places, there was the attitude of the masters who if not in most cases actually encouraged drinking, did nothing to prevent it whatsoever. And so on'. No wonder the *Sunday Dispatch* had carried a pocket cartoon in which the Head Master was shown admonishing not only a class but a form master: 'I said take your class for Gym and French — not Gin and French!'

Howard Ward, who died in 1958 at the tragically early age of twenty-two, was succeeded at Christmas 1954 as head of school by Brian Howard, now a Governor of the school, one of the monitors not implicated in the drinking and smoking scandal. Howard made the sensible assertion that in fact there were too many boys in senior positions — 127 when there were only 200 Sixth Formers.[2] Obviously it is not necessary for a Sixth Former to be an option;

equally obviously, boys need preparation as options in order to merit promotion to monitor. But if as many as 127 boys are either monitors or options the likelihood is that some will not be up to the mark. Indeed, such numbers devalue the role of options, or as Howard more crudely put it, 'Boys who would have been petty criminals were now in a position to lead and influence others'. To the extent that Seaman bore any responsibility for the fiasco, he certainly had too many unsuitable boys in office, beginning, one has to say, with his head boy; he also perhaps tended unrealistically to place boys on their honour not to break rules, for he was a man of high ideals himself who found it difficult to expect the worst of others. Brian Howard was made of sterner stuff, and began his reign as head of school by giving '3 cuts each' to two boys caught skipping chapel.

The Sanderson's monitor who had kept his nose clean, Michael Morris, now Lord Naseby, says he liked Seaman, that in fact he was 'one of the few who did. His unpopularity stemmed from placing too much emphasis on academic attainment, not holding in balance the sporting dimension'.[3] Morris was at Bedford from 1950-55, somehow managing (probably because Redburn and Farrar's were full) to sneak into Sanderson's, where he was beaten by the house sadist, while still in the Lower School. 'I loved school', he states quite simply, and makes no bones about having previously been failed by Tonbridge. Reverting to Mr Seaman's unfortunate headmastership, Morris says he saw the action of the monitors who confessed to crimes that had not been unearthed as a challenge to Seaman's authority, a challenge 'no Head Master could have ignored. It made an indelible impression on Seaman, who was really a man ahead of his time. I think he might have been a brilliant Head Master forty-five years later'.

One reason why Morris enjoyed school so much was because he succeeded at a wide range of activities; he became head both of Sanderson's and Ashburnham in addition to being appointed senior monitor, he was head of the chapel choir and played for the 1st XV and the 2nd XI. After Cambridge he cultivated a variety of business interests, and in 1974 he was elected Conservative Member of Parliament for Northampton South, losing his seat in the Labour landslide of 1997. For the last five years of his Commons career, Michael Morris had served as a deputy speaker, and loathe to lose his parliamentary experience, John Major invited him to accept a life peerage. It was in 1982 that the boy Tonbridge had turned their backs on became a Bedford School Governor, and in 1989 chairman of the Governors.

Today there are separate heads of boarding and school houses, and if the head of school happens to be a boarder, as Gareth Graham was in 1998 (at Sanderson's), he is quite likely to step aside to allow another boy the chance of being head of the house. (Gareth was succeeded as head of school by another

Ashburnham boarder, Anthony Macpherson, a rare and prestigious achievement for Sanderson's.) The numbers of options is currently confined to some three dozen, and monitors, including the head of school, the deputy head and the senior monitor, to a mere fifteen or so. And a very engaging bunch these days they are, quite devoid of the pomposity and self-importance so often attached to monitors when they marched into the Great Hall at assembly armed with canes and permission to strike any boy on the head who might be whispering or fidgeting. They still award drills for infringements of school rules, and pride themselves on 'cracking down heavily' on smoking, but they try to find creative drills for boys to do, like helping to stuff mailing shots. They see themselves as some sort of stepping stone between boys and staff, and regard the enhanced status they enjoy as privilege enough. They belong to a generation whose boarders may sign out on a Saturday evening to go to a restaurant, and whose Upper Sixth boys are allowed to visit a list of approved public houses.

In 1955 Clarence Seaman could not have been sorry to leave the unreliable Bedford hierarchy of his day to their own devices, responding positively, as Edward King had done in 1910, to an invitation to return to his own school as Head Master. And oddly enough, the Governors chose as his replacement the first Old Bedfordian ever to become Head Master, Grose-Hodge's former head boy, William Brown. Born in 1914, Brown went into the Inky as a St Cuthbert's day boy when he was seven, and remained at Bedford for 12 years, the first seven of which were spent under the headmastership of Reginald Carter. During his last year he was taught by Seaman. He took a First in Modern Languages at Pembroke College, Cambridge and taught at Wellington College for 11 years; he was also a housemaster, and among the boys he drilled in the Corps was another future Bedford master — John Eyre. In 1947 Brown was appointed Head Master of King's School, Ely, and eight years later, when he arrived at Bedford, he inherited 962 boys and the fifth largest public school. To succeed a great Head Master can be hard enough; to follow one whose tenure of office has been controversial and not very happy can present an even greater challenge. Brown remained at Bedford for a steady twenty years, and baring minor scraps with staff, his dealings with boys and most masters were shot through with compassion and trust.

Bill Brown, as he liked to be called, provided both stability and a bridge between tradition and progress. When he arrived at Bedford as Head Master little regarding the general ethos of the school had changed since it quit St Paul's Square over half a century before. In a lively unpublished memoir deposited in the school library, the account written by David Heald of life at Redburn between 1949-1958 could have been mirrored by those of hundreds of boys in similar houses — and over a much longer period. William Brown's task was gently to steer the school away from a culture of unquestioned authoritarianism, from a climate in which success in life could almost automatically be guaranteed simply by having attended a public school; the challenge he faced was to transform the school into an educational establishment capable of training boys to make their way in a world that was to change radically during his headmastership. On the horizon was looming the so-called Permissive Society. The odd fairly harmless pint of beer and drag on a fag behind the Pavilion were to give way to the temptation to experiment with drugs. And a dismantling of the Empire and a drastic reduction in the armed forces meant a diminution of two previously fruitful sources of employment for Bedford boys, whose career prospects in future would increasingly depend on a mastery of technology.

For an Old Bedfordian like David Heald, a return visit to Bedford today is to enter a very different atmosphere indeed. Looking back on his own school days he has recalled, 'There were times when only my CCF regulation greatcoat stood between me and death from hypothermia in the freezing dormitory. During those ghastly February nights, without any central heating whatsoever, the windows thrown wide open (and if they were closed, at the risk of a flogging, the housemaster would come in and open them again), I became convinced that there was nothing between Bedford and Siberia. There were times when I was bullied, and bullied others in turn. I was caned and slippered times without number for offences trivial and occasionally grave. One would be summoned from one's last refuge, one's bed, in the middle of the night to be flogged'.

David's maternal grandfather, two great-uncles and an uncle had all been at Bedford, but although he had been a boarder elsewhere since the age of six he seems to have arrived innocently unprepared. On his first day as a fag he was told by an older boy to carry his cases to his study. 'That'll be two and six', said David jokingly, intimating he expected a tip. He got a caning instead — for insolence.

But he *was* innocent. Boarding school life at Bedford during the 1950s was an era, he says, 'which, looking back, I increasingly remember with affection as a curiously innocent era, when people were not yet fully "enlightened" or "liberated", obsessed with sex, television and the mindless pursuit of material gain. By no means everybody had a house, a car (my father never owned one, and cycled to work in Jersey), a television, a microwave oven, washing machine, home computer, deep freeze or even a telephone'. Today, with permission from the Head Master, senior boys can drive their own car to school, and many boys are equipped with a mobile telephone; computers are de rigueur.

Geoffrey Grose-Hodge, the Head Master's brother, was David's first housemaster. He had 'grey-white hair, wore double-breasted suits and had a strong, kind face and humorous eyes. In the evenings, in the dormitory, he would lie down on a bed and challenge us to restrain him, holding him down by his arms and legs. We boisterous nine-year-olds would accept the challenge, "Botty" Briggs always being delegated to go for the legs. I never saw Geoffrey break out of our grip, but perhaps he wasn't trying too hard. Such mildly eccentric behaviour on his part would doubtless today be frowned upon by the portentously smug "child psychologists" and "educationalists" (and even some parents) who blight our lives.'

Richard Roseveare, from 1973-77 Vice-Master, took over from Geoffrey Grose-Hodge in September 1950, and remained at Redburn for 15 years. And for his final two years, David Heald had Anton Barber as form master, a Double First he describes as a remarkable character. He was, like Galbraith and Eyre, a teacher who inspired many of his pupils. 'In some ways', David Heald has written, 'he was a rebel, who disapproved of many aspects of public school life. Because he did not "fit" he was seen as being rather "pink" in his views. I remember he admitted to me that he had had to overcome his sense of outrage at my "extreme reactionary" views before awarding me the Irving French prize! He hated having to give permission to boys to leave class early for away games of cricket or rugby, believing this to be a melancholy proof that Bedford School regarded games as more important than the cultivation of the intellect … Anton was an excellent teacher. His lectures on German and French literature were marvellous'.

It has always been remarkable how many years so many people have devoted to Bedford. One such was Sgt Major S P Jackson, originally of the Middlesex Regiment, who instructed boys in swimming, fencing and gymnastics for 32 years, only retiring at Easter 1960 after suffering a heart attack. Immensely strong yet graceful, and far superior in gymnastic feats to most of the far younger boys whose fear of heights and bruises he helped to master, he never exhibited a sense of superiority. Nor did he believe in wasting time calling an ambulance when a boy dislocated his toe in the swimming pool. With one swift and decisive jerk he realigned the offending limb before the boy had time to yell. RSM John Whitelaw, whose Scots humour was always lurking just below the surface of an upright military bearing, was another legend in the gymnasium. He died in 1975 after instructing generations of boys in fencing, boxing and gymnastics.

Howard Ward's reference, while writing up the great monitorial scandal of 1954, to boarders having nowhere to meet in the late afternoon can be explained by the fact that in most boarding houses there was only one communal room, used for recreation, meals and prep. When the tables were being laid, the room was cleared of boys, and short of congregating in the changing rooms they had nowhere to go. Studies were at a premium; properly equipped study bedrooms did not exist. The lack of general amenities in the boarding houses was one reason why a decision was made in 1965 to provide centralised catering, one of the major innovations of Mr Brown's head-mastership. The plan has achieved two advantages and one disadvantage. On the plus side, day boys mingle with boarders much more, and the standard of catering, provided on a professional basis, and inclusive of vegetarian and Halal meals, is far higher than in the past. The disadvantage is that lacking any boarding house discipline at meal times, boys tend to rush through their meals and to ignore some of the basic social graces attached to eating. At any rate, for better or worse new dining halls, which received a Civic Trust award, were constructed, and Queen Elizabeth the Queen Mother, swathed in tulle, arrived by car on 28 June 1966 to open them. An Inky boy, William Hitchins, presented a bouquet, and Queen Elizabeth inspected a guard of honour. After announcing that she had asked for the school to have an extra two days holiday she toured the kitchens and then tucked into tea with a group of senior boys, leaving by helicopter after a visit lasting one and a quarter hours.

There was change in the air all round. In the summer term of 1960 Compline had first been experimented with in the chapel, at 8.45pm on Sundays. 'It is a curious service', D W Rice noted in his report book, 'and I think it is not popular with many boys. But some of it is fine'. [4] There were sophisticated changes too in the pranks boys got up to in order to court disaster. 'Shirking house games' (1917), 'Climbing through Boat Club window when told not to' (1918), 'Breaking School Rules' (1922) had given way by 10 February 1969 to two boys, who shall be nameless, receiving two cuts each from the head of school for 'Exhibition and abuse of contraceptive during library period'. How they abused the contraceptive is not recorded.

As far as the boarding houses were concerned, it was during Bill Brown's progressive and pastoral 20 years as Head Master that very considerable alterations to the accommodation were carried out. Centralised dining arrange-ments had released space in the houses for extended recreational purposes. Armchairs and television sets were introduced. Brown recognised that the boys for whom he was responsible had far more money than he ever had when at school, and needed to be trusted with limited facilities to enjoy the occasional drink; in came bars in boarding houses. He realised too the advantage of weaning boys as they grew older off the traditional sometimes rather rowdy and enervating camaraderie of the large dormitory to the greater privacy, in preparation for university, of shared, or even single, study bedrooms. (When Marlborough College opened in 1843 there were thirty-five boys in one dormitory; Bedford's boarders were never sandwiched on quite that scale, but anything between a dozen and twenty boys to a room was normal.)

The expense and initial upheaval of transforming the physical structure of the houses is generally regarded today as having been worthwhile, although, in a perverse sort of way, the more intimate the accommodation provided for boys the greater seems to be their need to conform to perceived patterns of correct behaviour. In the old days, no posters or photographs would ever have been displayed. Once boys began to share smaller rooms they were permitted to decorate them according to personal taste, that taste inevitably being dictated by prevailing (and majority) fashions in sexual mores, sport or entertainment. Provision of rooms for four boys, provided they get on well, is on balance probably preferable to dormitories for 14; the privilege of a single room for a head of house, or other senior boys, sets them apart as young men rather than boys, which today is what effectively many of them are, and provides not only privacy for serious study but a proper distance between them and the younger boys whose conduct they are expected to monitor. What may strike some as dubious is the idea of two adolescent boys being closeted in one room. To his credit, Brown at any rate realised that a more liberal regime would make life more civilised, encouraging 'social activity and a more responsible attitude among senior boys'.[5]

No seventeen-year-old boy could feel sensibly dressed wearing a cap on the back of his head, and despite opposition from some housemasters the cap was faded out and at weekends holiday clothes were faded in. A number of monitors began to voice objections to beating. On the academic side, no assessment of Bill Brown's stewardship could be bettered than by quoting from an appreciation compiled for the *Ousel* on his retirement:

In a period of rapidly changing educational theory and practice new ideas have to be sifted, tested and applied with discretion and discernment. Departments were given every encouragement to experiment but always within a balanced and practical framework. Major changes included the introduction of a 'block' time-table, allowing a greater variety of choice in the Sixth Forms, and a gradual extension of the subjects taken below 'O' Level, especially on the Science side, thus opening up a wider range of courses during a boy's early years in the Upper School and avoiding the danger of premature specialisation. The extension of General Studies helped to broaden the curriculum still further; the addition of Computer studies, World Affairs, Statistics, Economics and Russian indicated an awareness of contemporary needs; the development of Nuffield Science projects, Language Laboratories and new methods of examination and assessment encouraged fresh ideas of pupil engagement and staff involvement in what had previously been a more set and formal pattern of teaching.[6]

William Brown, an accomplished watercolourist, believed implicitly that education, too, was an art, not a science. It was through this belief that he brought such humanity to his task. He took some seven or eight classes a week in French and German, and made a point twice a week of teaching the bottom Fourth Form, 'to bring them up to scratch'.[7] He enjoyed teaching too much to allow administration entirely to rule his life, and it was by regular appearances in the class rooms that he got to know individual boys so well. He was blessed with two priceless assets for a Head Master; a very good memory and a genuine liking for people. On Sundays, he and Elizabeth Brown entertained boys to lunch, usually to meet a visiting preacher. He was both a pastoral and formidable Head Master, formidable in the sense of successful, not frightening. And without pomposity or pretensions of any kind he was able through the force of his personality to influence both boys and staff for good. Like Grose-Hodge, he had a deep religious faith, and it was no great surprise when a year after retirement he received holy orders, and settled down in Norfolk to the dedicated life of a non-stipendiary parish priest.

He handed over to his successor a school containing 1,000 boys, a school which, in his last summer, he was able to report on Speech Day had enjoyed 'our best "A" Level results since the GCE was introduced over 20 years ago. Not only was the percentage pass-rate our highest — eighty-seven per cent — but of the passes gained, half were Grades A and B'. In his final report to the Governors of the Harpur Trust, he noted: 'There has been much criticism of "streaming" in recent years, but I see little evidence of this having any depressing effect on the boys; the really able can go at a pace made possible through little need for repetitive instructions, and they have time for reflection and productive exploration; the less able gain confidence by going at a pace more suited to their needs. Some years ago when we experimented with reduced steaming it was the less able who clamoured for a return to the status quo!'

Under Bill Brown new workshops were added to the school estate. In 1960 the Hayward Wells Building, incorporating a new Geography Department, was opened, and in 1975 the foundation stone of a new Biology Department was laid by an Old Bedfordian, Sir George Godber. At school 1920-27, Godber had served as Chief Medical Officer from 1960-73. Sir George's family were remarkable in many respects. In 1898 his father, Isaac Godber, the youngest of eleven children, settled at Willington, five miles to the east of Bedford, and the connection remains to this day; and no less than nineteen of Isaac's children (of whom he had seven) and grandchildren attended Harpur Trust schools. Like his brother Rowland, who was two years younger, Sir George was originally entered at the Modern School, where in his last year he had the misfortune to lose an eye in a playground accident. In 1920 both boys were switched to Bedford, 'because,' Sir George has explained, 'the science teaching and facilities were far better there — as was the chance of scholarships to university.' [8]

Sir George duly won an Oxford scholarship, and remembers his school days 'with a certain whimsicality.' In particular he recalls how he and Rowland, who became a rubber planter in Malaya and survived the horrors of a Japanese prisoner of war camp, 'met the then quite venemous hostility to "the Modern" and to "train boys." The school was only beginning to adjust to boys from outside the town, other than boarders, and to begin to make provision for them.' He says it is difficult to appreciate today the 'snobbish hostility' displayed by Bedford boys towards the Modern School. At Henley (Sir George rowed in the 1st VIII) he offered to help carry in the defeated Modern School's boat 'and was rebuked by our captain!'

The second child of the family, Joyce Godber, who went to the High School, was to become historian of the Harpur Trust, and three other brothers, Geoffrey, who died in 1999, Joseph and Frank, were all entered at Bedford from the start. In 1936 Frank, alas, was 'requested to leave,' but redeemed himself by his heroism in the RAF, and was awarded the DFC. After a career in politics, in 1979 Joseph received a life peerage, taking the title Lord Godber of Willington.

With a new Geography Department in place, it may or may not have been by chance that William Brown was succeeded as Head Master, in 1975, by a Geographer, Ian Jones. Born in 1934, Mr. Jones was educated at Bishop's Stortford College and St John's College, Cambridge, returning to his old school after national service as head of the Geography Department. After a decade in the post he was appointed vice principal of King William's College on the Isle of Man, the school where Frederick Farrar, Master of Marlborough and author of the Victorian best-seller, *Eric; or Little by Little*, was educated. Not only was Jones the first specialist in Geography to become Head Master of Bedford; it is probably safe to say he was also the first Head Master to have been capped for hockey 17 times.

Ian Jones's arrival at Bedford coincided with a reduction in the age of majority, enabling boys to enter a public house at 18; hence he had the task of squaring school rules with parliamentary legislation. He took the sensible and pragmatic view that senior boys might be given the right to drink in moderation on a Saturday evening, but that there was no question of a boy of 18 marching off to a pub in the middle of a school day. By the same token, he saw no good reason why parents should be allowed to override school rules. 'After all', he told the *Ousel* in June 1975, 'they do delegate responsibility in these matters to the school'. Another topical issue on which he was immediately asked his opinion was whether Sixth Formers should be allowed to opt out of sports to concentrate on academic study. 'In general, No,' he replied. 'It's up to the school to organise its system so that work and sport are happily balanced and kept in perspective.'

But it seems somewhat academic to hazard a guess what concrete plans for the school Ian Jones had turned up with. For hardly had he been given time to look around, to assess the situation and decide on a list of priorities, than he faced a crisis of almost overwhelming proportions. After all, as he has written himself, 'How ... do you explain to your Governors that the Main Building of the school for which you are responsible has burnt down?' [9]

ELEVEN

Arson

1979–1981

THE FIRST of thirty-six telephone calls reporting a fire at Bedford School on 3 March 1979 was made from a public telephone kiosk in Kimbolton Road. It may have been made by the young man who started it; he had previously telephoned a victim to warn her anonymously that her house was on fire. His name was Ian Ludman. At his trial at Bedford Crown Court on 23 July 1979 he was charged with possessing cannabis, obtaining money by deception and with six counts of burglary and three of arson. So far as the charge of arson relating to the school was concerned, he had destroyed almost the entire main building save its outer walls, and most of the contents.

Ludman, who was twenty-four, lived in Church Lane, Goldington. He was a serial arsonist and no stranger to prison. In 1974 he had been sentenced to eighty-four days detention and discharged from the army for setting fire to a jeep. Three years later he served six months for drink and driving offences. Four weeks before burning down the school he had stolen a television set from a friend, setting fire to her house in Howbury Street and causing £7,500 worth of damage. Nine days after destroying the school, Ludman broke into a restaurant in Harpur Street to steal food, and started a fire causing £1,800 worth of damage. The destruction for which he was responsible at the school was estimated at £2.5 million. He was sent to prison for life.

Whoever it was who was the first person to raise the alarm, at 11.58pm, said he thought it was the chapel that was on fire. Kimbolton Road is scarcely a hive of activity at midnight. Had the caller been a passing motorist he would surely have turned into Glebe Road to make a proper reconnaissance. At 11.40pm one of the dining halls staff drove along Pemberley Avenue, and saw no sign of fire. It had taken hold in the eighteen minutes prior to the first call, eighteen minutes being all the time Ludman would have needed to start the fire, make his escape and reach a telephone box in Kimbolton Road on foot. If the caller was not Ludman or an accomplice it was someone who must almost have bumped into him.

At about the time of the call to the fire brigade from Kimbolton Road, two Burnaby boys, having returned late from a dance, roused their housemaster and his wife, and the head of Kirkman's likewise woke up his housemaster. No one had any need to alert the housemaster of Farrar's; from across the school playing fields he was actually woken by the sound of the fire, which had taken hold and spread with astonishing rapidity. The crews of the first two fire engines to race to the scene could actually see the flames from the Embankment. An eyewitness living in Kimbolton Road said that by midnight the flames were thirty or forty feet higher than the roof, and by the time fire engines had been summoned from Luton the flames were visible from Barton-le-Clay, 10 miles distant.

The Glebe Road Gates had been padlocked, and this caused delay. When the fire engines did gain entry to the grounds they carried only 400 gallons of water, and already the armoury, the Science Building and even houses in Glebe Road were threatened. Eventually all thirteen fire stations in Bedfordshire turned out to help, and eighteen fire appliances of one sort or another arrived to fight what was in effect a battle lost almost before it had begun. Pressure from hydrants was inadequate to reach the flames — the building stood ninety feet high — and water pumped from the swimming pool was soon exhausted. A hosepipe was even run to a hydrant as far away as the Granada Cinema in St Peter's Street. But almost by the time the first fire engine had arrived the main conflagration was inextinguishable, and efforts were concentrated on preventing the spread of the fire — to adjoining property and the west end of the building. The steel reinforced fire doors played a valuable role.

With hindsight, it can be seen how combustible the building was, even to the extent of containing velvet curtains to conduct flames to the tinder-dry beams in the ceiling, caked as they were by another perfect conductor of fire — eighty years accumulation of dust. Much of the Great Hall's decoration was oak. The chairs were oak. Once the flames had made a meal of the timber, the Victorian bricks behind the panelling grew white hot, emitting a furnace of heat of their own in addition to the scorching effect of the flames. It was rather as if Mr Phillpotts and his boys had generously constructed a giant Guy Fawkes bonfire for their descendants, who stood helplessly by as the school virtually exploded before their eyes. It was twenty-six hours before the last fire-fighting crew withdrew from the wreckage, from the scarred and blackened smoking shell of a building created by a great visionary headmaster and destroyed by an inadequate, unemployed arsonist.

Bedford was by no means the first school to be set on fire. At Eton in 1903 two boys died in an arson attack. In 1939 St Cyprian's at Eastbourne, a famous prep school whose alumni included Cyril Connolly, Cecil Beaton, George Orwell and Gavin Maxwell, the author of *Ring of Bright Water,* was burned down, and in 1950 Radley suffered a series of fires, all started by a boy at the college. At Ludman's trial it was stated by the prosecution that after setting fire to the school he had gone to a public house and later watched the fire raging from a friend's flat. 'He was laughing, cheering and shouting, "Burn, you bastard, burn".'[1] But no public house would have been open at that hour. It is however common practice for arsonists to want to witness the fires they have started, and it was reported in the official account of the fire that Ludman 'admitted that he had been present, and that he had cheered and jeered when the tower fell.'[2]

Among the appalled spectators was Ian Jones, Head Master since 1975 and the twenty-seventh holder of that office. He had been returning from a party when he was diverted by the sight of the flames from School House to the school itself, and was one of the first on the scene. He believes it to be true that Ludman was present and that he jeered in the mistaken belief that the boys would be happy to see their school razed to the ground, receiving a well-merited thump from a monitor. It was widely reported that Ludman's arsons were instigated in order to cover his tracks when committing burglaries, but in the case of the school there must be some doubt on that score; he was never charged with theft on the day of the fire, and his theft of a slide projector and viewer worth £350 from the Science Block was made a week before he broke into the main building, which he almost certainly ignited for no good reason whatsoever.

Initially there was much anguished speculation that a projectionist might have failed to switch off all his equipment, that the fire was a tragic accident for which someone in the school was responsible, but Mr Jones swiftly stamped on any such pointless hand wringing and — quite correctly, as it transpired — exonerated anybody of blame. Ludman was essentially a chronic attention seeker, who boasted of his exploits and made no attempt to destroy incriminating evidence like the hoarding of press reports of the fire, and he was arrested without much difficulty at the King's Arms in St Mary's Street.

Once it was clear the west end of the school building, which housed his study and the Bell Room, were saved Mr Jones was given permission to enter and to attempt to salvage as many papers as possible. They included detailed records of 720 Upper School boys for a start. And as so often happens on these occasions, a farcical incident had to intervene. Thinking to save a valuable offset litho machine, two of the rescue party attempted to manhandle it down the stairs only to drop it, causing considerable damage; left where it was, it would have remained quite safe, despite the fact that 90 per cent of the building and its contents had been destroyed or severely damaged.

Mr Jones had lost the heart of his school — the physical heart, that is; virtually every classroom, every desk, ruler, pencil, chair, table, and of course the Great Hall itself. And it was highly unlikely the academic year — or the next two or three academic years, come to that — would stand still for the benefit of Bedford School. Boys were preparing to sit 'A' and 'O' levels, and there were boys queueing up behind them. Fortunately a good many notebooks and textbooks had been retained by the boys, either at home or in their boarding houses, but the business of a school is to teach, and the first thing Mr Jones had to do was whistle up thirty classrooms.

He got his priorities right from the start. After attending Holy Communion he paid a visit to the dining halls to talk to boys having breakfast. Then he convened a meeting at School House for 10am. Teaching areas were assigned, and they included boarding houses, the dining halls, the pavilion, the chapel and even the rifle range. School headquarters — the Head Master's study, the Bell Room and so on — were from now on to be found at 6 Burnaby Road. That very day, 4 March, Jones had dictated a letter to every parent. 'It is our firm intention that school will continue as normal with the minimum disruption,' he told them. 'The school has a very fine staff and a first rate set of boys, and all of us will now be working harder than we have ever worked before to get the school back into first rate order in as short a time as possible.'

Already he had had notices posted explaining that on Monday morning (the fire had occurred in the early hours of Sunday) school would commence as usual at 9am. The Lower School would meet in the gymnasium. Fourth Forms would go to the Science Block, Removes, Fifth and Sixth Forms to the chapel. Hence on Monday morning the majority of the Upper School was assembled in the chapel, when the Head Master addressed them. 'Stunned, shattered, horrified, shocked, bewildered, tragic- these are just some of the words which can only inadequately describe our present feelings,' he began. But the first priority was to see that school continued. An assessment of the contents lost would be made. Then, 'we shall need to make our permanent plans for the future'.

He asked the boys to be determined and courageous, to remain optimistic, cheerful and helpful. 'Hold your heads up high both inside and outside the school,' he said, 'during term and in the holidays, so that when we look back on this darkest of hours we can justifiably be proud of our efforts and the cooperation which, provided there are no weaknesses in the chain, will pull us through.'

If there was one ray of sunlight it was the thought that only two weeks of term remained. At least the coming Easter holiday would give the Head Master and his staff time away from teaching activities to concentrate on future strategy. Jones had already endured the nightmare of watching his school burn down. Initially, he did something many people do who have lost their home by fire, he returned to pace around the charred remains. Was this perhaps a method of exorcising as swiftly as possible his own personal anguish so that he could get on with healing the wounds of his staff and pupils, and lending constructive leadership at a time when for him to have wavered might have proved fatal? One can imagine Phillpotts or Grose-Hodge managing to cope, but not every headmaster is called upon to face such a challenge to his reputation. Ian Jones's immediate grasp of the situation had all the hallmarks of a man capable of decisive decision-making in a time of crisis. A touching testimonial to his leadership during that last fortnight of term was presented by the head of school in the form of a gigantic greetings card signed by every Upper School boy.

Twenty-two huts were ordered to serve as classrooms, and they formed a sort of temporary teaching village between the Science Building and the chapel. These were for the Upper School. The Lower School moved into the Howard and Craig Buildings, and were given two temporary huts as well. And for the next seven terms the entire school tramped through fields of mud. Lorries were everywhere. Soon the builders had their own site huts to erect. To add to the chaos, at the time of the fire the new Recreation Centre, being built at a cost of £500,000 raised by subscription, was in the course of construction not fifty yards from the main building.

Many people in the town rallied round. Exams were held in the Harpur Centre, former home of the Modern School, when an eighty-six per cent pass rate in 'A' levels was achieved. *Twelfth Night* was staged in the garden of 39 De Parys Avenue. The Girls' High School twice loaned their hall for prize giving. It was not until September that the gutted main building had been cleared of rubble, for one of the first decisions made was to retain the outer walls once it was ascertained they were safe, hence the charred timbers and all the rest of the debris had to be removed by hand.

There was a momentary temptation to call off work on the Recreation Centre in order to facilitate the rebuilding of the main school block, but in the event it was decided to forge ahead. The result is a sports hall, interior swimming pool, four squash courts, a theatre and facilities for badminton, karate, weight training, basketball, volleyball, table tennis, water polo and fencing. On 9 September 1980 the chairman of the Sports Council opened the building and that summer it was possible to use the sports hall as a temporary examination room.

Meanwhile, Ian Jones had set a limit on the time he believed the school could survive undamaged academically or socially while slumming it; two and a half years. It concentrated minds wonderfully, and a deadline for restoration work was set for September 1981. Two firms of architects were invited to make presentations; Frederick Gibberd and Partners, who had recently designed the interior of the Harpur Centre, and Arup Associates, whose founding partner, Philip Dowson, knighted the following year, so impressed the Governors with his comprehension of the needs of the school that his firm was appointed. The complex problems of administration that beset a modern scholastic institution had not begun to surface in 1891, and Dowson realised immediately that what was required was a building adapted to modern requirements encased within a Grade II listed shell; an amalgam of old and new.

Some of the features a school of the future needed were clearly defined areas for different disciplines, the installation of audio-visual and computer equipment, and space for administration, for private studies and displays. A major issue was how to allocate space to a central hall, so vital to the corporate nature of any school, without allowing it to consume such a disproportionate amount of available accommodation as the old Great Hall had done, extending as it did from ground floor to the roof. For once it had been decided to retain the outer walls it seemed, in theory, as if everything everybody wanted to have incorporated would have to fit into the confines of Phillpotts's old building. The overall measurements remained constant; the challenge was to rethink the most creative way of utilising the space available.

Two departments were fairly quickly turfed out, and greatly to their own advantage; the Bursary, now housed at 10 Glebe Road (together with the Old Bedfordians Club), and Religious Studies, currently flourishing in renovated houses in Burnaby Road named after John King. And then Philip Dowson had the brainwave of creating a hall on the principle of the Italian *piano nobile*, its floor at first-floor level, with an approach by means of a grand staircase linked to a new porch at the centre of the south front. In the previous Great Hall, massive windows at first floor level had allowed light in but provided no view; with his new concept, Dowson saw that the same windows could provide the hall with a vista across the playing fields. And he would be left with all the space hitherto wasted in the rafters for extra ground floor accommodation beneath the hall. It is difficult today for anyone who did not know Phillpotts's arrangements to realise that in order to travel at ground floor level to the east or west ends of the building it was invariably necessary to pass along the south side of the Great Hall. Hence for most of each day the Great Hall was little more than a glorified thoroughfare. But now not only would space beneath the Hall be available for constructive use; roof space on the south side of the building not required by the Hall could be utilised to provide a third teaching floor, into which the English and History departments were to move.

Phillpotts's building was insured, in 1979, for £2.15 million.[3] A down payment of £1.9 million prior to an eventual final insurance settlement meant the school could begin to accrue £300,000 over two years by investing the £1.9 million. This still left a considerable shortfall, for no insurance payout could hope to meet the cost of every item it was hoped to incorporate if the fire was to yield its own dividends. Eventually a maximum expenditure of £3.5 million was agreed. By June 1979 construction costs alone were estimated at £2,125,000, and what with VAT and design fees the eventual costs looked as if they could soar to £3.5 million without any difficulty and in no time at all.

The strain all this imposed on the Head Master must have been considerable. Construction work scheduled to take place throughout 1980 could not afford to lag behind if the school building was to be operational by September 1981. And all the usual hazards associated with construction work began to make themselves manifest. There was bad weather that spring; in June there was a shortage of bricklayers; and by September 1980 delays to the roof had put the schedule behind by nearly a month. But as the internal reconstruction began to take shape it was at least possible to walk round the new Hall and visualise the final results; to watch, for example, the tracery being renewed. Not only had the original 19th century designs been unearthed, stone was being used from the very quarry that had supplied the builders in 1891.

As if to create beacons of hope and encouragement, various ceremonies were performed along the way. A stone tablet commemorating the restoration work was unveiled by Sir John Howard, president of the Old Bedfordians Club, and present was a core of people who had done most to speed the process: Mr A C W Abrahams, chairman of the Harpur Trust and the Restoration Committee, and in 1998 elected President of the Old Bedfordians Club; Mr H O Shallard, chairman of the Bedford School Committee; the managing director of the constructors, John Laing; the architect, Sir Philip Dowson; and of course the Head Master. Once the roofing was completed and the new spire was ready to be placed in position the traditional ceremony of topping out took place. In the workshops a time capsule of black fibreglass had been constructed, immersed, by Texas Instruments, in pure dry hydrogen and then hermetically sealed. It was, after all, intended to survive until the year 2552, when the school would be 1,000 years old. Those who eventually open the time capsule will discover inside evidence of life at Bedford School in 1981: there is a copy of the *Ousel* describing the fire, a detention form, a list of school rules, an aerial photograph of the shell of the main building, a facsimile of *Risen!*, commissioned from John Tavener for the Restoration Year Concert,

Oxford and Cambridge Examination Board papers, Tobler-Suchard wrappers, a street plan of Bedford, an Ashburnham tie, a box of chalk and much more besides, including a prize-winning essay by fourteen-year-old Nicholas Tinworth, part of whose elevation to fame involved a trip with the Head Master in a crane to the very pinnacle of the school itself, there to lodge his essay describing what life may be like at Bedford School in 2552.

One of the few items lost in the fire which no one seriously mourned was the inadequate electronic organ in the Great Hall (at morning assembly, Dr Probert-Jones had played a piano on the platform), but expert consideration was given to the new hall as a venue for concerts and recitals, and after much inspection and experimentation a four-manual electronic instrument was installed with three manuals complete and the fourth prepared for. Funds raised at a Restoration Ball in fact enabled the fourth manual to be completed straight away, and all four manuals voiced within a year.

Over the new south porch was incorporated a conference room. By a miracle, the school, town and New College shields were away being cleaned at the time of the fire, and these were now hung above the grand staircase. All the portraits of the Head Masters had been lost, and with the exception of a portrait of Phillpotts, an original previously in the possession of the family, they were replaced by copies. King's is a copy of one at Clifton; Brown's was repainted by the original artist, Bernard Dunstan. Totally irreplaceable were the commemorative chairs, but the new ones chosen after much debate suit the modern design of the hall pretty well. By 1980 it was realised that the entire project was going to cost £4 million. In an attempt to raise £600,000, an appeal was launched, and among the patrons were Sir Adrian Boult and Sir John Betjeman. Had it not been for the fact that eventually the rebuilding programme was zero-rated for VAT purposes there would have been a major loss to be recouped; so complex can financial transactions appear to the layman that a paragraph on the subject from *Bedford School and the Great Fire* is best reproduced verbatim:

As a result of the VAT verdict the final financial equation was to come out rather better than might have been anticipated. The total cost came, if by a somewhat roundabout route, to the very £3.5 million figure originally agreed. Construction costs had increased by some £175,000 since the Design Scheme presentation due to rising inflation and the difficulties associated with the completion of the contract. The addition of landscaping, new fittings, telephones and Great Hall staging had, with other elements, further inflated the total to around £3.9 million when the VAT judgement intervened to reduce the final figure to some £3,502,942. Of this, £3 million was covered by insurance moneys, including interest, and a bank loan financed from the endowment, leaving £500,000 to be raised from the Appeal. Even allowing for any extra costs for the additional car parks and the levelling and re-seeding of the temporary classrooms area the excess was negligible ... On 28 August the restored building was handed over, 100 weeks after the Governors had accepted the Architects' final Design Scheme — four weeks late! It was a near record achievement.

The building was opened on 10 September, and on 15 October the Bishop of St Albans conducted a service of dedication and thanksgiving. The first person to give a recital on the new organ, on 17 October, was none other than George Thalben-Ball, and two days later Tavener's new work, dedicated to the boys of Bedford School, received its premiere by the school's First Orchestra and Choral Society, conducted by the director of music, Andrew Morris. Scored for brass, timpani, percussion, piano and strings, *Risen!* is a work based on the Orthodox Easter exclamation, 'Christ is Risen!'. The guest of honour at the new Hall's first Speech Day, on 21 October 1982, was Lord Home, prime minister for a year from October 1963 to October 1964. He spoke in a building that had received commendations for design, craftsmanship and use of space from the Civic Trust and the Royal Institute of British Architects.

For Old Bedfordians returning to the school for the first time since the fire, the interior of the building they used to know almost always comes initially as a shock. How could it not? It is quite simply an entirely new school. Nostalgia for Phillpotts's school may also linger, and again, why not? So many precious mementos of the past were destroyed. But much that was always familiar remains; the piles of books and equipment hurled down at the east and west entrances, the two Thompson 'mouse' tables saved from the flames, the cloistered quiet during periods of school work and the sudden stampede of feet when the bell rings, and those wretched swing doors, so heavy to push, so useful when a fire is raging.

To have retained the outer shell, almost by necessity, was nevertheless a stroke of genius; it stands, twice scarred by fire, as a reminder of the past and of the stupendous efforts made by Phillpotts in transplanting the school to its present site. Once you have gained your bearings indoors, the awesome transformation can be seen as a blessing, a successful blend of wood and tiles, clean lines and purposeful perspectives, modern but not brash, serviceable but friendly. In terms of teaching methods alone, more than a mere generational gap separates Old Bedfordians who knew the old school and boys who were never taught there, and it is in fact almost inconceivable that today's pupils could have received a satisfactory modern education in the Victorian building. The fire of 1979 seemed at the time a disaster — which it was; what would have been truly catastrophic would have been to buckle under it. It took a very considerable cooperative effort to enable good to come out of evil, but Ian Jones's admonition to the school to remain optimistic, cheerful and helpful paid off very handsomely indeed.

Above All rowed fast, but none so fast as stroke. Bedford Regatta is one of the most popular in the country
Photograph: Bedford County Press

Left Tom Smith, perhaps a little overdressed for Registration

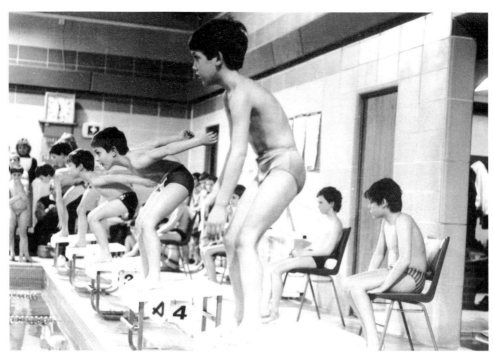

Above Young competitors poised for the off in the new indoor swimming pool
Below A headless referee is not the only one who has failed to realise the ball
has already been retrieved from the scrum, and may even now be half
way down the field, no matter in which direction he points
Photograph: Tony Woodcock

Above In 1992 Leroy Knowles takes the high jump in his stride
Below The same year, Ben Hughes scores in spectacular fashion
against Stowe

It's never too soon to learn. Four Prep School boys debate the rules of croquet

Right A budding carpenter puzzles out how to make a pencil holder
Photograph: Tony Woodcock

189

Above LBW presumably

Right In 1993, at the age of ten, Nathan Rice represented England at badminton and went on to become the most brilliant badminton player so far produced by Bedford
Photographs: Tony Woodcock

Philip Matias, whose beautiful
baritone voice and mature musicality
enhanced many school concerts and
entertainments during the late 1990s

Andrew Morris, appointed Director
of Music in 1979 and whose
contagious enthusiasm has helped
raise the school's musical standards
to unprecedented heights
Photographs: the author

In 1996 a galaxy of Old Bedfordians gathered at the Reform Club to enjoy a lunch in honour of their former history master, John Eyre. Seated are Michael Brunson and Mrs Eyre, and behind from left to right Andrew McCulloch, Richard Lindley (their host), Professor Quentin Skinner, John Percival, the Rt Hon. Paddy Ashdown, Professor Robert Hewison, Carole Stone and Sir Michael Burton
Photograph: Richard Lindley

TWELVE

First Division

1981–1998

NOT CONTENT with a brand new main building, Bedford School entered the decade of the 1980s in an ever-expansionist mood. The Library was refurnished and rearranged, eventually the whole of Burnaby Road was acquired, and further exciting new building projects lay in the not so distant future. As well as finding time to sit on the governing bodies of five prep schools, Ian Jones initiated a staff training day on the last day of the school holidays, partly in preparation for current social problems any modern Head Master now had to face; he was obliged to send one boy home to Hong Kong, and to expel two others for involvement with drugs. Unfortunately, he was also obliged to sack a member of staff for shoplifting, an offence the culprit had cheerfully admitted! On a happier note, several members of his staff were later appointed to headmasterships. Michael Hepworth went to Birkdale as Head Master, David Jarrett to Reeds School at Cobham, Pat Briggs to William Hulme's School, Manchester; Brian Rees was appointed to Pilgrim's, Winchester and Paul Ramage became Head Master of a famous London prep school, The Hall in Hampstead.

Having steered the school through the gravest crisis it had ever faced Ian Jones gave consideration to his own future and in 1986 he moved on to a second headship as Principal of the Royal Naval College, Dartmouth. An editorial in the *Ousel* for November 1986 prophetically stated: 'A history of the school is overdue; the last was written more than sixty years ago, but when eventually an update is written the account will quite correctly lay emphasis on Ian Jones's role in the massive extension of facilities that occurred during his years at the school. It will also stress that but for his leadership in the crucial days following 4 March 1979 the school would have come close to going under. It is easy today to take for granted that such a disaster was avoided, but no one present at the school in those days will forget that he ensured not only that we survived the fire but that we emerged both materially and spiritually better equipped to face the future ... The vision that created an environment in which boys had the opportunity to develop their talents and their self-confidence is perhaps what most characterises the headmastership of Ian Jones.'

One unique feature of that headmastership was that it furnished a school in which sport had always played a major part with a Head Master who was himself a very considerable sportsman. In 1956 Ian Jones had represented Great Britain at hockey in the Rome Olympics, and again at the Olympics in Tokyo in 1960, having played hockey for Cambridge 1958-9 as captain. At cricket, tennis, rugby, athletics and squash he also excelled. As the *Ousel's* appreciation of Mr Jones put it, 'Sport was clearly Ian Jones's main delight; he saw it not as an arena for gladiatorial display but as a way of generating a spirit of communal respect, a sense of fair play and a pulse to beat regeneration within the heart of the school.' An unusual sporting event over which he presided was a tour of Germany in 1985 of the Boat Club, ostensibly to celebrate 125 years of rowing at Bedford. The 1st and 2nd VIIIs spent a fortnight in Berlin and Hamburg, financed by appeals for money sent to Old Bedfordians and to various trust funds. When a final £2,000 was still needed — it was planned to transport two buses and 20 boys — parents rallied round.

Anyone who remembers passing through the German borders before the collapse of the Berlin Wall will not be surprised to learn that it took the crews one and a half hours to get through, nor that 'the guards never once broke into a smile'. Like everyone else who visited the infamous wall, the boys were deeply moved. They also went to see the Olympic Stadium in which Jack Beresford had received his 1936 gold medal from Hitler. The tour was varied in the extreme, although a certain amount of rowing does appear to have taken place; on the itinerary was a visit to the 14/20th Hussars and to East Berlin itself, a wretched ghetto of Communist deprivation in contrast to a champagne breakfast and other culinary delights laid on by their West Berlin hosts. To his credit, the club secretary, Richard Young, communicated in fluent German. A shock awaited the oarsmen in Hamburg. Having been invited to a lavish reception, the Bedford contingent was informed they would have to contribute £100 towards it! And when they got down to some serious racing on the Alster See it seems that pleasure cruisers most annoyingly had the right of way. All in all it was a turbulent jaunt, 'with everyone clearly worn out by the general pace of the tour and its timetable of events'.

Sporting tours are now a regular occurrence, organised on a rota basis. In 1987 the Boat Club flew off to the USA; the following year the Hockey XI toured Kenya. And in 1989 the 1st XV, who had previously been to Portugal and Spain, embarked on another overseas commitment — to New Zealand and Fiji, a far cry from their usual round of fixtures against Oundle, Rugby, Dulwich, Stowe, Uppingham and Haileybury. Twenty-eight boys went on the tour, and they played seven matches, five in New Zealand and two in Fiji. It was in a way a reward for a team who embodied a tradition of rugby which by any standards is outstanding, for over the years Bedford School had by this date produced 16 International players, three British Lions, twenty-nine Barbarians and twenty-one Blues.

The earliest rugby game played by Bedford against an away opponent is believed to have been in 1870, against Christ's College, Cambridge. The school's first rugby coach of standing was E H Dasent, in charge of the 1st XV 1884-1909, and it was he who established Bedford as a formidable rugby school. At one time in the late nineteenth century Bedford remained unbeaten by any other school for eight consecutive seasons, and photographs of some of the early teams may explain why; they feature burly boys of strapping proportions. The year 1907 seems to have been a record breaker; the 1st XV amassed 1,027 points, Mill Hill going down to an 89-nil defeat, St Paul's to an 84-nil defeat. In 1941 the 1st XV won every single match and scored 354 points to a mere 26 accumulated by their opponents. This was a period also when the school were finalists in the Public Schools Sevens three years in succession, winning twice.

Certain names have become bywords for Bedford School rugby. One is that of Leo Oakley, who scored eight tries in 1941 in a match against Stowe, and five in a match against Uppingham the following year. At Bedford 1932-43, Oakley may justly be regarded as the best all-round games player the school has ever produced, excelling not only at rugby but at cricket, boxing, gymnastics and athletics. He played in the 1st XV in 1941, 1942 and 1943, during three years when no inter-school match was lost. In 1942 he scored thirty-seven tries in twelve matches. During his second year in the 1st XI Oakley scored two centuries, and by the time he left school he was captain of Football, Cricket, Boxing and Gym. When he died in 1981 a contemporary, Sir Peter Parker, proposed a Leo Oakley Award to enable a Bedford School boy to attend a games coaching course or to help pay his expenses on a school team tour. D P Rogers (Budge Rogers), at school 1949-57, regarded by another famous Old Bedfordian coach, Murray Fletcher, as 'perhaps Bedford School's greatest player', went on to play for England against Ireland, France, Scotland, Wales, New Zealand and Australia a total of thirty-four times, on several occasions as captain. When he was made OBE in 1969 he became the first person to be honoured for services to rugby.

No account, however truncated, of Bedford's sporting achievements could be penned without special reference to Murray Fletcher, who died in 1996 at the age of seventy-three and whose name is now incorporated in the Leo Oakley Award. He was another of those people who devoted their entire life to the school, as boy, Old Bedfordian, master and coach. His actual connection with the school lasted 62 years, for he was 10 when he entered the Inky in 1934. In his last year he was captain both of the 1st XV and the 1st XI, and after army service and teacher training he immediately returned to the school, taking on, and retaining until he retired, the lower stream Fourth Form, for he had a great gift for encouraging less able boys and motivating them beyond their own expectations. He succeeded Owen Bevan as coach of the 1st XV, and was, in the words of Budge Rogers, 'a wonderful coach, who by his enthusiasm, patience and example both in attitude and skill brought out the best in both team and individual'. [1]

Fletcher became housemaster of Redburn, and was one of a new generation of masters who took seriously his role as surrogate parent for two-thirds of every boy's childhood, making sure that whereas discipline was maintained, one purpose of school life was to have fun. He spent his last six years at the school as Registrar, and in 1989 he became president of the Old Bedfordians Club. It was during his time, in the 1980s, that soccer was introduced as a minor sport, an addition to the Easter activities.

In April 1994 the Under Fifteen XV had the excitement of playing at Twickenham in the finals of the *Daily Mail* Cup, having beaten five schools in the preliminary rounds to meet Wellington College, a triumph only slightly marred by the outcome, a disappointing draw. And then in October 15 boys set off on a cricket tour of South Africa, playing eight matches in fifteen days. Writing in the *Ousel* for March 1996, David Money (on the staff 1947 - 78) recalled the cricketing achievements of Michael Allen, at school from 1944-50, who had died that year. He thought he was 'almost certainly the most successful spin bowler to play for the school'. Allen joined the 1st XI in 1949, when he was 16, and in two seasons his left-arm spin brought him 75 wickets. In 1950 he took 52 of them at an average of 12.73. After leaving school, his first-class career lasted some 20 years.

Lest it be assumed that Bedford's sporting successes all lie in what many young Bedfordians will today regard as the dim and distant past (Budge Rogers and Leo Oakley were born between the two world wars) a new Bedford star was born in 1992 — or to be precise, in 1983, the year of Nathan Rice's birth. He began his dramatic career at the age of nine by winning the singles event at a Buckinghamshire Under-12 county badminton tournament, and within six years he had progressed to international level. By the summer of 1997 Rice had represented England ten times; by the age of fourteen he had been national champion three years running, and in 1997 he held the singles, doubles and mixed doubles titles at Under 14. In his own age group in singles, between October 1995 and June 1997 he did not lose a match in domestic or international tournaments, winning well in excess of 100 matches.

In July 1996 it was the turn of hockey enthusiasts to go abroad — again to South Africa. Contemporary hockey dates from the codification of rules by the Hockey Assocation in 1886, and hockey was played at Bedford in the late 19th and early 20th centuries, the *Ousel* recording Blues and Internationals. It was reintroduced at the school in 1974, and is now, together with rowing, rugby and cricket, one of the school's four major sports. After problems of acclimatising to an altitude of 2,000 metres in Pretoria, the Bedford 1996 team got off to a commendable start by beating the Northern Transvaal team 4-0. They had been cold while staying at St Albans College, Pretoria; when the Bedford boys arrived at St John's School, Johannesburg it snowed for the first time for fourteen years. St John's is a school with a strong hockey tradition, so Bedford did particularly well to beat them 4-1.

The team moved on to Zimbabwe, as the guests of Prince Edward School at Harare, and emerged from a grass pitch 3-2 victors. They then saw off a boarding school called Peterhouse 2-1. Several members of the team had by now succumbed to food poisoning, so when they faced Northwood High School at Durban it was amazing they won 5-0, two goals being scored by Miles Harris, who normally kept goal, head of school 1996-7. Astonishingly enough, Bedford went on to win their next four matches as well, two of them by 2-1 and 4-1, the last two by 6-0. It was a memorable tour, which encompassed visits to Table Mountain and Victoria Falls, and included two nights in a Zulu village and close encounters with elephant and wildebeest. Two factors stand out, quite apart from the school's prowess at hockey; the ever-increasing opportunities Bedford boys were being given to travel while participating in competitive sporting activities, and the continued tradition of all-round excellence. The same boy, Tim Foster, contributed articles to the *Ousel* on both the rugby match at Twickenham and the hockey tour of South Africa.

Two afternoons a week are devoted to compulsory sports, rugby being played in the autumn term, hockey in the Easter (although it is also played indoors during the autumn) and cricket of course in the summer, although again, the school's sports facilities are now so extensive that cricket can be played indoors during the Easter term. As for rowing, this is now virtually an all year round activity. Due to a proliferation of minor sports — sixteen, all of which obtain school fixtures — fewer boys indulge in major sports than in the past, and traditional Bedford sports like fencing and fives now compete with weight-training, water polo, canoeing and even golf. In 1998 a Lower Sixth boy, Chris Mayson, bade cricket a sad farewell (as he was a member of the 1st XI it could not have been an easy decision) in order to concentrate on golf, for as an England Under-18 golfer he was playing off a handicap of one. Not surprisingly, *The Times* was predicting for him 'a glittering future in the game'.

The popularity of basketball can be attributed to the enthusiasm in particular of boys from south-east Asia. Some 50 boys play badminton. There is less coercion than ever before for a boy to take part in a major sport if his inclinations lean elsewhere. A boy with a beautiful singing voice, who was contributing a great deal not only musically, managed in 1997 to persuade the Director of Sport and Activities that his participation in any sport would be a total waste of time, so he and five other boys were given permission to play croquet — an extraordinary and commendable example of Bedford's contemporary flexibility.

The days when the school could depend exclusively on masters to coach have gone. Staff are under increasing academic pressure from league tables, and at a time when the school is hard enough pressed to recruit a first-rate mathematician or physicist they can hardly afford to turn one away because he does not offer sport at a high level. Almost all members of staff are involved in sport for at least two terms a year. Some female teachers are happy to help with rugby and rowing, but rowing still only survives by the school employing 15 outside coaches. Quite how rugby, soccer, cricket and athletics survive on fields that have been trodden under foot for 100 years is a real mystery; top soil has been eroded, drainage affected, and in a perfect world the school sports fields would be left fallow for a couple of years. It has become a moot point, whether work or sport has come under the greater pressure in recent years, partly because both exist in an ever-increasingly competitive world. Two changes very apparent to older Old Bedfordians must be the minor importance attributed these days to house matches and the abolition of the nightmare cross-country race, from which boys either returned in the last gasps of acute dyspepsia or failed to return at all; today they take part in a civilised eight-mile relay. They will be glad to know, however, that although academic and creative work have become highly prized, sporting success is still regarded as important, and successful sportsmen retain a large measure of prestige. Their activities are nothing if not wide-ranging. The year 1997–8, for example, produced junior internationals at cricket, hockey, rowing, rugby, golf, badminton and go-kart racing! It is increasingly common, however, for boys to excel both at work and games.

Although the 1st VIII were naturally disappointed to lose to Bedford Modern School in a race on the Ouse in 1998 for a new cup presented by the Prince of Wales, no one could accuse the Boat Club of resting on their oars. Two weeks later, at Henley, the 1st VIII beat Shrewsbury and Emanuel School in the first two heats of the Princess Elizabeth Cup. In 1989 an OB, Damien Rimmer, had won a gold medal at the Junior World Championships, racing in the coxless Fours event. Two years later another Old Bedfordian, Richard Young, became the first man to win a rowing Blue for both Oxford and Cambridge. At Henley in 1994 the school reached the final of the Fawley Challenge Cup, the following year the 1st VIII won the Open Eights at Bedford Regatta, and at Henley in 1997 two Old Bedfordians triumphed, James Edwards in the Brittania Coxed Fours and Alex Henshilwood in the Ladies Plate, Henshilwood going on to win silver and gold medals at Munich. At the town regatta in 1998 the 1st VIII set a course record when they beat St Edward's School, Oxford.

On the departure in 1986 of Ian Jones, who had done much to replace the Anglo-Indian connection by encouraging educational contacts in Australia, Malaysia and Hong Kong, the Governors alighted on Sidney Miller, the third Head Master of Bedford to have been educated at Clifton College, where he had been deputy head of school. A classicist, at Jesus College, Cambridge he took a Double First, and spent time at Harvard University as a Knox Fellow before returning to Clifton to teach the Classical Sixth. For five years he was head of the Classical Department at Eton. From there he became deputy headmaster of Bridgewater Hall Comprehensive School, and in 1977 he was appointed Head Master of Kingston Grammar School.

In the event, Mr Miller only remained Head Master for eighteen months, during which time he dismantled streaming, introduced setting for most major subjects and officially abolished caning; the practice of beating boys had been gradually fading out but required a positive sentence of death, and interestingly enough, parliament did not get around to banning caning officially in the private sector until March 1998. He initiated Technology from the age of 11 and did much to further links between the school and industry — surprising moves, perhaps, for a classical scholar. Just as importantly, he set up the line management in existence today, creating for Richard Miller, who had joined the staff in 1982 as head of History (he had previously taught at Alleyns and Lancing), the post of Director of Studies, a position ranking third in seniority after the Vice-Master.

On grounds of ill health, Sidney Miller resigned in March 1988, and Michael Barlen, Vice-Master since 1977, was appointed acting Head Master and then Head Master, but it was evident his appointment was a stop-gap measure, for he was due to retire in any case in 1990 following thirty-four vigorous and creative years on the staff, spending a decade as head of History. But that retirement was cut tragically short in 1991 when, on a walking holiday in Switzerland, he died at the age of sixty-one.

Not since the headmasterships in the seventeenth century of John Allanson and William Willis had a Head Master remained in office only a couple of years; for two successive Head Masters to serve for so short a time was not only unprecedented, it was seriously unsettling for the school. In fact, by 1990 morale was at a low ebb, for no matter what Mr Barlen's sturdy qualifications may have been, no school thrives properly under a caretaker. It was essential that the Governors make a wise choice to succeed him; indeed, any Head Master chosen at this time would have been well aware how much was expected of him. From among some 50 applicants, of whom, with the aid of a former headmaster from outside recruited as a consultant, ten were interviewed, there emerged a shortlist of three, one of whom was Philip Evans, for the previous 15 years an assistant master at St Paul's, and for the past six years head of the Chemistry department.

The fact that Dr Evans is a chemist could have told against his chances of appointment, for in that respect he was an unusual choice for Head Master of Bedford. He was also a state grammar school boy. Born in 1948, Dr Evans is a true child of post-war Britain, who finds it difficult to credit conditions in boarding houses experienced by any Old Bedfordian boarder over 50. He graduated at Churchill College, Cambridge with a First in Natural Sciences, and both he and his wife are doctors of philosophy. As a Welshman, it is hardly surprising that he lists among his interests music and poetry; but it came as something of a shock to his colleagues to discover his preference for cricket over rugger. What appealed to the Governors when they selected Philip Evans was his 'drive, obvious academic excellence, powers of communication and Welsh impishness'. [2]

Dr Evans's appointment coincided almost exactly with the centenary of the school's removal to its present site, and in 1991 gates to commemorate that centenary were erected at the eastern end of the chapel path. That somehow epitomised the new Head Master's desire to look simultaneously backwards and forwards, to nurture tradition while urging progress. While Ian Jones had been so nervous of getting a boy's name wrong he tended not to address his pupils by any name at all, under Dr Evans the almost universal use of boys' first names has become the norm — and not just by the staff. When surnames alone were used, it was rare for a boy to know another boy's first name unless they were close friends.

Philip Evans arrived at Bedford School with a deep curiosity about its past, a desire to stabilise the school whilst reassuring the staff, and a determination to secure for the school a reputation for academic excellence without which it could not hope to compete in what had become an education market. Parents were no longer putting down the names of their sons at birth; they had got into the habit, accompanied by their boys, of touring a number of schools before deciding which one was up to scratch, boarding house and games facilities being high on their order of priority. Senior boys are nowadays detailed to show parents and their offspring round. Fees, which inevitably rise year by year, were £300 per annum for a boarder in Grose-Hodge's time; by 1998 Upper School tuition and full boarding fees had risen to £12,720 a year, and facilities of every kind are now expected for that sort of money. Just as Grose-Hodge had himself arrived at a kind of crossroads, so had Philip Evans; the world was modernising at an alarming pace, and he knew that Bedford School had to keep abreast if it was to fill sufficient places to retain financial viability — which it has succeeded in doing, the number of boys remaining around a fairly constant 1,100 over the past decade. There is a general trend to send boys to school as boarders later than was the case in the past, but senior boarding houses have retained something like a 98 per cent capacity at a time when boarding is less fashionable at every age, and these figures can not be attributed solely to an influx of students from overseas, whose total share of the school population has been fixed by the Governors at approximately 10 per cent.

With the advent of Dr Evans's arrival gone for ever was the luxury of being allowed to coast along in the sure and certain knowledge that the world was every public schoolboy's oyster. The world of the last decade of the twentieth century owed no one a living, and boys were coming under increasing pressure to secure sound academic qualifications. Apart from his major building programme, Dr Evans's great achievement to date has been to make hard work respectable.

Although he believes it is essential to keep somewhat aloof from the rough and tumble and to accept the inherent loneliness of the job, the Head Master misses his academic teaching, likes to mingle with the boys as much as possible, and can sometimes be seen taking lunch in the dining halls, not hesitating to join a table where boys are sitting rather than staff. He has a shrewd Celtic assessment of a boy's character, seldom being fooled by the angelic charms of a potential trouble maker, and is immensely proud of his senior boys — and bitterly disappointed when he has to discipline one, as he did in the spring of 1999, when a monitor was demoted for drinking in an unauthorised pub. Of personal pomposity, so often the mark of a senior pedagogue, he has none, being quite liable to kneel on the gravel to tie up the shoelace of a little boy in the Prep School, who doubtless has only the vaguest idea who he is, although in fact Dr Evans visits the Prep School once a week, just as he continues Grose-Hodge's habit of interviewing every boarder, to discuss their half-term report. His criterion of a good school is one where 'academic excellence and a satisfying breadth of education are not mutually exclusive'. [3] Among the staff who recall the school before he arrived he is regarded as having provided a strong rudder; he hopes he is fair and not afraid to take difficult decisions; whilst the boys perceive him as tough but humane, a Head Master whose displeasure is not easily earned but once experienced can leave a sense of remorse. Philip Evans is the first Head Master since King to have a doctorate and the boys call him Doc Evans. He is also the first Head Master to have featured in an honours list, being made an OBE in the 1999 New Year Honours List for services to the Qualifications and Curriculum Authority.

It is extraordinary the degree of loyalty to Bedford School that Head Masters recruited from elsewhere so swiftly seem to acquire (Dr Evans attributes this to a genuine sense of community). Yet the crucial thing for a new Head Master to do, especially one whose appointment has been critical, is to establish his own agenda. This Dr Evans lost no time in doing. Having taken stock of the Governors' views at that time he decided very swiftly that the Lower School, separated from the Inky yet not properly integrated within the main building, had served its purpose. Thus he took the plunge, and in 1992 the Lower School and the Inky merged to become a new Preparatory School for boys between the ages of seven and thirteen. This meant that new accommodation would be required, for the old Inky building could not cope with 400 boys. Eagle House, with accommodation for thirty-four boarders, was purpose built, with bedrooms for four, five or six boys and what the school prospectus describes, without exaggeration, as 'en-suite facilities'. With Eagle House commissioned, Nash's could then be used as classrooms for boys aged seven and eight. The nine and ten-year-olds would continue to be taught in the old Inky building, and the Wells Building, named after Colonel George Wells, at the school 1884 - 94 and a former Governor, was extended for the senior Lower School boys. This newly enhanced Wells Building was opened by Betty Boothroyd, Speaker of the House of Commons, on 13 November 1993. Miss Boothroyd had a busy day, for she was asked at the same time to lay the foundation stone for a superb new Prep School building, the Erskine May Hall, adjacent to the Recreation Centre's theatre. Capable of seating 475, the Erskine May Hall provides a centre for Prep School assemblies and also serves as an adaptable concert hall and theatre. It was opened on 9 December 1994 by the Warden of New College, Oxford, Dr Harvey McGregor, but it had to wait until 14 October 1995 for its final touch, a series of splendid stained glass windows designed and made by Peter Sutton and unveiled by Chris Woodhead, HM Chief Inspector of Schools.

The school has particular cause to be grateful to Colonel Wells. In 1938 he purchased Ickwell Bury, seven or eight miles south-east of Bedford, an estate with roots going back to the thirteenth century and once the property of the

Knights Hospitallers of St John. When in 1971 the Colonel's widow died the estate was bequeathed to the school, and now serves as a conservation area. More than 20 years on dead trees and undergrowth are still being cleared, and a ten-year plan at present in operation aims at reclaiming the Bury for a wide variety of wild life. A river has already been dredged, a lake cleared of logs and reeds, and much superfluous ivy has been cut down. For many boys the Bury has become almost a place of pilgrimage.

Having muddled along for so many years in the Upper School building, former Lower School boys were now more than handsomely accommodated, and once the Lower School and the Inky were combined it meant that the smallest boys in the school could expand from their 100-year-old building on St Peter's Street; the Prep School now had, for the first time, its own design technology workshops and an Information Technology suite equipped with networked computers. A further addition to the Prep School compound was the acquisition of a house next door to Nash's, named Palmer's after Donald Palmer, the former Inky Head Master. This provided an art room, a science laboratory and music rooms, where much vital coaching takes place in preparation for Prep School boys to take their places eventually in the school orchestras.

School houses for the Prep School were devised separately from the Upper School houses: Bunyan, Harpur, Howard and Whitbread. From the age of seven all the boys are taught French and design technology, and they take up a second modern language when they are thirteen.

The academic year 1994-5 was a testing time for the school. They had been selected for inspection, and in theory they had been given a generous seven months notice of the fact. But as the information arrived towards the end of the 1994 Easter term, and the school inspectorate wanted School Information Details by mid-June, the school effectively had just 10 working weeks in which, 'on top of all else that had to be done in a pressured term, to produce the most complete written statement of the work of the school that had ever been written'.[4] Heads of departments, housemasters and the Bursary were duly alerted, and for five days the inspectors spent twelve hours a day attending lessons and investigating almost every aspect of school life. Thanks to stalwart cooperation from pupils as well as staff the school came through with flying colours, the verdict being that 'The academic standards are high in relation to the ability of the pupils and to schools of a similar kind'.

Philip Evans had soon clarified his mind about his ambitions for Bedford School, and they appeared in an Academic Statement published in September 1996.

Bedford School aims to develop the possibilities within each of its boys by using to the full the opportunities provided by its long history and high investment in staff and facilities. These possibilities exist in academic endeavours, in a sense of community, and in recreational, sporting and cultural activities. Developing intellectual excellence is paramount, and it complements and informs all else that is undertaken.

Through its staff the school aims to provide expertise and commitment. In the admission of its boys it aims to recruit those who will make best use of what it offers in academic, communal, recreational, sporting and cultural areas, and who will contribute most towards them. The school is the community of its staff, boys and parents; understanding of this drives much of its character.

Sensitive to its past, the school has a commitment to innovation and to the best contemporary practices. It aims to provide equally for those of any racial or religious background, to integrate its rich mixture of boarders and day boys and, while retaining the benefits of single sex education, to develop strong links with its sister schools and with the community beyond its estate. It helps pupils develop a sense of their own worth and to value others, to delight in achievement, to experience hard work and to see its results, to find lifelong pleasure in sport, drama, music and art, and to leave the school with their ambitions extended.

By this time the school had adopted a tutorial system, and the daily management of each boy's progress was being organised by his tutor, boys other than fourth formers remaining with the same tutor throughout their school career. In charge of the curriculum, 'as broad as we can make it', is the Director of Studies, who oversees all the work of the academic departments, manages staff appraisal and operates subject options. He also monitors applications to universities, and claims to be available to all parents, boys and staff at all times, which cannot be quite true, remarkably available though he is; he actually teaches as well.

While the majority of Upper School boys enter at thirteen, mainly from prep schools, a recent innovation is to take boys into a Lower Sixth Form at sixteen; generally they are required to have six passes at GCSE (grade C or higher), with B grade passes in the subjects they have chosen for 'A' level study. Whilst 'no boy is admitted to the school on academic criteria alone' the 'academic requirement is nonetheless of primary importance'. The majority of Sixth Formers go on to higher education in the October of the year they leave school; in 1995 120 Upper Sixth boys achieved the necessary grades for university entrance, the humanities and social sciences predominating. A distinctive feature of Bedford today is the high percentage of boys leaving with outstanding grades in mathematics and science.

With justifiable pride, Dr Evans was able to write in an Introduction to his Sixth Form Prospectus for 1998-2000, 'The achievements of Sixth Formers at Bedford are notable. Our pass rate at 'A' level is in excess of ninety-nine per cent, and approaching 70 per cent of these are at grade A or B. There are similar grades from the 'AS' levels that are taken. This performance places the school firmly in the published First Division of Schools. As a result, almost all

Sixth Formers proceed from Bedford to universities of their choice and many gain Oxbridge places (129 in the last ten years and twenty-one this year).' In December 1998 Dr Evans was able to inform parents that the percentage of Fifth Year GCSE candidates gaining five or more starred A to C grades was 99.3 per cent, with the *Daily Telegraph* table of top independent schools placing Bedford 79th out of 312.

Unfortunately, however, once at university the former Sixth Formers' struggles are far from over. In 1999 annual university grants were due to be halved to £810 at a time when it was estimated that nine out of ten students would leave university with debts of £7,500, and that only forty-three per cent of students were likely to find work within six months of graduating. With employment and financial prospects like these it requires enormous incentive, if not courage, to persevere while at school. Between the wars it was common practice to go up to Oxford merely to drink and hunt; someone like Edward Sackville-West, at Christ Church 1920-24, had no need of a degree and knew if he sat for one it would probably be a very poor one indeed. When a wealthy contemporary, Peter Ralli, took his History finals in 1922 he obviously had every intention of being ploughed, for he produced one, immortal sentence: 'Her subjects wanted Queen Elizabeth to abolish tunnage and poundage, but the splendid creature stood firm.' Those were the days!

Within a year of his arrival Dr Evans was compelled to take note of the 1989 Children Act, which came into force in October 1991, and purported to create a safer environment, and a fairer one, for 'children at risk', 'children in need' and boarding pupils. One thing the school's implementation of the Act has done is squash once and for all the notion that a bachelor will ever again be appointed as a housemaster. The school's policy statement categorically states that 'Boarding houses are run as family houses, and in residence are the housemaster and his family...' And it goes on to state, 'The housemaster works in conjunction with his pastoral team of wife, tutors, matrons and senior boys...' In other words, in deference to a society with 'child abuse' on the brain, bachelors need not apply, and an embarrasing hiatus concerning an unmarried housemaster in the 1990s seems to have clinched the matter. 'Parents expect a family unit,' says Dr Evans. 'In terms of PR it would be unwise to employ a bachelor housemaster, however gifted pastorally.' [5]

When it comes to disciplinary procedures things could also not be in greater contrast to the recent past: 'The pupil [who has transgressed] will be provided with an opportunity to explain his case to the appropriate member of staff in the Line Management who will then make the decision as to what disciplinary action is to be taken. The pupil may, if he wishes, be accompanied and represented during a disciplinary interview by a fellow pupil of his choice. The member of staff conducting the interview may also request the presence of another person employed by the school. A pupil may request one or both parents to be present during a disciplinary interview.' Not so easy if they live in Brunei.

Now that caning has been abolished the range of disciplinary measures available to the school seems meagre: for a 'minor offence' a verbal warning, drill or academic detention; for 'more serious offences' gating, or receipt of a report card; 'more serious still', exclusion for a specified time; 'Gross misconduct' and a boy can expect 'Permanent Exclusion', or in other words, expulsion. At the same time, monitors and options are reminded that 'punishments should always be applied carefully and fairly', and that 'leniency is often a sign of strength rather than weakness'.

It is really only on the question of illegal drugs that the school exercises a heavy hand. 'The school sees that it is part of its professional responsibility to provide support and counselling for any pupils and their families who encounter problems with drugs; at the same time it will take any necessary disciplinary or other appropriate action. Those involved in the selling and distribution of drugs, in the use of drugs on the school estate, and those encouraging others to take illegal drugs should expect the severest of penalties. The police and other appropriate external agencies will be informed of any drug-related incidents.'

Clarence Seaman (1951-55) would have been the last Head Master not to be plagued by the drug culture that began to take hold in the early 1960s; William Brown (1955-75) would have been the first Head Master who needed to be aware of the problem. It is something of an irony that the drug under whose influence boys are still most likely to fall is alcohol, and many a pair of bleary eyes can be seen weaving their headache-driven way to school on a Monday morning, now that freedom unknown to their predecessors enables many unsupervised day boys to indulge in an excess of drinking over the weekend. This, to the unsophisticated outsider, is only one surprise to be encountered among the modern headmaster's catalogue of concerns; for all the talk of an enlightened age, it is remarkable that boys can still find it in their hearts to bully other boys. The cynic will no doubt reply that boys will be boys, but in so many other aspects of their behaviour, late-twentieth century public school boys are more courteous towards one another than ever they were in the past. Nevertheless, as a precautionary and socially educative measure anti-bullying workshops are held at Bedford for all boys between the ages of eight and fifteen. Likewise, staff attend training days on bullying, and on 'child abuse'. The truth is that with the nation currently held to ransom by political correctness no school can afford to give hostages to fortune, although compared to the past boys today do not know what bullying is.

Bedford's guide to the Children Act lists no fewer than 14 possible worries or complaints boys might have, about which they are actively encouraged to complain. They include the possibility that a monitor may have treated them unkindly, and even the belief that they are being badly taught!

They are told:

It is particularly important for you to realise that if you are in trouble over something you can have your house tutor or a friend with you when you are talking with your housemaster, the vice-master or Head Master.

You do not have to inform staff or anyone else when you are complaining about them.

If the matter can't be easily settled to your satisfaction then you can make a formal complaint. You will need to do this by:

a) writing to your housemaster, vice-master or the Head Master, or telling your housemaster that you wish to make a formal complaint, then

b) he will then write the complaint in the complaints book held by the vice-master, then

c) if, within a week, you have not had the matter satisfactorily sorted out you may contact any of the people listed at the end of this booklet.

It was inevitable, given the climate of opinion in 1990, and the seemingly unstoppable swelling of the ranks of counsellors, that by the summer of 1992 a part-time school counsellor should have been appointed. He is a professional psychotherapist. Not surprisingly he sees more day boys than boarders, who have their own network of 'counsellors'; their housemaster, his wife and their house tutor. On the other hand, many boys, day or boarding, prefer to talk to someone who is not on the staff. He follows the normal code of ethics regarding confidentiality, only referring a case if he thinks that someone is at risk. He is also confident that physical bullying is relatively rare, but he sees the belittling of a boy, by another boy or a master, as a form of bullying.

Despite what appears to be an abundance of support — tutors, chaplains, housemasters — the school counsellor justifies his presence because he has the luxury of time. Boys may see him as often and for as long as they wish. When a Sixth Form boy was killed in a road accident his friends were bereaved, and turned to the school counsellor for befriending. He sees boys as young as seven, and is happy to see them with their parents if that is what the boy prefers. Unfortunately, he also sees many of the problems faced by day boys as emanating from the home; problems with step-parents, for instance, and whereas 40 years ago a boy whose parents were divorced would have been a rarity, today his situation is all too common.

The school counsellor is available 11 hours a week, usually by appointment. In the school year 1996-7 he saw forty-eight individual boys, who between them were involved in 320 appointments, about half a dozen appointments each. This would indicate fairly concentrated sessions of counselling. He is also available to staff. Fifteen per cent of the problems with which he had been presented concerned family and parents and eight per cent involved divorce or separation. Pressure of work accounted for eight per cent as well. Perhaps rather alarmingly, anxiety, fear or anger accounted for eighteen per cent, and depression for fourteen per cent. But happily, bullying by other boys amounted to only two per cent, and by teachers the figure was nil. There were no financial problems rearing their ugly heads, nor homesickness, although housemasters' wives undoubtedly have to cope from time to time with cases of loneliness affecting boys from overseas. 'Abuse', but of what nature was not specified in the figures released to staff, accounted for two per cent, and alcohol and other drugs a mere one per cent. Racism did not figure in the statistics at all — for the simple reason that at Bedford School there is none. That is not to say all ethnic groups settle in easily; but where problems exist this has to do not with the colour of a boy's skin but with his general demeanour and perceived unsociability.

These figures relate only to the incidence of appointments to see the counsellor. They bear no relation to the overall picture. A questionnaire on bullying distributed to a large number of boys once elicited the information that 175 of them considered that at one time or another, and to some degree or another, they had been bullied. The value of anti-bullying workshops may well be to keep boys aware of the unpleasantness of bullying at any age and in any form. So much depends on definition. If during his entire school career a boy once receives an unsolicited hack on the shins and claims for the rest of his life he has been subjected to bullying, his evidence can scarcely be regarded as worth recording. But any remedial efforts being made today have to be an improvement on the tactics adopted by Noel Sutcliffe at Farrar's. If a boy was accused of being a bully in the 1940s the other boys were lined up in two columns and instructed to punch him as he ran the gauntlet.

In the 'good old days', and they were not so long ago, sex education at Bedford was confined to lectures delivered to the Sixth Form by a biology master. Today Prep School boys of 10 and 11 can expect to be taught the basic facts of sexual reproduction, and boys of fourteen and fifteen are treated to drama workshops by a touring company which covers issues of sexual health and personal relationships, the dangers of HIV and attitudes to homosexuality. In the role plays there is always a gay character, whose appearance, sad to relate, seems to engender homophobia among the younger boys, whose attitudes become more liberal by the time they reach the Fifth and Sixth Forms. The chances are that today there are few homosexual role models among the staff; but those believed to be gay are greatly respected. It is also the case that a combination of misinformation about the origins of AIDS together with a rampantly homophobic gutter press has created an issue where in the past no issue existed. Boys never used to be troubled by their own sexuality in the way they are today, for there were not the pressures to conform to heterosexual modes of behaviour. It must today be exceedingly difficult and painful for boarders to come to terms even with normal adolescent homosexual feelings, never mind with the concept that they may in fact be endemically homosexual, and for a boy to display any overt understanding with or sympathy for a gay character in a workshop is perhaps asking too much of any but the boldest.

Since 1986 the Upper School has employed a handful of women teachers, one of whom was placed in charge of sex and health education. It seems small wonder that rather than ask a question of her verbally boys felt compelled to write their questions anonymously on a scrap of paper. While it may well be true that boys are best taught about relations with women by a woman, there are many intimate details concerning male sexuality that no boy can feel comfortable discussing with a woman, and with the best will in the world the impression one gains is that in all but the purely biological field sex education at Bedford, as in most British schools, remains in its infancy. 'I was uncertain of what (sic) it would be like teaching in an all-boys school,' one of the half-dozen or so Upper School mistresses reported in a 1998 *Newsletter*. 'In fact I think some boys found it strange having a young female teacher. Once we all got over our initial shock there seemed to be no real difference, except some boys still occasionally call me "Sir"!'

It is no disrespect to Dr Evans's academic credentials to say that he is also a man who enjoys managerial skills. How else can the headmaster of a modern public school shoulder his responsibilities, which are immense? He is not unlike the captain of a battleship, responsible, in the case of Bedford, for the welfare and education of over 1,100 boys; responsible too for a teaching staff of at least 110, and for plant worth millions of pounds. There are seven boarding houses and six day houses alone, before you begin to count up the value of property comprising the main school building, the Prep School buildings, the Recreation Centre, chapel, Science Block. The more facilities the school lays on the more complex becomes the organisational structure, and there are two primary preoccupations representing the lifeblood of the school which will never go away; a satisfactory recruitment of new suitable boys and an examination pass rate which will impress the parents of potential recruits. There is today even a Marketing Manager.

The Head Master's day is punctuated with appointments, and unless he keeps abreast of paperwork he is liable to end up buried beneath a pile of it. This state of affairs is true for most of the assistant masters as well, particularly for heads of departments. Dr Evans enjoys helping boys with discipline and advice, 'turning around a cussed boy'. There is, he says, 'a subtlety in handling the young that is enjoyable'. [6] But to enable him to make time to take even a minimal pastoral interest in over 700 Upper School boys he has been known to resort to the last desperate measure of the politician, a working breakfast, and there are times when, under pressure, he makes himself available to staff in his study at 7.30 am. He interviews every new member of staff, and every boarder once a year. He tries to attend every major school event and if he is not free his wife will try to represent him. She has unfailingly attended every Festival of Music concert since she and Dr Philip Evans arrived. Dr Evans consults with his Governors over anything to do with money, but enjoys far more autonomy than any headmaster would in the state sector. And, it should be added, far more responsibility and a far heavier workload.

Dr Evans is warm in his praise of the strategic role played by the school's Governors. 'As chairman, Lord Naseby is supported by a group of talented individuals with wide experience, and it is the Governors who define the strategy for the school as well as providing the financial framework within which the Head Master operates. What happens is that ideas often emerge during lively discussions between the Head Master and the Governors, and are then taken forward and built upon by the school.'[7] The most notable recent initiative for which the Head Master gives full credit to the Governors was the creation of the new Prep School, for it was Lord Naseby, together with the deputy chairman at the time, Miles Young, who conceived the basic plan a year or so before his appointment.

It was the persuasive skills of the chairman, using his experience as a politician, that obtained agreement from the Harpur Trust for the required borrowing; the detailed implementation of the overall plan was then left to the new Head Master and his development committee — essentially his senior management team. It is clear there is a notable rapport between the present chairman of the Governors and the Head Master, and while a close control is kept over important strategy, a light touch can be seen operating on a day-to-day basis. It is very much a relationship built upon trust and mutual respect, a state of affairs that currently intersects the Board of Governors and the academic staff, whose elected Governor, for example, Patrick Shorten, commands high esteem in the commonroom, as does Richard Gordon, who, as chairman of the finance committee, helps provide the sound financial basis more crucial today than ever before.

What has become increasingly apparent since the middle of the twentieth century is the ever expanding role available to a Head Master's wife. There may not have been any particular reason why for many years no unmarried Head Master has been appointed (perhaps one never applied), but with the modern Head Master's workload, the constant requests he receives to attend events both in school and outside, and the consequent need for him to relax and unwind there would seem to be an almost overriding necessity for the Head Master to be married — and married to someone happily willingly to immerse herself in an almost ceaseless round of school activities. Philip Evans certainly has more than a married partner in his role as Head Master, for Dr Sandra Evans has achieved a dual reputation, as a thoroughly supportive wife to the Head Master and as a vivacious presence in the school on her own account.

THIRTEEN

Forecasting the Future

1998–2002

T HERE IS no doubt that boys at Bedford (and probably at most public schools) work far harder than in the past, but a mere glance at extra-curricular activities sometimes makes one wonder how they find the time to work at all. Quite apart from a range of 20 sports there are now some 30 clubs and societies in addition to organisations like orchestras, bands and the CCF, made voluntary in 1970 yet still surprisingly popular. Pythagoreans are 'A' level Maths students; Viewpoint is a Christian society. The Wine Appreciation Society meets at Redburn, the Young Enterprise Society has a chance to market its own products. The Babbage Society is into computers. There are Canoe, Chess and Bridge Clubs, a Poetry Society, a Cycle Club and a gathering for bee keepers. The Mitre Club, which regards itself as the school's most prestigious and intellectual society, treat themselves to talks on Japanese tea bowls. In December 1993 an especially bright Quiz Team achieved second place in a national cryptic quiz organised by the *Independent* and Sharp Electronics, winning for the school a word processor and laser printer. Five years later, having beaten, among other strong teams, Radley and Bedford Modern, the school Quiz Team were runners-up to King's School, Canterbury in the finals of the Schools Challenge competition, with a very impressive score of 850 points. In 1995 the Debating Society was in fine fettle. A report of their activities in the *Ousel* for June that year began: 'Condemn-nation, contraception, chauvinism, Catholicism, Protestantism, prostitution, profanation, flagellation, manipulation, racism, terrorism; this year saw a controversial but varied set of debates at which the quality of prepared speeches was yet again extremely high. The floor debates, though often starting slowly and somewhat reluctantly, showed intermittent flashes of rhetorical brilliance, not to mention savage insults.'

A good deal of fund raising goes on as well, under the umbrella of a Charities Committee. RELATE, formerly the Marriage Guidance Council, benefited by £300 when nine boys went on a sponsored walk early one frosty morning in November 1996. 1 December that year was World AIDS Day. Red ribbons were sold in the main foyer, in support of the Terence Higgins Trust, talks were given on AIDS during house assemblies, and £120 was raised, 'which', Rafik Taibjee, a monitor, wrote in the *Ousel*, [1] 'considering the sensitive issue and the reluctance of some, in my opinion, narrow-minded people, to what they believe is "supporting homosexuality", I felt was not a bad sum at all'. What Rafik lacked in genteel syntax he more than made up for with an admirable display of moral courage.

It is now impossible to pick up an issue of the *Ousel* without discovering some way in which the horizons of Bedford boys are being extended, be it intellectually or geographically. Quite apart from sporting tours, in recent years they have taken part in visits to Canada to ski, to Snowdonia to hill walk, to Calcutta for an 'educative cultural exchange', to Spain, to the battlefields of the Somme, to Cyprus to experience an RAF camp, to Nepal, to British Columbia to perform *Hamlet*, to Japan to tour *Romeo and Juliet*. As the authors of a report in the *Ousel* for March 1996 commented, 'Given the number of school trips taking place these days, it was gratifying to be able to collect seventeen boys for what was, essentially, an educational trip', their destination being Greece. In the summer of 1996 a boy was chosen for work experience in a cancer hospital in Lahore. Thirty-six others had set out on a Geography Field Trip to Switzerland. And one of the noticeable things about the reports boys write for the *Ousel* on their return is their readiness to thank not only sponsors but individual members of staff who have given assistance.

At an average age of forty-two (the age at which Philip Evans became Head Master, so that by the time he retires he will appear like an ancient don), the teaching staff at Bedford may seem on the youthful side to those Old Bedfordians who remember Aga Hodges and Daddy Dunn, but compared to other public schools it remains relatively high. In 1994 the average age of teachers at Malvern, Oundle, Uppingham and Sedbergh was 40, at Sherborne and Harrow 39, at Marlborough and Wellington 38; Radley's average age was 37, Stowe's 35, Cheltenham's 34 and Bradfield's a mere 33. There is no reason to believe these figures have risen substantially, if at all, and both the Head Master and the Director of Studies have said they would like to see Bedford's average lower than it currently is. [2]

A relatively youthful teaching team is not the only transformation in personnel to have taken place in recent years. It has been estimated that by 1996 there were 18,000 boys and girls from overseas studying in independent schools in the United Kingdom. Eton had 93, 20 from Hong Kong; Haileybury, as early as 1986, had taken in 130 overseas pupils out of a total school population of 672. One-third of pupils at Fettes are from overseas. Gordonstoun's intake of overseas students represents 28 per cent of its pupils and they come from some 30 countries. At Bedford, in 1998, out of 1,116 pupils, 138 were from overseas, and they came from Hong Kong (53), Brunei (18), Thailand (15), Japan (14), Malaysia (11), Nigeria (seven), Korea (five) and Germany (three), with just two boys each from Singapore, Uganda, China and Taiwan and Saudi Arabia, and one each from France, Spain, Pakistan and Zimbabwe. Most Sixth Formers from overseas go into Burnaby, which has now become a Sixth Form international boarding house, and the more junior boys are disseminated among the other boarding houses in such a way as to promote the use of English as far as possible; obviously a group of boys from Japan, for example, need to be discouraged from conversing together in Japanese. When boys arrive from countries currently at loggerheads they too are separated in order to discourage any possible friction.

Far from attempting to absorb those boys from non-Christian families into the Anglican ethos of the school, it is more likely that ethnic Christians at Bedford now try to learn about faiths other than their own. There is obviously no compulsion for a Muslim, for instance, to attend chapel (a chapel which in 1997 witnessed twenty-six boys being presented for confirmation and four adult baptisms), but for boys who strictly observe Ramadan there can be minor disruptions to school life; they will rise before five o'clock in order to eat before sunrise, and they will most likely forsake the swimming pool for fear, during the hours of fasting, they accidentally swallow some water.

It has in fact been an eye-opener to English boys to discover how devout boys are from other cultures, and how religious observance comes naturally to them. One consequence of the broadening of the school's ethnic base has been for Religious Education to be taught as a Theological discipline and in an objective manner, boys being encouraged to question, analyse and discuss; no longer is Religious Education simply a matter of imparting Biblical Theology. There is actually an increasing request from boys to study Theology and situational ethics, the curriculum stretching from Plato to Pope John Paul II. Within the teaching of Theology boys are encouraged to consider the ethics of subjects like abortion, euthanasia, genetic engineering and business, and there is a generally held belief in the Religious Education department that Theology complements the study of History, English, Geography and Science.

One of Dr Evans's initiatives relating to the increase in overseas students at independent schools throughout the United Kingdom was the opening in 1996 by Lady Chalker, then Minister for Overseas Development, of a Study Centre at 67 De Parys Avenue, Kirkman's boarding house before it transferred — as Phillpotts — to Pemberley Avenue. The Centre runs three ten-week terms and two three-week summer courses each year for boys and girls between the ages of eleven and seventeen, some of whom (but none of the girls, of course) will go on to full-time education at Bedford, some to other schools of their choice, but all of whom need to master sufficient English to take their place in an English independent school.

The Centre can cater for thirty resident students. There is a small dormitory for six of the younger boys, but most students share a double study bedroom, and senior students have a room to themselves. No class is larger than six, and students are taught English, Maths, Science and Information Technology in groups depending on competence in English, not age. Countries from which the students have been recruited more or less span the globe: Iceland, Japan, Russia, Angola, Taiwan. They are forbidden to converse with students from their own country other than in English, which may sound harsh but their parents are paying a fairly breathtaking £500 a week, so little time can afford to be lost in perfecting English. One reason fees are high is because a maximum of thirty students receive the undivided attention of a housemaster and his wife, a resident tutor and a matron in addition to specialised teaching staff, headed by an Old Bedford Modernian, Jonathan McKeown, appointed first director of studies. For a number of school activities, including meals, the Study Centre students have an opportunity to mingle with Bedford pupils, and trips are organised to help them acclimatise to the general ethos of English life. Within two years the Centre had shown a profit, with agents around the world busy recruiting, for only a very small minority of the students are referred to the Centre by the school.

The Study Centre may be thought to have made a tiny dent in Bedford's masculine armour (in 1998 there were six girls in residence out of a total of twenty-nine students) but although the majority of public schools are now co-educational, the chances of Bedford going down that path are extremely slim. In 1997 the historian and biographer Christopher Hibbert wrote, 'Apart from Roman Catholic schools (although not Stonyhurst) only twelve of the better known public schools will accept boys only. In addition to Eton, Harrow, Radley [he was writing a history of Radley College] and Winchester these are Bedford, Sedbergh, Sherborne, Shrewsbury, St Paul's, Dulwich, Merchant Taylors' and Tonbridge.'[3] The Clerk to the Harpur Trust, Desmond Wigan, says that a Harpur Trust school would only become co-educational 'if from an educational and philosophical point of view it seemed the right thing to do, and then the Trust might end up with two single-sex schools and one co-ed'.[4] The issue of co-education has been examined by the Governors of the Trust in recent years, but there seems no serious reason to encourage such a move. Not every boys' school which has embraced co-education has welcomed girls with open arms — more often than not with routine macho jeers — and some have wished they now had the courage to reverse the trend. It must be right for parents sending boys to a public school to have a choice between a single-sex school and a co-educational one, and any parent choosing Bedford can hardly imagine, with easy access to the town and with two girls' schools in close proximity, their son is about to join an enclosed monastic order. 'There is always a theoretical possibility that Bedford might become co-educational,' Mr Wigan, who is himself an Old Etonian, concedes. 'But it would be against the ethos, and I cannot imagine it happening in the forseeable future. Bedford is at present in as good shape as it has ever been. There is no financial crisis. It is well governed and well managed. Boarding has stabilised, and academically it is in the First Division.' [5]

One of the most astonishing developments to have occurred at Bedford during the second half of the twentieth century has been the establishment of a diverse musical tradition second to none. Dr Probert-Jones, Director of Music from 1937-57, was an unostentatious, rather reclusive organist, unlikely to inspire enthusiasm in those not already aware of their musical gifts. Once a week he attempted to conduct in the Great Hall what was called Musical Appreciation. On one occasion he took the Upper School, week by week, through Beethoven's Fifth Symphony, his words continually drowned by a hubbub of talking, the music inaudibly played on 78 rpm gramophone records in the gallery. But his lack of disciplinary powers during periods of enforced musical teaching gave no clue to his tenacity and artistry when rehearsing an orchestra or choir, and over a period of 20 years he established a groundwork of musical excellence on which others, initially Ted Amos, who taught at the school for 36 years and served as Director of Music from 1957-79, could build.

It is worth remembering there was always an annual school concert in the past, that boys won musical scholarships to Oxford and Cambridge, that the Christmas term carol concert was a highlight of the year; there were Sunday evening concerts during summer terms, and even, before the Second World War, a jazz band. In 1975 the retiring Head Master, Bill Brown, noted in his annual report to the Governors of the Harpur Trust, 'At times it has been suggested that music studies may interfere with a boy's academic work. It is of interest that in the top two [musical] grades ... the four boys who took 'A' levels this July passed in all subjects with six As, five Bs, one C, and the five 'O' level candidates achieved 55 passes between them!' Symphonies by Haydn and Schubert and concertos by Vivaldi and Bach featured in that year's Festival of Music.

Nevertheless, there is a contrast between the musical life of the school today and Humfrey Grose-Hodge's assertion that Alec Cook, his head boy 1937-8, was 'the only considerable player of the oboe the school had ever produced'. There are now two Upper School symphony orchestras, a Choral Society 150 strong, a dance band as well as a jazz band, a brass ensemble and a chamber orchestra. Forty-five per cent of boys take instrumental lessons and half the school is in some way involved in music making. Music is in fact probably the most popular extra-curricular activity, and by general consent the most sought after trophy is not striven for on the river or the football pitch but in the Great Hall, when the six school houses compete in the Annual House Singing Competition. To eavesdrop on a boarding house rehearsal of their chosen unison and part song can be an extremely moving experience; in the ghastly jargon of the day, you really can sense an extraordinary degree of bonding.

Under Andrew Morris's directorship the Music School is now staffed by an organist and assistant director of music, and heads of strings, piano, brass and woodwind. The Prep School, a fertile breeding ground for future talent among the string sections of the Upper School orchestras, has its own symphony and string orchestras. The 'string factory', as it is affectionately called, came about because Ted Amos believed that if a boy had two arms he could play a musical instrument, and it certainly seems as if sight reading, the great gift of British orchestral players anyway, comes as naturally to Bedford's Prep School boys as operating a computer. It was Amos who incorporated music into the school curriculum, and it is now a foundation subject along with Geography and History. The school is able to offer musical scholarships up to half a boy's school fees, and in 1988 Bedford was host to the Music Masters' and Mistresses' Conference, a tribute to the successful ambassadorial nature of the school's various orchestras.

A Dance Band has played at the Café Royal and the London Hilton; concerts have been staged in the Purcell Room, at St John's, Smith Square and the Royal Festival Hall. The chapel choir have sung at Canterbury, Lincoln, Salisbury, Winchester, Wells and St Paul's Cathedrals, Westminster Abbey and the cathedral in Prague, where the Head Master and his wife travelled to hear them during the summer holiday of 1998. They have made CDs. Music making on the ambitious scale now undertaken also affords opportunities for collaboration with other schools — with the Dame Alice Harpur School, for instance, in a production of *The Magic Flute* in 1991, and with both Harpur Trust girls' schools and the Modern School in Britten's *War Requiem* in 1995, a performance conducted by Owain Arwel Hughes in the Birmingham Symphony Hall. In 1997 the School Choral Society came together with the Prep School's senior choir and Bedford High School to sing Brahms's *Requiem* in German.

The same year saw the staging of a seven-day event, the school's Silver Jubilee Festival of Music, marked unfortunately by the death of Ted Amos a few days earlier. His own achievements had included performances of *Belshazzar's Feast*, the *St Matthew Passion* and Beethoven's *Choral Symphony*. The first festival, held in 1973, consisted of three concerts; the twenty-fifth mounted seven concerts in as many days. The chapel choir sang *Zadok the Priest*, Palestrina, Purcell, and Britten; the second orchestra performed no fewer than ten works in one concert; there was a concert for half a dozen solo prize winners; there were contributions to the festival from the School Band, the Dance Band, the Brass Ensemble and a Dixie Group, who called themselves 'Pure Genius', eight boys who could not on this occasion be accused of blowing their own trumpets too loud. Out of courtesy, perhaps, to one of the festival's patrons, Ursula Vaughan Williams, the First Orchestra played two works by her husband, his *Norfolk Rhapsody No 1* and his *Fantasia on a Theme of Thomas Tallis*.

Musical performances of every kind by Bedford boys these days are never less then exciting, often thrilling. Those schools like Uppingham, who have always prided themselves on their high musical standards, are beginning to look to their laurels. It is encouraging, however, to note that music does not take precedence over sport or the academic curriculum, rather that it seems to have become a unifying force throughout the school, and it is a well known fact that while men or boys are making music (martial music excepted, perhaps) they do not as a rule resort to combat. And neither has the upsurge of musical activities edged out the other arts, which appear to be flourishing as never before. Examples of painting and sculpture are constantly on display in the foyer. Following a visit to the Art School in 1996 Michael Jones, a professional photographer, reported for the December *Ousel* that year, 'I was delighted and very impressed by clear evidence of individual development; by the varied and exciting use of materials, and a clear commitment by both students and staff to aim for a very high standard'.

An occasional essay finds its way into the *Ousel*, but poetry abounds. It is inevitable that schoolboy poems will differ widely in the degree of success they attain — and that many will very nearly hit it off but not quite. It is actually quite remarkable for a schoolboy to write an entirely successful poem, notwithstanding that poetry seems to be a natural artistic medium for the young, for some reason for boys especially. And for a schoolboy to attain the measured and mature poetic technique to be able to sustain with complete success such a sophisticated poem as *Not For Long*, printed in the *Ousel* in June 1994, is a rare achievement indeed. It was, however, achieved by Robert Mills.

Someday I'll cry when I try
to remember you.
For now, I have the real thing,
but not for long.

Someday I'll look through
those old photographs,
and feel how I feel for you now.
But not for long.

Someday we'll meet again,
when we're older
and we'll laugh and talk,
but not for long.

On 22 September 1997 the school celebrated the 500th anniversary of the birth of Sir William Harper. It did so with an appropriate mix of pomp and informality, worship and hospitality. A service in the chapel was attended by the Lord Lieutenant of Bedfordshire, the Bishop of Bedford and the Lord Mayor of London, lunch was served in the Great Hall, and the guests were entertained by brief dramatic excerpts ranging from Shakespeare to Pinter, and by some brilliant musical performances from the Brass Ensemble and the Dixie Group. Philip Matias sang Dowland like an angel and Thomas King like an archangel.

How in his wildest dreams could Sir William ever have envisaged the results of his deed of gift? Four and a half centuries later the Harpur Trust is responsible for the education not of a handful of scruffy Bedford boys bent on learning Greek and Latin but for 4,000 boys and girls studying a curriculum spread across the sciences and humanities. As recently as October 1988 yet another Scheme came into force to regulate the Harpur Trust, bringing up to date the scope of its educational and charitable purposes. Most importantly, the Trust is now empowered, still within the spirit of Harper's original intentions, to make grants to other institutions and to provide scholarships and bursaries for educational purposes. £400,000 a year is allocated, on a means-tested basis, to no fewer than 60 boys at Bedford School alone; some reduction in fees is arranged for families on an income of less than £30,000 a year, and a boy from a home producing no more than £10,000 per annum may, if he lives within Bedfordshire and is considered likely to benefit, be entered at Bedford free.

While the Harpur Trust schools operate autonomously, it is the duty of the Trustees to see they do not step out of line. For example, they may not borrow money against security without permission, nor alter the age of entry into the school without consent. In 1997 the Trust moved from the Harpur Centre to the Pilgrim Centre in Brickhill Drive, where plans soon got underway to extend its work by building a new school for children under seven, and to convert a block of the former school premises into which the Trust had moved into a centre for the arts. Where the Harpur Trust is now empowered to branch out beyond the promotion of education and the relief of the aged, sick and poor, as originally intended by Harper, is in the field of Recreation and Leisure Activities. In the year 1996-7 the Trust made grants totalling £850,000 — to schools in Stewartby, Kempston and Biddenham, to a Bedford Family Group which cares for the elderly, disabled and underprivileged, towards the establishment of a Bedford centre for MENCAP. Their largest single disbursement to date was £350,000 in 1998 as a contribution to £1 million needed to build a Special Needs Training Project for young people with learning disabilities.

A staff of 23 administer a charity that employs 900 people and manages assets producing a gross endowment income of over £3.7 million a year, and with a school fee income of over £21 million per annum Sir William Harper's Bedford Charity is now one of the largest local charities in the country. Whilst its Trustees are a good deal more forward looking than some of their predecessors, they do not hesitate to recall the past when it seems appropriate. And remembering one of Dr Brereton's most talented pupils, Charles Piazzi Smyth, who in 1845 had been appointed Astronomer Royal for Scotland and pioneered high altitude observing and solar astronomy, they decided in 1997 to contribute to the construction of an Observatory to be named after him. It was due to be built at a cost of £140,000, and opened at the end of 1999 on a site at the northern extremity of the school estate, to the rear of Phillpotts. The Piazzi Smyth Community Observatory, with its sixteen-inch reflecting telescope, will be available for use by other local schools – indeed, by the community as a whole.

Not even such a farsighted boy as Nicholas Tinworth, he who wrote the prize-winning essay on Bedford School AD 2552, included in the time capsule sealed in 1981, imagined the building of an Observatory in the grounds of the school. But such a prediction would have been reasonably easy to make by comparison to some sort of medium range forecast regarding the possible structure and ethos of the school in the early years of the new millenium. Tensions exist already between those parents of day boys who would prefer a five-day school week and those who are paying full boarding and tuition fees and naturally expect the maximum facilities possible for their money. But how long will any school like Bedford remain viable as a boarding school? A financial crisis hit the far eastern stockmarkets even as this book was being written, and if boys who have been so welcome from communities like Hong

Kong were prevented from attending schools in England, new sources of boarders would need to be tapped.

But already the boarding side of Bedford's life is only kept buoyant by boys from overseas at a time when more middle class families than ever before have begun to turn their backs on boarding schools, partly for economic reasons, partly because they just prefer to have their children at home with them 12 months of the year instead of four. Like so many other institutions we have taken for granted for so long, the great public and grammar schools face an uncertain and almost certainly changing future. A large number of conflicting factors arise, and to keep so many balls in the air at once requires a cool nerve and a gift for second-guessing: how to balance the priorities of sport and academic work; what sort of academic work will equip the prep school boy of today for his entry into the workforce in 2010; how to encourage an appreciation of art in all its modernist forms while retaining respect for the musical and literary giants of a past that is inevitably receding further and further into the distance.

Any Head Master who thought for one moment he was capable of planning a five-year strategy for his school single-handed these days would be seriously deluded, and at Bedford there is currently a process of staff discussion and consultation so that views about the future are heard from everyone concerned before a major plan of campaign is submitted to the Governors. This is no panic measure, merely the application of common sense to extremely complex issues, many of which, it is hoped, will be solved by financing much needed redevelopment of the Music School, an extensive enhancement of the Art Department and school theatre and the provision of an entirely new library and Resource Centre. As the school approaches its 450th anniversary in 2002, even Humfrey Grose-Hodge, who half a century after his retirement would find the school's atmosphere a strange if exhilarating one, would not begrudge those who have some awesome decisions to make a small element of that invaluable bonus he did not hesitate to offer to his own pupils — good luck.

The Letters Patent

EDWARD VI BY THE GRACE OF GOD KING OF ENGLAND FRANCE and Ireland defender of the faith and in earth supreme head of the Church of England and Ireland TO ALL to whom these letters shall come Greeting KNOW YE that We on the humble Petition of the Mayor Bailiffs Burgesses and Commonalty of the Town of Bedford to us made for erecting and establishing a free and perpetual School there for the institution and instruction of Boys and Youths of our special grace and of our certain knowledge and mere motion Also by the advice of our Council Have granted and given licence and by these presents do grant and give licence for Us Our heirs and successors as far as in Us lies to the said Mayor Bailiffs Burgesses and Commonalty of our said Town of Bedford and their Successors That they or their Successors may and shall erect make found and establish a free and perpetual Grammar School in our Town aforesaid for the education institution and instruction of Boys and Youths in Grammar Literature and good Manners to endure at all times for ever And the same School to be and consist of one Master and one Usher to continue for ever And that the said intention of the aforesaid Mayor Bailiffs Burgesses and Commonalty of the Town aforesaid may take better effect of Our more abundant grace We have granted and given Licence and by these presents Do grant and do give Licence for Us Our Heirs and successors aforesaid so far as in us lies to the said Mayor Bailiffs Burgesses and Commonalty of our Town aforesaid that they or their successors may and shall have enjoy perceive acquire purchase and receive Lordships Manors Lands Tenements Rents Reversions Revenues Services and Hereditaments whatsoever and other possessions whatsoever to the annual value of £40 above all charges and reprises of the gift grant bequest demise or assignment to any person or persons whatsoever willing to give grant bequeath or assign the same to them Although the same Lordships Manors Lands and Tenements to be held of us in capite or otherwise mediately or immediately or be held of other person or person TO HAVE AND TO HOLD to the same Mayor Bailiffs Burgesses and Commonalty of the aforesaid Town and their successors in and to the sustentation of the said Master and Usher and for the continuance of the said School for ever For marrying poor maids of the said Town and for nourishing and educating poor boys of that place and also for alms of the remainder or surplus of the premises accruing and remaining unto

the poor of the said Town for the time being to be distributed AND ALSO
WE HAVE GRANTED and given licence and by these presents Do grant and
do give licence for Us Our Heirs and successors by the advice and assent
aforesaid That the Warden or Keeper of the College of the Blessed Mary of
Winton in Oxford commonly called New College Oxford and the fellows of
the same for the time or the more part of them for the time being from time
to time when there shall be necessity or just occasion shall require by their
discretion may nominate elect and admit the said Master or said Usher of the
said School in the said Town and for good just and reasonable causes and
occasions may and shall change and remove them from time to time and
nominate elect and admit other fit and proper men into the said places or
offices of Master or Usher of the aforesaid School And to the same person or
persons that he or they may give grant bequeath or assign Lordships Manors
Lands Tenements Rents Revenues Reversions Services and Hereditaments to
the annual value aforesaid to the said Mayor Bailiffs Burgesses and
Commonalty of the said Town for the time being to be holden by them and
their successors as is aforesaid by the tenor of these presents In like manner
We have given and do give special Licence without hindrance impeachment of
trouble of Us or Our Heirs or successors Justices Escheators Sheriffs Coro-
ners Bailiffs or other ministers of Us or Our Heirs or any other persons
whatsoever And without any other Royal Letters Patent or any Inquisitions
upon any Writ of Ad quod Damnum or any other royal mandate on this behalf
in any way to be had prosecuted or taken The Statute of mortmain or any
other Statute Act or Ordinance thereupon to the contrary made published or
ordained or any Grant or Grants to the said Mayor Bailiffs Burgesses and
Commonalty of the said Town by Us or any of Our Predecessors before these
times made in these presents not made or being or any other thing cause or
matter whatever in any wise notwithstanding And this without any fine or fee
to us to the premises or any of the premises to be rendered paid or done in our
Hanaper or elsewhere And that although express mention of the true yearly
value or of any other value or certainty of the premises or any of them or of
other gifts or grants by Us or any of Our Predecessors unto the said Mayor
Bailiffs Burgesses and Commonalty of the Town aforesaid before this time
made in these presents be not made Any statute act ordinance provision or
restriction thereupon to the contrary made published ordained and provided
Or any other cause or matter whatsoever in any wise notwithstanding In
Witness whereof We have caused these Our letters to be made patent
WITNESS Ourself at Ely the Fifteenth day of August in the Sixth year of Our
reign.

Head Masters of Bedford School

EDMUND GREENE	1548-73	MATTHEW PRIAULX	1718-39
WILLIAM SMYTH	1573-77	GEORGE BRIDLE	1739-73
FRANCIS WHITE	1577-87	JOHN HOOKE	1773-1810
? CHAMBERS	1587-97	JOHN BRERETON	1811-55
RICHARD BUTCHER	1597-?	FREDERICK FANSHAWE	1855-74
HENRY WHITAKER	?-1601	JAMES PHILLPOTTS	1874-1903
ROBERT BARKER	1601-10	JOHN KING	1903-10
DANIEL GARDENER	1610-36	REGINALD CARTER	1910-28
WILLIAM VARNEY	1636-56	HUMFREY GROSE-HODGE	1928-51
	1660-63	CLARENCE SEAMAN	1951-55
GEORGE BUTLER	1656-60	WILLIAM BROWN	1955-75
JOHN ALLANSON	1663-65	IAN JONES	1975-86
JOHN BUTLER	1665-72	SIDNEY MILLER	1986-88
JOHN LONGWORTH	1672-77	MICHAEL BARLEN	1988-90
WILLIAM WILLIS	1681-83	PHILIP EVANS	1990-
NICHOLAS ASPINALL	1683-1718		

Notes and References

One: An Eagle Displayed

1. Founded in 1379, New College may have been so dubbed almost from the start in order to differentiate it from an earlier foundation, Oriel, also dedicated to St. Mary; Oriel, the House of the Blessed Virgin, was founded in 1326.

2. A common fallacy, that a royal charter was granted to Bedford School, should be laid to rest once and for all. Nothing was granted to the school itself; it was to the leading citizens of the town that letters patent were granted, by Edward VI on the advice of his privy council. To the town a charter had been granted in the twelfth century by Henry II.

3. The *Ousel* for 21 February 1942 opted for Scole Lane; in *A Brief History of Bedford School*, published in 1952 'in connection with the Fourth Centenary Celebrations', Schole was preferred.

4. The term Master remained in use until the school grew large enough to justify the employment of teaching staff in addition to an usher, when the Master became Headmaster or Head Master. Both Headmaster and Head Master appear to have been acceptable in the nineteenth century, but Head Master has become the preferred term at Bedford throughout most of the twentieth century.

5. There is no authoritative definition of a public school. Before Bedford School dropped the name Grammar in 1917 it was referred to as both a grammar and a public school, the terms apparently being interchangeable. Winchester's claim to be the oldest public school is disputed by Westminster, refounded by Elizabeth I.

6. It has sometimes been surmised that an alteration from Harper to Harpur was the result of some sort of Victorian snobbery. This is not so. In 1856 James Wyatt published *The Bedford Schools and Charities of Sir William Harper*, retaining the original spelling throughout the text; in the index he also identifies Dame Alice as Lady Harper. James Phillpotts, Head Master from 1874-1903, favoured Harper. The change to Harpur officially occurred in 1764, when a Latin inscription was inserted on the new facade of the school building, and can only be described as a Georgian conceit; Harper, they thought, looked more convincing as Harpur in Latin, and this alternative spelling became incorporated in Harpur Street, the Dame Alice Harpur School and the Harpur Trust. In literature commemorating the five-hundredth anniversary in 1997 of Harper's birth the school spelt his name Harper, and in this minor matter the school and the Harpur Trust appear to be locked in disagreement, and doubtless will now always remain so. Perhaps in another 500 years' time the dispute over the spelling of Sir William Harper/Harpur's name will have become an encrusted and greatly cherished tradition.

7. In *The Harpur Trust: 1552-1973* (The Harpur Trust, 1973) Joyce Godber traces Harpers living at Southill, one of them a William Harper; a Harper family resident in Ickwell, Cople and Renhold; and in about 1500 a William Harper residing in Bedford, who was churchwarden at St. Paul's in 1510. He may well have been the father of Sir William Harper, who in his lifetime was inconsistent in the spelling of his name, sometimes choosing Harpar.

8. *The Diary of Henry Machyn* (ed J G Nichols, 1848).

9. Godber, ob cit, believes the total purchase came to 13 acres and 3 rods.

10. *Bedford Schools and Charities*, ob cit.

11. Although she twice remarried after Harper's death, his second wife chose to be buried with him. Alice Harper's supposed burial in Bedford is a myth. There is however a stained glass window in St. Paul's Church, Bedford 'in memory of Sir William and Lady (Alice) Harper'. It was commissioned by the Harpur Trust and was dedicated on 24 June 1976.

12. For the first 100 years or so there is not universal agreement about the names and dates of some of the Masters. See Author's Note.

13. *The Counties of Britain: A Tudor Atlas* by John Speed (Pavilion, 1988).

14. *A History of Bedford School* (F R Hockliffe and T Fisher Unwin, 1925).

15. First published and performed in 1773.

16. For a history of Bedford Modern School see *Bedford Modern: School of the Black and Red* by Andrew Underwood (Bedford Modern School, 1981).

17. Sargeaunt, *A History of Bedford School*, ob cit.
18. For a comprehensive account of life at Eton, Harrow, Rugby, Westminster, Winchester, Shrewsbury and Charterhouse between 1800-64 see *Boys Together* by John Chandos (Hutchinson, 1984).
19. *Buildings of Bedfordshire* (1968).
20. Hooke, who is buried at St. Peter's Church, Bedford, had a son at the school who became a Fellow of New College, dying at the age of 26. Other instances of Head Masters sending their sons to Bedford include James Phillpotts, Edward King, Reginald Carter, Humfrey Grose-Hodge, Ian Jones, Sidney Miller and Philip Evans.

Two: Steak and Porter

1. Ob cit.
2. Quoted in *The Poisoned Bowl* by Alisdare Hickson (Constable, 1995).
3. *An Account of the Public Charities of the Town of Bedford* (Merry).
4. Sargeaunt, ob cit.
5. The works by Erskine May most frequently appealed to today are *Standard Parliamentary Procedure* and *The Constitutional History of England Since the Accession of George III*.
6. Wyatt, ob cit.
7. A preparatory school, where for the first time girls could be educated, was opened in 1815. Within the Edward Blore complex were housed the Writing, English and Commercial Schools, together with a home for poor children, called a Hospital.
8. Ob cit.
9. Sargeaunt, ob cit.
10. Ob cit.
11. Sargeaunt, ob cit.
12. There is even disagreement over where the riot began. Sargeaunt says it was Goldington Green, Godber a six-acre playing field to the north of the town.

Three: The Chief

1. See *Headmaster: The Life of John Percival, Radical Autocrat* by Jeremy Potter (Constable, 1998).
2. A rather charming example of naïve schoolboy honesty cropped up in 1997 in the Bell Room book in which boys late for school are required to record the reason. It simply read, 'Overslept'.
3. *Bedford Grammar School: Old and New*, 29 October 1891. School archives.
4. Ibid.
5. Ibid.
6. Old Bedfordians Club *Year Book*, 1943-44.
7. School archives.
8. Sargeaunt, ob cit.
9. 'There is no doubt that the Boer War was seen by many apologists as a vindication of the entire public school system.' Peter Parker, *The Old Lie: The Great War and the Public School Ethos* (Constable, 1987).

Four: A Regular Parade of Admirals

1. *Aspects of Anglo-Indian Bedford* (The Bedfordshire Historical Record Society, volume 57, 1978).
2. Godber, ob cit.
3. Bell, ob cit.
4. The High School for Girls and the Girls Modern School had been opened in Bromham Road in 1882. The Girls Modern School moved in 1892 to St. Paul's Square and in 1938 to Cardington Road, and in 1945 it was renamed the Dame Alice Harpur School.
5. Quoted Bell, ob cit.
6. Bell, ob cit.
7. Recollections of Charles Linnell, a pupil at Bedford Modern School 1888-95, quoted Bell, ob cit.

8. Quoted Bell, ob cit.

9. *Old and New*, ob cit.

10. *Hesketh Pearson by Himself* (Heinemann, 1965).

11. Michael Holroyd, biographer of Lytton Strachey and Bernard Shaw, believes that 'from the early 1930s to the early 1950s [Hesketh Pearson] was by and large the most popular biographer in England'. Letter from Michael Holroyd to the author, 26 November 1997.

Five: The Man in his Flying Machine

1. *The Bedford Grammar School Souvenir*, school archives.

2. Chapel Minutes, school archives. Initially Bedford Modern School boys were confirmed in the chapel.

3. Prices quoted for the purchase of land by Phillpotts, King and Carter are inclusive of stamp duty and legal fees. The actual cost of the Pemberly Estate, for example, was £7,650.

4. For information about Henry Grierson's life the author is indebted to Mr David Money, an honorary Fellow of Grierson's Forty Club.

5. Sargeaunt, ob cit.

6. Ibid.

Six: Conspicuous Bravery

1. Letter from Mr & Mrs Blythe to the author, 27 October 1997.

2. *Verse, Letters & Remembrances of Sub-Lieutenant Arthur Walderne St. Clare Tisdall, VC* (The Naval and Military Press, reprinted 1992).

3. It should be recorded that many Old Bedford Modernians served in both world wars with distinction and gallantry. In the Great War, in addition to the posthumous Victoria Cross awarded to Major G G M Wheeler, twenty-three DSOs were won, thirty-four MCs, two DSCs, one DCM and one DSM. Seventy Old Boys were mentioned in dispatches. In the Second World War one Old Modernian was awarded the DSO and bar, another the DSO, and there were twenty-three MCs awarded, two DSCs, one DFC and bar and a further thirteen DFCs, two AFCs, one DSC and one MM. Sixty-five Old Boys were mentioned in dispatches. 1,082 OBMs are known to have served in the First World War, of whom 166 were killed. Over 1,230 OBMs served in the Second World War, of whom 126 were killed. While serving with the Gloucestershire Regiment, who fought with great distinction during the Korean War, Lieutenant D A Simcox, at Bedford Modern School 1939-45, was killed at the Battle of the Imjin River.

    For the facts about Major George G M Wheeler, VC the author is indebted to Mr Andrew Underwood, archivist at Bedford Modern School, who passed on information gleaned from an Old Bedford Modernian, Mr Barrie Thorpe.

4. *Chronicles of Bedford House: 1931-57*, school archives.

5. Ibid.

Seven: The Test of an Educated Man

1. 'In 1914 all ranks, all ages in the Navy and the Army were 19th Century people, men born in the reign of Queen Victoria: the boy-midshipmen in the boats at Gallipoli, the boy-subalterns who came forward in droves from the public school and the grammar school OTCs, Boy First Class Jack Cornwell who won a posthumous VC at Jutland at the age of sixteen, and a regiment of first-class boys who gave false ages to the Recruiting Officers and lie beside the men in the War Cemeteries - they were all Victorians. The gulf between them and the people of the 1990s is already virtually unbridgeable, and widens every day. Two elements above all others separate the 1914-1918 people from ourselves: patriotism and religion.' John Terraine, in his Introduction to *The Bickersteth Diaries: 1914–1918*, edited by Bishop John Bickersteth, KCVO (Leo Cooper, 1995).

2. William Kimber, 1972.

3. Old Bedfordians Club minutes.

4. Letter to the author, 5 November 1997.

5. School archives.

6. Ibid.

Eight: Hitler's Oak

1. Not 1936, as stated in the 1928-38 *Supplement to the Ousel*.
2. 1928-38 *Supplement to the Ousel*.
3. Ob cit.

Nine: Taught to the Highest Standards

1. Godber, ob cit.
2. 1939-45 *Supplement to the Ousel*.
3. The *Ousel*, 27 July 1946.
4. In conversation with the author.
5. Privately acquired.
6. In conversation with the author.
7. Letter to the author, 3 September 1997.
8. Ibid.
9. 4 July 1997.
10. In conversation with the author.
11. Ibid.
12. In his *TES* interview Paddy Ashdown wrongly attributed the organisation of the lunch to Michael Brunson. It was in fact both organised and paid for by Richard Lindley.

Ten: Forty-Four Rebels

1. School archives.
2. Ibid.
3. In conversation with the author.
4. School archives. Today the Eucharist is celebrated with incense.
5. The *Ousel*, November 1975.
6. Ibid.
7. In conversation with the author.
8. Letter from Sir George Godber to the author, 19 October 1998.
9. *Bedford School and the Great Fire* by M E Barlen, M P Stambach and D P C Stileman (Quiller Press, 1984). From this exemplary account of the fire the author has mined much of the information to be found in the following chapter.

Eleven: Arson

1. The *Daily Telegraph*, 24 July 1979.
2. *Bedford School and the Great Fire*, ob cit.
3. Values and insurance premiums rise all the time, but by way of comparison it may be interesting to note that in 1998 the main school building was insured for £13.5 million.

Twelve: First Division

1. The *Ousel*, June 1996.
2. Lord Naseby, in conversation with the author.
3. *The Ousel*, December 1994.
4. R G Miller, Director of Studies, writing in the *Ousel*, March 1995.
5. In conversation with the author.
6. Ibid.
7. Ibid.

Thirteen: Forecasting the Future

1. March 1997.
2. In conversation with the author.
3. *No Ordinary Place* (John Murray).
4. In conversation with the author.
5. Ibid.

Index

Italic type denotes boarding houses; entries in bold type denote other schools.

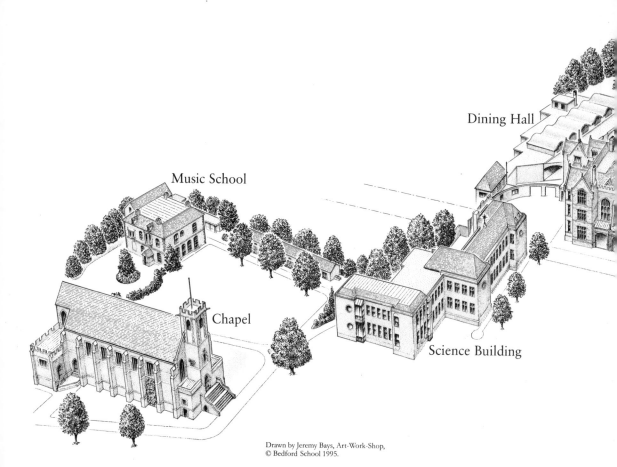

Music School

Chapel

Science Building

Dining Hall

Drawn by Jeremy Bays, Art-Work-Shop,
© Bedford School 1995.